History

for the IB Diploma

Evolution and Development of Democratic States (1848–2000)

Authors: Jean Bottaro and John Stanley

Cambridge University Press's mission is to advance learning, knowledge and research worldwide.

Our IB Diploma resources aim to:

- encourage learners to explore concepts, ideas and topics that have local and global significance
- help students develop a positive attitude to learning in preparation for higher education
- assist students in approaching complex questions, applying critical-thinking skills and forming reasoned answers.

CAMBRIDGE
UNIVERSITY PRESS

CAMBRIDGE
UNIVERSITY PRESS

University Printing House, Cambridge CB2 8BS, United Kingdom

Cambridge University Press is part of the University of Cambridge.

It furthers the University's mission by disseminating knowledge in the pursuit of education, learning and research at the highest international levels of excellence.

Information on this title: education.cambridge.org

First published 2011
Second edition 2016
Reprinted 2016

Printed in Dubai by Oriental Press

A catalogue record for this publication is available from the British Library

ISBN 978-1-107-55635-5

Contents

Introduction 1

This book is designed to prepare you for Paper 2 Topic 9, *Evolution and development of democratic states (1848–2000)* in the IB History examination. It will examine various aspects of four democratic states in different regions of the world between the mid-19th century and the end of the 20th century.

Overview

You will learn how basic democratic principles were applied in four different contexts during this period.

Germany

The unification of Germany in 1870 changed the balance of power in Europe, for under the leadership of the kaisers (emperors) and their chancellors, Germany became a growing industrial power and an enthusiastic, aggressive, colonial and military power.

In 1918 Germany saw the autocratic imperial government of Kaiser Wilhelm II replaced by a democratic, parliamentary republic. The Weimar Republic was formed during a period of military defeat and social revolution. It seemed to offer Germany the opportunity to develop a liberal democracy and escape from a militaristic past.

However, Germany was beset with serious problems, leading many either to withhold support from the new parliamentary democracy or to seek actively to destroy it. The extreme left and much of the right provided the republic's most vitriolic opponents.

When economic crises overwhelmed Germany after 1930, the republic was undermined and by 1933, a Nazi dictatorship was established and the experiment in democracy advocated by Weimar was finally crushed.

Twelve years of Nazi dictatorship under Hitler ultimately led to Germany's defeat in the Second World War. Soviet forces occupied eastern Germany, while the United States, Britain and France occupied the western half of the nation. This political division of Germany into a democratic West Germany and a one-party communist state, East Germany, subsequently became permanent and reunification did not occur until 1990. Under Konrad Adenauer, however, West Germany (BRD) brought about an economic miracle, built a strong democratic consensus and was integrated fully into Western Europe by 1955, as a sovereign state in NATO.

India

Until the Second World War, most of Africa and much of Asia formed parts of the colonial empires of European powers. In the decades following the war there was an extension of democracy as these empires were dismantled and former colonies gained their independence.

In India, this was the result of a long struggle against British rule by the Indian nationalist movement in which Mohandas Gandhi and the Indian National Congress played a dominant role. After independence, a Constituent Assembly drew up a democratic constitution, which transformed India into a federal republic. The establishment of a secular (non-religious) state, based on sound democratic principles, was a notable achievement of the first government led by Jawaharlal Nehru. This happened in spite of the violence and bloodshed that had accompanied independence and the partition of British India into India and Pakistan, when fifteen million refugees crossed the borders between the new states. However, on some occasions, acts of political extremism posed threats to secular democracy in India. Many of these were related to religion, language rights and nationalism.

The new government introduced policies to promote economic growth, extend education, improve health services, provide social welfare, improve the position of women and end the caste system. Although poverty and inequality remain features of Indian society, democratic institutions have survived. Today, India is the world's largest democracy, with a population in 2015 of nearly 1.26 billion people and an electorate of 814 million.

The United States

The United States faced tremendous domestic challenges and underwent immense changes throughout the period 1890–1975. The USA grew from being a recently industrialised and growing economic power into to the world's economic superpower with both an atomic capability and pervasive international military and cultural influence. From a Progressive era of social reform up to 1920 under Theodore Roosevelt, William Taft and Woodrow Wilson, it then experienced both an unprecedented financial boom under the Republican presidents of the 1920s followed by a stock market crash in 1929. Laissez-faire and the free market thus gave way to state intervention under Franklin Roosevelt's New Deal, which placed the USA on the road to economic recovery, from a point in early 1933 when the whole financial system and democracy itself was potentially imperilled.

Post-Second World War Americans worked hard to attain the modern, prosperous lifestyle known as the 'American Dream' in the 1950s, but the liberalism and reforming zeal of America in the 1960s under Kennedy and Johnson was partnered by divisive political conflict. Set against the backdrop of a war in Vietnam and the growing campaign for African American civil rights, there was much debate about the idea that the federal government should expand its social and economic role, offering greater security and protection for those in need.

While the United States witnessed the development of Lyndon Johnson's 'Great Society' (the largest ever programme of social legislation), the USA still had to eradicate much poverty and extricate itself from the disastrous Vietnam War, which had a huge impact on domestic politics.

The period from 1961 to 1973 was also paradoxical for the presidency. It saw the office of president gaining increasing power and authority, to the extent that by 1970 many thought of the USA as having an 'imperial presidency'. Yet these years also witnessed the humbling and the subsequent destruction of two of its office-holders – Johnson in 1968 and especially Nixon in 1973–4 with his resignation after the Watergate scandal.

Thus the USA entered the mid-1970s troubled by social and domestic problems, assailed by campaigns for peace in Vietnam, for women's rights and for ethnic minority rights; at the same time weakened by the onset of an international oil crisis and recession. Democracy still prevailed, however, and the United States managed to avoid revolution.

South Africa

The end of the Cold War in 1990, followed by the collapse of the Soviet Union, caused another extension of democracy as countries in Eastern Europe adopted democratic constitutions. The end of the Cold War also had a significant impact on Africa, where superpower support for autocratic regimes ceased. This encouraged moves towards democracy in a number of African states, where multiparty democracies replaced one-party regimes in the early 1990s.

The end of the Cold War was a key factor leading to the collapse of apartheid in South Africa, where discriminatory laws had denied democratic rights to the majority of people. The establishment of a democratic government under the leadership of Nelson Mandela in 1994 signalled the end of white minority rule in South Africa, where it had continued long after other former colonies in Africa had gained independence under majority rule. This political transformation was the result of a successfully negotiated settlement that put an end to white domination and established a constitutional multiparty democracy.

SOURCE A

This is how Nelson Mandela described South Africa's first democratic election in 1994:

Great lines of patient people snaking through the dirt roads of towns and cities, old women who had waited half a century to cast their vote, saying they had felt like human beings for the first time in their lives, white men and women saying they were proud to live in a free country at last ... it was as though we were a nation reborn.'

From N. Mandela (2003), The Illustrated Long Walk to Freedom, *London: Little, Brown Book Group, p. 199.*

However, although fundamental political change took place in 1994, it was harder to bring about meaningful economic and social transformation. The new democratic government faced significant challenges. It introduced ambitious policies that improved the daily lives of millions of people, but fundamental economic and social transformation was more difficult to achieve. Twenty years after the advent of democracy, poverty and inequality remained two of the biggest challenges facing South Africa.

Themes and case studies

Themes

To help you prepare for your IB History exams, this book will cover the themes relating to democratic states as set out in the IB History Guide. It will cover the themes in four detailed case studies, one from each of the regions specified in the IB History curriculum. Each case study is dealt with in a separate chapter.

Figure 1.1 Voters queue patiently to cast their votes in the 1994 South African election

The three broad themes relating to democratic states are:

- The emergence of democratic states, which includes information on the conditions that led to the establishment of democracy, the role played by political parties and leaders, and how democratic institutions functioned.
- The development of democracy, which examines factors that influenced this development, the response of the government to domestic crises and issues relating to equality and civil protests.
- The impact of democracy on society, which includes information on social and economic policies, the extent to which citizens benefitted from them and the cultural impact of democracy.

Each of the detailed case study chapters has units dealing with these three themes, so that you will be able to focus on the main issues. This approach will help you compare and contrast the roles of individual leaders and parties, and the main developments in the various states covered – and to spot similarities and differences.

Case studies

The case studies in this book cover:

- Germany
- India
- the United States of America
- South Africa

All the main events, turning points and key individuals in each of these case studies will be covered in sufficient detail for you to be able to access the higher markbands – provided, of course, that your answers are both relevant and analytical.

Where appropriate, each chapter will contain visual and written sources, both to illustrate the events or issues under examination, and to provide material for exam-type questions to help you gain practice in dealing with the questions you will face in History Papers 1 and 2.

Key Concepts

To perform well in your IB History exams, you will often need to consider aspects of one or more of six important Key Concepts as you write your answers. These six Key Concepts are listed below:

- Change
- Continuity
- Causation
- Consequence
- Significance
- Perspectives

Sometimes, a question might ask you to address two Key Concepts: 'Evaluate the reasons for and the immediate impact of the partition of India in August 1947.'

It is important to note that although the word 'causes' doesn't explicitly appear in the question, words such as 'reasons' or 'why' are asking you to address Causation. Similarly, words such as 'impact 'or 'results' are asking you to address Consequence. To help you focus on these and gain experience of writing answers that address these Key Concepts, you will find a range of different questions and activities throughout these chapters.

Theory of Knowledge

Alongside these broad key themes, most chapters contain Theory of Knowledge links to get you thinking about aspects that relate to history, which is a Group 3 subject in the IB Diploma. The Democratic States topic has clear links to ideas about knowledge and history. The decisions, actions and policies of different governments and leaders have been the subject of differing interpretations by historians. Thus the questions relating to the availability and selection of sources, and to interpretations of these sources, have clear links to the IB Theory of Knowledge course.

For instance, when trying to explain aspects of the emergence and development of democratic states and the impact on society, historians have to decide which evidence to select and use – and which to leave out – to make their case. But in selecting what they consider to be the most important or relevant sources, and in making judgements about the value and limitations of specific sources or sets of sources, how important are these historians' personal political views? Is there such a thing as objective 'historical truth'? Or is there just a range of subjective opinions and interpretations about the past, which vary according to the political interests and leanings of individual historians?

You are therefore encouraged to read a range of books offering different interpretations of the structure and strength of democratic institutions, the role played by leaders (such as Nehru in India and Mandela in South Africa), and the effectiveness of the policies adopted by the states covered by this book, in order to gain a clear understanding of the relevant historiographies.

IB History and regions of the world

For the purposes of study, IB History specifies four regions of the world:

- Africa and the Middle East
- The Americas
- Asia and Oceania
- Europe

Where relevant, you will need to be able to identify these regions and to discuss developments that took place within them. These four regions are shown in Figure 1.2, which also indicates the states covered in the case studies.

Remember, when answering a question that asks you to choose examples from two different regions, you must be careful – failure to comply will result in limited opportunities to score high marks. Every year, some examination candidates attempting this kind of question select two states from the same region.

Exam skills needed for IB History

Throughout the main chapters of this book, there are various activities and questions to help you develop the understanding and the exam skills necessary for success. Before

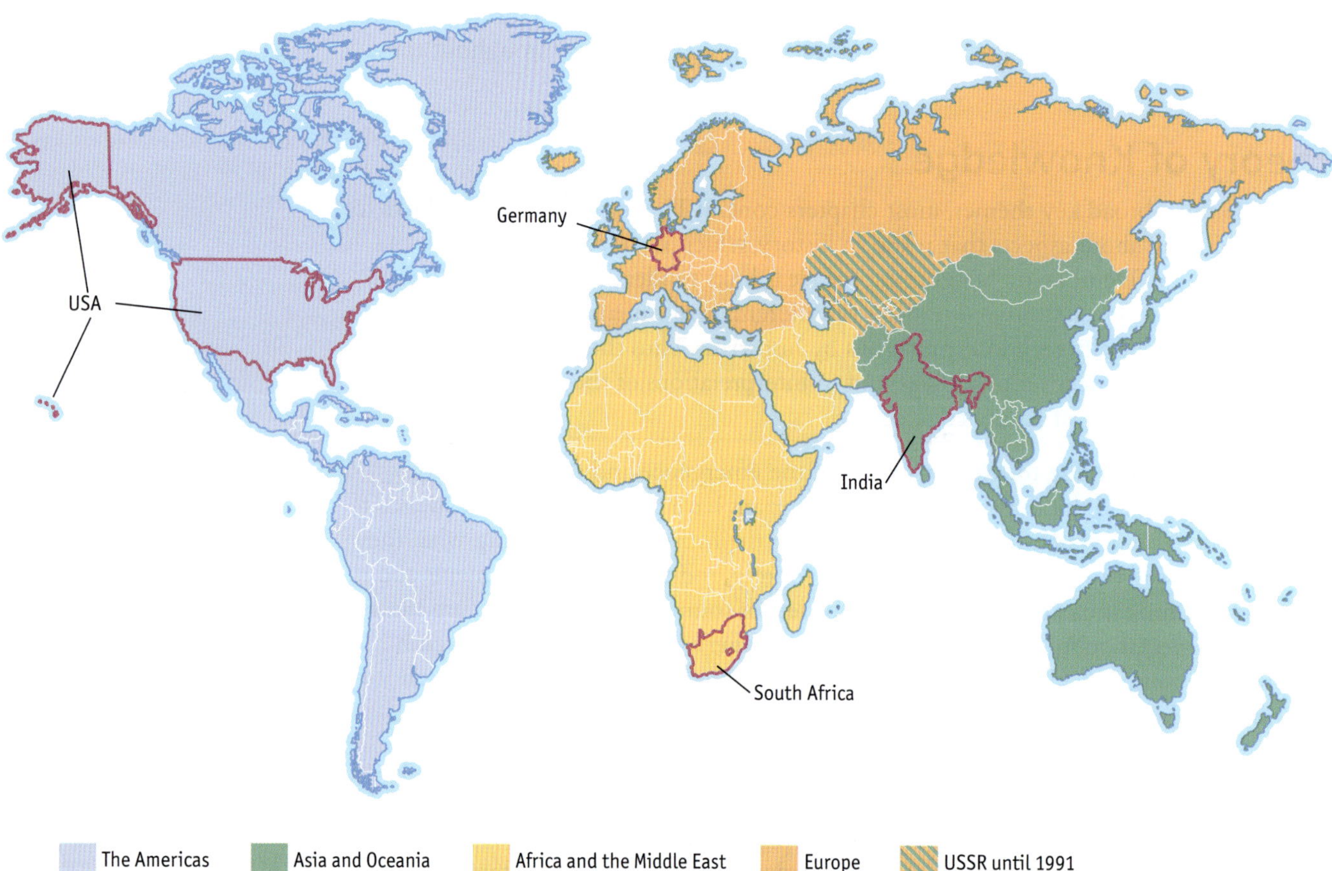

Figure 1.2 The four IB regions are shown on this map, along with the four countries covered by case studies in this book

attempting the specific exam practice questions at the end of each case study, you might find it useful to refer to Chapter 6 first – this suggestion is based on the idea that, if you know where you are supposed to be going (in this instance, gaining a good grade) and how to get there, you stand a better chance of reaching your destination!

Questions and mark schemes

To ensure that you develop the necessary understanding and skills, each chapter contains a number of comprehension questions in the margins. In addition, three of the main Paper 1-type questions (comprehension, reliability/utility and cross-referencing) are dealt with at the end of Chapters 2 to 5. Help for the longer Paper 1 judgement/synthesis questions and the Paper 2 essay questions can be found in Chapter 6 – the final exam practice chapter.

For additional help, simplified mark schemes have been put together in ways that should make it easier for you to understand what examiners are looking for in your answers. The actual IB History mark schemes can be found on the IB website.

Finally, you will find examiner's tips and comments, along with activities, to help you focus on the important aspects of the questions and answers, and to avoid simple mistakes and oversights that every year result in some otherwise good students failing to gain the highest marks.

Terminology and definitions

In order to understand the nature and structure of democratic states, you will need to understand the meaning of various terms and concepts relating to the functioning of a democracy.

Features of a democratic state

Although the nature and structure of democratic states may vary, there are certain key features of a modern democracy. These are:

- a parliament elected by universal franchise (meaning that all adults have the right to vote), in regular elections by secret ballot (meaning that the voter's name does not appear on the ballot paper);
- a constitution that determines how a specific democratic state will operate;
- freedom of expression, allowing public debate and criticism of government policies, and ensuring that the media are free of government control or restrictions;
- freedom of association, permitting the formation of political parties and pressure groups;
- the 'rule of law' (meaning that the state is governed according to its constitution and laws, and not according to decisions made by leaders or political parties);
- the 'separation of powers', ensuring that the three branches of government – the **legislature**, the **executive** and the **judiciary** – do not overlap.

The **legislature** (parliament) makes the laws; the **executive** (the government) administers the laws; the **judiciary** (law courts) upholds the laws.

Types of constitution

A constitution is the basic framework of a democratic state. It will determine, for example, the frequency of elections, and the basic structures of and relationships between the legislature, the executive and the judiciary. It will also clarify how much power the central government has over lower levels of administration (such as states, provinces, counties or cities). It may be a unitary constitution, giving most power to the central government and very limited power to the provinces (as in South Africa), or it may be a federal constitution, in which individual states retain certain powers but the central (federal) government has control over matters such as foreign policy and defence (as in the United States).

In most countries, the constitution is a written document, which is often drawn up as the result of painstaking negotiations by a constitutional (or constituent) assembly, as was the case in India where the Constituent Assembly took nearly three years to write the constitution. In other countries, there may be no written document at all, as in Britain, where the constitution gradually evolved over several centuries and is based on previous interpretations, rulings and judgements.

Elections and electoral systems

Regular elections are usually held every four or five years to elect representatives to the legislature (or parliament), and voting is by secret ballot. Although in modern democracies there is a universal franchise (with all adults having the right to vote), this was not always the case. In most Western countries, women were only given the right to vote after the First World War; most people living in colonies only gained the right to vote after independence from colonial rule; and in South Africa, black people were barred from voting at all until 1994. In many countries the voting age was lowered to eighteen from twenty-one after student protesters in the 1960s demanded a greater role in society for young people.

There are two main types of electoral system. In one, the whole country is divided into constituencies, or voting districts, in which the voters elect a member of parliament to represent them. The candidate who wins the most votes by a simple majority in each constituency is elected to parliament. Britain and the United States use this method, which is sometimes referred to as the 'first past the post system'. The other main electoral system is proportional representation (PR), where each party gains representation in parliament according to the proportion of total votes it receives in an election. In this system, which is the one used in many European countries, voters do not vote for individual candidates but for the party whose policies they support. As countries in other parts of the world drew up democratic constitutions they selected one of these systems. For example, India uses the constituency system, while South Africa chose proportional representation.

Figures 1.3 and 1.4 contrast the actual results of the 2015 General Election in the United Kingdom, which used the 'first past the post system', with the results that would have occurred under a simple system of proportional representation. The crudest version of proportional representation (PR) would give all parties seats in parliament based directly on their share of the vote; in practice, the countries that employ the PR system have thresholds in place in order to screen out the smallest parties.

If one of the larger parties fails to win an outright majority, it may be forced to form a coalition government with another party or several smaller parties. This is a temporary alliance in which parties cooperate to form a government together, but each party retains its own name and identity. Coalition governments are more common where a system of proportional representation is used because a greater number of parties generally gain representation in parliament under this system. Coalition governments may also be formed as a result of a pre-election agreement between parties – for example, in the interim

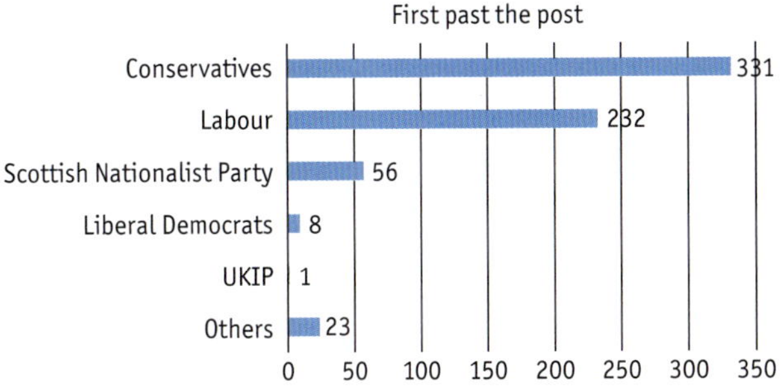

Figure 1.3 This graph shows the actual result of the 2015 UK General Election, based on the 'first past the post' system. This gave Conservative Party leader David Cameron a 12 seat majority, based on 650 seats up for election.

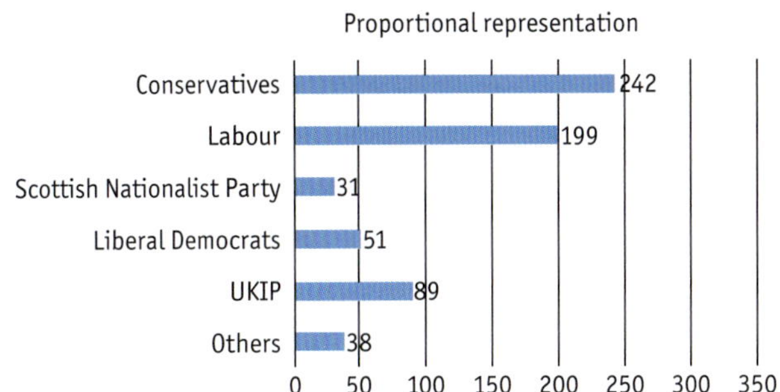

Figure 1.4 This graph shows how the 2015 UK General Election results would have looked if they had been based on a form of proportional representation. The result would have been far closer, with no overall majority for the Conservatives – 326 would have been required.

constitution drawn up before South Africa's first democratic election, it was agreed that there would be a coalition Government of National Unity for the first five years.

In some democratic systems, certain decisions are not made by the elected parliament but by the electorate themselves in a referendum. This is where voters are asked to vote 'yes' or 'no' on a specific issue, sometimes involving a change to the constitution, and the issue is decided by a simple majority.

Political parties and ideologies

In multiparty democracies there is usually a variety of political parties, ranging from left-wing (radical) to right-wing (conservative). These terms date from the time of the French Revolution when the more radical political groups sat on the left side of the National Convention and the more conservative ones sat on the right.

Those in the middle of the political spectrum are often referred to as 'moderates' or 'centrists'. However, it is important to remember that these terms are relative – a party that might be seen as radical in one country might be considered conservative in another context. Liberals, for example, are moderates who favour gradual progress and the improvement of society for all, by changing laws rather than by revolution. With a commitment to equality (viewed as left-wing) and a positive attitude to individual effort and freedom of choice (viewed as right-wing), they are usually seen as being in the middle of the political spectrum. However, many liberals would consider themselves to be 'radical' (wishing to make substantial changes in society), rather than 'in the middle'.

Communists and socialists are both left-wing parties, and the two ideologies are often confused. Communism is a political and economic belief that the state should own and control the means of production (such as land, mines and factories), and organise labour and industrial output to benefit all people, so that all levels of society can be equal. Communists believe that, in this way, everyone will contribute as much as they can and earn as much as they need. Socialism is a political and economic system in which the production and distribution of goods are controlled mainly by the government rather than by private enterprise, and in which cooperation rather than competition guides economic activity. There are many varieties of socialism. Some socialists tolerate **capitalism** as long as the government maintains the dominant influence over the economy; others insist on the abolition of private enterprise. All communists are socialists, but not all socialists are communists.

Capitalism: an economic system based on private ownership, minimal government intervention in the economy, free enterprise and competition; a free market economy in which prices and wages are determined by supply and demand rather than by government policy.

The political parties who fail to win an election form the parliamentary opposition. Opposition parties play an important role in a democracy by maintaining a critical watch on government policies and raising questions in parliament about government expenditure and other issues. Outside parliament, pressure groups can also play a watchdog role or try to influence government policies. They may represent a range of different interests, such as religious groups, trade unions, business leaders, environmentalists and other civil society organisations.

Summary

By the time you have worked through this book, you should be able to:

- understand the key features of a democratic state;
- explain the terms and concepts associated with democracy;
- understand the importance of a constitution;
- compare electoral systems;
- show an awareness of the role and significance of leaders and political parties in a democracy;
- understand the emergence of democratic states in different global contexts and the factors that influenced the evolution of democracy in them;
- show an awareness of the challenges they faced in maintaining and extending democratic practices;
- understand how they responded to social, economic and political issues and crises;
- understand key economic and social policies regarding education, social welfare, policies towards women and minorities, and the distribution of wealth;
- understand the impact of the freedom of expression bestowed by democracy to those in the world of the arts and media, and the benefits and problems that have naturally ensued;
- compare the emergence, development and impact of democracy in three democratic states from more than one region.

Germany 2

From empire to democracy: the emergence of a democratic Germany Unit 1

KEY QUESTIONS

- What conditions led to the establishment of democracy in Germany?
- What role did leaders and political parties play?
- How did democracy function in modern Germany by 1955?

Overview

- Germany changed from a Prussian-dominated monarchy, with little democracy in 1871, to a modern multiparty democracy by 1955.
- The Kaiser (emperor), as monarch, had immense influence in state affairs.
- Wilhelm II (reigned 1888–1918) in particular largely preserved the existing, rigid German political system, which operated to the detriment of many political parties and social groups.
- To many, the birth of democratic politics came with the emergence of the Social Democrats as the largest party in the 1912 Reichstag elections.
- Germany's defeat in the First World War brought a revolution in November 1918 that ended the monarchy and led to the establishment of the democratic Weimar Republic.
- The republic was headed by a president, and administered by a chancellor (prime minister) and a cabinet of ministers.
- Weimar became unworkable by 1932, leading to the dictatorship of Adolf Hitler and the Nazi Party (1933–45).
- After 1945, democracy gradually took root again in the western part of Germany.
- In 1949 West Germany was created when three occupied Western zones (USA, Britain and France) were absorbed into a new state, the Federal Republic of Germany (BRD).
- The Soviet zone – East Germany – became the communist German Democratic Republic (DDR).
- The BRD, under democratically elected chancellor Konrad Adenauer, became a full member of NATO and a sovereign state by 1955.
- The BRD became a major western ally and founder of the European Union (EU) in 1957.

TIMELINE

1871 New German Reichstag elected.

1888 Wilhelm II becomes kaiser.

1890 Fall of Bismarck. Power now in hands of kaiser and military.

1914 First World War breaks out.

1918 **Nov:** Germany signs armistice emerging defeated from the war. Kaiser abdicates.

1919 **Feb:** National Assembly meets at Weimar: Ebert chosen as president of new German (Weimar) Republic.

1925 Ebert dies. Hindenburg elected president.

1930 **Sep:** Reichstag elections; Nazi Party, wins 107 seats.

1933 **Jan:** Nazi Party's Adolf Hitler invited to be chancellor.

Mar: Enabling Act; end of Weimar Republic; start of Third Reich.

1945 **May:** Second World War ends. Germany in ruins, occupied by four Allied powers: USA, USSR, Britain and France.

1945 **Jun–Dec:** The four powers allow formation of political parties: SPD, CPU, KPD and LDPD.

1948 **6 Jun:** The Six Power Conference agrees outlines of new federal state in West Germany.

20 Jun: The new Deutsche mark introduced in western zones.

1949 **24 May:** Foundation of BRD (Bundesrepublik Deutschland)

15 Sep: Konrad Adenauer of CDU elected chancellor.

7 Oct: Foundation of DDR in East Germany

1952 **May:** Adenauer signs General Treaty with Western allies. Germany's 'occupied territory' status formally ends.

1953 Adenauer re-elected.

1955 **May:** BRD officially a democratic, sovereign state; joins NATO.

2.1 What conditions led to the establishment of democracy in Germany?

From empire to democracy: a contextual background

Figure 2.1 Political map of the German Empire 1871–1918

Germany is situated geographically in the centre of Europe. It is a federal, parliamentary, democratic republic, with a population in 2014 of around eighty-two million people. Germany is the most populous state in the **European Union (EU)** and also has the largest national economy in Europe. As recently as 1990, this modern 'Germany' was formed with the amalgamation of the former German Democratic Republic (DDR or East Germany) and the Federal Republic of Germany (BRD or West Germany) into a single entity, with its capital in Berlin.

European Union (EU): comprising twenty-eight European member states, the EU is a political and economic union that evolved out of the European Economic Community (EEC) of six nations, created in 1957.

Up to the early 19th century, Germany had meant the 'Holy Roman Empire of the German Nation' (the Roman Empire restored by the Christian King Charlemagne), a feudal state comprising numerous small territories with different cultures and ethnicities, governed by relatively independent rulers. By the late 1860s, Germany was a confederation of thirty-nine states, and politicians focused on the question of whether or not there should be a single 'Germany'.

The German Confederation finally united and created an empire in 1870. Accordingly, the German Reich (Empire) was proclaimed under the leadership of Prussia and its Kaiser (emperor) Wilhelm I. The unification of Germany changed the balance of power in Europe, for under the leadership of the Kaisers and their chancellors – notably **Otto von Bismarck** – Germany became a growing industrial player, a modernising nation and an enthusiastic, aggressive, colonial and military power.

Paradoxically this new, unified Germany was a largely illiberal nation where democracy struggled to flourish, its political structure dominated by autocratic, landed elites. From 1888 to 1918, Germany's ruler was Kaiser **Wilhelm II**, and there was a stormy marriage in the Reich he inherited between democracy and the Prussian monarchy.

Wilhelm II took advantage of the constitution of the empire (see below) to manipulate the chancellor (prime minister) to secure the funds he wanted from the Reichstag for the army and navy. In short, despite the existence of a parliament (or Reichstag), it was the Kaiser who introduced laws, selected the ministers, declared war and made peace. He only allowed the Reichstag to change laws occasionally and, although there were several political parties, he ruled Germany with virtually complete power. Germany's defeat in the First World War in 1918, however, brought major changes. A naval mutiny in November 1918 precipitated a revolution that led to Germany seeking an armistice with the western Allies – and to the Kaiser being replaced by a liberal, democratic republic. Named after the town where the first constituent assembly took place, the Weimar Republic had an elected president as head of state, with daily government being administered by a chancellor and cabinet of ministers; the Weimar Republic heralded a dramatic change for Germany after the First World War. But having emerged from a national defeat and a revolution, this liberal democracy never fully escaped the difficulties of its conception and was beset by unfavourable national and international financial crises. Ultimately, it failed in the early 1930s and led directly to the dictatorship of Adolf Hitler and the Nazis (1933–45). The failure of the Weimar Republic was the failure of the first truly democratic parliamentary system in Germany.

The twelve years of Nazi dictatorship under Hitler led to even greater loss and defeat in the Second World War by 1945. From the ruins of Hitler's defeated state, Soviet forces occupied eastern Germany, while the United States, Britain and France occupied the western half of the nation. This political division of Germany into a democratic West Germany and a one-party communist state, East Germany, subsequently became permanent and epitomised the **Cold War** in Europe for more than forty years. Reunification did not occur until 1990.

Democracy was rekindled with the formation of the Bundesrepublik Deutschland (BDR) in western Germany in 1949. Under the leadership of chancellor Konrad Adenauer and his economics minister Ludwig Erhard (see section 2.2, The Federal Republic of Germany) the BRD underwent an impressive post-war reconstruction, achieving the so-called 'economic miracle' of the 1950s.

By 1955, West Germany was finally deemed to be a fully democratic and sovereign state (see below), and by the 1960s the BDR was a trusted Western ally, a liberal democracy and dynamic, industrial state. But democracy did not prevail in all of Germany, and the eastern part – the Deutsche Demokratische Republik (DDR) – remained a one-party communist state within the Soviet sphere of influence until 1989.

By 1990, German reunification was once more a reality, following the dissolution of the communist-led DDR in 1989, with the end of the Cold War. On 3 October 1990,

Otto von Bismarck (1815–98)

He was a Prussian statesman and chief minister who became the first chancellor of the new united Germany in 1871. Bismarck aimed to build a powerful central European state with a unified national identity. He wanted the German Empire to be the most powerful in Europe. In 1890 he resigned as chancellor after disagreeing with the new Kaiser, Wilhelm II. It ended a career of long service: twenty-eight years as Prussia's prime minister followed by nineteen years as the German chancellor.

Wilhelm II (1859–1941)

He was the eldest son of Prince Friedrich of Prussia and his wife, Princess Victoria – eldest daughter of Queen Victoria of Britain. He became Kaiser in 1888 and immediately fell out with his chancellor, Bismarck. An immature and jealous man, Wilhelm was obsessed with outshining his British relations. Being militaristic, he wanted to expand the army and navy so that it exceeded that of Great Britain. He was forced to abdicate in 1918, when Germany was defeated in the First World War. He fled to Holland and lived there in exile until his death.

West and East Germany formally joined together and were reunified for the first time since 1945. When German federal elections took place two months later, it was the first free and universal election in all of Germany since 1933, with electors in the eastern part of the country included and free to choose. Thus the wheel had come full circle from unification in 1870 to reunification in 1990.

Cold War: hostilities short of direct armed conflict, consisting of spying, threats, propaganda and supporting conflicts by proxy. This term was applied specifically to the state of affairs between the Western powers (USA, Britain and France) and the USSR, between the end of the Second World War and the collapse of the communist regimes in Eastern Europe in the late 1980s.

The establishment of democracy has been neither easy, nor consistent. This study now examines how circumstances and conditions in Germany at different times led to the establishment of democracy; first by assessing the extent to which it was present by the time the First World War broke out in 1914; then looking at attempts to establish democracy between 1919 and 1933 in the period of the Weimar Republic; and finally seeing how democracy rose from the ashes of Nazi tyranny to re-establish itself securely in the BRD, or West Germany, by 1955.

How democratic was Germany by 1914? Between German unification in 1870 and the outbreak of the First World War in 1914, Germany transformed itself from a confederation of disparate and largely agrarian states into Europe's leading economic power. During this period, German steel production had increased eightfold, whereas Britain's had only doubled, and by 1914 Germany was poised to outstrip Britain as Europe's superpower. But Germany fell behind Britain and several other countries with regard to its democratic credentials.

Prussia was the largest and most powerful of the German Empire's constituent parts – comprising 60 per cent of the Reich's population of forty-one million – and its power and influence dominated the new **constitution**. It was also the most reactionary state.

Constitution: the rules and principles governing a state.

Federalism: a type of government where individual states retain a considerable degree of power, but where the central or federal government has control over such matters as foreign policy and defence.

Unitary state: a government where the constitution has given strong powers to the central government and limited power to provinces or states within a confederation.

The constitution of the German Empire

The constitution of the German Empire drawn up by Bismarck in 1871 was a compromise between the forces of conservative **federalism**, and liberals who wanted a more **unitary state**.

Federalism was enshrined in the Bundesrat (Federal Council), which consisted of fifty-eight representatives from the various state governments. In theory, it was the key decision-making body, representing all parts of Germany and the independent interests of these states. It alone had the right to make changes to the constitution, and the agreement of the Bundesrat was necessary for all legislation. With the assent of the Kaiser, the Bundesrat also had the authority to declare war and settle disputes between states.

But Prussian dominance was overwhelming, having being apportioned seventeen of the seats at the Bundesrat council table; yet any military or constitutional issue could be vetoed by the opposition of fourteen votes. So Prussia guaranteed its privileged position within the political structure of the Reich.

The Imperial Parliament or Reichstag is somewhat more ambiguous. In what appeared to be a real concession to liberal democracy in the new constitution, the Reichstag was directly elected by both secret ballot and universal male suffrage. Its assent was required for all legislation, including the periodic renewal of the military budget. It was also made up of a wide variety of independent political parties, representing the full spectrum of political interests; moreover, it had the power to question the chancellor and to debate his policies.

But the Reichstag lacked most of the powers associated with full democracy. Neither the chancellor nor any other minister was responsible to the Reichstag for their actions.

Moreover, it could not introduce legislation, but only discuss or ratify bills or proposals put forward by the Bundesrat and the imperial government.

They had no direct control over foreign policy, nor – beyond the voting of the military budget – over the conduct of the army. In short, the Reichstag was a representative assembly – albeit relatively democratically elected for the time – but it possessed no real power, and the political parties within it could play no direct role in the formulation of national policy.

This was exactly how the Kaiser wanted it to be, as he enjoyed great authority as of right. He had the final word over the conduct of German foreign policy, he was commander-in-chief of all armed forces in the Reich during peace and war, and he alone could appoint and dismiss the chancellor and the key state secretaries who made up the imperial government. It also meant that the appointed chancellor was not dependent on the confidence of a parliamentary majority. The Kaiser thus had immense powers at his disposal, should he so wish to exercise them, and Wilhelm II made full use of this.

Bismarck's constitution as drawn up in 1870–1 embraced two different political mentalities; one firmly planted in the roots of **liberalism**, the other acknowledging the authoritarian government pre-eminent in the German states before 1870. German democracy depended upon which mentality blossomed.

Liberalism: a political doctrine that views the promotion and protection of the freedom of the individual as integral to politics. Liberals believe that government is a necessity in order to protect individuals from harm by others; but they acknowledge that government itself can pose a real threat to liberty.

Another problem was that the Reich had no mass political parties with broad support bases. Many of the parties were more or less closely intertwined, or represented a distinct section of society, whose narrow interests were usually advocated. The most striking challenge came from the Social Democratic Party of Germany (SPD) after 1890.

Bismarck had viewed socialism as a menace and used two assassination attempts on Kaiser Wilhelm I in 1878 to introduce a law banning meetings aimed at spreading socialist principles. He did not ban the Social Democrat Party, but outlawed trade unions and closed forty-five newspapers, which crippled the SPD. After Bismarck resigned in 1890, his anti-socialist laws lapsed. This led to the meteoric rise of the SPD in parliament.

It promptly organised itself nationwide, and in the seven Reichstag elections between 1887 and 1912 the SPD jumped from 11 to 110 seats out of 397. It was the largest political party in Germany at the outbreak of the First World War.

Kaiser Wilhelm II himself pursued policies that maintained the dominance of narrow social élites, despite changes elsewhere in Europe. He opposed those with liberal sympathies and remained steadfast in his desire for personal rule. In 1913 the Kaiser commented that 'the German parliamentarian becomes daily more of a swine', and the four chancellors succeeding Bismarck were essentially dependent upon Wilhelm II for their political survival. When the Kaiser's personal involvement was often erratic, hot-tempered and blundering, this made for difficult government.

The election results of 1912 had ensured that the conservatives in parliament were on their guard against the rising tide of socialism; but the very nature of the constitution and the dominance of reactionary Prussians meant that Germany in 1914 remained largely conservative. There was indeed a rapid growth in social democratic politics, demanding a transformation of society; but in practice, many SPD deputies in the Reichstag were content to preach the rhetoric of revolution while working for change within the existing system.

Theory of Knowledge

History and ethics:
Look at the Kaiser's views on members of the German parliament. What do you think of them and his tone? Is it acceptable for an unelected, hereditary head of state to interfere so strongly in the daily running of a country? There is a saying that 'the end justifies the means' – but does it always? What exactly does this phrase mean? Is it ever right for any government or leader to use undemocratic or unlawful methods to achieve what is viewed as a justifiable and correct outcome?

There was a fervent message from the Kaiser and the government that this was a united nation-state named Germany. Yet Polish speakers in eastern Germany, French speakers in Alsace-Lorraine and stubborn independent Bavarians in southern Germany felt anything but German or united, while many Germans living in Austria and elsewhere were not included. Such ethnic and cultural divides later returned to haunt the nation. But Germany in 1914 was relatively stable, economically strong, largely autocratic and only notionally democratic. Perhaps apart from the SPD, no party yet believed that any lasting benefits might come out of constitutional change, and in Germany generally there existed a cautious, almost ambivalent attitude towards parliamentary democracy.

Constitutional monarchy: where the monarch has limited power within the lines of a constitution, and political power is in the hands of a civilian government.

Fact: Germans were war-weary by 1918. Millions were on the edge of starvation due to an Allied blockade; influenza was ravaging a weakened population; and riots erupted following a naval mutiny at Kiel. The Imperial Naval Command in Kiel ordered a fleet to sea for a final battle against the British Royal Navy. This edict triggered a mutiny on 24 October among the sailors, and then a general revolution. They refused to risk injury or death when the war was so obviously about to end, thinking it futile.

How democratic was the Weimar Republic in its government and structure?

Germany went to war in 1914, with the support of most people, but by 1917 morale had slumped. There was a bleak military situation, food and fuel shortages, increasing civilian mortality, and shop prices double those of 1914. In 1918, social discontent grew against the Kaiser and politicians who had demanded total war. General Erich Ludendorff, a key military leader, sensed the likelihood of defeat and wanted to steer Germany towards becoming a **constitutional monarchy**, with the Kaiser or another member of the royal family on the throne, while establishing a more democratic government.

Ludendorff hoped that it would prevent a revolution and make the Allies more sympathetic to a democratic government. It might also shift the responsibility for defeat away from the leadership of 1914–18 and place responsibility in the hands of a new administration. In the last month of the war, a moderate chancellor was appointed: Prince Max of Baden, known in Europe for his work with the Red Cross and possessing more liberal views. Wilhelm II relinquished his powers over the armed forces, the chancellor and his ministers were now made accountable to the Reichstag instead of the Kaiser, and armistice talks began with Britain, France and the USA. But hopes of a transition to democracy via constitutional monarchy unravelled when naval mutinies at Kiel and Hamburg led to a general revolution, sweeping aside the monarchy.

On 9 November 1918, the Kaiser abdicated and went into exile in Holland. His departure paved the way for talks between Germany and the Allied powers, and the war ended two days later. A revolutionary climate existed in Germany, but unlike Russia, where a communist government emerged out of their 1917 revolution, the Social Democrats (SPD) – as the largest political party – took the helm of government and proclaimed Germany a democratic republic. **Friedrich Ebert**, the SPD leader, replaced the Kaiser as the national leader. Following an interim period, elections subsequently confirmed Ebert as president. He then convened a conference in the southern town of Weimar, away from riot-torn Berlin, to discuss how best to run Germany.

Friedrich Ebert (1871–1925)

He was the first Weimar Republic president of Germany, a post he held from 1919 until his sudden death in 1925. Ebert had to deal with a loss of national morale following the country's defeat and the imposition of the Treaty of Versailles. He also presided over economic depression, the Ruhr Crisis and the devastating impact of hyperinflation in 1923. After 1920 – when Weimar's first parliament met – Ebert lost support among the German people, who believed that Versailles was simply a non-military way of destroying their country.

The new Weimar Constitution

The new Weimar Republic born in 1919 had political parties and was elected on the basis of **proportional representation (PR)**. This raised hopes of true democracy following wartime humiliation.

Germany had a newly written Constitution, which was democratic and fair. The Weimar Constitution was strongly influenced by liberals who played a key part in its preparation. All Germans had the right of free speech and equal rights. Everybody – men and women – over the age of twenty had the right to vote. This was very forward-looking, given that in Britain at that time only women over twenty-eight years of age could vote. The new constitution created a bicameral assembly – a parliament made up of two layers. One layer (the Reichstag) represented the whole nation and made national decisions, while the upper house (the Reichsrat) represented the regions.

Proportional representation (PR): a system of electing a government that allocates seats in parliament in proportion to the number of votes cast by the electors.

A major break from the undemocratic tendencies of Bismarck's constitution can be seen in relation to the Reichsrat. Unlike the Prussian dominated pre-war Bundesrat, the Reichsrat were now subservient in all respects to the Reichstag. The people elected the president and the politicians who sat in parliament by direct vote. Germany was established as a federal state with regional states (Länder), retaining much autonomy.

The head of state was the Reich president, to be elected by popular vote every seven years. He was the commander of the armed forces and was considered to be a ceremonial president or more of a figurehead, supposedly removed from the day-to-day running of the country. But he had the authority to dissolve the Reichstag and to nominate a chancellor (prime minister), who could command the support of the majority of the Reichstag. But in a crisis he could rule alone, since, under Article 48, the president could declare a national state of emergency and rule by presidential decree. He was also empowered to veto any Reichstag that he disapproved of.

The parliament was elected every four years using PR. This made it virtually impossible for one party to get an overall majority (more than half the votes). There were twenty separate coalition governments between 1919 and 1933, with the longest-serving government surviving two years. This instability caused many Germans to be dismayed by the new democratic system and played into the hands of those who opposed the Weimar Constitution. But the democratic credentials of the Weimar Constitution were strong.

Unlike the unrepresentative nature of the parliaments in the German Empire between 1870 and 1918, forty political parties were represented in the Reichstag, and they embraced groups and opinions from all sides of the political spectrum; but they also differed in their degree of support for, or opposition to, the democratic constitution.

The constitution also outlined individual freedoms in a Bill of Rights guaranteeing personal liberty, the right to free speech, religious freedom and conscience, the prohibiting of a state Church, no censorship and equality of the law for all Germans. A Supreme Court was created in order to settle different interpretations of the law.

Inter-party squabbling soon led to difficulties in passing legislation and to weakened, indecisive government. So alternative parties with more extreme ideas evolved. But this fragmentation of political power was only partly due to the peculiar parliamentary system adopted by the Weimar Republic; it was also due to economic challenges facing both German democracy and the wider world. President Ebert reminded people what the country had endured and argued for the permanent establishment of liberal democratic traditions in German government.

But since PR made the decision-making process very slow and divisive, people started to resent the system of government. In the public mind, the constitution became linked to the surrender in 1918. Its politicians became the 'November Criminals' – men who had betrayed the fatherland by surrendering to the Allies. Little wonder then that some of the older aristocratic families, army generals, judges, industrialists and academics longed for 'the good old days', with one strong leader running the nation, as was voiced by one old soldier in Source A.

SOURCE A

Politicians! What is this democracy? We never used to have democracy. We had strong leaders like the Kaiser. We never voted for him and was Germany ever so weak under the Kaiser? I spit on freedom – it's the patriotic thing to do!

From the BBC series History File: Nazi Germany, *in A. Wilkes (2006),* Germany 1918–45, *Haddenham: Folens Publishers, p. 11.*

QUESTION

How did people feel towards the new Weimar Republic and its constitution? What problems might this lead to when it was in government?

KEY CONCEPTS ACTIVITY

Change and Continuity: Re-read this section, then draw up a chart to summarise the main differences between the constitutions of imperial Germany and that of the Weimar Republic. Indicate where change or continuity is represented.

In section 2.2, an examination of the challenges and opposition to Weimar Germany will show that this fledgling democracy survived its troubled birth, and from 1924 to 1929, enjoyed a period of relative stability and limited prosperity. Indeed, this period of democracy lasted longer than Hitler's Nazi dictatorship, although its democratic credentials were highly compromised after 1930 when President Hindenburg used the Weimar Constitution to invoke Article 48, by which he could declare a state of emergency and rule by decree without the Reichstag.

The significance of the Weimar Constitution

Historians have different views on the Weimar Constitution. A.J. Nicholls sees it as a true democratic advance for Germany, bringing a more representative democratic system into being. Conversely, Gordon Craig views it as part of an 'aborted revolution' that failed to change basic political attitudes. Eberhard Kolb views the constitution as a halfway point between progressive political ideas and protecting more traditional elements, noting that the provisions for presidential rule by decree in Article 48 might be seen as making the president 'a kind of "ersatz emperor"' and reflected the mistrust that the fathers of the Weimar Constitution felt towards a fully parliamentary system on a democratic party basis.

The constitution had its weaknesses; for example, Article 48 – also the relationship between the president and the Reichstag – and then the potential pitfalls of PR. But it was a not fatally flawed document and Germany was transformed into a democratic republic. It offered a new approach and as such it was passed in the Reichstag in July 1919 by 262 votes to seventy-five. What the constitution could not control were the circumstances in which it had to operate, but it was a remarkable attempt to fashion out of defeat a constitution that would be the antithesis of authoritarian imperial Germany. Weimar Germany was initially seen as the most progressive democracy in the world and in the vanguard of constitutional modernity, where democracy had fallen into the lap of a shattered nation.

Democracy and sovereignty: Germany 1945–55

Following the end of the Second World War in Europe and the unconditional surrender of Nazi German military leaders in May 1945, Germany was badly damaged by Allied bombing campaigns and military battles. Its economic infrastructure had collapsed, as transport systems and factories almost ceased to function. Sovereign authority had passed to the victorious occupying Allied powers and would not be restored until 1955 to the western part of Germany.

The US, Britain, France and the USSR divided Germany into four zones (see Figure 2.2), with Berlin, the former capital, part of the Soviet zone, but partitioned into four sectors

Figure 2.2 Germany divided into four occupation zones, 1945

for administrative purposes and placed under the joint authority of the four powers. Soon, growing differences between the Soviets and the Western Allied powers inevitably led to the permanent division of Germany; and by 1947 it was evident that the USSR would not allow free, multiparty elections throughout the whole of the country. Alarm bells had sounded when, in the previous year, SPD leaders in the Soviet zone opted to amalgamate with the Communist Party, a move condemned by the SPD in the western zone. Consequently the Americans and the British merged the administration in their occupation zones in order to create greater efficiency and hopefully encourage speedier economic recovery. This resulting unit was called Bizonia, and its federal structure would serve as the prototype for the West German state, with the Social Democrats and the Christian Democrats soon establishing themselves as the major political parties. Then, in an attempt to halt growing political and fiscal integration between the western zones, the USSR blockaded western Berlin between June 1948 and May 1949. During this period, politicians from western Germany began to draft a new constitution and ultimately the Basic Law was passed on 23 May 1949. This law ratified a new constitution for the Federal Republic of Germany (Bundesrepublik Deutschland, BRD) and so heralded the start of the second German democracy in the 20th century. The Basic Law, or Grundgesetz, stipulated that it was designed only for interim purposes, to provide a temporary but authoritative guideline until all the German people had agreed to its provisions and freely adopted it. But this democratic constitution was ultimately enacted only in one half of Germany. The eastern part of Germany became the DDR – a one-party communist state operating within the Soviet sphere of influence – and this split brought to an end the unified state created in 1871, until the reunification of 1990.

QUESTION

What type of problems were going to be created by the geographical division of Germany among the four Allied powers?

The Bonn republic and its constitution

The Constitution of the BRD is called the Basic Law or Grundgesetz and was drawn up in Germany after the Second World War. The new constitution of the BRD specifically sought to avoid repeating the experience and problems of the Weimar Republic Constitution and tried to correct those defects. The Basic Law was conceived under unusual circumstances, since it was drafted under Allied occupation and with the Allied powers' influence.

It was drafted on the heels of the disaster of Nazi rule but, most significantly, it was drafted under the circumstances of the territorial division of Germany that occurred after 1945, with disagreements between the Western Allied powers and the Soviet Union, in their respective zones of occupation. Until German reunification in 1990, the Basic Law applied only to West Germany. The eastern part was under the DDR, in effect a one-part communist state and Soviet satellite.

The city of Bonn was selected as the capital of the BRD, and the head of state was to be a largely ceremonial president, elected for five years by parliament and allowed no more than two terms in office. Parliament was made up of two houses: the Bundestag (federal parliament) and the Bundesrat (upper house). The electoral system no longer comprised just PR, but allowed for 50 per cent of the Bundestag to be elected by a majority vote. The new constitution helped the BRD to lay the basis for the creation of a stable democracy at the second attempt.

2.2 What role did leaders and political parties play?

The nature and structure of democracy in Germany were shaped at various times between 1870 and 1955 by key political parties and leaders. In this section, these political forces and important personalities will be examined.

The Social Democrats in imperial Germany

Political parties in pre-1914 Germany had a limited role. A political party is usually defined by its constitutional ability and readiness to assume power and achieve its aims through the political structure present in that society. Political parties also usually have outstanding or instantly recognisable leaders. This did not really apply in Germany, since political parties had limited opportunities to exercise power. The Kaiser and his government largely operated independently, and governments were frequently unrelated to the strength of political parties as expressed at elections. Historian Peter Nettl states that 'the political parties in Germany before 1914 can better be described as politically organised interest groups, attempting to exert pressure on the Government in order to gain sectional advantages'.

From 1870 until Bismarck's resignation in 1890, the Reichstag was dominated by either the Liberal Party or the Centre Party.

The Liberals were traditionally the party of economic and political liberalism and represented bankers and industrialists who shared Bismarck's desire for a centralised state; but they were at variance with him in their support for progressive social and constitutional legislation.

The Centre Party, formed in 1871, upheld the interests of the Catholic Church. Its appeal was therefore denominational rather than class based. But David Blackbourn has showed that the Centre Party became increasingly less clerical and began to attract lower-middle-class interests and held the balance of power between left and right from 1890 to 1914.

Then came the Social Democrats (*Sozialdemokratische Partei Deutschlands*, SPD). They grew rapidly between the elections of 1887 and 1890, increasing their seats from eleven to thirty-five. By 1912 they had more than a million members and were the largest party in the Reichstag, with 110 seats. It was a meteoric rise after years of persecution were ended by the lapse of Bismarck's anti-socialist laws in 1890.

The SPD argued for a total collapse of the existing order, and based its policies on that assumption. Unsurprisingly it was seen as a pariah, as historian Peter Nettl comments in **Source B**.

SOURCE B

For twelve years, from 1878 to 1890, it was illegal; after Bismarck departed and the special anti-socialist legislation was repealed, the SPD never lost the conscious feeling of being an outcast, and adopted attitudes accordingly.

P. Nettl (1965), 'The German Social Democratic Party 1890–1914 as a political model', Past and Present, *No. 30, pp. 65–95.*

QUESTION

What does **Source B** tell us about the nature of German society in general?

But by 1914, the SPD was a nationwide mass party, using friendly newspapers to argue for more democracy, highlighting how the courts and the police were used as instruments of repression. The SPD lampooned the personal failings and personalities of leading figures in sympathetic publications, yet privately party officials were moderate in their everyday politics out of necessity – but remained radical in principle.

Historians have suggested that the growth of the SPD and its demands for democracy were the imperial government's major internal concern up to 1914. SPD growth in the Reichstag is certainly indicative of dissatisfaction emanating from the working classes. From time to time, the SPD forced the government to adopt policies that would gain support from their followers. They achieved educational and health care improvements while advocating better rights and conditions for industrial workers. Yet in order to maintain presence and influence, the SPD sometimes worked with, rather than against, the government. For example, in 1913 the SPD supported increased taxes designed to fund the Kaiser's desired military expansion.

Real democracy had not been established by 1914, but the SPD had come to prominence. Extending democracy throughout the economy and society was seen to be the primary task of their movement, as it represented the equality and classlessness at the heart of their project.

The Weimar Republic 1919–23

Friedrich Ebert and the Social Democratic Party

Friedrich Ebert (1871–1925) was the first president of Germany under the Weimar Republic from 1919 until his sudden death in office. As an apprentice saddler from a very modest background, he was involved in trade union work and administration for the socialist movement. He entered the Reichstag in 1912 and was soon the chairman of the SPD. When Germany collapsed in 1918, he wanted a democratic parliamentary government with a constitutional monarchy along British lines, but events moved rapidly: the Kaiser abdicated, the elites of the defeated monarchy and army were depressed and had dispersed; and political power in post-war Germany fell into the lap of the largest pre-war political party, the Social Democrats (SPD). As Ebert accepted the chancellorship, it fell to him and the SPD to cope with the repercussions of the war and build a democracy.

His task was enormous in a parliamentary system that had come into existence through military defeat and national humiliation. But as historians such as Geoff Layton have pointed out, it was a real achievement to manage to hold the first truly democratic German election, which led to the Constituent Assembly and the creation of the Weimar Constitution.

Building a democratic Germany from the despair of defeat required decisive measures that would not satisfy extremes on both the left and the right. Ebert was condemned by the far left for not being revolutionary enough, while the extreme right regarded the entire SPD as too radical. To loyal supporters of the Kaiser, he represented the ineffectual and hated democratic system; while to the army generals and nationalists, he was the man who quit the war and humbled Germany to the Western powers. His hopes in maintaining democracy were immediately tested with the communist Spartacist Uprising in January 1919 and the right-wing Kapp Putsch of March 1920. These were the first threats to the democratic republic.

The Spartacists were founded in 1915 and were a group of radical socialists led by Rosa Luxemburg and Karl Liebknecht, from those who left the SPD when it supported the war. In January 1919, they founded the German Communist Party (*Kommunistische Partei Deutschlands*, KDP), refused to participate in parliamentary elections and mounted an armed rising in Berlin with the aim of overthrowing Ebert and creating a workers' style soviet republic. After three days of street fighting and more than one hundred

Figure 2.3 Freikorps soldiers in the streets of Berlin during the Kapp Putsch in 1920, when they attempted to overthrow the Weimar Republic and bring back the Kaiser

Fact: The Kapp Putsch was a right-wing threat to Weimar's democracy, which occurred in Berlin in March 1920. It was led by Wolfgang Kapp and a group of Freikorps, opposed to what they saw as the liberal democracy of Ebert. They seized Berlin, proclaiming Kapp as chancellor of a right-wing nationalist government. Ebert temporarily moved out of Berlin and called for a general strike. This ensured that Kapp's supporters could not move around Berlin. This paralysis caused the Putsch to fail and the conspirators fled Berlin.

killed, the revolt was crushed by the government with help from the Freikorps; but controversially, Luxemburg and Liebknecht were murdered while in custody.

Both Ebert's support of the democratic constitution and his opposition to communism were evident when he crushed the Spartacists, although he was condemned for using the army and the **Freikorps** to suppress the far left. Moreover, this earned him the everlasting hatred of the communists and also put him in a position of dependency on the far-right. But his commitment to democracy is demonstrated by his mobilising of the left to precipitate the general strike that thwarted the Kapp Putsch.

Freikorps or 'free corps': right-wing nationalist soldiers who acted as paramilitaries, and were used by Ebert to help crush communist activity.

Pressure came from outside Germany too, when in January 1923, Germany defaulted with reparations payments required by the Allies under the terms of the Treaty of Versailles. French and Belgian troops occupied Germany's main industrial region, the Ruhr. They then controlled the majority of mines and manufacturing outlets. So German workers went on strike, and also sought to encourage other forms of passive resistance. The stand-off lasted eight months yet damaged the Weimar economy much further, which in turn helped to fuel hyperinflation.

Ebert was clearly not averse to playing off one group against the other. This suggests a clever, calculating politician, but it also highlights the problems faced by a fundamentally decent man of integrity; a patriot who truly wanted to maintain democracy and stability and who successfully managed the SPD.

Fact: The Treaty of Versailles was the peace settlement between Germany and the Western Allies (USA, Britain and France), signed at Versailles near Paris, in June 1919. After agreeing to an armistice in November 1918, Germany believed that it would be consulted by the Allies on the contents of the treaty. This did not happen and Germany was in no position to continue the war. This lack of consultation angered Germans, as did the terms when they were made public. Apart from major land losses, Germany had to accept the 'War Guilt Clause', acknowledging responsibility for starting it and paying heavy reparations.

Ebert's SPD always won at least one hundred seats during each of the Weimar elections and so was the largest and most successful mainstream political party during this era. The SPD was a solid and consistent supporter of the republic and its democratic constitution; SPD deputies were included in all Weimar cabinets, and also provided three of the chancellors. But by 1932 its voter base had halved as the Nazis became the largest political party and ex-SPD voters felt disappointed with their party in government and its lack of achievement.

In reality, Ebert was handicapped from the outset, being blamed for the shame of the lost war, along with the politicians working with him from the centre-left; and from 1920 – the year of Weimar's first parliament – the republic slowly lost support among the people. Although Weimar appeared more stable when Ebert died suddenly in 1925, the republic still faced pressures. In section 2.5 you will read more about the pressures Ebert had to overcome; but above all, it is testament to both the SPD and to Ebert's personal integrity that democracy kept working.

Gustav Stresemann (1878–1929) was very influential during the republic, and is viewed by historians as a politician who helped to consolidate democracy in Germany's darkest financial days. In the early years of his political career, however, Stresemann was a staunch nationalist and supported the Kaiser's **Weltpolitik**, openly avowing the restoration of the monarchy. His democratic credentials were also not apparent when he formed the German People's Party (*Deutsche Volkspartei*, DVP) in 1918. He was right-wing and approved of the Freikorps, expressing relief at the communists' defeat in the German revolution. However, as right-wing groups became increasingly violent, Stresemann the nationalist began to side increasingly with Ebert, and accept the legitimacy of the republic.

Weltpolitik (World Policy): the imperial policy pursued by Kaiser Wilhelm II to make Germany a great overseas power.

Stresemann became chancellor in August 1923, when the entire German economy was teetering on the edge of collapse. He was then determined to tackle Germany's economic and social crisis, following hyperinflation, so between November 1923 and April 1924, he made two key decisions. He resumed reparations payments to the Allies; and he tackled inflation by establishing a new more stable currency – the Rentenmark – in December 1923, which was well received.

Fact: Munich Putsch – or 'the Beer Hall Putsch' – of November 1923 was an attempt by Nazi leader Adolf Hitler to take advantage of the crisis facing the Weimar Republic by starting a revolution in Munich. He hoped it would spread and lead to the overthrow of Ebert, and establish a right-wing nationalist government in its place. Poor planning and misjudgement resulted in failure and the subsequent imprisonment of Hitler.

Historical debate:
There has been debate among historians as to Stresemann's commitment to democracy, fuelled by his apparent change of heart between 1918 and the early 1920s. Liberal historians have viewed him as a democrat who wanted stability, reintegration into the world community, and as a confirmed European who put cooperation before confrontation. Henry Turner describes him as essentially a 'pragmatic conservative', while Eberhard Kolb believes that he was motivated by economic security. Those on the Marxist left argue that Stresemann was an archetypal capitalist, pushing for a deal with the West in order to shore up support for future anti-Soviet plans.

Criticised by the left over his unwillingness to deal firmly with Nazi leaders after the Munich Putsch, Stresemann resigned. But in a new government he became foreign minister and in Unit 2.2 you will read about his skilled statesmanship, integrating Germany back into the international community. He died suddenly in October 1929.

Stresemann's time in high office shows him as a committed supporter of constitutional government, and a loyal patriot. He probably never abandoned his preference for monarchy, but he knew that Weimar was the best guarantee against communist revolution or dictatorship of the far right; supporting the republic out of necessity.

SOURCE C

The main role in (Stresemann's) plans was played by Germany's economic potential, not the least important feature being close economic co-operation with the USA; he realised at an early stage that an American stake in Germany would confirm the interest of the world's leading power in the peaceful evolution of conditions in Europe.

E. Kolb (1988), The Weimar Republic, *London: Routledge, pp. 175–6.*

The Federal Republic of Germany (BRD)

Konrad Adenauer

The nature and structure of post-war democracy in western Germany was shaped by Konrad Adenauer (1876–1967). He was a lawyer's son who became mayor of Cologne in 1917, and was influential nationally as president of the Prussian State Council during the Weimar Republic. A devout Catholic, he had joined the Centre Party in 1906, and was a firm believer in the democratic will of the electorate. As such, he made a major miscalculation in the early 1930s, arguing that Germans should ignore Nazism and concentrate on the communist threat. Underestimating Hitler, he argued that the Nazis should be part of the government, based on election returns and the democratic verdict of the people. Adenauer was replaced as mayor of Cologne after the Nazis came to power in 1933, being imprisoned briefly both in 1934 and 1944. He aimed to bring democracy back to Germany, regain sovereignty and create prosperity and security.

He was nearly seventy years old in 1945 when he set up the Christian Democratic Union (*Christlich Demokratische Union*, CDU). He hoped that this new political party would help bring post-war reconciliation and unite both Roman Catholics and Protestants, promote Christian principles in a liberal democracy and prevent a resurgence of Nazism.

By 1946, Adenauer was CDU chairman in the British zone of post-war occupation, based in his hometown of Cologne. Eventually the CDU spread to all the four zones of the Allied occupation. But the Soviet Union was highly protective of their zone in eastern Germany, promoting the Communist Party and obstructing the Allied Control Council, which ran the general administration of Germany. So Britain, France and the USA decided to give their three occupation zones a federal-state organisation.

In 1948, Adenauer was made president of the new Parliamentary Council that produced a provisional constitution for the western zones (which became the BRD in May 1949). Consequently, Adenauer took office as head of the first post-war democratic German government, the first steps on a road to international recognition when West Germany finally became a sovereign state as the BRD in 1955.

Adenauer and the CDU dominated the BRD, but also helped to give the state stability. He bound Germany's future to that of association with the Western alliance, and obtained BRD membership of the Council of Europe (1951). He also helped to initiate the European Coal and Steel Community (1952), and negotiated Germany's entry into NATO (1955). Democracy was now irrevocably rooted in the BRD and Adenauer personally won four elections in the Bundestag as CDU party leader up to 1961, as the BDR itself underwent a period of great economic revival. He stood down as chancellor in 1963, being succeeded by the economics minister Ludwig Erhard. When he died in 1967, Adenauer was honoured with a state funeral.

Adenauer led the West Germans back to international respectability, transforming a divided, devastated and occupied country into a much-sought-after and respected democracy.

Geoff Layton comments further on Adenauer's rule in **Source D**.

Figure 2.4 CDU election poster for 1949

SOURCE D

During his time in office, Adenauer's style of government and leadership was labelled 'chancellor democracy' a term which is interpreted in positive or negative terms depending on your political standing. Yet, Adenauer had a strong personality and he was self-confident enough to withstand it ... His long years as the Mayor of Cologne in the Weimar Republic had taught him everything he needed to know about democratic processes and the need to lobby support. As a committed Catholic, he had disapproved of the political ideologies of communism and Nazism and had kept his moral and political integrity throughout. He was not easily impressed by 'opinion polls' or 'expert comments'. Instead his rather practical, sober approach to politics and a good instinct for the feasible helped him to integrate different interest groups in government and in parliament.

G. Layton (2009), Democracy and Dictatorship in Germany 1919–63, *London: Hodder, p. 338.*

ACTIVITY

Look at **Source D** and the previous information about Konrad Adenauer. What insight does it give us into Adenauer's personality? How was he able to secure such a powerful position in the BRD?

Ludwig Erhard

Dr Ludwig Erhard (1897–1977) was instrumental in helping the BRD consolidate its democratic credentials after 1949, and he is credited with the decisions that resulted in its impressive economic recovery. He was the economics minister of the BRD from its inception in 1949 until he succeeded Adenauer in 1963 as chancellor until 1966. Erhard was born in Bavaria and worked as a commercial apprentice until he was conscripted into

Figure 2.5 Children playing amongst the ruins of Berlin c.1948

the German army in 1916. He was badly wounded in the First World War, and after it ended, he became an economics student at Frankfurt University. He eventually joined a business school in Nuremburg and became director, but in 1942 the Nazis removed him from his position. He had refused to join the Nazi Party.

Erhard's evident anti-Nazi stance, together with his reputation as an economics expert, led to him being appointed to key administrative posts set up by the Western Allied government that occupied Germany after 1945. Initially Erhard headed the reconstruction of the war-ravaged industries of Bavaria, and then became economics minister in the Allied-run Bavarian state government. But by 1948, Erhard was director of the Economic Council of Bizonia – established by the British and US to coordinate economic activities in their respective zones of occupation: a key post.

As the creation of BRD grew ever-nearer, Erhard oversaw the creation of the new Deutsche mark. He joined the CDU and in the first Bundestag election in September 1949 was elected as a member. Immediately appointed as Adenauer's minister of economics, for the next fourteen years he guided the BRD economy through a recovery that outpaced the growth of those European countries that had won the war. Erhard wanted to create a stable economic background conducive to revival and growth, unlike that of the Weimar Republic.

He sought to manage the economy by constructing a 'third way' between unrestrained capitalism and an overregulated socialist economy. He wanted to promote political and economic freedom with social justice and security, where a strong democratic state ought to be able to intervene in the free market in order to protect the common interests of the individual. By the time the BRD became a sovereign state in 1955, influential commentators were talking about a German 'economic miracle', and the long-term foundations that enabled the BRD to become an economic giant, were secure. Erhard is thus widely admired for bringing economic stability to West Germany and – in partnership with Adenauer – playing a major role in re-establishing democracy.

Kurt Schumacher

Dr Kurt Schumacher (1895–1952) was a student of law and politics who had been seriously wounded in the First World War and had lost an arm. He was further tortured by the Nazis as an SPD opponent, and was held in various concentration camps between 1933 and 1945. A former newspaper editor and SPD representative in the old Reichstag, he set about rebuilding the SPD after 1945 and became its leader. In 1948 he had a leg amputated, but Schumacher still ran in the 1949 election against Adenauer as SPD leader. He committed the SPD to nationalisation of key industries and campaigned for a democratic, reunified, neutral and largely demilitarised Germany; therefore he was opposed to what he saw as Adenauer's subservience to the West. He also blamed the communists for the rise of Hitler. He died in 1952, much missed by the centre-left and regarded as one of the key figures in democratic post-war German politics.

2.3 How did democracy function in modern Germany by 1955?

The first election to the West German Bundestag was on 14 August 1949. Adenauer and his Christian Democrats emerged as the strongest party over the revived Social Democrats (SPD). In a close contest, the CDU won 139 seats to the SPD's 131. CDU leader Konrad Adenauer later became the first federal chancellor of the German Federal Republic or BRD, governing in coalition with the Free Democrats (FDP) who had won fifty-two seats. At the same time, FDP politician **Theodor Heuss** became the first President of the Republic.

It marked the onset of a period when the BRD witnessed increased industrial production, the creation of employment opportunities, and the availability of consumer goods that West Germans had wanted for years. These were also achieved against the backdrop of a stable democratic parliamentary system which enabled the BRD to achieve its full sovereignty in 1955.

Theodor Heuss (1884–1963)

He was an ex-journalist who fell foul of Nazi press laws, and after 1945 entered politics as a liberal. He helped draft the new constitution for the BRD and was a popular choice for first president of the BRD from 1949 to 1959. His post as head of state was largely ceremonial, but Heuss helped to shape the office of president and give it respect by his diplomatic and non-partisan governing.

The constitution

The Basic Law or Grundgesetz is the name given to the new constitution of the BRD, which was drafted in 1948–9 by the Parliamentary Council in the western zones of Germany and headed by Konrad Adenauer. The Council met in Bonn, the future capital, and its work was monitored closely by the Allies. They intervened on several occasions to ensure particular outcomes; for example in areas of basic rights and on issues of fiscal administration and taxation. The Parliamentary Council approved the draft Basic Law on 8 May 1949, elections were held for the Federal Parliament on 14 August, and its first session took place on 7 September. The following week its members elected Konrad Adenauer as the first BRD chancellor. Above all, the Council had tried to avoid a repeat of the problems caused by the Weimar Republic constitution.

To summarise, the constitution's main points were as follows:

- The new constitution upheld the **pluralism** of political parties as a necessity for a stable, functioning liberal democracy: thus, the banning of political parties (as had happened in Weimar) was prohibited.
- The use of direct votes on laws and other important issues (referenda or plebiscites) was not permitted. The Nazis had used such methods to influence people.
- The president as head of state (Bundespräsident) would be elected for five years by parliament – not by popular vote as in Weimar – and could only be re-elected once. He or she would have mainly ceremonial functions and very limited powers in the case of emergencies. So there was no Article 48 in evidence here, and no repeat of the powers given to the president under Weimar.
- The parliament was two-tiered in structure, like Weimar. But there were far more democratic checks now in place.

Pluralism: the idea that democratic parties are a fundamental part of any constitution and cannot be abolished. Specifically, Article 20 of the BRD constitution states that if a party acts, aims or conspires against the constitution and is anti-democratic, it can be forbidden.

- The Bundestag was the federal parliament. It had to approve the chancellor and so gave the chancellor definitive authority and responsibility. Moreover, it could not bring down a government by a simple vote of no confidence and destabilise the system.
- The Bundestag could only bring down the chancellor's government by using a 'constructive vote of no confidence' – thereby removing one of the blights of Weimar, when the old Reichstag could remove an individual or a head of government.
- It now required the opposition to pass a vote of no confidence on the chancellor and his cabinet as a whole, and to have a successor nominated at the same time as an alternative government. This has ensured the strong position of the chancellor in the German system of government since 1949 and brought stability.
- The Bundesrat was the upper house or council of the parliament, with members appointed by members of the Länder governments. It assisted in the assent of legislation and in the election of federal court judges.
- The electoral system was changed. No longer was there straightforward PR, as it had led to difficulties in forming a coalition.
- The system was modified to allow half of the seats in the Bundestag to be elected by a majority vote in their constituencies (as operates in the UK), and the other half from party lists, through PR.
- In 1953, this was modified to state that any party winning less than 5 per cent of the popular vote was barred from parliament. The electoral system was thus tilted towards the larger parties, in the hope of forming more stable and enduring coalitions.

QUESTION

What strengths and weaknesses do you see in the constitution of the BRD? Where does it differ from the Weimar Constitution?

The Basic Law provided for a government with a strong executive, subject to democratic control, combined with a large measure of devolution to the federal states (Länder). The constitution of the BRD gave the state a federal structure and decisively helped to bring about stable democracy in Germany at the second attempt; although there was some criticism of the 5 per cent rule, together with complaints about the banning of left- and right-wing extremist parties. But the fact that the new constitution was operating in more positive economic climate meant that, by 1955, under Adenauer's leadership, the BRD became a fully sovereign state.

The first government of the BDR

Adenauer dominated German politics as leader of the CDU and as chancellor for fourteen years, although many people thought that he would only be a caretaker chancellor, being aged seventy-three.

Party	Seats won	% of votes
CDU/CSU	139	31
SPD	131	29
FDP	52	11
Communist	22	5
Others	65	22

Table 2.1 Table of election results, 1949

His first administration was a coalition between the CDU and its Bavarian counterpart, the Christian Social Union (CSU), with the FDP or Free Democrats. The election statistics suggest that it was a close election; the Social Democratic Party ran Adenauer close, while the communists polled more than 5 per cent and were the fourth-largest party. But the remaining 22 per cent comprised a wide range of splinter groups, single-issue causes and regional interest parties. In this election, six of these smaller parties obtained less than 5 per cent of the vote and were allocated seats under PR; but after 1953 when the 5 per cent rule was introduced, it lessened the chance of fragmentation.

Ultimately Adenauer put together a coalition of 208 out of 402 members, although on 15 September 1949 he was actually voted in as chancellor of the first government with a majority of just one vote. But by 1953, he was re-elected comfortably with the CDU/CSU gaining nearly 15 per cent more of the votes, while the 1957 election brought him more than 50 per cent. Unlike the days of Weimar, there was continuity under a strong leader, but one who was a democrat. As such, Adenauer's aspirations were evident in his very first government.

Adenauer had two principal aims: to rebuild the BRD economy – which he left in the capable hands of Ludwig Erhard – and to achieve full sovereignty for the BRD, which in 1949 had remained under the guidance of the three Western Allied commanders. They reserved the right to intervene in the internal affairs of the BRD if they deemed it necessary, and initially they refused to allow the BRD to conduct its own foreign relations. So one of the key driving forces for Adenauer was to secure the rights of a normal sovereign state, quickly. He knew that the speediest way to ensure this was by showing support for the ideals and interests of the Western powers, and then to consider reuniting all of Germany at some time in the future, from a position of greater strength and trust.

Political parties

Christian Democratic Union

In 1945, the Christian Democratic Union (CDU) and its Bavarian counterpart the Christian Social Union (CSU) were formed by a group of both Catholics and Protestants, who included academics, business figures and trade unionists. The party wanted to break with the denominational nature of pre-1933 politics and espoused a broad, Christian democratic approach that rejected both Nazism and communism. The CDU/CSU initially talked of central economic planning and nationalisation for essential industries as a means of initiating the revival of Germany's devastated economy; but this was dropped in the western zones by 1949, when the party came under the control of Adenauer. It thereafter advocated a more centre-right policy – the social market economy – which married corporate capitalism with an extended system of social welfare. Adenauer correctly believed that this would attract a majority of the electorate. Indeed, the coalition of the CDU and CSU proved itself successful in uniting conservative, Christian, middle-class voters, who felt comfortable with Western liberal democracy under the umbrella of partnership with the West.

Social Democratic Party

The Social Democratic Party (SPD) was Germany's oldest political party and had dominated the politics of the Weimar Republic, but was then banned by the Nazi regime. By 1949, under Kurt Schumacher, the centre-left SPD had re-established itself and became rooted in the interests of the working class and the trade unions. The SPD advocated state running of the economy and nationalisation of major industries. Schumacher was a nationalist and patriot who he believed Adenauer's pro-Western policies were a sell-out. Schumacher wanted to unify Germany, even if that meant compromising with the Soviet Union, although he opposed communism and blamed it for the growth of Nazism. But the SPD saw itself as the only party serving the interests of all Germans. Unification under democratic socialism was their key aim. Despite an SPD membership of almost one million, it failed to defeat Adenauer's CDU. Schumacher's death in 1952 and a succession of electoral failures thereafter caused the SPD to reassess its policies and overall political platform in order to make it more attractive to voters.

Free Democrats

The Free Democrats (FDP) was much smaller than the CDU/CSU or SPD, but it had great importance in the political life of the newly formed BRD, providing its first president Theodor Heuss. Founded in 1948 by the members of pre-war liberal parties, the FDP served in coalition governments with the CDU/CSU from 1949 to 1956 and again from 1961 to 1966, under Adenauer and Erhard, so was continually at the centre of the political decision-making process, usually holding the balance of power. It added to the stability and continuity, with FDP ministers building up a detailed knowledge of government procedures over the years, unsurpassed by most other parties.

In Adenauer's first coalition cabinet, the FDP had three ministers in key offices, including the vice-chancellor and the ministers for housing and justice. It was significant that on major issues of economic and social importance, the FDP backed its CDU/CSU partners; but being the liberal party they were, the FDP also urged a more secular approach to education and accused other parties of creeping clericalisation in the BRD.

Communist Party

The Communist Party or KPD began to reorganise in the western part of Germany after 1945. At a time when the Western powers set about to partition Germany, the KPD consistently supported the need to keep Germany unified. It also campaigned in the 1949 election on nationalisation of industry, the introduction of democratic land reform, and the setting up of a progressive system of social security. It received almost 6 per cent of the popular vote in the BRD election of 1949, but by 1953, it won only just over 2 per cent and lost its seats. The KPD was poised to mount an election challenge in 1957, but found itself banned in 1956 by the Constitutional Court of the BRD. In the following years, many communists were brought to trial in the BRD and imprisoned.

Historical debate:
Interestingly, although the KPD was weak politically and from an organisational viewpoint, at grassroots level it was very strong numerically in the Ruhr, in Hamburg and Kiel dockyards and at major steelworks like Krupp's at Essen. It was almost as strong as it had been around 1930 in the Weimar Republic. Yet by 1956, the BRD's highest court had banned it. Why? This has puzzled historians and it shocked some people at the time. After all, the BRD was keen to identify itself as a modern liberal democracy. Patrick Major comments that the west German KDP became distracted by becoming too involved in the campaign to reunite the whole of Germany, and was perceived as falling under the influence of communists in eastern Germany. It then appeared to be involved in a flawed campaign to prevent West German rearmament. At the same time, the party was obviously pilloried by the Western powers and was heavily shunned by a largely anti-communist BRD, who associated it with the one-party East German DDR. It was never to make any major impact nationally on the politics of the BRD in its transition to democracy and sovereignty.

QUESTION

Why is the banning of the KPD by the German Constitutional Court in 1956 a surprise? Why might it not be wholly surprising given the time and date?

The BRD in 1955

When the BRD was founded in September 1949, it was not actually a sovereign state. The occupying powers of the US, Britain and France had appointed three high commissioners who had permanent residence in Bonn, to oversee and intervene as necessary, during the transition to democracy. In reality, their influence diminished and became less necessary during this period of transition. Adenauer's stable administrations, together with the rapid economic revival, meant that the BRD could develop without the lack of hinterland that proved so devastating to Weimar.

The BRD – West Germany – was officially given back its sovereignty on 5 May 1955 and finally recognised by the Western Allies as a full sovereign state. The continued stationing of Western troops in the BDR remained, in order to guarantee the BRD's security, while the full reunification of Germany remained an open topic for the foreseeable future. But the BRD was also admitted to NATO, a key moment in its reintegration into the international community; then the Bundestag amended the Basic Law to create a federal army or Bundeswehr – with conscription being introduced for all men over eighteen years.

Figure 2.6 Adenauer swears in the first recruits to the BRD army (Bundeswehr), 5 May 1955, as West Germany finally becomes a sovereign state

Fact: NATO – the North Atlantic Treaty Organisation – was a Western military alliance created in 1949 and included USA, Britain, France, Canada and seven other countries. The BRD joined by invitation in 1955, thus securing its place as a rehabilitated country and a trusted Western ally. In response, the same year an alarmed USSR formed a rival organisation: the Warsaw Pact, made up of its East European satellites.

Theory of Knowledge

Historical information and interpretations:
Consider the issues surfacing at the time of the foundation of the BRD. In pairs, discuss why there were such different viewpoints about the unification of Germany. Should it be sought immediately? Ought it to be left until the BRD was stronger? Also, should Adenauer have tied himself so closely to the Western Allies? Or was Schumacher right in advocating a more independent Germany? How does hindsight affect our understanding of the direction taken by those who established the BRD between 1949 and 1955?

Chancellor Konrad Adenauer proudly announced that 'almost ten years after the military and political collapse of National Socialism, the era of occupation has come to an end for the Federal Republic of Germany'. The BRD had emerged as a stable and successful democracy – a notable achievement given the hideous situation it faced in the ruins of the Second World War a decade earlier.

End of unit activities

1 Explain the significance of each of these in the move to democracy in Germany: pluralism, liberalism, proportional representation and Basic Law.
2 Construct a mind map to illustrate the factors that led to the establishment of a democratic state in the BRD between 1949 and 1955.
3 Research activity: use the information in this unit, as well as additional information from books or websites, to write an obituary for either Friedrich Ebert, Gustav Stresemann or Konrad Adenauer, evaluating his contribution to the establishment of democracy in Germany.
4 On the basis of the information in this unit, how accurate is it to describe the democracy in Germany as 'weak' in the period 1870–1955? Explain your opinion clearly by giving appropriate reasons.
5 Draw up a table like the one below to summarise the role of the main political parties in West Germany in the period 1945–55.

Name of political party	Who supported it?	What were its beliefs and its vision for the BRD?	How significant was it in terms of influence or support?
CDU/CSU			
SPD			
FDP			
Communists			

2 Unit The development of a democratic state in Germany: 1919–33 and 1949–55

TIMELINE

1918 **Nov:** Germany emerges defeated from the war. Kaiser abdicates and flees to Netherlands. Friedrich Ebert, head of the SPD, replaces Kaiser.

1919 **Feb:** National Assembly first meets at Weimar; Ebert chosen as president of the new German (Weimar) Republic.

Jul: New democratic constitution based on proportional representation.

1933 **Jan:** Nazi party's Adolf Hitler invited to be chancellor.

Jul: All political parties other than Nazis banned. Fascist dictatorship replaces democracy.

1939 **Sep:** Second World War begins.

1945 **May:** Second World War ends. Hitler's Nazi state defeated. Germany in ruins, occupied by the four allied powers of USA, USSR, Britain and France, and each zone prints its own currency.

Jun–Dec: The four powers allow formation of political parties: SPD, CPU, KPD and LDPD.

1947 **Jan:** British and US occupation zones form a unified economic zone: Bizonia.

1948 **6 Jun:** Six Power Conference in London agrees outlines of a new federal state in West Germany.

20 Jun: The new Deutsche mark is introduced in western zones.

24 Jun: Blockade of Berlin by USSR begins.

1949 **12 May:** Berlin blockade ends.

24 May: Foundation of BRD (Bundesrepublik Deutschland) in West Germany (German Federal Republic).

15 Sep: Konrad Adenauer of the CDU, elected chancellor of BRD following first Bundestag election.

7 Oct: Foundation of DDR in East Germany (German Democratic Republic).

1953 Adenauer and the CDU re-elected.

1955 **May:** BRD officially becomes a democratic, sovereign state and joins NATO.

KEY QUESTIONS

- What factors influenced the evolution of democracy in Germany?
- How did the government respond to domestic crises?
- How did the government react to demands for equality and other protests?

Overview

- The introduction of democracy after Germany's defeat in the First World War was riddled with problems, not least that of trying to develop a democratic and republican culture among people who had lived for decades in an autocratic, imperial system.
- Hatred of the new republic by the extreme left and right played a significant and sometimes destructive role, while the twin struggles to achieve financial stability and shake off the stigma of defeat, were major features of German politics.
- The creation of the BRD in 1949, after the Second World War, provided no less a challenge for a devastated Germany; with occupying Western allies and German politicians alike anxious not to repeat the constitutional and political mistakes made in 1919, which later proved so destructive to the Weimar Republic.
- The leaders of the BRD had to galvanise a disparate workforce, build morale and try to put Germany's recent Nazi past to one side as they tried to build a vibrant economic state out of one devastated by war, filled with refugees and where a black market economy dominated.
- The 'economic miracle' of West Germany in the 1950s was seen to have its roots in the necessity and urgency of the BRD having to restart from scratch; combined with the social market economy of Adenauer and Erhard.
- The role of women and the nature of suffrage in both Weimar and the BRD is highlighted, likewise the threat posed by external factors.
- Demands by different groups for specific rights in both Weimar and the BRD forced these democratic elected governments to reflect on the reasons for their own existence, and how they might build a better state.
- Weimar's obstacles and crises between 1919 and 1933 were far greater than those of the BRD, which operated in the more conducive economic climate of the 1950s.

2.4 What factors influenced the evolution of democracy in Germany?

This chapter examines how democracy developed in the Weimar Republic after 1919 and in West Germany (BRD) after its formation in 1949.

German democracy in the 20th century was punctuated by autocratic rule and its development faced the problem of developing a culture of democracy among people who had not experienced this. From German unification in 1870 to the outbreak of the First World War in1914, the imperial government of Germany was a virtual military autocracy; what Ralf Dahrendorf, has called an 'industrial feudal society'.

After Germany's defeat in 1918 and the abdication of the Kaiser, it was a parliamentary democracy; the Weimar Republic, led by the largest political party – the Social Democratic Party (SPD).

But Weimar failed under difficult circumstances, and by 1933 democracy was dead. Germany became a one-party Nazi state under Adolf Hitler, who subsequently led the country to war and defeat in 1945. Then, Germany became divided as tensions between the occupying powers (USA, Britain, France and the USSR) ushered in the era of the Cold War (see Unit 2.1).

In 1949 the western part of Germany became a democratic federal republic and a sovereign state – West Germany (BRD) – while the eastern zone, occupied by the USSR, evolved into a one-party communist state – East Germany or the DDR. Both Germanies were finally reunited democratically in 1990.

So in both 1919 and 1949, these new democratic states – the Weimar Republic and the BRD – had to cope with problems at the outset of their existence, as they attempted to consolidate their status. This chapter examines some of those issues.

The Weimar Republic (1919–33)

The military and political crisis of October 1918–January 1919

Germany's defeat at the end of the First World War in 1918 led to the establishment of a republic and its first democratic constitution, together with its first democratic elections and a coalition government led by the Social Democratic Party. It evolved rapidly, out of necessity and in exceptional circumstances, as a rapid succession of unforeseen events proved to be the crucible of this first German democracy.

By September 1918, General Ludendorff and the Supreme Army Command (OHL) recognised that the war was unwinnable. The Kaiser was advised to sue for an armistice and imperial Germany began to democratise, hoping that a more constitutional Germany would win an advantageous negotiated peace settlement with the Allies. Many in the OHL wanted a constitutional monarchy, so Kaiser Wilhelm II relinquished his powers over the armed forces, while the chancellor and his ministers were now made accountable to the Reichstag, not him. But a naval mutiny at Kiel on 29 October 1918 triggered a revolution, which accelerated events.

Within days, there was unrest in towns and military bases across Germany; while revolutionary councils urged an end to hostilities, greater political reform with democratic representation; greater economic fairness and, crucially, the abolition of the monarchy. Radical revolutionaries also demanded the trial of the Kaiser; support for whom was haemorrhaging among the military and his personal advisors. Wilhelm II hesitated, but on 9 November he was forced out when his own abdication was announced by Chancellor Max von Baden, who then promptly resigned himself in order to precipitate peace negotiations with the Allies. The Kaiser fled to the Netherlands and the war ended on 11 November, thus completing a rapid pace of change, which led to a democratic republican Germany emerging from the defeat of war. The reins of power fell into the hands of SPD leader Friedrich Ebert (see section 2.1, How democratic was Germany by 1914?) as the leader of the largest political party. Germany was duly declared a republic and Ebert formed a government, which spent the last month of 1918 finalising the armistice and organising elections for a national assembly. Meanwhile, the **Spartacists** were preparing for an armed uprising and, on 5 January 1919, mounted an armed takeover of Berlin; but the mobilisation of around 3,000 Freikorps crushed the uprising (see Unit 2.2, The Weimar Republic 1919–23). This did not prevent a further uprising in April 1919 in Bavaria, nor a later Freikorps uprising in Berlin in 1920 (see next section).

Spartacists: a radical socialist group led by Karl Liebknecht and Rosa Luxemburg, whose members were also founders of the KPD (German Communist Party). They were named after Spartacus who led a slave rebellion against the Romans in 73 BCE. Their attempt to overthrow the Weimar Republic was suppressed mercilessly and their leaders were murdered after being arrested and probably tortured.

But the fledgling republic had survived its first weeks of existence and by June 1919, Germany was slightly calmer. Elections for the National Assembly had taken place on 19 January, although the disorder in Berlin had meant that the Assembly's first meeting was moved to the town of Weimar. But the elections produced an impressive turnout of more than 83 per cent of the electorate. More than 75 per cent had voted for pro-democracy parties, so enabling the SPD (with 165 of the 423 Reichstag seats) to form a coalition with the German Democratic Party (seventy-five) and the Centre Party (ninety-one). This was significant in the evolution of democracy.

However Ebert and his SPD had aroused long-term dislike among left-wingers, by cooperating in government with the business community and working with the army and extreme right-wing groups in order to prevent a revolution. For many on the far-left, the SPD had betrayed the workers. Instead of developing a worker-friendly state like Soviet Russia, they had created a middle-class democracy, dependent on old institutions.

Figure 2.7 German delegates at Versailles in June 1919 in the main conference chamber to sign the treaty

To those on the far-right, the republic had betrayed Germany. There was a belief that the German army might have continued fighting, but that they had been 'stabbed in the back' by German politicians – mainly Social Democrats – who had sought the armistice, and were going to sign the Treaty of Versailles. **Source A** reveals the depth of this feeling.

SOURCE A

In the eyes of the right, the Republic was associated with the surrender, a shameful and deliberate act of treachery, and the peace treaty, a further act of betrayal. The fact that the new republican institutions were democratic added to the hostility. It was openly said that loyalty to the fatherland required disloyalty to the republic.

A. Bullock (1962), Hitler: A Study in Tyranny, *Harmondsworth: Penguin Books, pp. 58–60.*

Democracy had arrived in Germany by 1919, but almost accidentally. Geoff Layton suggests that Ebert had overexaggerated the threat from the left, while H. Stuart Hughes feels that it is more accurate to talk of 'a potential revolution which ran away into the sand than the genuine article'. In reality, it represented a compromise where German conservatives and industrialists had ceded power to the Social Democrats to avert a Soviet-style revolution, whilst Social Democrats had allied with demobilised officers of the Kaiser's army to crush the revolution. Walter Rathenau, the first foreign minister of the Weimar Republic, commented wryly : 'Now we have a Republic, the problem is we have no Republicans.'

SOURCE B

There is only one master in this country. That, am I! Who opposes me I shall crush to pieces.

Kaiser Wilhelm II, speaking in 1912.

SOURCE C

The German Commonwealth is a Republic. Political authority is derived from the People.

The Weimar Constitution, 6 February 1919.

QUESTION

What do **Sources B** and **C** suggest about the nature of the changes in German political life brought about by the end of the war in 1918? To what extent do they enlighten us about the task facing the Weimar Republic?

The Ideas behind the Weimar Constitution

The Weimar Constitution drafted in 1919 sought to devise a democratic political system (see section 2.1, The new Weimar Constitution). Having tolerated an autocratic kaiser who largely disregarded parliament, many on the left wanted an unrestricted people's parliament; but those on the right were nervous of an over-powerful parliament. It was also crucial that the position and powers of the president, as head of state, were determined carefully.

Many on the centre-right looked to the US constitution. It was more than one hundred years old and appeared to work well. It embraced democracy, federalism, had checks and balances applied to the branches of government, contained a Bill of Rights and provided for strong leadership with the president. Others – notably many socialists and SPD members – looked more closely at the doctrine of parliamentary sovereignty as seen in the British system, which sat well with the constitutional ideas they had avowed. There was little doubt that a democratic ethos would prevail, but many wondered whose version of democracy would prevail? How ideological might it be? Would it satisfy most if not all?

When the Weimar Constitution was finally ratified and adopted by the National Assembly on 31 July 1919, it had the appearance of a great democratic document. As you learnt in Unit 2.1, it was federal in structure, with seventeen Länder or states sharing power and responsibilities with the central government; there were elections by proportional representation (PR) – inherently democratic – and voting for all citizens (male and female) over the age of twenty. It had a Bill of Rights outlining broad freedoms such as speech, religion and equality before the law.

In it there was also mention for social rights such as land reform and welfare provision. This facilitated the passage of legislation to assist war veterans, such as the Decree on Social Provision for Disabled Veterans and Surviving Dependents in 1919: progressive, democratic ideals, enshrined in the constitution and bearing the distinct imprint of socialists and liberals. But on closer examination, liberalism was not consistent throughout the constitution. Conservatism prevailed with the creation of a powerful executive presidency.

Apart from being directly elected by the people – and thus independent of parliament – the president could be re-elected indefinitely every seven years, could intervene in the legislative process by ordering a referendum and, most crucially, was given considerable emergency powers, allowing him to bypass the elected Reichstag under Article 48 of the Weimar Constitution and 'take all necessary steps … if public order and security are seriously disturbed or endangered'.

Some on the far-left expressed misgivings and asked what if a general who had supported the autocracy of the Kaiser was now head of state, or was defence minister and could influence the president?

But others in the centre and on the right were anxious to have a safeguard in case an unrestricted parliamentary system one day brought a socialist majority or even the communists into power. Some historians have argued that he was a 'substitute emperor' and that this marks an element of continuity with the imperial past.

QUESTION

What do you think is meant in **Source D** by the term 'ersatz emperor'? Why might the provisions of the Weimar Constitution convey this impression?

SOURCE D

The provisions which made the president a kind of 'ersatz emperor' reflected the mistrust that the fathers of the Constitution felt towards a fully parliamentary system on a democratic basis … The SPD although very much the largest party in the Assembly, was able to impart to the document very little of its own constitutional and social programme. There were several reasons for this … the need for compromise imposed by the conditions of the governmental alliance … the fact that the Social Democrats had no clear-cut constitutional theory of their own … and it was impossible to forecast clearly how the provisions of the constitutions would work out in terms of political and social reality.

E. Kolb (1988), The Weimar Republic, *London: Routledge, p.19.*

The Weimar Constitution had elements of liberalism and conservatism; unsurprising in a swiftly drafted constitution that needed to clarify the terms for a progressive democratic republic, but which also had to acknowledge historical traditions of autocracy and conservatism.

The PR voting would rule out any prospect of a majority government and fill the Reichstag with many small, sectional, regional and often undemocratic parties. The powers given to the president under Article 48 almost invited exploitation. Vestiges of imperial Germany remained in this autocratic office in the way his relationship to the Reichstag was set out in the constitution. Nonetheless liberal democracy was established in Germany in 1919, although the old imperial concepts of conservatism, militarism, nationalism and faith in autocratic government were seldom far away and would prove testing to Weimar as the republic sought to allow democracy to grow and strengthen.

The influence of external events, 1918–20

The evolution of democracy in Germany was also influenced by external factors that created both political and economic consequences for the fledgling republic. First, the Weimar Constitution was influenced by that of the United States of America (see above) with its executive president, federal nature and separation of powers. But many Germans were unhappy with the fact that their new constitution was modelled on that of a wartime enemy, complicit in exacting such harsh punishment on their defeated country. Also the powerful position of the president created future problems.

The other external influence was the Treaty of Versailles, viewed by most Germans as a foreign-dictated peace or Diktat, since German representatives were not allowed to negotiate at the peace conference.

The terms agreed by US President Woodrow Wilson, British Prime Minister David Lloyd George and French President Georges Clemenceau had a direct effect on both the short-term and the long-term evolution of the democratic state. When the requirements were announced in June 1919, the republic suffered a loss of confidence, as did the politicians who had been instrumental in its creation. Ridicule and mistrust were heaped on these men, not least Ebert.

This feeling was reflected in a poor performance by parties supporting the republic in the 1920 elections. So there began a series of weakened coalitions. No longer did political parties push through reforming legislation and govern Germany in such a way as to build stability and confidence. Instead they bargained, fought off defeat and tried to pass legislation that was constantly being blocked in its passage through the Reichstag.

Arguably, the evolution of true democracy in Germany was hindered by the decisions of other countries, as Germans felt vulnerable, betrayed and weakened in all areas; but the inclusion of the war guilt clause, forcing Germany to accept that the German nation bore sole responsibility for the First World War, meant that the Weimar Republic would have to provide compensation for any damage caused. Many Germans believed that they were neither responsible for the war, nor that they had been defeated. Right-wing nationalists who wanted a strong nation were enraged at Germany's perceived decline from the key power in Central Europe to second-class status, this decline being part of the inheritance of the Versailles Treaty.

The end of the war had also brought a lack of capital and a large trade deficit, which was exacerbated by the loss of important industrial regions to France and Czechoslovakia. Germany ended up paying only a small portion of the reparations

Fact: The Treaty of Versailles was the main peace treaty at the end of the First World War, signed near Paris in June 1919, between Germany and the Allied Powers of Britain, France and the USA after completion of the Paris Peace Conference. Germany was not consulted and the representatives of the new republic were summoned to sign the terms. Germans were shocked: a guilt clause blaming Germany alone for the war; the army reduced to 100,000; conscription, tanks, U-boats and aircraft banned; the high seas fleet to be surrendered to Britain; reparations set at £6,600 million; the Rhineland demilitarised; German overseas colonies taken away; Alsace-Lorraine lost to France; territory given to Poland, Belgium, Denmark and Czechoslovakia. The politicians of the republic who signed the armistice in November 1918 and then this treaty were ridiculed and called the 'November Criminals'.

Theory of Knowledge

History and ethics:
In relation to the Versailles Treaty and its impact upon the Weimar Republic, discuss in pairs whether a foreign government (or state) is right to intervene in the running of another state – and thereby indirectly affecting people's lives – and if so, to what extent and under what circumstances? Can you think of any modern-day examples?

KEY CONCEPTS QUESTION

Significance: What was the significance of the actions or ideas of other countries between 1918 and 1920 on the newly established German republic?

officially demanded. However, the reparations would damage the republic's economy by discouraging market loans and forcing the government to finance its deficit by printing more money, causing hyperinflation in 1923. The impact of this will be examined in the next section, when we consider the response of the republic to domestic crises and their impact.

Figure 2.8 In Munich, more than 30,000 Germans protested against the decisions of the Versailles Conference in June 1919

The Federal Republic of Germany (BRD) (1949–55)

Occupation and division

Following the collapse of Nazi Germany in 1945, the Allies – who had sought Germany's unconditional surrender on all fronts – were not fully certain what should be done with the defeated state. Frank B. Tipton points out that the four Allies sought to restructure both German government and society, but – more significantly – they disagreed over both the specific policies to be implemented and the manner of their implementation. This was underpinned by the tension and suspicion between the Soviet Union and the Western powers. It led inevitably to an international ideological and political division in the Cold War; and to Germany's division in 1949 into the democratic BRD (West Germany) and the communist DDR (East Germany). It was what historian Mary Fulbrook in *The Divided Nation* called 'an ad hoc unintended result of the emerging Cold War between the superpowers, rather than the outcome of conscious allied plans for Germany'.

The framework of Germany's political division – which occurred in geographically distinct zones – reflected the military situation in 1945. The USA, USSR and Britain were each allocated an occupation zone equal to the area conquered in 1944–5, with France being granted a smaller zone adjacent to their border with Germany. Berlin, the strategically important capital, was itself divided into four zones, although it was located in the centre of the Soviet zone.

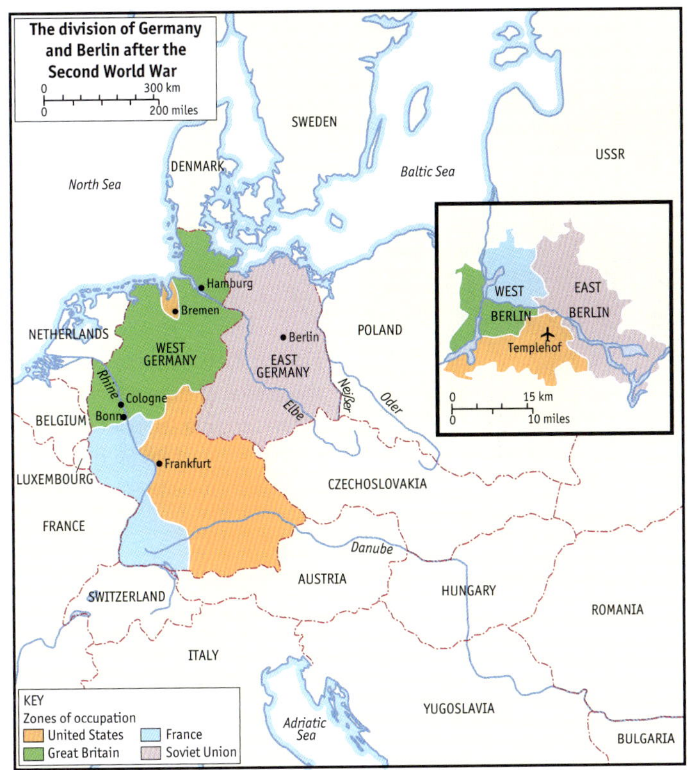

Figure 2.9 The division of Germany and Berlin after the Second World War

Fact: On 23 June 1948, Britain, France and America introduced a new common currency into their zones of occupation. The Soviets cut off all rail and road links to West Berlin within twenty-four hours. To the West, this was an attempt to starve Berlin into surrender, and they immediately launched an airborne supply service to west Berlin. The Berlin Blockade lasted 318 days, but for all of this period supplies were delivered around the clock. On 12 May 1949, the Soviets abandoned the blockade.

By late 1945, the Western powers (USA, Britain and France) had developed a framework for government and administration in their occupation zones, and in western Berlin. These reflected their liberal democratic traditions, with a capitalist economy. In the eastern zone and in eastern Berlin, the occupying Soviet authorities implemented a political order more akin to that practised in Moscow, with Soviet communist ideology predominant.

All four powers had initially emphasised their desire for parallel development throughout Germany, especially in preserving the country's economic unity. But the differences between east and west – and thus the future of Germany – were determined by a rapid deterioration in relations between the USSR and the West between 1946 and 1949. Things came to a head when the USSR cut off all road, rail and freight traffic to West Berlin. The supply of electricity from Soviet east Berlin to the west was also stopped. This blockade from June 1948 to May 1949 was an attempt to halt the growing political and fiscal integration between the three occupied western zones (see section 2.1, Democracy and sovereignty: Germany 1945–55).

KEY CONCEPTS QUESTION

Causes and Consequences: What were the causes and consequences of the division of Germany into two states in 1949?

The result was the massive Anglo-American Berlin Airlift in which fuel, food and other key supplies were flown into West Berlin for more than a year. The blockade was finally called off by the USSR, but this situation also hastened the creation of a separate state out of the three western occupation zones. The Bundesrepublik Deutschland (BDR) was born and the new democracy of West Germany officially came into existence in September 1949.

The shaping of the BRD, 1949–55

The creation of the BRD in 1949 was largely determined by the developing international tensions and contrasting ideologies in the Cold War. With the general deterioration in Soviet–Western relations, and the blockading of Berlin, the military protection of the

Figure 2.10 People watch the arrival of on a transport plane carrying supplies to people in West Berlin during the Airlift of 1948/9.

Western Union: a defence organisation and a precursor to NATO, this union was established in March 1948 when Britain, France, Belgium, Luxemburg and the Netherlands signed the Treaty of Brussels. It aimed to guard against armed aggression in Europe; whether from Germany, or against any other members.

Fact: The North Atlantic Treaty Organization (NATO) was the military alliance organised by the West as a response to the perceived Soviet threat, following its takeover of Eastern Europe and the Berlin crisis of 1948–9. Five European states had formed the Western Union in 1948, but by 1949 it was felt that an American presence was needed. Established by the North Atlantic Treaty in Washington, DC, April 1949, NATO included the five Treaty of Brussels states plus the USA, Canada, Norway, Denmark, Iceland, Italy and Portugal. The USA then assumed leadership.

Fact: The Warsaw Pact, or the Warsaw Treaty Organisation (WTO), was the defensive military alliance formed between the Soviet Union and its East European satellite states, shortly after the BRD (West Germany) was allowed to join NATO and rearm in May 1955. The Soviet Union was alarmed by this rehabilitation of the BRD and cemented the formation of an opposing alliance.

western zone had become the chief goal of the USA, Britain and France. In 1948, the **Western Union** defence organisation was inaugurated; and by 1949 the North Atlantic Treaty Organization (NATO) had been founded, since security policy and defence strategy was dominating the European political landscape. This was eventually completed by the creation of the East's Warsaw Pact in 1955; so the BRD was at the epicentre of a continent dominated by two adversarial political and military alliances.

For Western Europe, German survival was crucial. Germany's integration and rehabilitation into European and world affairs was both desirable and necessary. Then came the key role German industry might play in the wider regeneration of Europe's industry and economy. Finally, a democratic Germany was vital for the preservation of the balance of power.

But if Cold War ideology and international events were significant in the BRD's birth, German politicians across the spectrum also contributed to the division of their fatherland and the growth of a democratic West Germany. In fact, the permanent division of Germany was probably sealed as early as April 1945 with the forced amalgamation in the Soviet controlled zone of the German Communist Party (*Kommunistische Partei Deutschlands*, KPD) and the Social Democratic Party (*Sozialdemokratische Partei Deutschlands*, SPD) to form the Socialist Unity Party (*Sozialistische Einheitspartei Deutschlands*, SED).

Other non-communist political parties now faced insurmountable opposition from this amalgamation of the left. A change of outlook by the Western powers in Germany was detectable when the US secretary of state James Byrnes visited Stuttgart in September 1946 and commented that the presence of the Western Allies in Germany was less of an occupation than a means of protection against the further advance of communism.

The Western European and Soviet social systems were also very different. The German Communist Party leadership – itself recently returned from exile in Moscow during Hitler's Nazi regime – had worked with the occupying Soviets to ferment political and social change. Pursuing what they referred to as an 'anti-Fascist upheaval', all political and social functions were run by German communists and their sympathisers. Communist leader Walter Ulbricht proclaimed that 'it has to look democratic, but everything must be in our hands'.

The nature of the BRD was similarly determined immediately after 1945. In the western part of Germany, allied authorities undertook a programme of denazification, and encouraged the development of democratic institutions; while organisations such as the American Federation of Labour actively worked to help their German counterparts with reconstruction. Western ideas, in particular American attitudes, impacted strongly on the political culture of the western occupation zones.

Konrad Adenauer of the centre-right Christian Democratic Union (CDU) was strongly pro-American and he, like many Germans, believed that future prosperity and success meant alignment with the USA. Some on the centre-left in western Germany blamed capitalism for many of the ills of war and a number Germany's Social Democrats (SPD) wanted more state directed social and economic planning. But the first BRD elections in 1949 brought Adenauer to power, and with him, the notion that a free economy would best stimulate recovery.

His governments over the next fourteen years helped to bring about what would be described as West Germany's economic miracle, building a national consensus, and striking an appropriate blend of free-market and social-market policies, while integrating the BRD into Western Europe by 1955, as a sovereign state in NATO. There was also no real possibility that the BRD might eventually be unified with Soviet-dominated eastern Germany; and reciprocal formation of the DDR (Germany Democratic Republic) in the east with Communist Party leader Walter Ulbricht at its head, was as inevitable as that of its western counterpart.

The favourable economy of the BRD in the 1950s also facilitated the swift integration of almost nine million displaced persons from parts of eastern Germany, either now occupied by the Soviets or forming part of the former eastern territories of the Hitler's Reich. Refugees from the Sudetenland, parts of Hungary, Poland and even Southeast Europe were accepted more easily. This helped to smooth out differences of class and religion in the new BRD and it stifled the attraction of radical nationalist parties, although social problems did exist as a consequence of division, defeat and war. But the newly formed major democratic parties, such as the CDU/CSU and the SPD now had a wider electorate and became major popular parties, which helped to stabilise democracy in the BRD and steer it towards full sovereign state recognition in 1955. But the eastern part of geographical Germany, the DDR, remained a one-party Soviet satellite.

2.5 How did the government respond to domestic crises?

From its inception in 1919, the Weimar Republic faced numerous political problems, including profound social divisions within Germany, frequent political instability and economic crises. Problems accumulated for the new government between 1919 to 1923, when it experienced a particularly intense period of domestic upheaval, threatening the new democracy.

Less acute in comparison, but equally important in the formative years of Germany's second democracy, were the problems facing Konrad Adenauer and the BRD between 1949 and 1955; for even by 1951, post-war economic recovery was by no means yet guaranteed, with more than two million West Germans unemployed – over 10 per cent of the workforce. Adding to this was a continual influx of immigrants. Adenauer and many ordinary West Germans feared that potential social discord and economic uncertainty could find expression once more in political extremism as it had done for the Weimar government between 1919 and 1923 and after 1929.

The Weimar Republic (1919–33)

Political extremism posed a serious challenge to the stability and authority of Weimar at a time of economic fragility and social division, with challenges to the fledgling democracy coming from both the far-left and far-right.

Left-wing opposition

As seen in Unit 2.1, a left-wing attempt to overthrow Weimar took place in January 1919 when the Spartacists attempted to topple Ebert and establish a workers' republic by means of an armed uprising in the capital, Berlin. However they lacked support and their revolt was brutally suppressed by the right-wing Freikorps. The significance of this uprising lies in the government response; an SPD centre-left government allowed right-wing Freikorps to suppress the Spartacists – so the Communist Party detested Ebert and Weimar even more deeply.

A more fruitful revolt happened in Munich in March 1919, when Bavaria was proclaimed a Soviet (communist) Republic. A Red (communist) Army was then set up to protect the communist revolution. But on 1 May 1919, Ebert called upon the Freikorps to quell the uprising, as he did again in March 1920 with another uprising in the Ruhr, Germany's industrial region. Clearly, the democratic republic was fragile and faced intense and violent left-wing opposition; but by using those who despised Weimar (i.e., the Freikorps) to suppress these uprisings, Ebert's government increased its dependence on far-right forces. However, this did not mean that the far-right supported Weimar.

Right-wing opposition

Right-wing attempts to overthrow Weimar were rooted in the belief that Germany had been 'stabbed in the back' by its politicians – mainly social democrats – who had surrendered and signed the Treaty of Versailles. The Treaty of Versailles weakened Germany, militarily, territorially and colonially. Finally, the Treaty had incorporated into its terms the infamous war guilt clause, forcing Germany to acknowledge that it bore full responsibility for the war and were obliged to compensate the damage caused. Many Germans – especially nationalists – considered this anathema and were enraged at Germany's perceived decline from the key power in Central Europe to second-class status.

In March 1920, Dr Wolfgang Kapp, with Freikorps support, launched a putsch (revolt) in Berlin in order to overthrow the government. The right-wing revolutionary group managed to take over Berlin, which, as a socialist city, was unlikely to support Kapp wholeheartedly. The government, fleeing the capital for safety, called for a general strike and the workers responded accordingly. Without essential services, such as transport, gas and electricity, Kapp was unable to govern. The rebellion failed and he fled. However, if it had not been for the far-left's general strike, Kapp might have seized power.

The centre-left was able to mobilise to curtail the revolt, while internal divisions within the extreme right – for example, between civilian politicians and paramilitaries – undermined its efficacy. Significantly, the army did little or nothing to try to stop Kapp from seizing power (clearly indicating where the army's sympathies lay). Once again the republic had been saved by those who despised it. This undermined its future long-term stability, while the army that was supposed to be supporting the republic had refused to act against Kapp and his supporters.

Historical debate:
The legacy of Germany's defeat in World War One and its impact on the new democratic republic has provided historical debate for many years. The Treaty of Versailles is seen as responsible for most of the hatred directed at the Weimar regime. Nick Fellows in *Peacemaking, Peacekeeping: International Relations 1918–36*, says that instability in Germany was caused by the very act of signing the Treaty, and in *Germany from Bismarck to Hitler 1890-1933*, Geoff Layton notes that the Treaty of Versailles became an integral part of the internal economic and political conflict that evolved in Germany after 1919. But A.J.P. Taylor in *The Course of German History* suggests that the Treaty could have been much more severe, given the desire for revenge among the victors, and that Germany would not even have been able to negotiate peace if the Weimar government had not signed. He also sees the bigger problem as being the failure of all political parties – especially the Social Democrats – to accept what had happened and move forward. He states that 'instead of placing the blame for defeat on the old order... they helped the old order back into power and bore the burden of its disaster'. The debate still continues.

QUESTION

Why can it be said that both the extreme left and extreme right contributed to the instability of the Weimar Republic?

The Weimar government faced more right-wing opposition in the form of political murders and violence. In 1922, the assassination of Walther Rathenau, the foreign secretary, caused great shock and 700,000 people took to the streets of Berlin to protest at his killing. This protest demonstrates that the republic did have supporters prepared to defend it vigorously, as in 1920 with the Kapp Putsch. Yet many were increasingly pessimistic, arguing that Rathenau's assassination highlighted the government's vulnerability and proved that support for Weimar was weak. The situation worsened when the government failed to prevent Germany's economic crisis.

Fact: Foreign Secretary Walter Rathenau (1867–1922) was murdered on 24 June 1922 by three right-wing extremists belonging to a secret group called Organisation Consul. His chauffeur-driven car was overtaken, and Rathenau was then shot at close range with a machine-gun before a hand grenade was thrown into the car. Rathenau believed Germany should fulfil the terms of the Treaty of Versailles and acknowledge the new communist government in Russia. Two weeks before his killing, he had signed the Treaty of Rapallo with the USSR, which fulfilled this. His murder shocked Germany, and until the Weimar Republic ended in 1933, the date of his killing was commemorated publically, with the assassination viewed by many as a sacrifice for German democracy and for international decency.

Hyperinflation – Weimar's greatest domestic crisis

The demands placed upon Germany for payment of war damage were eventually fixed by the Allies at 132,000,000,000 Deutsch marks (£6,600,000,000). Weimar was unable to maintain the economy, but continued to print currency. Rampant inflation ensued and provided Ebert with reasons for withholding the second instalment of the reparations. France decided to force payment by sending both French and Belgian troops into the Ruhr, to collect outstanding reparations from Germany's industrial heartland. **Passive resistance** from the workers of the Ruhr was urged by Germany's leaders, which accelerated a further collapse in the economy, as the government was forced to print more paper money to pay the strikers. At this point Germany's industrial heartland had been decimated and the country was not producing anything. Meanwhile, more notes were circulating, currency soon became worthless and prices were constantly rising. The result was hyperinflation. (In July 1914, the US dollar was worth about four marks, while by November 1923 its equivalent in marks was 4,000,000,000,000.)

Passive resistance: a policy of non-cooperation or non-compliance with the decrees or directives issued by a government or an occupying power. Used as a means of protesting against what is seen as an unlawful authority, or against a perceived injustice; it usually takes the form of fasting, boycotting, setting up blockades, creating sit-ins, refusing to work or theatrical and media protests.

The hyperinflation of 1923 led to Weimar's greatest social and domestic crisis. The German middle classes lost all their savings and pensions, while the working classes (who had no savings and no income when made redundant) faced extreme poverty, with no adequate benefits system to support their families. Millions became unemployed.

Figure 2.11 Unemployed unskilled workers hold up their identification cards to attract attention in the crowded offices of Berlin's unemployment agencies in the early 1920s, during the Weimar Republic's post-war economic crisis

In September 1923, Gustav Stresemann called for Germans to cease their passive resistance in the Ruhr, so that the economy might start moving again. Although his response might be viewed as a positive development, many saw it as further political humiliation, with Germany being forced to do what the French wanted.

The extreme right reacted. Nazi leader **Adolf Hitler** attempted to overthrow the government in the Munich Putsch of November 1923. He wanted to show that not all Germans accepted the situation. But Hitler was arrested when the police broke up the revolt. The extreme left also acted. In Saxony there was a communist uprising against the republic and a communist regime was briefly established. Stresemann ordered them to resign or be charged with treason. The Ruhr crisis precipitated economic collapse, deepened the political humiliation, and undermined the republic. People starting to look towards extreme solutions.

Adolf Hitler (1889–1945)

Austrian by birth, Hitler moved to Munich and fought in the German army in the First World War. He later became leader of the right-wing German Worker's Party. It was an extreme nationalist organisation that later became the Nazi Party. It targeted left-wing groups and those who had 'stabbed Germany in the back' by signing the armistice in 1918. In 1923, Hitler's attempted Munich Putsch failed. He was imprisoned and wrote *Mein Kampf (My Struggle)*, in which he set out his nationalist, anti-democratic and anti-Jewish views. Upon his release in 1924, he reorganised the Nazi Party, using the democratic process to achieve power, although violence and intimidation was used against opponents. By 1932, the Nazi Party was the largest in the Reichstag, and in January 1933, Hitler became chancellor. Within 18 months, he had turned Germany into a Nazi dictatorship and was its Führer (leader).

Yet the republic survived and moved towards a period of greater economic and social stability between 1924 and 1929. Neither left- nor right-wingers were able to strike the fatal blow at this point in time. But there still remained a general hatred of the new system, with the political issue of the Treaty of Versailles, and the republic's identification with its acceptance, remaining the most important single reason for opposition from both left and right.

For right-wing nationalists, it was the political terms of the treaty and the territorial loss that had made Germany a second-class power, while for the far-left the greatest source of resentment was the reparations, which had led Germany into an economic abyss, causing social tensions and personal distress. These economic and social problems led to unemployment and civil unrest. The SPD then joined forces with the army, the business community and extreme right-wing groups in order to prevent revolution. This in turn triggered opposition from communists, who believed the SPD and their allies were betraying working people. Resentment continued to fester and to undermine the stability of the republic throughout the 1920s.

Having survived the insurrections from left and right and the growth of separatist elements in parts of the Ruhr, Rhineland and Bavaria, coalition governments held together in the mid- to late 1920s when it came to dealing with the problems associated with Versailles. But this fragile unity fell apart in 1930, following the Wall Street Crash, and arguments over social policy. Workers' power – and that of the left (which held firm over the Kapp Putsch) – was much more divided by the early 1930s. As massive unemployment spread within Germany, industrialists, the military and the rural–agricultural–Protestant interests, all anxious for a solution, were in the ascendant. They were very much in sympathy with the Nazi Party, which was now efficiently funded, organised and, since 1930, electorally strong and so became the unified vanguard of the nationalist right.

The Federal Republic of Germany (BRD) (1949–55)

The BRD did not have an easy start. Konrad Adenauer secured the chancellorship by the smallest of margins, so his governing CDU/CSU coalition needed support from other parties. He faced a number of key domestic challenges; many of which were underpinned by geography – namely West Germany's front-line territorial exposure to the Soviet Union and its satellite states. Moreover, as the BRD came into existence in 1949, the Soviet Union had successfully tested an atomic bomb. Soviet Bloc armies also outnumbered those of the West. Then in 1950, communist North Korea attacked

Western-backed South Korea. To West Germans living in the BRD, the parallels were inescapable; so Adenauer needed to show strength and build morale, although many at the time had limited faith in his government's survival.

The 'status' and the future of the BRD

The BRD's Basic Law permitted Adenauer to cope with his fragile coalition, as it strengthened the federal chancellor within the political system and undoubtedly helped to reinvent western Germany as a liberal-democratic nation that had learnt its lessons from the demise of the Weimar Republic. But despite Adenauer and his pro-American credentials, the BRD still faced suspicion within Europe after 1949. The relationship was not going to be entirely smooth or straightforward.

For example the Western Union of 1948 had seen Britain, France, Belgium, Luxemburg and the Netherlands all form an alliance against future aggression, whether from Germany, or against any other members. Germany's recent history therefore automatically placed constraints on German politicians. Even more importantly, the BRD did not immediately gain full independence or sovereignty; allied troops occupied Germany, and West German politicians had to gain the approval of the Allies in governmental areas such as internal security and trade. The Ruhr region was under international control and France administered the Saar coal-mining region. The BRD was even forbidden to manufacture weapons or to rearm. This meant that the rulers of the new democratic state had much to prove and were highly accountable both to their own electorate and to the occupying Allies.

Domestic controversy

Many in the Allied camp believed that the German 'national character' suffered from serious flaws, and that many still needed re-education after the horrors of Nazism and the Holocaust. But Adenauer was determined to put the Nazi past behind the BRD, sharing a commonly held view that denazification was victor's justice. Consequently broad amnesties were put in to place in 1949 and 1954 and convicted war criminals were set free again.

Former Nazi civil servants were re-employed and many Nazi supporters were able to continue their careers in the BRD as long as they supported the new political order and remained quiet about both Nazi ideas and their own past. Many of these officials had administrative experience and Adenauer urgently needed this in the fabric of his new democracy.

Moreover the perceived threat was soon seen to come from the East and its communist ideology. German prisoners-of-war in the Soviet Union were increasingly seen as victims of the war, not just the Jews. This did not mean that neo-Nazism was tolerated in the BRD: it was not, and there was an acute redrawing as to what was politically acceptable on the right. But Adenauer knew that in order to survive, the BRD had to reinvent itself, distance itself from its past and try to reconcile many disparate groups, in order to forestall domestic crises of the sort that undermined Weimar. The economy would prove to be his salvation, but initially proved to be a great test.

Economic challenges

Unsurprisingly, Adenauer and his economics minister Ludwig Erhard knew that progressive economic growth and prosperity was the key to the survival and evolution of the BRD as a democracy. They had lived through Weimar and witnessed the trauma of economic failure. They inherited a delicate economic situation in 1949.

The Western Allies had withdrawn the existing currency and replaced it with a new 'Deutsche mark' in June 1948 at the rate of one new mark for ten old marks. It was intended to protect the western zones from potential hyperinflation and to curtail the increased bartering and black market economy where American cigarettes were used as currency.

This exchange rate immediately cancelled out more than 90 per cent of governmental and private debts, yet it wiped out the personal savings of individuals. Since the Nazi era, prices and wages had been controlled, but cash had been abundant. Consequently many people had accumulated large amounts of paper currency, and the black market had dominated an economy fuelled by unofficial cash transactions.

Price controls were abolished and they soon rose by more than 25 per cent; yet labour unions had to accept a wage increase of only 15 per cent. The BRD thus inherited a Western-imposed, competition-based market economy. The result was that export prices were low, while profits and earnings from exports soared and were reinvested back into the fledgling, post-war economy. But while the currency reform might have filled shop windows and restaurants, Erhard's economic management of the BRD increased the divide between the haves and the have-nots in the short-term.

Three years in to his chancellorship, Adenauer was still grappling with West Germany's post-war inheritance, and then had to battle a recession. But then he and Erhard had inherited a difficult economic situation in 1949.

In the West, farm production had continually fallen since 1945, while food supplies were eventually cut off from Soviet-controlled eastern Germany. Moreover, shipments of quality food and produce once guaranteed from conquered Nazi territories such as France, Denmark, the Netherlands and Poland, had ceased.

The overall living standard had by 1949 regressed to a pre-1914 level, and food was in short supply. Inflation had risen quickly in 1948–9, with the retail prices of manufactured consumer goods increasing by 18 per cent and food prices by 29 per cent, and a black market had distorted the economy.

Galvanising the workforce was also proving problematic. More than six million of the forced labourers working for the Nazis in Germany had now been repatriated to their own native land, but about fourteen million Germans had come in from the east since 1945, many living for years in displaced persons camps. It also took nearly a decade for all German prisoners of war to return home and reintegrate into the workplace, with many of those held captive in Soviet Russia lost forever.

To add to this, there was a continual flow of civilian refugees – almost half a million alone between 1951 and 1953 – who brought all the problems inherent with their social and economic integration, while the BRD itself still faced housing shortages.

Two million West Germans (12 per cent of the labour force) were still unemployed by 1951, with unemployment being especially high in predominantly agricultural states with a high number of refugees and expellees, Adenauer and Erhard shared a gnawing concern that social and economic dissatisfaction might find a voice in renewed political extremism. After all, unemployment had helped Hitler to power in 1933.

Yet the so-called '**economic miracle**' or Wirtschaftswunder of the 1950s eventually unfolded. It was not just about increased production and employment opportunities for Erhard and his advisors renamed their economic policy as 'the social market economy', a market economy with a social conscience. The government would provide a 'social net' of minimum living standards through which no one in the BRD should fall, simultaneously providing support for the millions of war widows, veterans, orphans and disabled who lost their assets and their livelihood. By 1955, trade unions and employers' federations worked together increasingly for the benefit of the economy. A strong currency, together with a non-adversarial industrial policy and a focus on improving wages and working conditions within the framework of a capitalist market economy, helped to deliver greater prosperity, and stability. This was a key factor behind the small number of strikes in the 1950s. Indeed, Article 20 of the Basic Law of 1949 gave all Germans an obligation to maintain the republic as a 'democratic and social federal state'.

Economic miracle: a phrase first used by *The Times* of London in 1960 – and added to international economic parlance – to denote the rapid rebuilding and subsequent development of the BRD's economy in the decade following 1949. Adenauer and Erhard were seen as the architects of this period of low inflation, efficient labour practices and growing confidence in the newly introduced Deutsche mark currency.

Karl Hardach calls the period after 1952 the 'consolidation phase' of the German economy. **Source E** explains this.

SOURCE E

By the second quarter of 1951, however, the balance of payments crisis was essentially under control, owing to the cresting of the worldwide raw materials boom, and the continued fast growth of German exports ... the six years from 1952 onwards were a period of relative tranquillity compared to the preceding time of hectic developments. Germany's economic upsurge continued with few tendencies towards higher prices throughout the fifties, and her GNP increased in real terms between 1952 and 1958 at an annual average rate of 7.6 percent, while the unemployment ration fell from 6.4 percent to 1.7 percent leaving virtually no further reserves on the labour market.

K. Hardach (1981), The Political Economy of Germany in the Twentieth Century, *Berkeley and Los Angeles: University of California Press, pp. 185–6.*

QUESTION

What domestic problems did the BRD face when Adenauer and Erhard assumed office in 1949 and how effectively did they respond to them?

2.6 How did the government react to demands for equality and other protests?

The Weimar Republic had to cope with issues other than those exacerbated by economic or political problems, facing civil protests and demands for specific voting rights (suffrage) and greater social equality, while the BRD had to reconstruct a ruined post-war Germany, faced with a significantly increased female population, looking for a more equal post-war role, and the politicians had to look towards bringing about a greater harmonisation of living conditions, which in itself would depend on economic stability and prosperity.

The Weimar Republic (1919–33)

The situation before 1919

Ironically, although imperial Germany between 1871 and 1914 had a repressive political system, other cultural factors favoured the development of women's movements. Women were encouraged to bolster German cultural life and spread the use of German language, traditions and customs in the new unified state. It contained many different nationalities and languages. The government had encouraged the formation of several such organisations, all of which were concerned with strengthening German nationalism. The middle-class women's movement in Germany founded the Federation of German Women's Associations (BdF), as an umbrella organisation in 1894.

Within the BdF, the state of motherhood was viewed as a crucial link between the organisation's commitment to promoting nationalism and education; and wider female demands for greater social freedom and political emancipation. But to the eyes of the imperial government, family, motherhood and domesticity played a key role in constructing 'Germanness'.

Politically, the Social Democrats had adopted causes such as the female vote and equal pay by 1900. Significantly they had recruited more than 140,000 female members by 1913, following the Citizenship Law of that year failing to change a ruling that women's citizenship followed their husbands'.

Figure 2.12 This poster by Karl Maria Stadler calls for a public gathering of women on 8 March 1914. The text reads: 'Give us women's suffrage. Women's Day….come all, you women and girls, to the 9th public women's assembly on Sunday, March 8, 1914, at 3pm'

Many women on the political left now stated that 'women have no fatherland' and they disapproved of what they saw as a male-centred perception of gender relations, a widening of separate spheres and the continuation of a male-dominated public state with no female right to vote. But the German socialists were not committed feminists, but rather viewed women as natural allies in a wider undertaking to transform the political system. Also, we must remember that Germany was not a democracy and, as such, the socialists had been banned for some years by Bismarck. In fact the voting rights possessed by men carried only limited influence.

As in Great Britain and many other countries, the outbreak of war in 1914 then put the campaigns for women's rights on hold; but German feminists were determined to press their case when peacetime resumed, in order to achieve equal rights with men. Defeat in the First World War accelerated this development by replacing the Kaiser's rule with the democratic Weimar Republic.

Suffrage and equality for women in the Weimar Republic

Before 1914, politics and class had kept different German women's movements apart, in spite of overlap on the desire for political and legal equality. But female suffrage would prove to be the product of the Weimar Constitution, rather than any movement.

The enfranchisement of women affected about half of the population and was a radical step. Approximately 10 per cent of the delegates to the 1919 National Assembly in Weimar were women, while the calculated turnout of women at these first democratic elections was almost 90 per cent – an unprecedented, unrepeated level of participation.

Women were viewed by Ebert as a key group, but to many on the right, they were seen as a potentially unsettling constituency who might subvert the old order of pre-war Germany! Political parties thus adopted a cautious attitude towards women, knowing that they were more successful in getting women's votes when they emphasised culture, religion, education and welfare. So they largely moved away from programmes of women's reform and emancipation. The desire to pursue women's equality was also inhibited by the desire of most political parties not to 'rock the boat' and keep to the middle ground, policy wise.

After the adoption of the 1919 constitution, women were officially guaranteed equal status in terms of voting rights, and their financial and legal standing. But many felt that this progress amounted to mere token gestures of appeasement and remained largely theoretical. Also, the 1919 constitution was never made mandatory by legislation, and the Civil Code of 1900 – which was highly reactionary and restrictive – still controlled many of their legal rights. As historian Claudia Koonz states: 'Weimar leaders grafted a democratic state onto a traditionalist and conservative social structure and a thoroughly capitalist economy.'

Double standards for men and women were often common practice, and much progress on women's issues stalled. Yet girls were now educated on the same basis as boys, and in spite of deep-rooted conservative and patriarchal tendencies, women made greater progress towards equality in Weimar Germany than in any other state at the time, with 2,500 female physicians and 300 female lawyers in practice by 1930.

However the reality for most was vastly different from that of the 'New Woman' they supposedly wished to emulate. With under-promotion in the workplace, and political parties sending out a traditional message about their role, many women continued to embrace the ideal of child-bearing, home-making and attending church. Notions of political liberation were also tenuous. Despite gaining the vote in 1918, they had little or no representation at the top levels of Weimar German political parties.

Undoubtedly, following the First World War, the number of working women did increase and more married women worked for wages. It was now acceptable for young single women to live and work on their own in the city. But illegal abortion was also widespread, and the birth rate continued to decline. In short, the position of most women in Germany did not improve greatly.

Where there was change, it was superficial. Behind apparent progress remained deep-rooted conservatism, as social change – particularly the role of women – later became a prominent part of a much wider debate. Consequently in Weimar Germany the struggle for women's equality continued in spite of what appeared to be a state of parity with men, and it was hampered by the necessity of compromise on the part of politicians locked into a system where coalitions and minority governments ruled the day.

Theory of Knowledge

History and reason:
Regarding political instability from 1919 to 1933, it has been said that the extreme right had a far greater reason for hating the Weimar Republic than the extreme left. Discuss in pairs whether this statement is correct. Now look back at this unit and the relevant pages of Unit 2.1. Identify and briefly explain two key reasons for each side to be hostile towards Weimar.

Civil unrest and protests

Weimar Germany never faced a single massive popular uprising or manifestation of civilian protest that threatened the survival of the fledgling democratic state. Even though thousands protested in Berlin against the terms of the Treaty of Versailles, rather Weimar faced ongoing protests; its early years being ones of nervousness and intermittent political instability.

In 1919–20 there were radical uprisings from both left and right extremists, with attempts at revolution by Spartacists on the far-left and with the Kapp Putsch on the far-right. This was followed by sporadic political assassinations and intermittent attempts at rebellion. As Germany's international position deteriorated, resistance to the Allies' reparation plans led to a Franco–Belgian occupation of the Ruhr in January 1923, where strikes and civil disobedience incited extremists. Hyperinflation and the Munich Putsch, both in 1923, further destabilised the political system.

A period of recovery after 1924 was halted with the **Wall Street Crash** of October 1929, which sent the Germany economy into crisis. The USA recalled the loans it had made to the Weimar Republic. This created the stressful economic conditions in which democracy broke down and the Nazi Party was able to rise to power. Such pressures could overload any governmental system, let alone one tainted by the circumstances of its creation, and by its inheritance of weak democratic values.

Wall Street Crash: the sudden and heavy fall in the prices quoted for shares traded on the New York Stock Exchange, reaching its lowest point in October 1929. The resulting bankruptcies and financial devastation led to a worldwide depression as the US economy collapsed.

Weimar's political structure failed to produce the required loyalty necessary from Germans to help it through the crises it faced. The **Great Depression** quickly eroded any remaining vestiges of confidence placed by the public in the republic's political system.

Great Depression: the economic downturn felt internationally throughout the 1930s as a result of the chaos of the 1929 Wall Street Crash. It was felt very heavily in Central Europe, especially in Germany, where the Weimar Republic lacked the democratic traditions to meet the social challenges of economic depression. This led many Germans to turn to communism or Adolf Hitler's Nazi Party.

The Federal Republic of Germany (BRD) (1949–55)

Suffrage and equality in the BRD

Figure 2.13 German women clear rubble from the streets of Berlin, 1945

During the war, German women assumed responsibilities traditionally undertaken by men. After the war, the so-called **Trummerfrauen** (women of the rubble) helped to tend the wounded, buried the dead and generally initiated the arduous task of rebuilding the nation by clearing away the rubble.

Trummerfrauen (women of the rubble): the women who physically helped to clear and reconstruct some of the German and Austrian cities bombed by the USA and Britain during the Second World War. With an absence of menfolk – many of whom were dead, away or in captivity – the task fell largely on women. Hundreds of towns and cities had been reduced to rubble through round-the-clock bombing and firestorm damage; as well as street fighting and ground shelling. These women gained almost legendary status for their heroic and hard physical labour.

With the creation of the BRD in 1949 came the establishment of a bipolar party system with the CDU and the SPD representing different interpretations of Germany, but acknowledging a common democratic framework and continuing the precedent of suffrage for women, first introduced under Weimar in 1919.

But political and social life in the early years of the BRD was conservative in character, as reflected by the domination of Adenauer and Erhard and the CDU, following the first democratic elections. A pro-American party that focused on economic growth and drew upon the support of established business interests and local elites, the CDU was faced with important post-war demographic changes with women constituting a larger proportion of the electorate than for several decades. Indeed Adenauer wanted to make the family the keystone of the emerging post-war social order, with the state being the servant of a vibrant, stable family life – not its master as in nazism and communism.

SOURCE F

Article 3 of the Basic Law stated categorically that women and men were equal, and for the first time in German history women could determine their citizenship independently and regardless of whom they married. But even the so-called Equality Law of 1958 still made the rights of women to gainful employment dependent on its compatibility with their 'duties in marriage and family'. Protecting motherhood and its values of domesticity and clean living became one of the leading themes of postwar German reconstruction.

S. Berger (2001), Inventing the Nation: Germany, *London: Hodder Arnold, pp. 177–8.*

Unsurprisingly, this meant that women had poor representation in government; indeed even in the 1980s, they comprised only just in excess of 10 per cent of the representatives in the Bundestag. Moreover, the average woman's wage in the late 1950s was still 40 per cent less than the average man's. Within a few years of the BRD becoming a sovereign state in 1955, feminist issues really began to rise to the surface of public consciousness. Feminist writers in the USA and Britain were soon translated into German, and the 1960s thus witnessed the emergence of another band of German feminists campaigning for social change. But in 1955 – and beyond – real emancipation remained distant.

QUESTION

How effectively do you think the government of the BRD dealt with the rising importance of women in post-war Germany?

To Adenauer and Erhard, the key to achieving greater equality in the BRD, was by developing and maintaining political, social and economic stability for this post-war generation; at the same time, ensuring that people became 'participants in the new republic', becoming more involved in politics and held their politicians more accountable. Indeed, there was almost a demand for such participation, equality and accountability after the excesses of Nazi dictatorship.

Politically, the Basic Law hoped to erode the contrast between state and society, by giving all the BRD's political parties a dynamic role at the centre of the new constitutional and political order. This helped to promote inter-party consensus and collaboration. So there was a greater feeling of equality as opposition parties also began to view themselves as having a stake in the affairs of government; sharing responsibility rather than opposing and criticising.

Federalism and the legislative involvement of opposition parties in the working committees of the Bundestag motivated all parties into making their influence felt. The posturing and factionalism of Weimar had led to political deadlock: this was now largely removed and in the view of some historians, it moved West German political parties away from the narrow sectional or exclusively short-term electoral concerns prevalent between 1919 and 1933.

Economically, Erhard knew that he had to deliver the economic goods, both figuratively and literally. Opposed to centralised state planning, but not governmental inactivity, he advocated 'prosperity through competition' in a social market economy. Here, the market would allow citizens of the BRD to accumulate property, while active social engineering would insure against the negative consequences of economic change.

In conclusion, the BRD's democratic party-state was reinforced by such policies and approaches, with a kind of levelling taking place. Geoff Layton observes that by the 1960s 'ideological gaps got smaller as the new materialism forged a bond of common values. Workers gradually adopted the lifestyle and values of the middle class. That is not to say that it was a classless society, but West Germans appeared rather homogenously middle class.'

In Unit 3, attention will be focused further on the social and economic policies of both Weimar and the BRD, with an examination as to the extent to which its citizens benefitted from their government's programme and the cultural impact it had.

End of unit activities

1 Design a mind map to summarise the various challenges, crises and threats that the Weimar government in Germany faced between 1919 and 1933.
2 Reread this chapter. Note down and evaluate the criticisms of Weimar from left- and right-wing perspectives. Then using the internet or library for additional research, assess whether the Weimar Republic could ever have responded to a crisis in a way that would have satisfied all sides.
3 To what extent were German women in the BRD emancipated by the end of the 1950s?
4 Explain the significance of each of these in the context of modern German history: NATO; Basic Law; social market economy; repatriation; Trummerfrauen; economic miracle; 1958 Equality Law.
5 Draw up a table to summarise and evaluate the response of either the Weimar government or the BRD to the challenges posed by each of these issues. You can use this table as a model:

Issues	What was the underlying nature of the problem?	How successfully did the government deal with the issue?
Consolidation of democracy		
Suffrage and women's rights		
Political extremism		
Foreign influence		
Equality		

The impact of democracy on society in Germany, 1919–33 and 1949–55

Unit 3

KEY QUESTIONS

- What economic and social policies did the Weimar Republic and the BRD implement?
- To what extent did the Germans benefit from these policies?
- What was the cultural impact of the establishment of democracy?

Overview

- The economic and social policies enacted by the Weimar Republic and the BRD focused on economic growth, employment, health and welfare, the status of women, the development of education, and the distribution of wealth and resources.
- Two of the goals sought by the Weimar – the social protection of the working class and the reduction of unemployment – were never fully achieved, in view of the republic facing the most serious economic problems experienced by any Western democracy in history.
- The Weimar Constitution offered German women the promise of legal equality for the first time. Although that promise was not wholly fulfilled, German society was characterised by the emergence of a new kind of woman who had more freedom, but this led to a backlash as part of a much wider debate about morality and social status.
- Genuine attempts were made to modernise welfare and education, but many of these proposed reforms never came to fruition as the republic focused on its own survival;
- The BRD after 1949 faced immense challenges. There was an urgent need to create a stable and prosperous economy while developing a fairer society. But the progress made, because of political leadership and the engagement of the people, was remarkable, if not always ideal.
- The BRD had to rebuild from 'zero hour' with an inheritance of occupation and collapsed infrastructure. Restarting the economy and paying attention to health, social welfare, to denazifying the education system and improving everyday life, were urgent requirements.
- For both republics, democracy brought changes in the social and cultural life of Germany. The effect on minority groups is also considered.

TIMELINE

1919–33

1921 **Jan:** Allied Reparations Committee demands 33 billion marks in war reparations from Germany (equal to 26 per cent of all German exports for forty-two years).

1922 Youth Welfare Act.

1923 **Jan:** German non-payment; French occupation of Ruhr.

Jul–Oct: Hyperinflation.

Dec: Stresemann stabilises finances with a new currency, the Rentenmark; cuts in expenditure – 750,000 civil servants/public employees lose their jobs.

1924 **Aug:** Reparations adjusted under Dawes Plan.

1927 Labour Exchanges and Unemployment Insurance Law passed.

1929 **Jun:** Young Plan further adjusts reparations payment instalments over fifty-eight years.

Oct: Death of Stresemann; Wall Street Crash and Great Depression.

1930 **Mar:** Collapse of Grand Coalition over unemployment benefit.

1931 **May:** Collapse of Austrian bank Kreditanstalt; bank crisis in Germany; unemployment stands at four million.

1933 **Jan:** Nazi leader Adolf Hitler becomes chancellor. Democracy ends.

1949–55

1949 **23–24 May:** Basic Law comes into force.

Foundation of BRD (Bundesrepublik Deutschland) in West Germany (German Federal Republic).

15 Sep: Konrad Adenauer of the CDU, elected chancellor of BRD following first Bundestag election.

1951 Co-determination Law.

1952 The Equalisation of Burdens Law and the Works' Constitution Law are implemented.

Sep: Luxembourg Agreement regarding compensation to Israel and Jewish victims of Holocaust.

1955 **May:** BRD becomes a sovereign state and joins NATO.

The Dusseldorf Agreement on Education.

2.7 What economic and social policies did the Weimar Republic and the BRD implement?

The economic and social policies introduced by the Weimar Republic in 1919 and the BRD in 1949 tried to address the immense problems facing Germany. On both occasions, the country had been defeated in war. Challenges included unemployment, poverty, issues with refugees and other displaced persons, plus the need to examine the general distribution of resources within Germany.

In 1919 the Weimar was burdened with the terms of the Treaty of Versailles and its blame given to Germany. In 1949, the BRD was created out of the Western occupied section of a ruined and defeated Nazi Germany, while the onset of the Cold War and a lack of state sovereignty underpinned its founding.

Both democratic governments introduced policies to improve health, provide social welfare, boost education and improve the position of women. Underlying these was the desire to create a stable, prosperous economy, but also an equitable society. The outcomes for Weimar and the BRD were markedly different.

Figure 2.14 Prices of everyday food items rose astronomically with the hyperinflation in the Weimar Republic, 1923

Policies to promote economic growth

Weimar Republic, 1919–33

The Weimar Constitution provided for election by proportional representation (PR), which led to coalition government. Opposition from the extreme political left and right was constant. Weimar was famously called a 'democracy without democrats' and its leaders were challenged every step of the way. Ideas of 'national needs above party policy' were not in the political vocabulary. The situation inherited in 1918 was also significant. Because of inflation and the borrowing to finance the 1914–18 war, the German mark in 1919 was worth less than 20 per cent of its pre-war value. Tax revenue was also inadequate, so Weimar was economically vulnerable; as in 1923 and 1929–32.

The economic impact of the Treaty of Versailles was severe. Germany lost 13 per cent of its territory, 10 per cent of its population, 15 per cent of its arable land, 75 per cent of its iron and zinc ore, 25 per cent of its coal resources and its entire potash and textile industries. In addition, the reparations demanded were three times what Germany was able to pay.

The Allies gradually allowed restricted goods to be imported into Germany again, but these were too costly for many Germans to buy. So there was a growing shortage of basic everyday items. There was money in circulation and there were goods, but demand far exceeded supply. Inflation soon became a serious concern and as it crept upwards, currency became increasingly devalued.

Historian Volker Berghahn examined the economic situation in Germany when the first Versailles reparations payments were being made, and he described the problems as 'an unholy mess'.

In 1923, hyperinflation followed the French occupation of the Ruhr. The mark declined from four marks to the dollar to more than one trillion to the dollar. Although Weimar later experienced greater economic stability and international respectability between 1924 and 1929, the republic never enjoyed the full confidence of the public in its fiscal policy following hyperinflation. It was 'relative stabilisation' rather than major recovery.

To control inflation, the gap between government expenditure and income had to be narrowed. Two obvious approaches were to increase personal taxation and to cut government spending. But given the sluggish nature of Germany's post-war economy and the nation's fragility, this would deepen the problem and alienate much of the population. The government therefore adopted a policy of **deficit financing** by reducing taxation.

Deficit financing: also known as a budget deficit, this is the amount by which governmental or individual spending exceeds revenue, over a period of time. The shortfall is covered through borrowing or printing new currency. The method is sometimes used as a deliberate attempt by a government to stimulate an ailing economy, when it might lower taxes or increase public expenditure.

They thought this would give people more spending power and thereby increase the demand for goods. In theory, it should have provided work for returning troops and helped to reduce the national debt. However, as an integral part of a deficit financing policy, inflation had to rise. Combined with Germany's obligation to pay war reparations under the Treaty of Versailles, this provided a major flaw in the plan.

But it was not really until August 1923 – when the entire German economy was teetering on the edge of collapse – that the new coalition government formed by Gustav Stresemann really sought to radically tackle both Germany's economic crisis and the resulting social problems with the necessary determination and in a less partisan manner.

Stresemann made key decisions and in December 1923 a new stable currency, the Rentenmark, was well received. However, at the same time Stresemann ordered the government to cut expenditure in order to reduce the deficit. This led to almost 750,000 civil servants and other public employees losing their jobs, adding both to unemployment and resentment.

With the acceptance of the Dawes Plan in 1924, an influx of foreign capital enabled Stresemann to embark on a programme of public building. Eventually, industries flourished, new jobs were created and lost working days fell considerably.

Fact: The Dawes Plan proposed to resolve the situation when Germany had difficulty paying reparations agreed under the Treaty of Versailles. In 1923, French and Belgian troops occupied the Ruhr as a result of Germany failing in its treaty obligations, and massive inflation and increased unemployment followed. The Allied Reparations Committee asked a US banker, Charles Dawes, to look for a solution. Between 1925 and 1930, Germany received 25.5 billion marks in loans from the USA. This and other investments resulted in a dip in unemployment. Germany met its reparation obligations for the next five years, so initially the Dawes Plan was a great success.

Fact: An international commission devised the Young Plan (spearheaded by another US banker, Owen D. Young), which lowered German reparations to £1,850 million, due over the following fifty-nine years. Many Germans remained unhappy at the fact that Germany would still be required to pay an annual sum of £30 million to the Allies right through to 1988.

Yet Weimar was living beyond its means and this was 'borrowed prosperity', to quote Stresemann: as unemployment still hovered above two million and foreign indebtedness rose to more than half the national income. The financial influx between 1925 and 1930 appeared to enable Germany to sow the seeds of economic progress and by 1928 industrial production exceeded pre-war levels. Workers seemed to be the chief beneficiaries, and this was enhanced by Stresemann's introduction of the 1927 Labour Exchanges and Unemployment Insurance Act (see next section).

Further optimism arose in 1929, with the provisions of the Young Plan. But before this could be implemented, the New York Stock Exchange crashed and worldwide economic depression set in; Germany was again in debt.

This set the scene for disaster. Companies went bankrupt, unemployment rose and those who stayed in business had to tighten their budgets. Workers accepted pay cuts as vacancies went unfilled. The demand to raise employees' contributions to the Unemployment Insurance Fund (see next section) split the Cabinet, and led to the fall of Chancellor Müller's Grand Coalition in 1930 – the last with a parliamentary majority.

It marked the beginning of a slide towards dictatorship, and signalled the start of an authoritarian presidential regime, given that under Article 48 of the Weimar Constitution, the president could rule by emergency decree when required by the seriousness of any national situation. Government by decree did nothing to help the economic situation – quite the opposite, in fact. When major cuts to unemployment benefit were opposed at a time when millions were losing their jobs, the new chancellor Heinrich Brüning simply put the cuts into effect by means of emergency decree.

By late 1932, two successive chancellors had cut spending and raised taxes, thereby lowering demand and exacerbating the effects of the slump. The collapse of the major Danatbank in July 1931, and the demise of others, including Austria's leading Creditanstalt Bank, also had huge knock-on effects, raising unemployment to 5.6 million by 1932.

Even with the arrival of Adolf Hitler as chancellor in January 1933, the German economy experienced a prolonged period of uncertainty, which it only recovered from in the mid-1930s. Hitler reduced unemployment by introducing conscription, creating Nazi labour schemes that introduced huge public building programmes and phasing out many women's jobs. But there were still 2.5 million unemployed in 1936. Living standards did not improve until 1938, but democracy was replaced by dictatorship.

QUESTION

From **Source A** and the text, why do you think Weimar Germany was hit so badly in the aftermath of the Wall Street Crash? Explain your answer.

SOURCE A

The collapse of world trade and the withdrawal of foreign short term lending in 1930–32 exposed structural weaknesses and led to historically exceptional falls in employment, output and investment. The trough of the recession was reached in the autumn and winter of 1932–33.

P. Panayi (2001), Weimar and Nazi Germany: Continuities and Discontinuities, *Harlow: Pearson Education, p. 163.*

BRD, 1949–55

With the defeat of the Nazi regime in 1945, Germany entered a period known as Stunde Null (Zero Hour), when its ruined society and economy had to be rebuilt from scratch.

When the BRD was formed in 1949 living standards in western Germany had regressed to a pre-1914 level, with food shortages and a cash transaction-based, black market economy. The government also had to attend to returning soldiers, refugees and rebuilding morale. The men who guided Germany's post-war economy were Chancellor Konrad Adenauer and economics minister Ludwig Erhard. Once in office, Erhard adopted a 'social market' economy as Geoff Layton comments in **Source B**.

SOURCE B

Erhard believed that the aim of the 'social market' economy lay in rising consumption and economic growth. However he did not oppose state intervention … its aim was to combine political and economic freedom with social justice and security. While private property should be protected, and enterprise and investment supported with as many financial incentives as possible, a strong state should be able to intervene in the free market to defend the common interests of the individual.

G. Layton (2009), Democracy and Dictatorship in Germany 1919–63, *London: Hodder Education, p. 314.*

The BRD initially had a recession due to a lack of foreign currency and insufficient demand to sustain growth. But by 1952, job creation was rising, unemployment was beginning to fall (down to just one million, around 4.25 per cent, by 1955) and gross national profit (GNP) was rising to the point where it had doubled by 1955.

Adenauer also wanted to foster a sense of mutuality and shared responsibility between government, industry and the trade unions. This was evident in the 1951 Co-determination Law – which gave workers representation on managerial boards in the iron, coal and steel industries – and in the 1952 Works' Constitution Law, which provided for works councils for all employees in companies with more than 500 workers.

Unions worked as partners to employers, rather than posturing and being antagonistic, as in Britain and France. Industrial peace was also enhanced by the fact that the unions – in spite of a natural affiliation to the SPD – tended to rise above party politics.

The BRD were also able to benefit from the Marshall Plan and build factories, equipping them with up-to-date machinery. By 1960, overall industrial production had risen to more than twice the level of 1950 and the BRD was the third biggest trading power behind the USA and Britain. The social market economy had lifted the BRD into a position primed for unimagined growth, and it would soon be an economic giant, with its banking system the touchstone for fiscal stability.

QUESTION

To what extent does **Source B** support the idea that the social market economy of the BRD was actually an attempt to construct a third way between unrestrained capitalism and over-regulated socialism?

Historical debate:
Under the European Recovery Programme, better known as the Marshall Plan, the USA gave $13 billion to European nations affected by the war. More than $1.5 billion was assigned to Germany. Historians such as Layton and Fulbrook have argued that Adenauer, Erhard and the BRD's economic rebirth was helped enormously by the Marshall Plan, rather than Erhard's policies alone being the principal recovery factor. However, it has been estimated by economists that aid from the plan contributed less than 5 per cent to the BRDs national income during this time period and that Britain received twice as much as West Germany, although German growth continued over the years. Erhard's early financial reforms and the presence of good industrial relations in the BRD are now viewed as being more pivotal.

Policies to alleviate unemployment and provide social welfare

Weimar Republic, 1919–33

Throughout the Weimar Republic, the spectre of unemployment haunted government policies to improve the economy and control inflation. Ebert's republic had inherited an economic imbalance. After 1919, thousands of returning soldiers required reintegration into a defeated nation, itself needing transformation into a competitive peacetime economy. Nonetheless, the republic tried zealously to provide a better tomorrow.

In 1919, a maximum working week of forty-eight hours was introduced, with restrictions on night work and a half-day break on Saturday. Health insurance was extended to cover wives and daughters without income – crucial given the level of injured soldiers and the number of orphans and widows after the war – plus people incapable of finding employment. There was help for individuals working both in private and public cooperatives, while a series of progressive tax reforms were introduced, involving tax increases on investments and capital; plus a huge rise in the highest rate of income tax from 4 per cent to 60 per cent.

Then the government decreed that all aid for the disabled and their dependants should be controlled by the central government, plus they extended the role of the nationwide welfare relief organisations, so they might coordinate welfare for war widows and orphans in peacetime.

Following hyperinflation, Stresemann merged all forms of unemployment relief into a unified assistance scheme; then in 1925 he reformed an accident insurance programme. This allowed occupational diseases to be insurable risks in law. Housing construction was accelerated with more than two million new homes 'at an affordable price' being built between 1924 and 1931, while nearly 200,000 properties were renovated and modernised. Legislation was passed to regulate rents and increase protection for tenants in rented accommodation – especially those in a difficult financial situation due to unemployment.

Finally in 1927 the Labour Exchanges and Unemployment Insurance Act was introduced. It stipulated compulsory unemployment insurance for more than seventeen million German workers. It was the largest and most comprehensive scheme in the world at that time. Jointly funded by employers and workers, there was also a state reserve fund established to allow the scheme to cope with cyclical downturns in the economy. It was administered by a new body, the Reich Institution for Labour Exchanges and Unemployment.

However, the financing of this scheme was based on an assumed unemployment level of around 800,000 (lower than that reported at any point in 1928–33). It also made provision for a further 600,000 unemployed people using an emergency fund, to be 'drawn on in times of crisis'. In addition, state subsidies were available to build parks, playgrounds, schools, sports facilities and council housing. All these policies led to better conditions for the German people, but the benefits were short-lived.

By 1929 unemployment had risen to three million. The scheme soon had insufficient funds and its financial limits were reached within the year. The state was owed more than 300 million marks in government-loaned money. This caused outrage, with the National Association of German Industry attacking fiscal policy. It became clear that the republic could not sustain the type of welfare system it desired in order to look after the unemployed. Hostilities between left and right became more acute.

With the depression of 1930–2, government expenditure was reduced and there were many welfare cuts. Housing, basic nutrition, maternity and child health were prioritised, but none were ring-fenced. Shortage of funds made it impossible to maintain the genuinely comprehensive welfare programme the reformers had originally envisaged.

As studied in Unit 2.2, the overambitious unemployment insurance scheme helped to destroy the coalition government in 1930. Yet in a short period of relative stability, the Weimar reformers tried to tackle unemployment and welfare creditably. But its failure almost served as the demise of democracy.

SOURCE C

Just as state welfare had paid important political dividends for the republic in the 1920s, so the disintegration of the Sozialstaat (social state) had disastrous implications for it in the early 1930s. Above all, working class support for the Republic, which had been so crucial at certain periods in the past, now either ebbed away or sank into passive disillusionment.

S. Ogilvie and R. Overy (eds.) (2003), Germany: A New Social and Economic History Vol III Since 1800, *London: Hodder Arnold, p. 238.*

QUESTION

According to **Source C**, where was real disillusionment felt as the republic's welfare policy became unworkable? Who might find that advantageous politically?

BRD, 1949–55

As BRD's economy improved throughout the 1950s, Adenauer's government paid greater attention to improving the welfare state and consolidating West Germany's social, economic and political reconstruction.

In the years immediately following Nazi Germany's surrender in May 1945, welfare policy meant the Allies ensured that Germans had basic amenities such as water, food and shelter. The influx of nine million refugees from the East compounded a drastic humanitarian situation where cold, disease, malnutrition and black-marketeering were the norm. But the provisions of the Marshall Plan, together with the welfare side of Erhard's social market economy, gradually provided the base for a successful social policy that would provide dignity, encourage work and thrift, and ultimately nurture the BRD's economic miracle.

The private sector, working with the state, had built a million new homes by the mid-1950s. The post-war shortage was so acute that governmental involvement was vital. It provided employment to thousands through the building construction industry, and ultimately led to people acquiring homes to purchase or rent.

Erhard brought in strict rental controls and tenants' rights, to ensure security for families, and housing became one of the key aspects of the social market economy. Six million new flats were built in the decade from 1950, with more than half of the accommodation being social housing or local council property.

Erhard's social market economy had the state supporting and subsidising both the public and private sector in its efforts to alleviate the problems caused by war damage, unemployment and a severe shortage of family housing.

In 1952, the Equalisation of Burdens Law was passed. This permitted the government to impose a levy on capital and property unaffected by the ravages of war, in order to give help to those who had suffered great loss and impoverishment. In conjunction with the setting up of the War Victims' Relief Fund, it helped ease social tensions in an era when Germany's Nazi past and defeat was still very raw.

Erhard reintroduced unemployment benefit, based on the 1927 Weimar system, and later introduced legislation concerning accident and sickness insurance. Families were helped by tax-based child allowances and the introduction of child benefit. But the most significant social welfare reform was the introduction in 1957 of the so-called Dynamic Pension. In planning for several years, it index-linked the level of old-age pensions to wages and salaries: 60 per cent of final year earnings. In consequence of the economic boom in the BRD, pension value rose by more than 50 per cent in the next decade; thereby allowing a rising number of pensioners to enjoy its benefits.

Policies to extend education

Weimar Republic, 1919–33

In pre-1914 Germany, there was real contrast between primary education, which was available to everyone, and secondary education, which was the preserve of the better-off. Such divisions meant that most poor children were denied access to a secondary or university education.

Fact: Although the years after 1933 are outside the period of the Weimar Republic, it is worth noting the downward turn that education took after Weimar. This was largely due to Hitler. During his dictatorship, the Nazis used the education system to spread racist, right-wing ideology. By 1939, all but six universities in Germany had closed and more than 14 per cent of university professors had been dismissed due to disagreements with the regime. The number of school-leavers seeking higher education declined rapidly, partly because they were required to do two years' compulsory military service. Open, liberal education in Germany was destroyed.

Weimar introduced big changes, establishing universal, free, four-year elementary schooling (Grundschule). Most pupils then continued at these schools for another four years. Those who paid a small fee then went to intermediate school (Mittelschule) for one to two years, with a more challenging curriculum. If they passed an entrance exam after year four, pupils could enter one of the four types of secondary school.

The Weimar Constitution outlined broad legislative powers over education; standardised teacher training; compulsory primary school attendance; continuing education until eighteen; and free education. The Youth Welfare Act of 1922 required municipalities and states to set up youth offices for child protection, and also ratified further the fundamental right to education for all. Girls were educated on the same basis as boys and the teaching of religion and morality was made more flexible.

This seemed to offer Germany the chance to maximise the talents of its post-war generation, leading to greater equality of opportunity. But many of these reform proposals never came to fruition. The instability of different coalition governments meant political compromise. There were also clashes between left and right over the content of the material taught.

Political posturing was acute, but at least dissent was permitted. But as Weimar gave way to Nazism, this changed.

BRD, 1949–55

In 1945, the four occupying allied powers ensured immediately that Nazi ideology was eliminated from the German school curriculum. In western Germany, religious institutions regained their foothold in education, while the occupying authorities dismissed several thousand teachers, replacing them with those holding democratic values and untainted by Nazism. Inevitably, their respective occupation zones developed systems predisposed to their own social and political ideas.

When the BRD was formed in 1949, its new constitution, the Grundgesetz, devolved to the state governments or Länder, the authority to run their own education system. This led to very differing school systems, and sometimes made it difficult for children to continue the same level of schooling when moving between states.

But this was in part a reaction to recent history, with the rationale being to move far away from a rigidly, centralised state education system like the Nazis. It was also the outcome of disagreements between Britain and the USA in the western occupation zones as to what form the education system should take. The American approach prevailed, with an emphasis on re-educating German youth. Accordingly, West Germany focused on the democratic values of federalism, individualism and choice in education, through a combination of public and private institutions.

The curriculum and teaching methods of Weimar were resurrected, which pleased many West Germans. Primary school was still maintained and the selective system remained, with a choice between vocational schools and the equivalent of grammar schools. The accessibility of universities remained much as it was in the 1920s and 1930s, something of a preserve for an academic elite.

Education had a difficult beginning, given the lack of school buildings, a shortage of non-Nazi teaching material, a **brain drain** from the years under Nazism and the need for large classes owing to a scarcity of teachers. But enthusiastic students began to express themselves ever-more freely as the BRD stabilised and the economy grew.

Brain drain: the loss of skilled and educated workers. They migrate to other countries where working conditions and salaries are better, and – in the case of pre-war Germany – to countries where they had personal and political freedom. This was a particular problem for Germany in 1945, as it tried to reconstruct after the war.

In 1953 education throughout the *Länder was standardised,* and in 1955 the Dusseldorf Agreement defined examination standards, the length of school terms and the number of subjects examined. It would later lead to the abolition of all school fees and a more major overhaul of the school system by 1960.

Policies to improve health services

Weimar Republic, 1919–33

Weimar faced major health problems. The population was decimated by war, many lived in poverty, and hundreds of thousands suffered from famine. During the war, Germany lost two million soldiers, as well as 750,000 civilians largely due to the food blockade. Both the malnourished population and weary military then faced the influenza or 'Spanish Flu' pandemic that swept through Europe in 1918–19.

This virus created serious problems, claiming more than 400,000 lives in 1918. Curiously, in mid-1919, the pandemic suddenly ended, even though no cure had been found. However, its legacy at home and on the battlefront added to the difficulties faced in making health care provision.

The republic had inherited a basic welfare system from the 1880s, which was under strain by 1919. Medical professionals wanted a single, structured, national authority to oversee health and welfare administration, with wider public health services. Medical practitioners aimed not merely to treat diseases but also to prevent them. Gradually physicians, nurses, midwives and apothecaries became part of Weimar's expanding welfare network. Doctors now felt responsible for national public health as well as for the health of individual patients in their local communities.

Weimar passed laws to assist disease prevention, especially the fight against tuberculosis and established alcohol treatment centres. Other centres opened to advise people

Theory of Knowledge

Teaching history:
How acceptable is it for governments to authorise what is taught in schools? What is permissible and what is not? Does the teaching of history have a specific purpose? If so, what? Why did the BRD believe it was important to monitor what was taught in schools after 1949?

with social, financial and legal problems. There were advances in infant care and child development. Those without sickness insurance were given special payments to help them cover the cost of parenthood. Personal health education was promoted, and help existed for those who wished to discuss sexual matters. Meanwhile, the medical profession encouraged greater openness about issues such as contraception and menstruation.

One aspect overlapping both health care and social welfare was the treatment of disabled people. By 1930, increasing numbers of mentally and physically disabled people were being moved from their local communities into state-funded institutions, to monitor the national health of citizens and develop state care at all levels. This gave the state total control over their lives and well-being. In the wrong hands, this could prove fatal, which it did under the Nazis after 1933. However the republic ran out of energy, time and money. In the early 1930s it was forced to make major cuts in health and welfare because of the deep financial crisis. This was anathema to many in Germany who originally set out to do the greatest good for the greatest number.

BRD, 1949–55

In 1945, Germany was an occupied country with no civilian government and minimal infrastructure. It was inhabited by dazed, defeated Germans, as well as millions of refugees, homeless people and foreign armies. Large parts of the country were covered in rubble with no clean drinking water, electricity or gas. Hospitals overflowed with patients but had little in the way of medicines, medical staff, beds or bedding. In such circumstances, the potential for serious epidemics and public health disasters was high. So public health was soon identified as a major component in creating order and enabling the reconstruction of Germany.

One of the earliest problems was the health threat posed by arrivals at camps for displaced persons. Common ailments upon arrival included rickets, dysentery, intestinal and chest infections, tuberculosis, diphtheria, typhus and skin infections. Sexually transmitted diseases and pregnancies were also common. As displaced persons were often moved between camps, the chance of spreading diseases was high, so an emphasis was placed on controlling infections and immunisation. Also the government aimed to nurture the welfare of its citizens with a 'social net' through which no one in the BRD should fall. But what developed was not a welfare state in the same mould as that of Britain's National Health Service.

With the enormous wartime legacy facing the BRD, it is unsurprising that debates about a more egalitarian welfare state along the lines of Britain soon faded. Instead, social policy was advanced by the centre-right government of the Christian Democratic Party – and increasingly backed by the Social Democrat opposition.

Economic reconstruction, promoting house-building and integrating migrants into the BRD were viewed as the main priorities in social policy, followed by a gradual reform of social security. The Christian Democrats could have substantially changed health insurance and used the period of post-war reconstruction to instigate a radical overhaul of the medical system.

Instead, they remained strong supporters of self-governance by the medical profession – forsaking the opportunity to bring them into greater state accountability – and focused on improving sick-pay coverage and passing long-term care insurance.

Nor did the Social Democrats at this stage formulate policies for altering the financing, organisation, or level of control over national health insurance. Neither party considered shifting to a tax-financed system. Health insurance was deemed too important. The medical profession alone defined health care quality until the 1990s.

Rather than being solely a lesson about 'left versus right politics with the power of trade unions and the role of the government thrown in' – as in Britain, health care in the BRD reflected conservative forces in society. These included employers, churches and social welfare organisations. This is not to deny that the BRD had a welfare state or rather a 'social state'; it was enshrined in the 1949 constitution of the BRD as a key principle of the new democratic Germany. It was simply that the Pensions Reform Act of 1957 became seen as the cornerstone of the post-war German welfare state, and its attitude to health was not a National Health Service, as it was in Britain.

QUESTION

What health care and welfare provisions were available in Great Britain in 1950, under the newly created National Health Service (NHS)? How does it compare to the measures introduced in the BRD? Using the library and the internet, research this and present a report to the class.

Policies to improve the position of women

Weimar Republic, 1919–33

The Weimar Constitution offered German women the promise of legal equality for the first time, and they were a key group, comprising more than half of the electorate. However, many on the political right yearned for the order of pre-war Germany, viewing women as a destabilising force. But their emancipation considerably altered how women were viewed; likewise the roles they could undertake.

Forty-nine women were elected to the Reichstag (parliament) in 1919, showing that both women and men accepted their growing importance. But while suffrage and emancipation denoted a change in attitudes towards women, it was resisted. In many areas of Germany, the traditional values of pre-war society wished to preserve the previous social fabric.

The Weimar Constitution also retained laws that criminalised abortion and restricted access to contraception; laws seen as essential for promoting marriage and repopulating Germany.

Nonetheless 1920s society was characterised by the emergence of a modern German 'New Woman' who appeared to break from the traditional family-oriented stereotypes, exercising independence and greater social and sexual freedom.

Evidence supporting this has focused on a declining birth rate during the 1920s. In 1900 there had been more than two million live births per annum, but by 1933 the figure had dropped to below one million. Some

Figure 2.15 Portrait of the Journalist Sylvia von Harden by Otto Dix, 1926

viewed this as a catastrophe, whereas German social historian Ute Frevert has suggested it was more about 'a rationalisation of sex life'.

Writer Elsa Herrmann described the New Woman as refusing to 'lead the life of a lady and a housewife.' The 1926 Otto Dix painting *Portrait of the Journalist Sylvia von Harden* is a good example. Sylvia von Harden is depicted in an unfeminine manner, as an androgynous woman, publicly smoking and drinking in a café (see Figure 2.15).

War permanently affected families hit by bereavement and disabling injury. Wounded husbands and fathers often returned as long-term invalids, unable to resume traditional patriarchal roles. Indeed the war also left a surplus of 1.8 million marriageable women as well as many women who had to care for invalid husbands. These factors may also help to explain the fall in the birth rate.

With men away fighting, the father's role was replaced by that of the empowered German mother. So the post-war role of women as wage-earners became important; although they faced under-promotion and lower pay than men in the workplace.

Yet many politicians still sent out a traditional message, advising women to embrace a domestic ideal. Some had to leave the workforce after marriage in order to fulfil their traditional domestic roles – but not all. The position of most women in Germany, however, did not improve greatly. Where there was change, it was superficial, behind a deep-rooted conservatism.

BRD, 1949–55

For years a woman's role and responsibility in Germany was described as being the 3Ks – Kinder (children), Kirche (church) and Küche (kitchen). There had been changes under Weimar, when in 1919 women received the right to vote and the 'New Woman' of Germany emerged in many urban centres. But the experiences of Nazi rule and the war meant that women were now seen as essential in the survival and normalisation of post-war German society.

Women had looked after the injured and cleared the rubble of Germany's ruined cities. Yet German authorities initially stated that women with 'family responsibilities' should only work in the absence of male breadwinners. But by the 1950s, this changed. Women now outnumbered men and were poised to assume roles previously denied them.

Unsurprisingly, the Basic Law of 1949 affirmed that men and women were equal. Also, definitions of 'family responsibilities' changed as more women sought part-time work. However, women in this position were initially seen as a threat to the male breadwinner, and there were spats between women's associations and employers over women and paid work.

Even during Adenauer's 'economic miracle' of the 1950s, women could be dismissed from the civil service when they married and – despite a post-war shortage of young men that made marriage impossible for many women – church and state still espoused traditional marriage as society's ideal. Employment and welfare schemes were still constructed to the ideal of the male breadwinner.

But in 1957, the Law of the Equality of the Sexes allowed women to take up work without their husband's permission, and to retain control of their own property upon marriage. The economic boom also meant that women in the workplace were eventually seen as complementary to the male workforce, a valued addition and not a threat. Many young women also combined jobs with work and family, this being made easier with the arrival of new household gadgets, freezers and improved communications.

But the issue of part-time work was remained thorny, as many men had fixed ideas about paid female employment within domestic family life. Opinions in the Catholic Church also meant that a traditional female role defined by the 3Ks persisted well into the 1960s. Moreover a woman's pay on average was 40 per cent less than the average man's.

The BRD also turned to (predominantly) male migrants or immigrants, including a significant number of workers from Turkey, and to refugees from East Germany (DDR) to augment labour requirements for its booming economy.

QUESTION

It was once said the German women during the 1950s had opportunity given to them in one hand, and taken away in the other hand. What was meant by this? Explain your answer with reference to the text and to **Source D**.

SOURCE D

Women in the BRD continued to have 'their' social class measured primarily in terms of their father's or husband's occupation. Insofar as they took up paid employment outside the home, women tended to remain in lower-status, less well-paid, often part-time or temporary employment.

M. Fulbrook (2000), Interpretations of the Two Germanies 1945–90, *Basingstoke: Macmillan, p. 59.*

Policies to protect the rights of minorities

Weimar Republic, 1919–33

Ethnic minorities and their rights under Weimar were central in helping the republic establish its credentials and legitimacy. But Germany was not ethnically strong. Almost all churches in Germany were state churches, and there were no significantly large religious groups or sects other than Jews, gypsies and Jehovah's Witnesses. The gay community, for obvious reasons, was often discreet and invisible. But all groups had the potential to be useful scapegoats.

Jews

All men and women were afforded equal rights under Weimar, so legally the emancipation of Jewish women was assured. But the result was not social equality, as many 19th-century anti-Semitic prejudices prevailed. According to a 1925 census, 564,973 registered Jews resided in the Republic, with 71.5 per cent in Germany's largest province, Prussia.

Fact: In reality, there were fewer Jews in Germany before 1933 than many people might have imagined – at most about 1 per cent of the population. They were a relatively small group, but highly visible because they tended to live in the larger cities, and some played an important role in German cultural life; while many were visible on account of their refugee status.

An organisation unique to central Europe, the Gemeinde (or community) served as a focal point of German Jewish life. Created to centralise local Jewish activities, the Gemeinde embraced all Jews within the country, including non-citizens. They became public corporations, empowered by the government to organise local Jewish communal and ritual affairs.

They hired rabbis and religious functionaries, maintained synagogues, ran a variety of institutions (including newspapers, social associations, libraries, health facilities and charity funds), forwarded tax revenues (collected either by the government on behalf of the Jews or by the community itself) and supported communal activities.

Although many individual Jews enjoyed acclaim in the arts, activities such as music and theatre were rarely organised under Jewish auspices. But career-wise German Jews were strongly – and almost disproportionately – represented in areas such as journalism, law, medicine and retailing. Concentrated in a small number of professions, usually in urban areas, Jews became increasingly visible to their critics.

While most German Jews were middle class, a number of Jews living in Weimar Germany – many of them Yiddish-speaking refugees from Eastern Europe – eked out a humble existence as industrial workers, artisans or peddlers. The hyperinflation of 1923 and the economic depression greatly complicated the lives of virtually all German Jews.

For example, democratic political parties of the centre-left, often strongly opposed by the middle classes, were elected to parliament and, with them, leading Jews. They gained important posts in the administration, and in 1929 the philosopher Ernst Cassirer was the first Jew ever to become vice-chancellor of a German university. All these events led to rising anti-Semitism in Hamburg and other cities.

Figure 2.16 The Nazi Party revealed its anti-Jewish prejudices very early on, in this 1924 Reichstag election poster. It shows Germany enslaved by the Dawes Plan and being whipped by a wealthy Jewish businessman, under the slogan, 'Down with financial slavery – vote National Socialist!'

By 1930, anti-Semitic feelings were fuelled by the Nazis, while organisations, schools and churches began to follow. The SPD were so preoccupied with economic problems that they took no decisive action to counter increasing anti-Jewish feeling.

So no major organisation consciously supported German Jews. Only individuals offered their support as the Jewish population became increasingly isolated. Yet the strength of Jewish support for the liberal Weimar state set them apart from other Germans. With the economic crisis, the increasingly widespread idea that Jews were a 'problem', the steady collapse of state institutions and the growth of Nazi power, anti-Semitism became quite open.

Anti-Semitic attitudes found their way into German churches, both Protestant and Catholic, and Jews were now openly blamed for much of the social change and unrest that had taken place since 1914, as well as for their allegedly nefarious role during the war.

Anti-Semitism was easily adapted for use by an increasingly troubled Church. In response, Jews relied increasingly on themselves and their families, developing a distinct subculture. This in turn led to German Jews being highlighted as 'a race apart' and 'not German'. It increased hostility and was brutally exploited by Hitler after 1933.

Roma and Sinti

Under Weimar, laws against Roma and Sinti (gypsies) increased. For example, there were regulations requiring gypsy communities to register with local police officials, laws increasingly prohibiting free travel and by the early 1920s, they were forbidden to use parks or public baths. Some Roma gypsies were even sent to work camps.

Imperial Germany had opened a centralised agency for the surveillance of the Roma and by 1900 the first gypsy intelligence service in Munich had more than 3,000 files at its disposal. It became key to the republic's policy of monitoring and controlling gypsies. By 1923, they could obtain personal details on men, women and children, and also take both photographs and fingerprints.

Then in 1926 the Bavarian government passed a law for 'the fight against gypsies, vagabonds and those unwilling to work'. It gave the Bavarian authorities a legal right to take measures against people who had not even committed a criminal offence. Consequently they were increasingly seen as a criminal element. Sadly the existence of these laws formed a basis of information for the deportation, internment and mass extermination of gypsies after the Nazis came to power in 1933.

LGBT rights

Throughout Weimar, **LGBT** society and its subculture coexisted with the heterosexual society surrounding it. This was certainly true in Berlin, which became a cosmopolitan centre of art, music, theatre, film and jazz. Berlin was renowned for its LGBT nightlife, its raunchy cabaret scene, for nudity and for its subversive, satirical comedy. But the permissive nature of Berlin – especially its LGBT subculture – was not typical of Germany, being opposed in rural areas and, above all, in the deeply Catholic, conservative south. Many Germans were aghast at what they saw as a general collapse of moral and cultural standards. They also blamed it on the increased role in everyday life of socialists, Jews and the LGBT community.

LGBT: lesbian, gay, bisexual and transgender; a term used since the late 1980s to replace the phrase 'gay community', which it was felt did not accurately represent all those to whom it referred.

Prominent gay men – including actors, dancers, designers, academics, politicians and lawyers – had to live with a certain level of abuse and intolerance, but many had influence, financial clout and connections to the government. This bestowed protection. Generally, gay men lived undisturbed unless they fell foul of some law or were entrapped by the police or by blackmail.

Lesbians lived more freely, and lesbian magazines, bars and clubs flourished, especially in Berlin. Laws against gay men had been introduced under the Kaiser in Paragraph 175 of the 1871 criminal code and had never been repealed by Weimar, so technically sexual relations between men remained illegal. But there were no laws punishing sexual relationships between women.

But after 1929 and the rise of the Nazi Party, the sexual tolerance often associated with Berlin and other urban centres – such as Hamburg and Frankfurt – diminished. Many Germans now regarded the Republic's toleration of gay men and lesbians as a sign of Germany's decadence.

Hitler and the Nazis increasingly ridiculed the LGBT community and once in power, Nazi persecution of gay men would intensify and would include banning organisations, closing clubs and bars, and sending gay men and women to concentration camps. But, significantly, this growing intolerance became increasingly evident in the last two or three years of Weimar, and was underpinned by the republic leaving in place a criminalising law that it ought to have revoked, in accordance with the socially liberal tones it aimed to promote.

Jehovah's Witnesses

Jehovah's Witnesses first appeared in Germany in the 1890s, opening their first main German office in 1902. After the war in 1919 they attracted opposition based on the premise that they were communists and pro-Jewish. Known as Ernste Bibelforscher, or Earnest Bible Students, opposition grew and Bible Students were frequently arrested on charges of illegal peddling as they handed out pamphlets in towns and cities.

The Nazis then harassed them and broke up their meetings. In a three-year period up to 1930, nearly 5,000 Witnesses had charges brought against them, although many were acquitted. By 1931, Weimar had issued the Decree for the Resistance of Political Acts of Violence, which permitted state intervention where organisations, institutions or customs were 'abused or maliciously disparaged' by sects such as the Witnesses. Bavaria banned all their publications, then a later decree extended the ban nationwide.

When the Nazis took power in January 1933, more than 2,000 charges against Bible Students were pending in courts, so the prosecutions brought in under Weimar provided rich pickings for the Nazis.

BRD, 1949–55

Jews

During the pre-war years of Hitler's Nazi dictatorship, many Jews left Germany; around 315,000 between 1933 and 1939. But 215,000 still remained at the outbreak of war in 1939. More than 90 per cent died during the Holocaust, but around 15,000 German Jews survived the deportation to concentration camps by hiding or being married to non-Jews and escaping detection. These Jews were joined in Germany by approximately 200,000 displaced persons who had survived the Holocaust in Austria, Hungary and Poland.

In 1948, when Israel became an independent state, most of those in refugee camps emigrated there; however, around 15,000 Jews remained in Germany. Most of them were in the western occupation zone and after the formation of the BRD in 1949, they founded their own organisation – the Central Council of Jews in Germany. By the late 1960s, this community had grown to about 28,000 Jews.

The BRD's Jewish community was socially conservative and private in nature, having an older age profile. Few young adults had chosen to remain in Germany, but the BRD actually implemented measures to try to encourage the Jewish community in Germany.

The 1949 constitution had a specific clause that gave automatic German citizenship to those persecuted by the Nazi regime, or who had been stripped of their residency because of politics, religion and race. The law also applied this ruling to their offspring and other relatives, as part of a new liberal democratic political system that made a point of wanting to guarantee and cherish civil liberties.

Finally, the question of compensation had to be discussed. The BRD was honour-bound to pay compensation to Jews, as part of the agreement whereby the USA, Britain and France granted sovereignty to the BRD (which took full effect in 1955). Chancellor Adenauer declared in September 1951 that the BRD and its people were aware of 'the immeasurable suffering endured by the Jews of Germany and by the Jews of the occupied territories during the period of National Socialism'. He declared that both moral and material restitution was necessary.

So in March 1952, talks began between delegations representing BRD, Israel and an ad hoc organisation of other Jewish groups. This led to the Luxembourg Agreement of September 1952 signed by Adenauer, Israeli foreign minister Moshe Sharett and the influential president of the World Jewish Congress, **Nahum Goldmann**. Jewish delegations calculated that $6 billion of Jewish property had been pillaged by the Nazis, but argued that the BRD could never compensate for what they did to Jewish lives with any material restitution.

Figure 2.17 BRD Chancellor Konrad Adenauer signs the reparations agreement with Israel and the Jewish Claims Conference, representing world Jewry, Luxembourg, 10 September 1952

The BRD was obliged to pay Israel three billion marks for the slave labour and persecution of Jews during the Holocaust, and to compensate for Jewish property stolen by Nazis. It also obliged them to pay 450 million marks to various international Jewish groups, who acted as receptors for the payment to many individuals who had filed personal claims.

The impact both for workers in German industry and the Israelis was significant. The BRD built and installed five power plants between 1953 and 1956, quadrupling Israel's electric power-generating capacity. They also laid nearly 300 kilometres of pipelines for

Nahum Goldmann (1895–1982)

He was the founder of the World Jewish Congress in 1948, of which he was president until 1982. He was often described as a statesman without a state. Goldmann was born in Lithuania and raised in Germany until the Nazis came to power, after which he went to the USA via Palestine. Goldmann was the nearest person the Jewish community had as a leader until the formal establishment of the state of Israel in 1948. He was the main architect of the important agreement that committed the Adenauer and the BRD, to pay compensation both to Israel and to individual Jews for losses, thefts and other acts perpetrated during the Nazi years. He saw himself as an international, roving diplomat for Jewish affairs and through the medium of the World Jewish Congress, as an alternative international voice to that of Israel; the state in whose establishment he was instrumental, but of whom he was frequently critical, much to the irritation of the Israel leadership. Consequently Goldmann never sought political office in Israel.

the irrigation of the Israeli Negev Desert. Israel was also given sixty-five German-built ships, including four passenger vessels.

Roma and Sinti

One and a half million gypsies died from 1933 to 1945 in Nazi-controlled Europe and, like the Jews, many placed claims for compensation before the courts of the BRD after 1949. Yet the state judiciary of Baden-Wurttemberg issued a directive in 1950 to its judges hearing claims that 'Gypsies were persecuted under the National Socialist regime not for any racial reason, but because of an asocial and criminal record'. This suggests that the BRD had a single focus on the Jews as Nazi victims. It also meant that the Sinti and Roma gypsies suffered prejudice and ridicule for years.

The chief obstacle for gypsies seeking compensation was whether Nazi policies against them had been racially motivated as opposed to having been mere policing measures. The Nazi view that gypsies were essentially 'dishonest', 'asocial' and 'work-shy' was shared by many in the BRD. The surviving gypsy community thus had scant hope of legal redress and gaining recognition as deserving victims. It also shows that the BRD focused on compensating some victims while bypassing others.

LGBT rights and Jehovah's Witnesses

The BRD exhibited intolerance towards gay men and lesbians, believing that they contributed to a declining birth rate. Adenauer also inherited from the 1871 German Criminal Code Paragraph 175, making sexual acts between men a crime. Hitler had broadened the law so that the courts could pursue any 'lewd act' and the BRD retained it.

Consequently 100,000 men were involved in court cases from 1945 to 1969. Nearly half were convicted. With strong Church influences prevailing and socially conservative influences in the governing CDU, administrations either ignored or opposed LGBT rights, being content to stifle discussion.

In this sphere, the BRD was not dissimilar in thinking to Weimar Republic or even the Nazi regime. It was stated that there was a difference between a gay man and a lesbian, because men were more predatory than women. While lesbianism violated nature, it did not present the same threat to society as same-sex male relations, so it was not criminalised.

In 1949, Jehovah's Witnesses reconstituted themselves as 'The Watch Tower Tract Bible Society' and applied for corporate status under public law in line with the provisions of the Basic Law of 1949, which promoted religious freedom.

They were refused on the basis of the Witnesses' inability to satisfy the requirement of loyalty to the constitution: a cooperative relationship between the state and its Churches was required, whereby a declaration was called for. This declaration would affirm loyalty to the state, a willingness to partake in the democratic process, and an acceptance that service in the armed forces (or some alternative form of national service) might be required.

Jehovah's Witnesses assume a position of complete political neutrality, will not join the armed forces and consider their only allegiance is to God. Consequently, German courts repeatedly denied the Witnesses' request to become a corporate body under public law for various reasons, one of them being that their tenets would discourage their members from taking part in state elections.

Their status was unresolved, but they were free to hold meetings in the BRD, and in 1951 held a major 'Assembly' at Frankfurt where more than 47,000 people attended the final day of the gathering. This included members from the DDR, where the communists had banned them in 1950.

Policies to create a more equitable distribution of wealth

Weimar Republic, 1919–33

In Weimar Germany, the gulf between the 'haves' and 'have nots' widened at a time when the republic was trying to create greater fairness and a more equitable distribution of wealth and resources.

Politically fragile, Weimar saw prices that had doubled from 1914 to 1919 double again over just five months in 1922. There were complaints about the high cost of living. Factory workers pressed for wage increases. An underground economy developed, aided by a desire to beat the tax collector.

Under Stresemann, with help from the Dawes Plan, Germany's economy partially recovered after the hyperinflation of 1923. Jobs were created, living standards improved and state governments financed activities with the help of these loans. Interest rates were high and capital flowed in. But with the introduction of a new currency, the Rentenmark, people who had worked all their lives found that their pensions would no longer even buy coffee. As **Source E** notes, Germans were stunned.

SOURCE E

Pearl Buck, an American writer famous for her novels about China, was in Germany in 1923:

The cities were still there, the houses not yet bombed and in ruins, but the victims were millions of people. They had lost their fortunes, their savings; they were dazed and inflation-shocked and did not understand how it had happened to them and who the foe was who had defeated them. Yet they had lost their self-assurance, their feeling that they themselves could be the masters of their own lives if only they worked hard enough; and lost, too, were the old values of morals, of ethics, of decency.

Quoted in G.J.W. Goodman (1981), Paper Money *by 'Adam Smith', New York: Summit Books, pp. 57–62.*

Yet cashing in on apparent improvement, large firms borrowed money and depended heavily on American loans. But the so-called recovery was based on uncertain foundations and even before the Wall Street Crash of October 1929, the economy was in decline again, with little or no growth in German industrial production and unemployment at 2.5 million.

With the Crash, American demand for imports collapsed, and US banks saw their losses mount. German firms, heavily dependent on American bank loans, began to cut back drastically. Industrial production collapsed and by 1932 it was around 40 per cent of its level in 1929. Also, key Austrian and German banks went out of business in 1931, which made matters worse.

Theory of Knowledge

History, the present and the future:

The philosopher George Santayana once said: '*Those who don't study the past are condemned to repeat it.*' This suggests that it is possible and perhaps even wise, to decide our actions on what has happened in the past. What does a study of the policies towards minorities in both the Weimar Republic and the BRD reveal about human nature? Do you think that the failure of Weimar to take action on behalf of Jews, gypsies, the LGBT community and Jehovah's Witnesses impacts on how they were treated by the BRD? Did the BRD continue where Weimar left off? Can the past ever be used to justify present action?

QUESTION

Using books in the library or the internet, research about the effects of hyperinflation in 1923. Then look at how other countries have been hit since Weimar. Argentina and Zimbabwe are two examples you might want to investigate. Which other countries can you find?

By February 1932, 33 per cent of the workforce was unemployed, and many were no longer in receipt of unemployment benefit as state governments could not afford to pay it. The middle-class people found their savings wiped out again, while crime and suicide rates rose sharply.

The government cut spending in order to keep inflation under control and raised taxes, reduced salaries and cut unemployment assistance. This worsened the situation and the gap between 'haves' and 'have-nots' widened enormously. Both Nazis and communists thrived in this economic chaos.

BRD, 1949–55

In 1948, under Allied currency reform, citizens in the three occupied zones and in west Berlin, were each given sixty new Deutsche mark, at a rate of one-to-one for the old currency. It led to the impression that all people were starting equal. This ignored the fact that those West Germans who had non-monetary assets, such as land, jewellery and antiques, held an advantage over their compatriots.

But Adenauer and Erhard were keen to provide a social dimension to the new economic policy they were formulating, to stabilise the BRD. The so-called 'social economy' or 'social market economy' required legislation to alleviate the privations of refugees and the insecurities of the poor and vulnerable. If all sections of the population could coalesce in a form of social consensus, then not only might Germany prosper, but the possible threat of communism from the DDR would be countered.

The economic recovery that began in the early 1950s, led to a steep fall in unemployment and many workers in the BRD felt a renewed sense of optimism, that progress was being made and that now there was a greater equality of opportunity and social cohesion.

Subsidised savings programmes and tax relief schemes, to buy your own property, pushed up private demand and increased the number of house-owner-occupiers. People bought new domestic gadgets and started to take holidays, thus indicating increased prosperity. But many people lived modestly and, as of 1955, a third of Germans had never holidayed. Only 10 per cent of the population owned a fridge and half of the population lived in one-bedroom flats.

Over the next five years – as the BRD's economy continued to blossom and unions made demands for higher wages – living standards for ordinary Germans improved. But distribution of wealth and income remained imbalanced.

2.8 To what extent did the Germans benefit from these policies?

The policies of the Weimar Republic were thwarted by the political and financial backdrop against which it conducted its brave attempt to bring democracy to Germany, while the BRD emerged from the desolation of war in 1945 to bring an unexpectedly high standard of living and prosperity to West Germans. Both periods of time witnessed positive and negative policy outcomes.

Unemployment

Weimar Republic, 1919–33

The Weimar government introduced an eight-hour workday (a major achievement) and plants with more than fifty workers had to have workers' committees. This was cemented by the creation of a central national joint labour committee, a forum in which trade unionists and employers tried to agree common objectives to encourage economic growth.

Nor should it be forgotten that the working class downed tools in large numbers in order to defend the republic against the Kapp Putsch in 1920, so there was clear support for Weimar from the German labour force, doubtless as a result of policies towards workers' rights.

The introduction of the Rentenmark was largely well received, but government expenditure had to fall and cuts led to almost 750,000 civil servants and other public employees losing their jobs. This had a negative impact on working Germans and increased both unemployment and resentment.

The arrival of foreign capital through the Dawes Plan then gave Stresemann the chance to implement a public building programme. Workers benefitted through new jobs, more buoyant industry and the value of real wages increasing. Suddenly, the chasm of unemployment seemed to have receded. With exports 40 per cent higher in 1929 than in 1924, workers seemed destined to benefit even more in the future.

Then Stresemann's introduction of the 1927 Labour Exchanges and Unemployment Insurance Act, which introduced unemployment insurance, was a very important piece of legislation, which also appeared to enhance the security of ordinary Germans. But the financial limits of the scheme were reached within a year.

The collapse of the US Stock Exchange in October 1929, when combined with the political deadlock in the Reichstag, all but cancelled out the good intentions of the Weimar legislation.

By late 1930, unemployment exceeded two million and by late 1932, industrial production had fallen by 42 per cent from its 1929 level, with one in three workers unemployed. By July 1932, the Nazis were the largest political party in the Reichstag. The die was cast for Weimar democracy.

BRD, 1949–55

The Marshall Plan in 1947 marked a new beginning for Germany and helped to reassure the West about the political and economic future of the country. Economic reconstruction could commence, the existing distribution of private property rights would be confirmed and a market economy would be restored. The currency and economic reforms of 1948 then launched the social market economy. There was great scope for employment and the incentive to work was raised by the growing availability of consumer goods, plus Adenauer's decision to make overtime earnings tax-free.

Erhard's social market economy saw the state supporting and subsidising both the public and private sector in its efforts to alleviate the problems caused by war damage, unemployment and a severe shortage of family housing – and to create jobs.

ACTIVITY

Imagine you are living in Germany during the 1920s. Working in pairs, start by making individual lists of what you might consider to be your main concerns and fears for the future. Give yourself a particular job/profession. This might influence your outlook. What might be going well? What might not be going well? Now imagine you are looking for work. How do you see things around you in Weimar Germany? Exchange your lists and ideas with your partner, and discuss your findings.

Figure 2.18 Women workers in a textile factory in the Ruhr in the 1950s. They contributed much to the post-war economic miracle in the BRD

The cheapening of transport and communications also greatly increased the awareness of investment opportunities and meant that workers were encouraged to travel more readily in their daily commute to work. Work became much more plentiful and is evidenced by the fact that pre-war levels of GDP and industrial productivity (1936) had been attained in the BRD by the end of 1951.

But there remained the continual flow of civilian refugees – almost half a million alone between 1951 and 1953 – who required social and economic integration, while the BRD still faced housing shortages. Indeed two million West Germans remained unemployed by 1951, with agriculture suffering significantly. Yet gradually the BRD benefitted from having agricultural labourers who were often mobile and could be moved into industrial work without putting upward pressure on wages.

Refugees were integrated eventually. Two million had arrived from eastern Germany between 1946 and 1950, and this was further augmented by a procession of well-trained immigrants from East Germany. More than three million entered the BRD from 1950 up to 1962, and this inflow of trained labour allowed the BRD to allocate a much smaller proportion of gross domestic profit (GDP) to industrial training and education than was the case in the Weimar Republic. There was also a ready workforce and no negative consequences for economic growth.

The re-introduction of unemployment benefit, and provisions for insurance in case of sickness and accident, also encouraged workers to seek and remain in employment, as did tax-based child allowances and the introduction of child benefit. By 1955, unemployment had fallen to one million and so began a period of almost full employment that basically endured until the 1970s. Indeed so great was the creation of jobs and the need for workers, that the recruitment and immigration of foreign labourers or Gästarbeiter from Turkey later became a feature of economic and social policy in the BRD.

Education and welfare

Weimar Republic, 1919–33

The principal benefit to children from the Weimar's education policies was the outlining of a vision of learning guided by the state, and codifying further the fundamental right to education for all children. Unfortunately many proposals never materialised as financial catastrophe overtook Germany after 1929.

One aspect of welfare policy had a particularly worrying impact. Many people with learning difficulties lived in their local communities, but by the late 1920s, increasing numbers of mentally and physically disabled people were being moved into state-funded institutions, to monitor the national health of citizens and develop state care at all levels.

This gave the state total control over their lives and well-being. In the wrong hands, this could prove fatal. It would later do so after Hitler and the Nazi Party took power in 1933, with their firm belief in Charles Darwin's theory of natural selection and 'survival of the fittest' and their liking for the science of eugenics. Proponents of eugenics proposed 'positive' government policies such as tax credits to foster large 'valuable' families and 'negative' policies, such as forced sterilisation, for those who were deemed unfit to reproduce.

Weimar never adopted these ideas, but they were debated in Germany, and some welfare workers learned to separate the 'deserving' from the 'undeserving' when allocating scarce resources in the period from 1929 to 1933. When economic efficiency became the Weimar government's prime consideration after 1930, such decisions became a question of 'cost-benefit analysis'. Ultimately Weimar ran out of energy, time and money and was forced into making health and welfare cuts. This saddened many who wanted to do the greatest good for the greatest number.

Theory of Knowledge

History and ethics:
How does the idea of health care as primarily a question of 'cost-benefit analysis' fit in with utilitarianism and its concept of gross national happiness (GNH)?

BRD, 1949–55

Following a difficult start with resources, education became more invigorated by the mid-1950s, as the BRD stabilised. The reforms of 1953 ensured greater uniformity and standardisation across the Lander. This pre-empted a greater overhaul of education by 1960, when all school fees were abolished and the curriculum was expanded and modernised. Indeed, after 1962, investment in schooling and training doubled and nine-year school attendance was mandatory.

So, although the embryonic education policy of the BRD appeared rooted in the Weimar system (which it largely was), the stability, continuity and return to normality it offered, after the doctrinal teaching of Nazism, allowed young Germans to access an honest system. It lacked vibrancy and consensus, but at least children were being taught in a safer, de-Nazified environment. In that respect, it was an improvement on 1933–45. But there were significant weaknesses.

Germany's social welfare reform peaked with the 1957 Dynamic Pension. By index-linking old-age pensions to wages and salaries, a growing number of pensioners benefitted. No one piece of legislation pleased people more and economists declared it 'the most important social reform of the 1950s', being years ahead of its time. It ensured that pensioners received not just the minimum required for existence, but were more or less enabled to maintain their standard of living.

Women

Weimar Republic, 1919–33

In giving German women the vote, they had greater opportunity to partake in the life of the new democracy. They also found work in previously male-only jobs such as bus conductors and miners. There was also a demand for non-manual labour. Gender roles thus shifted with an acceptance of women's growing importance.

Employers were now keener to employ women, as they could pay a woman less than a male employee. Moreover, laws forcing women to leave the workforce in favour of men did not succeed to the degree that many hoped. Women postponed marriage until later in life and rejected exclusively domestic work. This is evidenced by statistics showing that 36 per cent of the workforce in 1925 was comprised of women in industrial, agricultural and clerical work.

But increased female employment did not mean gender equality. Women were often forced into lower-paid, lower-skilled jobs than their male counterparts, regardless of education or training. Reality for the majority of women in the Weimar Republic was vastly different from that of the 'New Woman' they supposedly wished to emulate.

They also had only modest political representation and a restrictive Civil Code of 1900 continued to control the legal and financial rights of women. Undoubtedly after 1919 the number of working women did increase and more married women worked for wages. It was now increasingly acceptable for young single women to live and work on their own in the city; but illegal abortion was also widespread and the birth rate continued to decline.

KEY CONCEPTS QUESTION

Change and Continuity: How did democracy bring both change and continuity for women in Germany between 1919 and 1933?

In short, the position of most women in Germany did not improve greatly, although ideas about the role of women in society were transformed. But where change came, it was superficial. Behind the apparent progress remained deep-rooted conservatism, which would rise to the fore under Hitler's Nazi dictatorship after 1933 when he envisaged more traditional roles for women.

BRD, 1949–55

With the creation of the BRD in 1949, the Basic Law of 1949 stated that men and women were equal. Yet women could be sacked from the civil service when they married; and employment and welfare schemes still assumed that the main worker in a family was male.

By 1957, the Law of the Equality of the Sexes encouraged female emancipation, enabling women to work without permission from their husband, and to retain control of their own property after marriage. The economic boom and the expanding civil service, the increase in office jobs and the growing service industry in the BRD improved career opportunities to women; but many men still retained very different ideas about paid female employment and the structure of domestic family life.

Yet the 1954 Weisser Report defined women in paid employment as a positive role model, compatible with middle-class West German society, in contrast to a negative symptom of economic necessity (as many trade unions and political parties on both the right and left had argued), It also stressed the need to get more women in the BRD into higher education. Female entry into higher education did increase somewhat throughout the 1950s, from a lowly 19 per cent at the inception of the BRD in 1949. Although by the late 1960s, it still remained modestly around 33 per cent. True female emancipation was still missing in the BRD of 1955.

The distribution of wealth

Weimar Republic, 1919–33

Weimar introduced a system of subsidies and social help, which did bring some redistribution of wealth. After 1923–4, wage rises were forced through by the increased strength of the unions and the system of compulsory arbitration. So wage rates from 1925 to 1929 took no account of declining productivity (especially after 1928), and when combined with the implementation of social benefits such as unemployment insurance, people's sense of security increased and to some extent acted directly as an instrument of redistribution.

But these factors also led to a growth in unemployment, which, for those made redundant, had a negative impact. It also led to surprisingly low levels of labour productivity. There is no real consensus among historians as to the reasons for this low productivity. Some feel that it was because of 'excessively high' wages, while others argue that unjustified subsidies played a major part. The dominance in German industry of a handful of giant corporations, almost forming a cartel, cannot have helped the situation either. This may have stifled entrepreneurship among industrialists and perhaps put off would-be investors. So 'who lost' and 'who gained' under Weimar? Was there a redistribution of wealth?

By 1924, inflation had certainly redistributed some of Germany's wealth. The segment of society that was hit the hardest seems to have been the middle class. The poor had little wealth to lose, while the rich were often able to keep their wealth in forms not adversely affected by inflation. But it has been argued that, under Weimar, there was a definite redistribution of wealth and resources, with inflation turning a significant section of the middle class into a proletariat, politically disoriented and disillusioned, and increasingly susceptible to Nazism.

Coping with a situation in which prices could double in a day also meant huge changes in the way people organised their financial affairs. Workers' wages were paid daily or several times a day; and people had to go out immediately and spend the money before it lost value.

The economic change is also debated by H. Mommsen, who argues that, whereas it was once thought that the working class became impoverished after 1919 and remained so, evidence suggests that after 1923 the workers' standard of living actually improved in certain important areas. Official salaries and some wages rose for a while in real terms, after hitting a trough in 1920. The levelling tendency was not restricted to official salaries, since the years of inflation and subsequent economic crisis led to reduced wage differentials between adolescents and adults, men and women, skilled and unskilled workers.

BRD, 1949–55

There was a more equitable distribution of wealth in the BRD, although not in the socialist sense of the word, by a narrowing of the income gap; rather that more ordinary people began to have their slice of Erhard's social economy and eventually joined the middle class.

The term 'social' in 'social economy' was important, because Erhard wanted a system that would enable entrepreneurs to prosper and fuel the economy, but also provide support for those who might not succeed or cope well with the competitive nature of a market economy. Erhard used 'social' and not 'socialist' in order to draw attention to the distinctive nature of the BDR's system from most in Eastern Europe, where state intervention and direction of the economy was seen as the government's right.

Unlike Weimar, the BRD had no massive reparations to pay – apart from compensation to Israel and some debts from the Marshall Plan and the Dawes Plan. But they were insignificant in comparison to the 1920s; nor did the BRD have defence costs, given that they were not allowed to form an army until sovereignty was granted in 1955. It meant that Erhard could allocate more funds for welfare and other types of social spending.

State investment for social housing and legislation to control rent gave more West Germans roofs over their head. This was crucial in helping restore the economy, but also in creating affordable accommodation to buy or rent. It created social cohesion, as well as alleviating feelings of inequality or inferiority. Overall, it made for an outwardly prosperous society, almost complacently so. West Germans were better-off and more secure, while class and ideological gaps seemed narrower. But 1.8 per cent of all households still controlled 35 per cent of private wealth by 1959. Disparity in the distribution of wealth and income clearly existed.

2.9 What was the cultural impact of the establishment of democracy?

Weimar Republic, 1919–33

Weimar's democratic tenets facilitated an enormous cultural change in reaction to the authoritarian and conservative Imperial years. The toleration and acceptance of alternative cultural, political and religious views was enhanced by minimal censorship, growing changes in media and communication, plus a shift in women's roles.

As the 1920s witnessed the worldwide emergence of radio, the car and talking pictures, so the liberal environment created by the republic stimulated an new openness to wider international influences in jazz, art and American-style consumerism.

Berlin had innovative street theatre and the growth of satirical cabaret in an atmosphere of artistic creativity and sexual promiscuity. Women wore short hair, make-up and smoked – supposedly American habits – generally turning away from traditional concepts of 'feminine' ways of behaving. Arnold Schoenberg founded musical modernism, artists and writers challenged religious, social and even political conventions, and modernist architecture was taught at 'Bauhaus' schools.

One of the bestselling books was the pacifist *All Quiet on the Western Front* published in 1929 by Erich Maria Remarque. He was an ex-soldier, critical of the First World War, which sat awkwardly with many nationalists. The era was also associated with such famous figures as film director Fritz Lang, actress Marlene Dietrich and painter Otto Dix. During the so-called 'golden years' of 1924–9, when the republic encountered some relative stability; Germany become the world's most prominent cultural centre for filmmaking, drama, art, architecture and design, music and literature, as **Source F** shows.

SOURCE F

Life seemed more free, more modern more exciting than in any place I had ever seen. Nowhere else did the arts or the intellectual life seem so lively ... there were new currents and fine talents.

William L. Shirer, European correspondent of the Chicago Tribune *quoted in G. Layton (2009),* Democracy and Dictatorship in Germany 1919–63, *London: Hodder Education, p. 78.*

But this also triggered fears of moral decay and the Catholic Church was shocked by the apparent encouraging of sexual freedom. It added to the ongoing left–right clashes about permissiveness, decadence and American 'negro' influences.

The right was also disgusted at the springing up of organisations concerned with sexual health, hygiene and contraception. In 1923, the Association for Sexual Hygiene and Life Reform was founded, and 1928 saw the establishment of the National Union for Birth Control and Hygiene. Rising numbers of women in the workplace, growing divorce and abortion rates, and a more liberal approach to sex and sexual imagery were all seen by some as proof of moral decline and the demise of the family.

But although society was polarised culturally by the end of the decade, it was not necessarily the open sexuality or Americanisation that threatened family life. Family stability was more shaken with the onset of economic crisis after the 1929 Crash, and the threat of Nazism was looming.

BRD, 1949–55

The post-war resurrection of cultural life in the BRD owed much to the presence of the occupying Allies and their policies. In many respects, the BRD was caught between cultural ideals represented respectively by Britain and the USA.

For example in the British zone of occupation after 1945, cultural policy from an early stage partly entailed the presentation of British traditions and society as a model for post-war Germany. Nearly three-quarters of all cinemas in the western zones were under British control. This empowered the British as an occupying power not only in deciding what films Germans might see, but it also led them to have great influence in drama and music programming; not least because of the international prestige of the London-based BBC.

Then, while no prohibitive 'black lists' were issued to libraries, there remained a monitoring of books at a local level, with the removal of titles considered unsuitable or too reminiscent of the Nazi past. Then, as the BRD was formed in 1949, there came positive initiatives for translating British and other Western literary works. Good contracts were negotiated with German publishers to assist in bringing out translations of pro-democracy, classical and contemporary works of fact and fiction.

Equally, with a pro-American, market economy-oriented government in power led by Adenauer and Erhard, it is obvious that the BRD would be Americanised to a degree. By 1949, the occupying powers – notably the USA – had granted licences to 169 newspapers and magazine titles in the BRD and west Berlin. Many from those early days still thrive today, such as the news magazine *Der Spiegel* and the newspaper *Frankfurter Allgemeine Zeitung*. The Allies collectively ensured that broadcasting was decentralised, following the state control of radio during the Nazi era. Public-service radio stations were established in the federal states such as Norddeutscher Rundfunk (NDR) in Hamburg and Bayerische Rundfunk (BR) in Munich. The British and Americans closely advised Adenauer's government about the setting up of television and it was funded and organised nationally through the ARD.

Article 5 of the Basic Law from 1949 guaranteed freedom of information and press freedom, although it placed restrictions on this freedom, naming specifically the protection of young people and, somewhat more ambiguously, the rights of an individual to maintain their 'personal honour'.

Figure 2.19 West Germany captain Fritz Walter and coach Sepp Herberger celebrate winning the World Cup in Switzerland in 1954. They beat Hungary 3–2 in the final. Millions of people in the BRD were able to watch the game on television for the first time, as media advances widened cultural and sporting boundaries

It is evident that both Adenauer and the Allies recognised that the cultural life of the BRD would now be influenced heavily by the media. Although there were imperfections, the granting of permission to introduce newspapers and public-service broadcasting was undertaken with painstaking care, especially after the Nazi removal of freedoms.

Adenauer was keen to direct federal support towards high culture as a way of re-establishing West Germany's status in the Western cultural community. Artworks had to expunge the Nazi past, but also had to be mindful of the BRD's geography in the context of the Cold War. Communism cast its shadow over many in the art community; hence art in the BRD was guided by the emergence of New York as the pre-eminent artistic marketplace.

Writers avoided anything politically divisive or confrontational; and with filmmakers eschewing social comment or anything controversial, the majority of West German films in this period did no more than entertain the audience. The defining genre of this period was arguably the Heimatfilm (homeland film), where stories of love, adventure and family problems were set in picturesque rural locations.

By 1955, when the BRD was granted its sovereignty, culture in the BRD had undoubtedly retained some distinctly German traits, especially in the regions; as would be expected in any country today. But American and British troops were still stationed in the BRD at the forefront of the Cold War, so their influences here are unsurprising. Moreover, many German writers, musicians and film directors had been lost when they fled to Britain and the USA to escape Nazism.

Popular culture had adopted American rock and roll, British theatre and a general mid-Atlantic tone. With exposure to Frank Sinatra and Elvis Presley, viewers in the BRD were perhaps becoming less German and more international. The continent of Europe was also linked through Eurovision, with TV and radio bringing foreign news reports,

KEY CONCEPTS ACTIVITY

Significance: Explain the significance of the role played by the Western Allied powers in overseeing radio and television in the BRD after 1949, and how it affected or changed cultural attitudes.

European club football and the eponymous Eurovision Song Contest into German homes. Cultural life in the BRD broadened.

Figure 2.20 Corry Brokken of the Netherlands sings the winning entry in the 1957 Eurovision Song Contest, hosted by West German television in Frankfurt

But what preoccupied the leaders of the BRD was that whatever their young generation were doing culturally, it was important that it should not be political or ideological! Fears of Nazism were always in the background. But the politics and the ideology would come later to the BRD, around 1968.

End of unit activities

1 Design a spider diagram to illustrate the economic and social problems facing the Weimar Government throughout the period 1919–33 and how the government tackled them.

2 Divide into two groups: one group should work out an argument to support, and the other group an argument to oppose, the following statement: 'Considering the historical context of Germany from 1945 to 1955, Adenauer's government did all that was possible at the time to improve the position of ordinary people in the BRD.'

3 Just how far did the BRD become Americanised under Adenauer and Erhard? Consider social and cultural influences as well as the obvious economic and political parallels.

4 To what extent did the supposedly liberal and open-minded Weimar Republic betray the different groups living under its protection? Consider your answer to this by making reference to women's rights, as well as Jews, Roma and Sinti, LGBT and Jehovah's Witnesses.

5 **Either** find out about and make brief notes on the position and importance of the migrant workers in West Germany from 1949 into the 1960s **or** find out what you can about the life of Dr Ludwig Erhard – the BRD's economics minister from 1949 to 1963 (consider his distinguished academic career, his work and life under Nazi German rule, his economic beliefs and his overall contribution to democracy in the BRD).

End of chapter activities

Paper 1 exam practice

Question

According to **Source A**, why is there debate about Gustav Stresemann's successes and failures as the prominent political figure of Weimar Germany? [3 marks]

SOURCE A

Stresemann has always been the focus of debate … praised for his staunch support of parliamentary government and condemned for pretending to be a democrat … portrayed as an idealist on one hand and an opportunist on the other. Stresemann achieved a great deal in a short time to change both Germany's domestic and international positions … by peaceful methods. However … circumstances in the years 1924–29 were working strongly in [his] favour. Also … he failed to achieve his aims to revise Versailles fundamentally and … Stresemann's policies failed to generate real domestic support for Weimar.

G. Layton (2009), Democracy and Dictatorship in Germany 1919–63, *London: Hodder Education, pp. 76–7.*

Skill

Comprehension of a source.

Simplified mark scheme

For each point/item of **relevant/correct information** identified, award one mark – up to a **maximum of three marks**.

Examiner's tips

Comprehension questions are the most straightforward questions you will face in Paper 1 – they simply require you to understand a source and extract two or three relevant points that relate to the particular question. As only three marks are available for this question, make sure you don't waste valuable exam time that should be spent on the higher-scoring questions by writing a long answer here. All that's needed are a couple of short sentences, giving the necessary information to show you've understood the source. Try to give one piece of information for each of the marks indicated as being available for the question.

Common mistakes

When asked to show your comprehension/understanding of a particular source, make sure you don't just paraphrase the source (or copy out a few sentences from it!). What's needed are a couple of sentences that briefly point out the view/message of the source.

Student answer

Source A suggests that Stresemann is viewed by some as an idealist and by others as an opportunist. This is one of the areas of debate about his career and reputation. Although he did change both Germany's domestic and international positions 'by peaceful methods', he still didn't manage to get wholehearted support for Weimar. In any case, much of his success was due to 1924.

Examiner's comments

The candidate has stated one of the areas of debate about Stresemann. They have selected one relevant piece of information from the source to argue that, although there was peaceful international and domestic progress for Germany, much of it was, perhaps, due to factors beyond Stresemann, who never had full support anyway. This is certainly enough to gain one mark out of three. However, the answer does not explain other aspects of his personality/career and merely paraphrases and quotes vaguely 'due to 1924' from the source. To gain the other two marks available, the student would need to give further explanation and show wider understanding of the argument about Stresemann and his supposed areas of strength and weakness.

Activity

Look again at the source, and the student answer above. Now try to write another brief sentence and identify/make two other comments to give an overall view of the message the author is trying to get across, regarding the other areas where Stresemann's actions/beliefs/policies have been debated.

Paper 2 practice questions

1 Examine the challenges facing the government of the newly democratic Weimar Republic between 1919 and 1923.

2 Evaluate the achievements of Ebert's government in its efforts to establish a liberal, democratic republic in Germany after 1919.

3 Evaluate the successes and failures of economic, welfare and women's policies during the government of the BRD between 1949 and 1955.

4 'The Weimar Republic government created greater equality in German society between 1919 and 1933.' To what extent do you agree with this statement?

5 With reference to **either** Weimar Germany 1919–33 **or** the BRD 1949–55, explain the cultural impact of democracy on that society.

6 Evaluate the successes and failures of the government of the BRD under Adenauer and Erhard between 1949 and 1955.

Further reading

Try reading the relevant chapters/sections of the following books:

Berger, S. (2001), *Inventing the Nation: Germany*, London: Hodder Arnold.

Berghahn, V.R. (2008), *Europe in the Era of Two World Wars 1900–1950*, Princeton, NJ: Princeton University Press.

Bullock, A. (1990), *Hitler: A Study in Tyranny*, London: Penguin.

Evans, D. and Jenkins, J. (1999), *Years of Weimar and the Third Reich*, London: Hodder & Stoughton.

Frevert, U. (1989), *Women in German History*, Oxford and New York: Berg.

Fulbrook, M. (2000), *Interpretations of the Two Germanies 1945–90*, Basingstoke: Macmillan.

Hiden, J. (1996), *Republican and Fascist Germany*, Harlow: Longman.

Kershaw, I. (ed.) (1990), *Weimar: Why Did German Democracy Fail?* Bath: Weidenfeld & Nicolson.

Kolb, E. (1988), *The Weimar Republic*, London: Routledge.

Koonz, C. (1988), *Mothers in the Fatherland*, New York: St Martin's Griffin.

Layton, G. (2009), *Democracy and Dictatorship in Germany 1919–63*, London: Hodder Education.

Ogilvie, S. and Overy R. (eds.) (2003), *Germany: A New Social and Economic History Vol III Since 1800*, London: Hodder Arnold.

Panayi, P. (2001), *Weimar and Nazi Germany*, Harlow: Longman.

Roseman, M. (1992), *Recasting the Ruhr 1945–1958: Manpower, Economic Recovery and Labor Relations*, New York: Berg and St. Martin's Press.

Tipton, F.B. (2003), *A History of Modern Germany Since 1815*, London: Continuum.

White, A. (1997), *The Weimar Republic*, London: HarperCollins.

Wighton, C. (1963), *Adenauer – Democratic Dictator*, London: Frederick Muller Ltd.

India 3

From imperial rule to democracy: the emergence of a democratic state in India Unit 1

KEY QUESTIONS

- What conditions led to the establishment of democracy in India?
- What role did political parties and leaders play?
- How did democracy function in independent India?

Overview

- This unit explains how India changed from being a colony under British rule to a multiparty democracy.
- As a result of its history, India had a rich mixture of languages, cultures, traditions and religions. The main religious groups were Hindus, Muslims and Sikhs.
- Until 1947, the whole area that now forms India, Pakistan and Bangladesh was under British colonial rule.
- Indian nationalists formed the Indian National Congress to fight for independence from British rule.
- The British government introduced constitutional reforms that gave limited representation to Indians. However, the pace of reform was too slow to satisfy the nationalist movement.
- There was disagreement over the nature of an independent India. Congress wanted a single united country, while the Muslim League wanted India to be partitioned into two separate states: one Hindu and one Muslim.
- As tensions rose, Congress reluctantly accepted the concept of partition. India and Pakistan became separate independent states in August 1947.
- Mahatma Gandhi and the Indian National Congress played a dominant role in the struggle for independence in India, while Jawaharlal Nehru played the principal role in the establishment of a multiparty democracy in independent India.
- Nehru led an interim government, which ruled India until a constitution was drawn up and elections were held.

TIMELINE

1858 India becomes a British colony.

1885 Formation of the Indian National Congress.

1892 Appointed Indian representatives in provincial legislatures.

1906 Formation of the Muslim League.

1909 Elected Indian representatives in provincial legislatures.

1919 Indian ministers in provincial legislatures.

1935 Government of India Act: provinces to elect local governments.

1939–45 Second World War.

1946 **Dec:** Inauguration of Constituent Assembly.

1947 **Feb:** Louis Mountbatten arrives as last viceroy of India.

15 Aug: Independence from British rule.

1948 **26 Jan:** Official Independence Day; India becomes a sovereign democratic republic.

Dec: Constituent Assembly completes work.

1952 **Feb:** First general election.

1957 **May:** Second general election.

1962 **April:** Third general election.

1964 **May:** Death of Indian prime minister Jawaharlal Nehru.

India

- The Constituent Assembly drew up a democratic constitution, which transformed India into a secular, federal republic.
- The first elections, held in 1952, were won convincingly by the Congress Party, which represented a wide range of political opinions, ranging from reformists like Nehru, who wanted to transform India politically and socially, to the conservative right-wing, which wanted to maintain traditions.
- Opposition parties also represented a range of ideologies, from the left-wing communist and socialist parties, to the conservative Bharatiya Jan Sangh, a Hindu nationalist party.
- Nehru served as prime minister until his death in 1964. He was widely respected both in India and internationally.

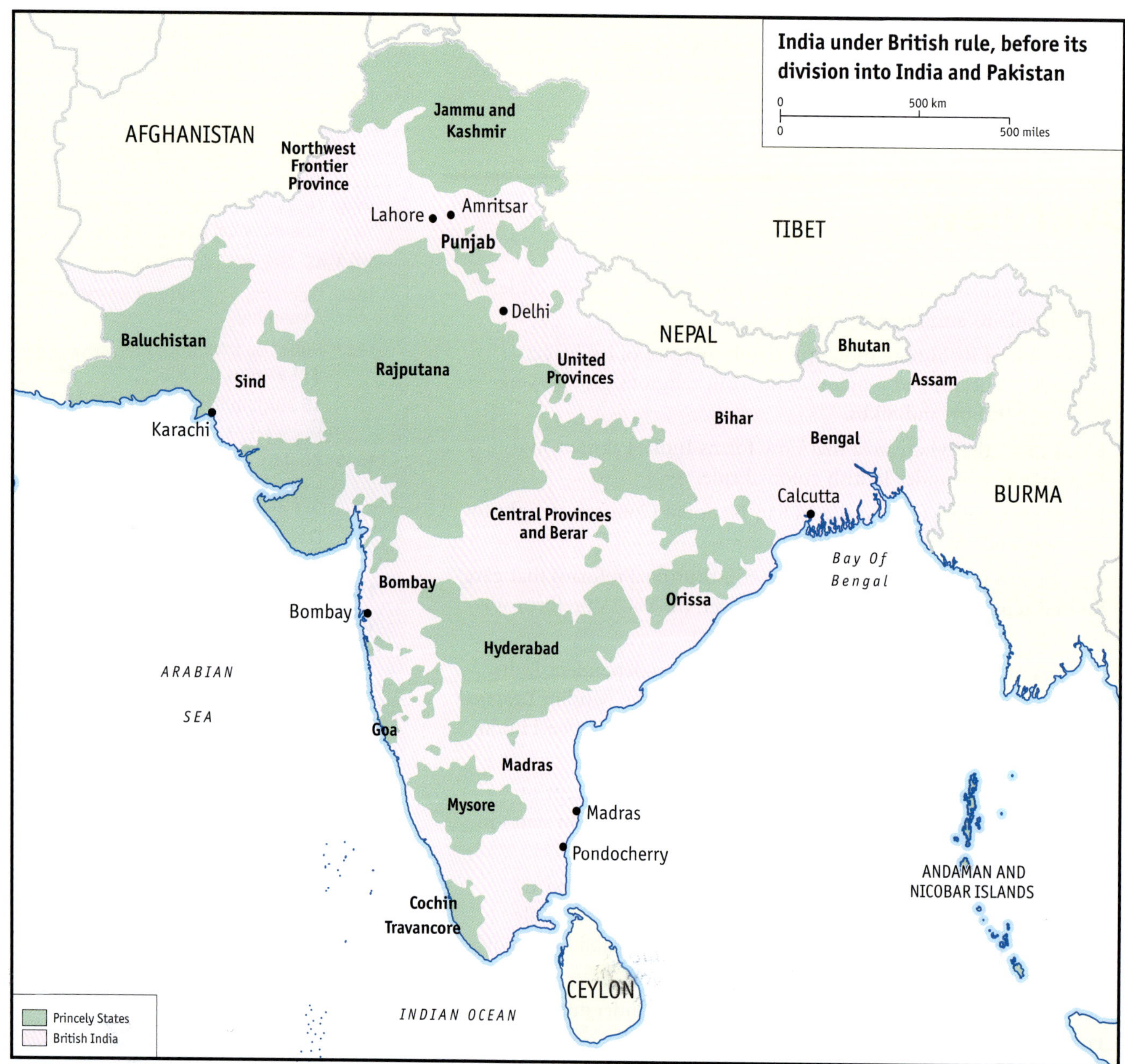

Figure 3.1 Map showing India under British rule, before its division into India and Pakistan

3.1 What conditions led to the establishment of democracy in India?

The area where India, Pakistan and Bangladesh are situated today is usually called the Indian subcontinent or South Asia. Over the centuries, many different people moved into this region, bringing with them their culture and traditions. By the early 20th century, about 75 per cent of the population were Hindu, just under 20 per cent were Muslim, and the Sikhs formed a smaller but significant religious group.

The area had been a British colony since 1858 and was ruled by officials sent from London, who provided efficient, but authoritarian, government. Change came in 1947, when British colonial rule came to an end and India became an independent democratic state. Today India is the world's largest democracy, with a population in 2014 of 1.26 billion people and an electorate of 814 million.

British rule in India

British interest in India began when the English East India Company (EIC) set up trading posts along the coast from the beginning of the 17th century. EIC rule gradually expanded into the interior and by the middle of the 19th century, the company controlled large parts of India. However, an uprising against EIC control in 1857–8 resulted in the intervention of the British government, which sent troops to crush the uprising and take over control from the EIC. After this, India became part of the British Empire. Large parts of the country were placed under direct British administration, but some areas remained under the control of hereditary Indian rulers, with whom Britain signed treaties that recognised their autonomy over local affairs. There were about 550 of these 'princely states', as they were called.

British rule in India was enforced by a **viceroy** and senior officials sent from London. Indians themselves had limited representation in this government, although they later formed the bulk of the junior staff in the Indian Civil Service. British control of more than 300 million Indians was enforced by a large army, staffed by British officers and Indian troops. The administration and the army were financed out of taxes paid by Indians.

The British brought certain benefits to India. These included an efficient administration and judicial system, a good railway network and Western education for some. However, British rule was always based on an assumption of racial superiority. The British believed that government should be firm and vigilant against the rise of any resistance to their rule. Above all, they wanted to prevent the formation of a united opposition movement. To this end, they stressed differences between people – significantly differences of religion, and also of caste. The result of this colonial policy was to create and intensify existing differences in Indian society.

Britain derived great economic benefits from its Indian empire. Money collected from peasants in the form of taxes was transferred to London to fund the British government's purchase of EIC shares, finance capital investments (especially railways) and provide funds for the administration of India. Critics felt that the money could have been better used for internal investments in India itself. Britain also benefited from the balance of trade with India, which supplied raw materials – mainly cotton, jute, indigo, rice and tea – to

Fact: In recent years, the names of some places in India have been changed. In this chapter, we use the names that were in use at the time of the historical events discussed. Bombay is now Mumbai; Calcutta is now Kolkata; Madras is now Chennai.

Viceroy: the highest official in the British colonial administration, who ruled India on behalf of the British monarch. Although there was a great deal of status, material comfort and wealth attached to the position, the viceroy had limited power to influence policy, which was decided by the British government in London and implemented by the secretary of state for India.

Fact: The caste system in India developed about 2,500 years ago. It divided society into a hierarchy of levels called castes. Status, occupation, rights, privileges and opportunities in life were all determined by the caste into which one was born.

British factories. In return, India bought manufactured goods such as textiles, iron and steel goods and machinery, and was the biggest export market for British goods by 1914. As a result, India under colonial rule was no longer an exporter of cloth to European markets. Instead it produced raw cotton that was manufactured into cloth in British factories and re-exported to Asia. Another disadvantage for India was that land formerly used to grow grains for staple foods was now used for commercial cash-crop production, making peasants dependent on foods grown elsewhere.

India also served Britain's political and economic interests in other parts of the empire. Indian soldiers, paid for by Indian taxpayers, were used to protect trade routes and serve British interests in China, East Africa and the Middle East. India also served as a source of indentured labourers for British colonies in the West Indies, Africa and other parts of Asia. In the 20th century, large numbers of Indian soldiers provided military support for Britain in both World Wars.

The nationalist movement

By the beginning of the 20th century there was a growing feeling among educated Indians that British rule in India should end. Many of them supported a nationalist organisation called the Indian National Congress, which had been formed in 1885. At first, it represented the interests of the wealthy middle class and it did not have mass support. Most of its membership was Hindu, although it also had Muslim members. In 1906, Muslims established their own political organisation, the Muslim League.

The person who transformed the Indian Congress into a mass nationalist movement after the First World War was Mohandas 'Mahatma' Gandhi. Promoting the tactics of civil disobedience, he led the opposition to British rule. Although the British tried to crush it by implementing harsh laws and jailing Gandhi and other Congress leaders, the resistance movement gained increasing support. (You will read more about Gandhi and the nationalist movement later in this unit.)

Constitutional developments

Although India was ruled as a colony, from 1892 wealthy Indians were given limited representation in provincial legislatures, to which they were appointed by the British government in India. From 1909, however, Indian representatives on provincial legislatures were elected. The 1909 reforms also reserved a number of seats for Muslims, in this way establishing the principle of separate **communal** representation. Although the right to vote was always subject to various economic and educational qualifications, over the next decades these gradually became less restrictive so that the number of Indians entitled to vote slowly increased.

Communal: serving one community; sectarian.

Fact: The Simon Commission consisted of seven members of the British parliament under the chairmanship of Sir John Simon. Although the Indian National Congress and other Indian political groups boycotted it, the commission produced a two-volume report that recommended representative government at a provincial, but not national, level.

In 1919, the British parliament passed the Government of India Act, which was regarded as a first step in the progress towards self-government for India, although at this stage only about 3 per cent of the population had the right to vote. Certain responsibilities in the provinces – such as agriculture, education and health – were given to Indian ministers, although the central government in Delhi remained under British control. Crucially, however, the British retained control of the police and the justice system. These tentative steps towards reform did not satisfy Indian nationalists.

In 1927, the British government appointed the Simon Commission to make recommendations for further constitutional reform. However, no Indians were included in the Commission, so the nationalists rejected it and called instead for **dominion status** and full self-government. When the British ignored the call and instead made vague statements about future constitutional developments, impatience at the slow pace of reform increased.

As support for the nationalist movement grew, the British government was forced to accept that more meaningful constitutional change was necessary. The 1935 Government of India Act gave each province the right to elect a local government, but with limited powers. Voting rights were extended to about 10 per cent of the population, with the electorate separated along racial and religious lines. The British viceroy had ultimate power, and the composition of his Executive Council was designed to emphasise and encourage divisions in Indian society, according to the historian Clive Ponting. It included separate representatives for Hindus, Muslims, Sikhs, Christians, Europeans and other minority groups. In addition, the act ensured that Britain retained control of the provinces through emergency powers, which could be imposed whenever it was deemed necessary.

Historian Robert Stern suggests that throughout this period there was a 'persistent British unwillingness to part with the substance of power' and that the British government periodically 'delivered packages of constitutional reforms in which ostensible concessions to nationalist aspirations were wrapped together with insidious schemes to protect British power from what it conceded' (*Changing India*, 1993, p. 144).

Although both Congress and the League condemned the 1935 reforms as inadequate, they decided to participate in the provincial elections held in 1937. The right to vote was based on a property qualification, and so was limited to thirty-five million of the wealthier part of the Indian population, including women. In the elections, Congress emerged as the strongest political force, with 70 per cent of the popular vote. In stark contrast, the Muslim League did not do well in the elections, winning barely 5 per cent of the total Muslim vote.

The outbreak of the Second World War in 1939 meant a postponement of the further constitutional reforms laid out in the 1935 Government of India Act. To the anger of Indian politicians, the viceroy declared war on Japan without even consulting them. During the war, Congress organised a 'Quit India' campaign to put pressure on Britain, and in response the British imprisoned hundreds of Congress leaders. The Muslim League, on the other hand, continued to cooperate with Britain and was consequently in a strong negotiating position at the end of the war. An alternative view during the war years came from those who saw it as an opportunity to force Britain to grant immediate independence. One such group was the **Indian National Army (INA)**.

The concept of partition

The situation in India was complicated by differences over the form that an independent India should take. Congress wanted independence as a single united nation, but the Muslim League wanted India to be divided. Muslims were a minority, forming about 20 per cent of the population at that stage, and they feared that their interests would be neglected in a Hindu-dominated country. They wanted a separate country, to be called Pakistan, to be created in the northern parts of the subcontinent, where most Muslims lived. The leader of the Muslim League, **Muhammad Ali Jinnah**, put pressure on Britain to support the partition of India into two separate states.

Dominion status: this gave colonies the right to rule themselves; they were linked to Britain as members of the empire but not ruled by it; Canada, Australia, New Zealand and South Africa had been granted dominion status.

KEY CONCEPTS ACTIVITY

Change and Continuity: Draw up a chart to summarise the main stages of constitutional reform. Indicate to what extent each stage represented change or continuity in British policy towards India.

The Indian National Army (INA): was formed by Subhas Chandra Bose, a Congress leader who disagreed with the views of Gandhi and Nehru on non-violent resistance. With Japanese help, he organised Indian prisoners-of-war and civilians in Southeast Asia to form the INA. The INA fought the Allies in Burma, and briefly captured parts of northeastern India.

Muhammad Ali Jinnah (1876–1948)

He worked with Gandhi and Nehru in the nationalist struggle for independence, but left the Indian National Congress and became leader of the Muslim League. He fought for partition and the creation of a separate Muslim state, and became the first leader of independent Pakistan.

QUESTION

Explain the difference in attitude towards the concept of partition between the Congress Party and the Muslim League.

The Congress Party, on the other hand, vigorously opposed partition. Gandhi himself was a Hindu but he firmly believed in religious tolerance, and he never put the interests of Hindus above those of any other group. Nehru supported the creation of a single, **secular** state, in which religious differences would not be significant. They tried very hard to persuade Muslim leaders that they would be safe in a united India. However, as tensions mounted, there were violent clashes between Hindus and Muslims.

Secular: not connected to any religion; secularism is the view that religion should be separated from government or public education.

In 1946, elections were held for provincial assemblies with a restricted franchise, in which 28 per cent of the adult population was allowed to vote. Historian Ramachandra Guha analyses the contrast between the election messages of the two parties in **Source A**.

SOURCE A

The world over, the rhetoric of modern democratic politics has been marked by two rather opposed rhetorical styles. The first appeals to hope, to popular aspirations for economic prosperity and social peace. The second appeals to fear, to sectional worries about being worsted or swamped by one's historic enemies. In the elections of 1946 the Congress relied on the rhetoric of hope. It had a strongly positive content to its programme, promising land reform, workers' rights, and the like. The Muslim League, on the other hand, relied on the rhetoric of fear. If they did not get a separate homeland, they told the voters, then they would be crushed by the more numerous Hindus in a united India.

R. Guha (2007), India after Gandhi: The History of the World's Largest Democracy, *London: Macmillan, p. 28.*

The partition plan

In February 1947, the British government sent Louis Mountbatten as the last viceroy of India to facilitate and oversee the handover of power by June 1948. He later brought the date forward to 15 August 1947. Therefore, in only six months, he had to decide whether power would be handed over to one, two or more states, where the borders between them would be and what was to happen to the 'princely states'. These were parts of India that had remained under the control of hereditary rulers with whom the British had signed treaties, recognising their local autonomy. Mountbatten's initial proposal, Plan Balkan, which suggested transferring power to each province separately, was rejected by Nehru, who was determined to avoid the '**Balkanisation**' of India.

Balkanisation: the division of a region into small states that are often hostile to each other. The term was first used to describe the situation in the Balkan Peninsula in Southeastern Europe after the collapse of the Ottoman Empire, and again with the break-up of Yugoslavia in the 1990s.

In an atmosphere of escalating violence, the Congress leaders reluctantly came to accept that partition was the only viable solution and that British India would be divided into two separate states. However, it would be impossible to draw the borders so that all Hindus would be in India and all Muslims in Pakistan. As Independence Day approached, millions of people began to flee their homes, afraid of being caught on the wrong side of the border.

Historians have different views about whether Britain was responsible for partition. **Source B** gives the view of historian Bipan Chandra.

SOURCE B

[H]aving unified India, the British set into motion contrary forces. Fearing the unity of the Indian people to which their own rule had contributed, they followed the classic imperial policy of divide and rule. The diverse and divisive features of Indian society and polity were heightened to promote cleavages among the people and to turn province against province, caste against caste, class against class, Hindus against Muslims, and the princes and landlords against the nationalist movement. They succeeded in their endeavours to a varying extent, which culminated in India's Partition.

B. Chandra, M. Mukherjee and A. Mukherjee (2000), India after Independence: 1947–2000, *London: Penguin, p. 18.*

Other historians blame Jinnah and the Muslim League for promoting the violence that led to partition. Ramachandra Guha explains this viewpoint in **Source C**.

SOURCE C

The violence of August–September 1946 was, in the first instance, instigated by the Muslim League, the party which fuelled the movement for a separate Pakistan … By starting a riot in Calcutta in August 1946, Jinnah and the League hoped to polarize the two communities further, and thus force the British to divide India when they finally quit. In this endeavour they richly succeeded.

R. Guha (2007), India after Gandhi: The History of the World's Largest Democracy, *London: Macmillan, p. 9.*

ACTIVITY

Compare and contrast the reasons suggested in **Sources B** and **C** for the partition of India into two separate states in 1947.

Independence

In August 1947, British rule came to an end when the subcontinent became independent as two separate states: India and Pakistan. Pakistan itself was divided into two parts, East and West Pakistan, separated by 1,500 kilometres (930 miles) of Indian territory.

On 14 and 15 August, hundreds of thousands of Indians came to Delhi to celebrate the handover of power and the creation of a new state. They listened to the words of their new prime minister, Nehru, as quoted in **Source D**.

Fact: The people of East and West Pakistan had little in common, except their religion. East Pakistanis resented the political and economic dominance of the western part. In 1971 they broke away and formed the independent state of Bangladesh. With help from the Indian army, they successfully fought off an attempt by Pakistan to reunite them.

SOURCE D

Long years ago we made a tryst with destiny, and now the time comes when we shall redeem our pledge, not wholly or in full measure, but very substantially. At the stroke of the midnight hour, when the world sleeps, India will awake to life and freedom. A moment comes, which comes but rarely in history, when we step out from the old to the new, when an age ends, and when the soul of a nation, long suppressed, finds utterance. It is fitting that at this solemn moment we take the pledge of dedication to the service of India and her people and to the still larger cause of humanity.

J. Nehru (1965), Nehru: the First Sixty Years Volume 2, *London: The Bodley Head, p. 336.*

Figure 3.2 A map showing modern India

Gandhi himself decided to mark India's independence with a twenty-four-hour fast. He was deeply saddened by the partition and by the widespread violence and bloodshed that accompanied it.

Theory of Knowledge

History and emotion/ language:

Nehru's 'tryst with destiny' speech (see **Source D**) is considered to be a landmark in the freedom struggle in India, and a masterpiece of oratory. How does Nehru use emotion and rhetoric to get his message across?

The factors that led to these changes

There are debates among historians about the importance of various factors that encouraged demands for democratic reform and led to independence and the subsequent establishment of a democratic state in India

- Some historians emphasise the leadership role played by Gandhi in the nationalist movement. He succeeded in turning what had been a small organisation dominated by elite middle-class leaders into a mass movement.

- Others believe that it was the sustained protest actions – in the form of peasant resistance, strikes by workers and mass civil protests and boycotts – by a wide cross-section of the Indian population that made the British position untenable in the end.
- Another view is that the constitutional reforms introduced by Britain, which gradually extended representation to a larger number of Indians, played a role in encouraging and facilitating the move towards full self-government.
- The Second World War was a critical factor: Britain was weakened by the war – both economically and politically – and after the war lacked the resources and will to maintain a large empire.
- In the post-war world, the United States and the Soviet Union were the new rival superpowers and, in their competition to gain allies in the wider world, neither was prepared to support unpopular imperial rulers

3.2 What role did political parties and leaders play?

Mahatma Gandhi (1869–1948) and the Indian National Congress

Gandhi and Congress played a critical role in the nationalist movement, which made it possible for India to become an independent and democratic state. Gandhi was both the political and spiritual leader of the movement. He was a London-trained lawyer who spent twenty-one years in South Africa (1893–1914), where he was involved in a struggle against discrimination towards the Indian community there. It was during this period that he developed his philosophy of *satyagraha* and the tactics of non-violent resistance.

On his return to India he became part of the nationalist struggle against British rule led by Congress. It was he who transformed Congress from an elitist organisation representing the English-educated middle class into a mass-based movement with wide appeal. He did this partly through his identification with peasant struggles and his promotion of schemes to promote rural upliftment, and also through the appeal of his non-cooperation campaigns of **civil disobedience**, which mobilised millions of people throughout India, to force the British to leave India. He was imprisoned several times during the independence struggle and, both inside and outside prison, he used hunger strikes as a form of political and social protest.

His firm commitment to liberal democratic principles, the emancipation of women and a reform of the caste system had a deep influence on the kind of democracy that India became. Although he was a Hindu, he was committed to the belief that India should be a unified and secular state. He devoted much time to trying to create greater understanding and tolerance between the Hindu and Muslim communities. He fought hard to maintain the unity of India, and he deplored the violence that accompanied partition. He saw **communalism** as one of the greatest threats facing India, and ironically it was this force that resulted in his assassination (which you will read about in the next unit).

Theory of Knowledge

History and ethics:
Gandhi's philosophy of non-violent resistance against oppressive measures was called *satyagraha*, which means 'soul force'. He believed that the authorities could be forced to give in by the firm yet peaceful demonstration of the justice of a cause. This philosophy earned him the name Mahatma, or 'Great Soul'. How could *satyagraha* be an effective moral force to bring about political change?

Civil disobedience: also called 'non-violent resistance', this is the refusal to obey the law as part of a political campaign. These tactics were used successfully by the Indian nationalist movement to force Britain to grant independence.

Communalism: a belief in promoting the interests of one ethnic, religious or cultural group rather than those of society as a whole. Communalist groups were responsible for promoting violence between Hindus, Muslims and Sikhs. Communalism is also referred to as sectarianism.

Jawaharlal Nehru (1889–1964)

The nature and structure of democracy in India were shaped between 1947 and 1964, under its first prime minister, Jawaharlal Nehru. Although he was twenty years younger than Gandhi, Nehru became his close associate, confidant and successor. Nehru came from a wealthy family, and was educated in England, at Harrow School and Cambridge University. Like Gandhi, he qualified as a lawyer in London. Together with many educated Indians of his generation, he deeply resented British attitudes, policies and actions in India. After his return to India, he was attracted by Gandhi's philosophy of active yet peaceful civil disobedience. He joined the Indian Congress in 1919, and devoted the rest of his life to politics. He was jailed many times because of his role as a Congress leader working for the independence of India, and he spent a total of nine years as a political prisoner.

Figure 3.3 Nehru, photographed in the early 1950s, with a crowd of supporters behind him

As the general secretary of Congress during the 1920s, Nehru travelled widely around India and saw at first-hand the conditions of poverty and oppression under which millions of people lived. This gave him a driving determination to improve the position of the peasants. He also travelled to Europe and the Soviet Union, where he came to believe that some form of socialism, in the form of central planning, would be the solution to India's social and economic problems. At the same time, he valued liberal and humanist ideas, and had a vision of India as a tolerant secular democracy. He became the leader of the left wing of the Congress, and was regarded by some of the more conservative members as a militant revolutionary.

Nehru became president of Congress in 1930. There were other more experienced politicians who were rivals for this position, but Gandhi saw qualities in Nehru that other Congress leaders lacked. He became Gandhi's political heir and was recognised as such from 1942 onwards. Together they formed a powerful partnership. While Gandhi mobilised the masses, Nehru attracted the support of the educated middle classes, intellectuals and young people.

A strong supporter of democracy and secularism, he advocated socialist central planning to promote economic development in India. He served as India's first prime minister, leading the Congress Party to victory in India's first three general elections.

In January 1964, Nehru suffered a stroke and died in May of that year. He had dominated Indian politics for decades, first as a leader of the nationalist movement alongside Gandhi, and then as the first prime minister of independent India. He is widely admired for his commitment to democracy and secularism, and for the role he played in establishing a united and democratic India.

Robert Stern comments on Nehru's legacy to the development of democracy in India in **Source E**.

SOURCE E

Were we to name a founding father of parliamentary democracy in India and the one-party dominance of the Congress … it would be Jawaharlal Nehru … He might have succumbed easily, as did many of his contemporaries in Asia and Africa, to the self-serving revelation that parliamentary democracy is for any number of reasons inappropriate to a 'third world' country and declared himself chief guide in a 'guided democracy', first person in a 'people's democracy', president-for-life, great helmsman, whatever. But he did not. Instead he led his party in India's first three democratic elections and tutored its electorate in parliamentary democracy, tolerated dissent within Congress, suffered the rivalry of opposition parties – left and right, regional and national, secular and religious; and bore the restraints that democracy imposes on executive power: by cabinet and party colleagues, a lively parliament, an articulate opposition, a free press, an independent judiciary, and an unpoliticized civil service.

R.W. Stern (1993), Changing India, *Cambridge: Cambridge University Press, pp. 186–7*

Other historians share similar positive views about the values Nehru prized, his qualities as a leader and his role in establishing a multi-party democracy in India. In their book, *A Concise History of Modern India* (2006), American historians Barbara and Thomas Metcalf observe that his solid support for democratic processes ensured that these became an entrenched feature of the way democracy functions in India. According to Indian historian Ramachandra Guha, in *India after Gandhi* (2007), Nehru represented the voice of democracy against dictatorship, and of secularism against narrow communal interests. In *India after Independence* (2000), another Indian historian, Bipan Chandra, provides a balanced view, describing Nehru as a visionary leader but one who failed to find a way of putting his ideals into practice. He cites some of the areas that were neglected by Nehru's government that created problems for the future. These included the education system, which was not reformed and failed to reach the majority of people; the failure to launch an effective mass struggle against communalism as an ideology; and the inadequate implementation of land reforms, leaving a legacy of economic inequality, social oppression and political violence in rural India. These were some of the political, economic and social challenges facing India, which you will read about in Units 3.2 and 3.3.

Some historians, such as Nehru's biographer Tariq Ali, believe that Nehru could have achieved his goal of transforming India more successfully if he had not been restrained by the right wing of the Congress Party. The British philosopher Bertrand Russell, who was a great admirer of Nehru, voiced this view in an obituary after Nehru's death (see **Source F**).

KEY CONCEPTS ACTIVITY

Perspectives: Compare the different perspectives of Stern, Metcalf, Guha, Chandra and Russell in their evaluation of Nehru's role. Suggest why historians hold such different views. Explain why evaluating different perspectives is important for students of history.

SOURCE F

After the independence struggle had been won, Nehru was hampered by the power of the right wing which increasingly came to dominate the Congress Party. This domination was only held in check by his own leadership and command over the population of India. The price, however, of having to reconcile the powerful economic forces which the Congress comprised with his hopes for democratic socialism, was the emasculation [weakening] of the latter programme. India has a slow growth rate and remains stricken with poverty and disease. Nehru's own efforts to alter this would have succeeded more had his party been forthrightly socialist with an opposition in Parliament representing the very forces which now dominate the Congress.

Bertrand Russell, quoted in T. Ali (1985), The Nehrus and the Gandhis: An Indian Dynasty, *London: Chatto and Windus, Hogarth Press. pp. 108–9.*

3.3 How did democracy function in independent India?

The first government of independent India was a coalition, dominated by the Congress Party but designed to be as inclusive as possible, to span the divisions that had threatened the whole process. Its main task was to rule India until a new constitution was written and the first elections could be held. The government was led by Jawaharlal Nehru and his deputy was another Congress Party veteran, the conservative **Vallabhbhai Patel**. After Patel's death in 1950, Nehru was able to consolidate his dominant position in the party and push through a more active policy of reform.

Vallabhbhai Patel (1875–1950)

He was a leading member of the Congress Party and a close associate of Gandhi. He served as deputy to Nehru and as home affairs minister in the first government of India, and was responsible for negotiating the successful transfer of the princely states. He played a leading role in drawing up India's constitution.

The constitution

India's constitution was drawn up by a Constituent Assembly, which met from December 1946, when India was still under British rule, until December 1948. It consisted of 300 members, 82 per cent of them members of the Congress Party, but the party itself represented a wide range of views. The public was also invited to make submissions, and large numbers were received, on issues ranging from the recognition of local languages and special rights for people from lower castes to the prohibition of cow-slaughter and special safeguards for religious minorities. The chief architects of the constitution were Patel, the minister of home affairs, and the law minister, B.R. Ambedkar. Nehru himself only took part when controversial matters were involved. Historians Hermann Kulke and Dietmar Rothermund observe that he had the ability to reconcile opposing views, conservative and radical, through his persuasive speeches.

The constitution came into effect on Independence Day, 26 January 1950. It adopted a British or Westminster form of government, with two houses of parliament, the Sabha (House of the people) with more than 500 members, and a smaller upper house, the Rajya Sabha (Council of States), chosen by the state assemblies. Elections would be held every five years, using a system of universal suffrage for all citizens of twenty-one years and older. This made India, with a population of more than 300 million people, the largest democracy in the world. The system of voting would be the constituency system, with seats won by a simple majority in each constituency. The government would be formed by the party winning a majority of seats in the election, with the leader of the party serving as prime minister. The head of state would be a president elected for a five-year term by members of parliament and the state assemblies.

The constitution gave India a **federal** structure, with a strong central government that controlled major issues such as foreign affairs and defence, but the individual states had a certain amount of autonomy. This, according to historian Bipan Chandra, met the demands for diversity as well as the need for unity, and allowed for decentralisation but not disintegration. Each state had an elected assembly, where the leader of the majority party became the chief minister for that state. An American idea incorporated into the constitution was a supreme court with the power to review legislation to ensure that it complied with the constitution. The constitution also listed a bill of fundamental rights, which included social and economic rights.

The constitution was completely secular. This meant that there was to be no state religion, a complete separation of religion and state, a secular school system and no taxes to support any religion. It recognised the equality and freedom of religion of all individuals, and any citizen could hold public office. Nehru was deeply committed to **secularism**. According to historians Bipan Chandra, Mridula Mukherjee and Aditya Mukherjee in their book *India after Independence*, Nehru defined secularism as keeping the state, politics and education separate from religion, making religion a private matter for the individual and showing equal respect for all religions and equal opportunities for their followers. He defended it vigorously against communalism, which he saw as a major threat to democracy and national unity.

The constitution had to take into account India's linguistic diversity, with its many hundreds of languages. Part of India's colonial inheritance was the use of English as the language of government, the law courts and higher education, as well as the language of the middle and upper classes. There was no single alternative language that was widely spoken all over India. The nearest was Hindi, used in the north, but it was spoken by only about half the people in India. Others, especially in the south, spoke Dravidian languages, such as Tamil and Teluga. The constitution recognised fourteen major languages, and made Hindi and English the official languages, although there was provision for Hindi to replace English as the sole official language by 1965.

Regarding India's international status, the Commonwealth prime ministers had agreed at a 1948 meeting in London that India could remain a member of the Commonwealth even if it formally adopted the constitution of a federal republic. This meant that it could have an Indian president as head of state, rather than the British monarch. This precedent was later followed by other former British colonies. In this way, India set a pattern for

Historical debate:
In the Indian constitution, Granville Austin describes the process of the framing of *The Indian Constitution* as a coming together of two different revolutions: a national or political revolution focusing on democracy and liberty, which had been denied by colonial rule; and a social revolution focusing on emancipation and equality, denied by tradition and religious belief.

Federal: a political system in which the central government controls matters of national importance, but individual states have control over regional affairs

Secularism: the view that religion should be completely separated from government and public education.

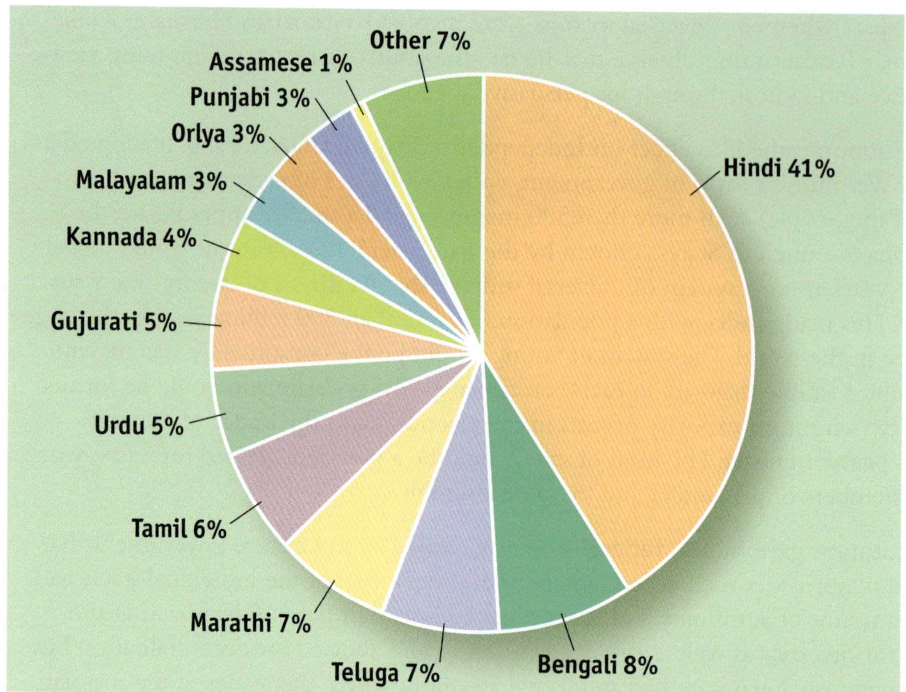

Figure 3.4 The percentage of speakers of the official languages in India, according to the 2001 census (Kashmiri, Sindhi and Sanskrit, which also have official recognition, are included in 'Other')

the peaceful transformation of the multiracial British Empire, according to historian Francis Wilson. Membership of the Commonwealth meant that India did not remain totally isolated, despite Nehru's determination to pursue a policy of non-alignment internationally.

The first election

In 1952, India held its first general election. More than 173 million voters, of whom 84 per cent were illiterate, cast their votes for 489 national parliamentary seats and more than 3,000 seats in the state assemblies.

QUESTION

Apart from the illiteracy of most of the electorate, what other challenges faced the organisers of India's first election?

The election was a triumph for the Congress Party, which won 75 per cent of the seats in the Lok Sabha, despite gaining only 45 per cent of the vote. This was because of the electoral system, which required a simple majority to win each constituency. The Communist Party became the main opposition. The extremist right-wing party, Jan Sangh, which supported communal interests, won only 3 per cent of the votes. A Turkish journalist, quoted by Ramachandra Guha in *India after Gandhi*, described the election as a victory for secularism, moderation and national unity, and a rejection of communalism and narrow regional interests. The Congress Party also won majorities in nearly all the state assemblies.

Political parties

The Congress Party won an overwhelming majority of seats in the first election, and also won the 1957 and 1962 elections, although with reduced majorities. It usually got between 42 per cent and 48 per cent of the national vote but, because of the

Figure 3.5 A man carries his blind, elderly father to vote in India's first general election at a polling station in the Jama Masjid area in Delhi, 1952

Table 3.1 Table of election results (1952)

Political party	Seats won	% of votes
Congress Party	364	45
Communists and Allies	23	4.5
Socialists	12	10.5
KMPP	9	6
Jan Sangh	3	3
Hindu Mahasabha	4	1
RRP	3	2
Other parties	30	12
Independents	41	16
Total	489	

QUESTION

How would a system of proportional representation (PR) have affected these election results?

electoral system, won 65 per cent to 75 per cent of the seats in the Lok Sabha. This dominance in parliament disguised the fact that the Congress Party never obtained a majority of the votes. It remained in power because the opposition was fragmented, and it managed to win successive elections during Nehru's lifetime, except in a few areas at a local level.

The Congress Party had enormous prestige as the leader and heir of the nationalist movement and because of its links with Gandhi. As such, its supporters came from a wide range of social, economic and regional backgrounds. It appealed to landowners and capitalists, as well as to the urban and rural working class. These supporters represented a range of political opinion, giving the party the character of a broad coalition, with the ability to include and reconcile different and sometimes competing points of view. Nevertheless, there were deep divisions between the left and right wings of the party, which was held together largely by Nehru's personality and leadership. Nehru himself represented left-wing opinion within the party, favouring socialist policies to transform India economically and socially. However, he was always mindful of the strong support within the party for more conservative policies and the influential leaders who supported these policies, such as Patel.

By the early 1960s, the Congress Party had lost some of its drive and idealism, and was failing to attract new supporters or to develop a new generation of leaders. Nehru himself had realised this, and had tried to introduce measures to revitalise the party before his death in 1964.

During the nationalist struggle for independence, the Communist Party of India had been part of Congress but had broken away in 1945. After independence, it promoted the idea of an armed struggle to liberate India from the rule of the Congress Party, which it accused of serving British imperial interests and of representing the princes, landlords and bourgeoisie. In 1948, it supported a peasant uprising in Hyderabad, which resulted in the death of thousands of party activists and peasants when the Indian army was sent to crush it. The party lost support after it was banned in several states for launching acts of terrorism. It was also weakened by internal divisions over policy and leadership.

At the end of 1951, the party changed its tactics, on the advice of the Soviet Union, abandoned its armed struggle and decided to participate in the first general election. Although it won less than 5 per cent of the votes, it emerged as the largest opposition party, and therefore the official opposition. Support for the Communist Party came from peasants, workers, students and the intelligentsia, and it was stronger in certain regions of India, especially in the south and in Bengal. In the 1957 state elections it won a majority in the southern state of Kerala, where it proceeded to launch land reform and educational reform programmes, before the communist chief minister was removed from office by the central government. On a national level, the Communist Party improved its position in the 1957 and 1962 general elections, winning nearly 10 per cent of the national vote in 1962. However, a surprise attack by India's communist neighbour later that year, when the Chinese army invaded parts of northern India, was a serious setback for the party

The Socialist Party had also been part of Congress but broke away in 1948 to function as a separate party. It accused the Congress Party of betraying the poor, and representing the landlords and capitalists rather than the workers and peasants. Historians such as Bipan Chandra believe that this decision seriously weakened the left wing of Congress, and made it more difficult for Nehru to introduce more radical reforms because of the strength of the conservative forces within the Congress Party. In the 1952 elections, the Socialist Party won only twelve seats in the Lok Sabha, although it gained more than 10 per cent of the votes, which was more than any other opposition party and twice as many as the communists. It later merged with another party formed by Congress dissidents, the Kisan Mazdoor Praja Party (KMPP), which claimed to be following more closely the teachings of Gandhi. However, later splits weakened the Socialist Party and support for it declined in subsequent elections.

Figure 3.6 A Socialist candidate campaigning in the streets of Jaipur before the 1952 elections; the Socialist Party won 10 per cent of the votes, making them the largest opposition to the Congress Party, although they won only twelve seats

The Bharatiya Jan Sangh (BJS) was a Hindu nationalist party that challenged the secular nature of the Indian state. Most of its leaders and active members also belonged to Rashtriya Swayamsevak Sangh (RSS), a militaristic Hindu nationalist group. Jan Sangh promoted Hindu culture, religion and traditions and, using the slogan 'one country, one culture, one nation', wanted to unite all Hindus. It did not have much support in the south because of its strong support for Hindi as the national language. It was strongly anti-Muslim, and treated India's Muslims with suspicion, questioning their loyalty to India. Initially it wanted the reunification of India by absorbing Pakistan, but it later abandoned this aim. It accused Nehru and the Congress Party of appeasing Muslims. At first Nehru saw Jan Sangh as a challenge because he knew that it expressed the views of some of the more right-wing members of Congress. However, in the 1952 general election, Jan Sangh won only 3 per cent of the vote, indicating that there was little support for a communalist Hindu party. The BJS was later succeeded by the Bharatiya Janata Party (BJP) as the main Hindu nationalist party.

QUESTION

Explain the difference between left-wing and right-wing in the context of Indian politics during the Nehru era.

The Scheduled Castes Federation was established in 1942 by B.R. Ambedkar, a respected lawyer educated in the United States and Britain. As an independent in the first government, he served as law minister and played a leading role in drafting the constitution. Although the Congress Party – and Nehru in particular – denounced 'casteism' and introduced legislation to raise the lower castes, Ambedkar criticised the Congress government for not doing enough. He believed that independence had

Theory of Knowledge

History and terminology:
In Hindu tradition, society was divided into a hierarchy of different levels, according to the caste system. Status, occupation, rights and opportunities in life were all determined by the caste into which one was born. Outside the caste system were the 'untouchables', who suffered many forms of discrimination. The British colonial administration referred to them as 'the depressed classes'. Gandhi fought for their rights and called them 'Harijans' (or 'Children of God'). The Indian government used the official term 'scheduled castes', but the people themselves prefer to be called 'Dalits' (which means 'oppressed').

What are the implications of each of these terms? What does this suggest about the use of terminology in the writing of history?

QUESTION

How successfully did India develop democratic institutions in the early years after independence?

not meant freedom for the 'scheduled castes', and he described the situation of these caste members as a continuation of the tyranny, oppression and discrimination that had always existed. The party stood in the 1952 elections but its candidates were defeated, mainly by Congress candidates, in the seats reserved for the scheduled castes. In the next election, the Congress Party won sixty-four of the seventy-six reserved seats. By this time Ambedkar had stopped playing an active role in politics. As a rejection of Hinduism and its discriminatory caste system, he converted to Buddhism and focused on persuading his fellow caste members to do the same. The situation of the scheduled castes was taken up again as a political cause by the Dalit Panthers in the 1970s.

Significance of the developments after independence

By the time of Nehru's death in 1964, India had emerged as a stable democracy – a notable achievement given the large size of the country and its population, the legacies of colonial rule and the difficulties encountered during the progress towards independence.

Robert Stern comments on the significance of this achievement in a country with such a vast and diverse population in **Source G**.

SOURCE G

Political development in India has been most notably of parliamentary democracy. In four decades, one of the world's few stable parliamentary democracies has been produced by a society that is more populous and diverse in every way than Europe's, scattered over more than half-a-million localities in a vast subcontinent, largely parochial and illiterate and fundamentally anti-democratic in its traditional institutions and cultural biases.

R.W. Stern (1993), Changing India, *Cambridge: Cambridge University Press, p. 184.*

End of unit activities

1. Explain the significance of each of these in the move to democracy in India: civil disobedience, communalism, secularism and partition.
2. Design a spider diagram to illustrate the factors that led to the establishment of a democratic state in India.
3. Research activity: use the information in this unit, as well as additional information from books or websites, to write an obituary for Nehru, evaluating his contribution to the establishment of democracy in India.

4 Draw up a table to summarise the role of political parties in Indian politics in the 1950s, using the headings suggested in the example below.

Political party or pressure group	Who were its main supporters?/Who did it appeal to?	What were its beliefs and aims/ vision?	How significant was it in terms of influence or support?
Congress Party			
Communist Party of India			
Socialist Party			
Bharatiya Jan Sangh (BJS)			
Scheduled Castes Federation			

5 Read **Source A** again. The writer claims that two different approaches are used by political parties to attract voters – the rhetoric of hope and the rhetoric of fear. Show whether this analysis can be applied in a modern context, using a general election in your own country as an example.

2 Unit The development of a democratic state in India

TIMELINE

1947 Aug: Independence and partition.

Aug–Sep: Refugee crisis in Punjab.

Dec: Start of war between India and Pakistan over Kashmir.

1948 30 Jan: Assassination of Gandhi.

1949 Jan: UN arranges ceasefire in Kashmir.

1952 Dec: Death of Andhra leader, Potti Sriramulu.

1953 Oct: State of Andhra Pradesh created.

1954 Nov: France hands over Pondicherry to India.

1956 Nov: Reorganisation of states along linguistic lines.

Provincial boundaries redrawn.

1959 Mar: Dalai Lama escapes to India where he is granted political asylum.

1960 May: Bombay split into Gujarat and Maharashtra.

1961 Oct: China invades India.

Dec: India annexes Goa from Portugal.

1963 Dec: State of Nagaland created.

1966 Nov: Punjab split into Punjab and Haryana.

KEY QUESTIONS

- What factors influenced the development of democracy in India?
- How did the government respond to domestic crises?
- How did the government react to protest movements?

Overview

- After independence, violence between Hindus and Muslims led to the flight of fifteen million refugees across the borders between the new states.
- The incorporation of the 'princely states' into India was a peaceful process in all but three of the states; the consolidation of India was completed with the peaceful withdrawal of France and the forced withdrawal of Portugal from their small coastal enclaves.
- Religion continued to play a significant and sometimes destructive role, and the struggle between secularism and communalism remained a feature of Indian politics.
- India and Pakistan went to war over the state of Kashmir, which was eventually partitioned between them by the United Nations.
- India followed a policy of non-alignment internationally but fought wars with Pakistan and China; the unresolved dispute with Pakistan over Kashmir led to further wars and ongoing tensions.
- The repatriation of thousands of women abducted during partition was not always successful and many were rejected by their own communities.
- Thousands of Hindu and Sikh refugees required land, jobs, accommodation and assistance; this was accomplished fairly successfully in Punjab but not in West Bengal.
- Acts of political extremism at times threatened secular democracy in India. Many of these were related to religion, language rights and nationalism. The assassination of Gandhi highlighted the threat posed by extreme Hindu nationalism.
- Demands by different groups for the recognition of their languages resulted in the reorganisation of state boundaries along linguistic lines.
- Ethnicity was sometimes linked to issues of language and religion, as in Sikh demands for greater autonomy.
- Rural protests included the ethnic struggle for recognition by the Naga people, and a peasant uprising in Hyderabad.

3.4 What factors influenced the development of democracy in India?

Even before India's constitution was drawn up, the new state had to cope with crises created by the abrupt partition of the subcontinent. Afterwards the government took steps to consolidate India's status as a unified, secular, independent state.

The refugee crisis after independence

Partition led to a severe refugee crisis as millions of people took to the roads, anxious not to be caught on the wrong side of the new borders between India and Pakistan.

The two areas where partition was most complex were in the provinces of Punjab in the west and Bengal in the east. Both had very mixed populations, so the decision had been made to divide each of them between India and Pakistan. Furthermore, the new border lines dividing these provinces were announced only a few days after independence. Millions of Hindus and Muslims found themselves on the wrong side of the border and tried desperately to get to safety. About fifteen million people abandoned their homes and belongings in a panic-stricken scramble to get to the other side.

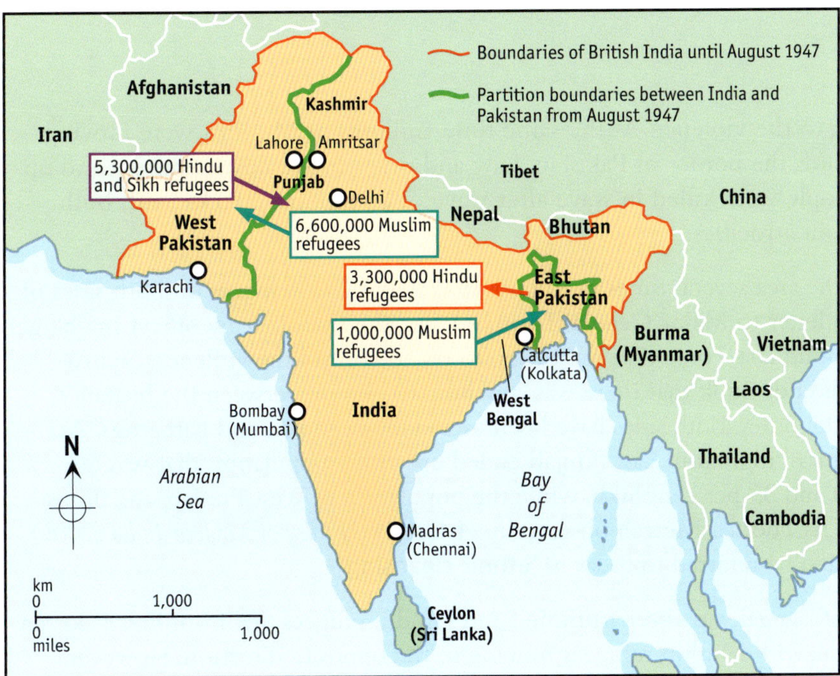

Figure 3.7 Map of India and Pakistan after independence, showing the flow of refugees

The situation in Punjab was further complicated by the presence of the Sikhs, who were scattered throughout the province. Their demands for their own state had been ignored, and they feared that the partition of the province would leave their community powerless and split between two states. When the border was finally announced, they streamed eastwards out of West Punjab, along with millions of

Figure 3.8 Trains crowded with desperate refugees were a common sight in India at the time of partition; both sides attacked such trains and massacred their passengers

Hindus, adding to the violence. At the same time, millions of Muslims were moving westwards towards the border of Pakistan. Law and order broke down entirely, and up to a million people were killed in wave after wave of communal attacks, with both sides carrying out atrocities.

Nehru visited the area several times in August 1947, talking to refugees on both sides of the border. In a letter to Major General Thomas Rees, the British army officer in charge of the Punjab Boundary Force that was set up to try to control the violence, Nehru wrote that he did not think that there was 'anything to choose between the brutality of one side or the other. Both sides have been incredibly inhuman and barbarous.' As a result of this mass migration, East Punjab ended up with a population that was 60 per cent Hindu and 35 per cent Sikh, while the population of West Punjab was almost totally Muslim. As Thomas Metcalf observes in *A Concise History of Modern India* (2006), this process would be referred to today as '**ethnic cleansing**'.

Ethnic cleansing: the expulsion of a population from a certain area; the forced displacement of an ethnic or religious minority. The term was first widely used to refer to events in the civil wars in Yugoslavia in the 1990s.

The province of Bengal was also partitioned and Hindu refugees fled from East Pakistan into West Bengal, with Muslim refugees moving in the opposite direction. However, the migration in Bengal was a more gradual process and not accompanied by as much violence and death as in Punjab.

By the end of 1947, the new governments of India and Pakistan had been able to contain the violence and restore order and control. Despite the mass migration, about forty million Muslims remained in India, and several million Hindus in Pakistan. The resettlement of refugees was a huge financial burden for the new states, which also had to manage the economic effects of the abrupt partition on existing patterns of communication, infrastructure, agriculture, irrigation and trade.

KEY CONCEPTS QUESTION

Causes and Consequences: What were the causes and consequences of the decision to partition India?

Issues relating to unity and consolidation

At the time of independence there were more than 550 'princely states', under the nominal control of hereditary rulers who had signed treaties with Britain. Their territory occupied about 40 per cent of British India (see Figure 3.1). In theory they were free to decide their own futures once the British had left. However, there were strong pressures on them to give up their independent status. They were tied economically to the surrounding areas that were now part of either India or Pakistan. In addition, Indian nationalists were opposed to the idea that independent India should be a patchwork, broken up by hundreds of tiny autonomous states. The issue was therefore given to Patel, Nehru's deputy, to resolve, which he did successfully using a combination of persuasion and, in a few cases, force. The integration of so many small states was regarded by many Congress leaders as an important feature of nation-building for the new state.

All except three of the princes voluntarily decided to join either India or Pakistan in return for generous pensions and the right to use their titles and palaces and to keep some of their extensive personal holdings. Two of the exceptions were Hyderabad and Junagadh, where Muslim princes ruled over large Hindu populations. Both these states were annexed to India by force, against the wishes of their Muslim rulers, in moves generally welcomed by their people. The third exception was the state of Kashmir, which presented a special problem (you will read about it later in this unit).

With the exception of the unresolved issue of Kashmir, the consolidation of India was completed with the final withdrawal of other European colonial powers that had held small parts of India. France agreed to withdraw from Pondicherry and other small French enclaves in 1954. And, when Portugal was reluctant to hand over control of Goa, the Indian army invaded and united Goa with the rest of India by force in 1961.

The challenges posed by religion

Religion has played a significant role in the history of modern India. You saw in Unit 3.1 how the fears and tensions between Hindus and Muslims led to partition, and then how hatred and panic resulted in the violence and bloodshed that accompanied it. When British India was divided, Pakistan was created as a specifically Muslim state, with Islam as its official religion. Even today, the population of Pakistan is 95 per cent Muslim.

In contrast to this, India became a secular state. The Congress Party had always supported secularism. In 1949, it passed a resolution on the rights of minorities, confirming its support for India as a democratic secular state where all citizens would enjoy full and equal rights, irrespective of their religion. Nehru, in particular, was committed to secularism, and saw communalism as the greatest danger facing India. He denounced it repeatedly in radio broadcasts, in parliament, in public speeches and in letters to ministers. The constitution adopted in 1950 established India as a completely secular state, with a separation of religion and state, and no official state religion.

However, more than 80 per cent of the population of India was Hindu, and Hindu nationalists and communalists believed that India should be a Hindu state. This is where political parties such as the Jan Sangh and pressure groups such as the Rashtriya Swayamsevak Sangh (RSS) found their support. Much of the opposition to the Hindu Code Bill and the subsequent legislation that gave women greater equality in marriage and property rights came from Hindu nationalists who saw the changes as a threat to Hindu identity and traditions (you will read more about these issues in Unit 3.3).

Theory of Knowledge

History and religion:
What role did religion play in the partition of India? In what ways can religion be both a positive and a negative force in a country's history?

ACTIVITY

Nehru is reported to have told the French writer, André Malraux, that the most difficult task he faced was creating a secular state in a religious country. Explain what he meant by this remark.

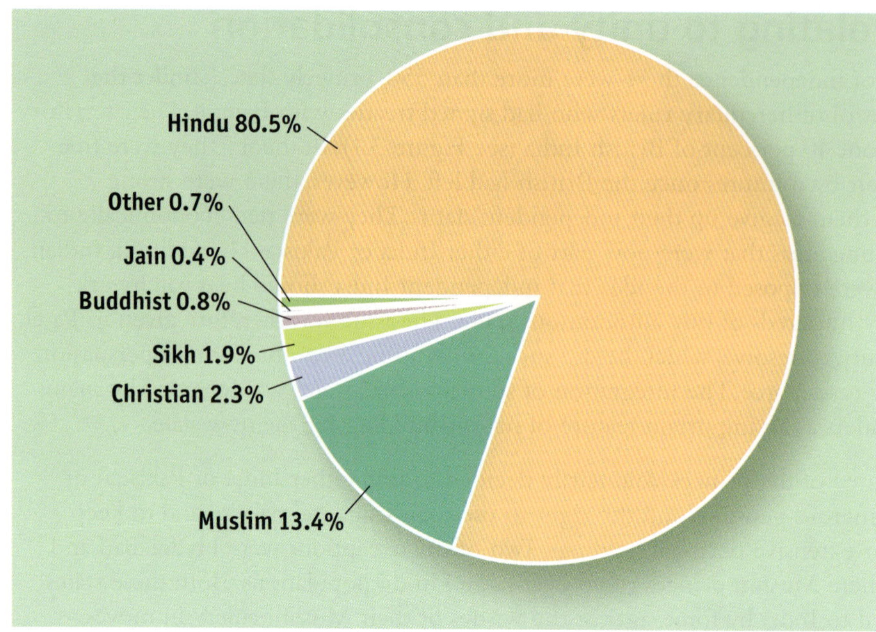

Figure 3.9 Indian religious affiliation according to the 2001 census: although the population was more than 80% Hindu, there were sizeable religious minorities, such as 138 million Muslims, twenty-four million Christians and nineteen million Sikhs. There are almost as many Muslims in India as there are in Pakistan

Although it did not play a significant role during Nehru's lifetime, the rise of Hindu nationalism and communal violence became a feature of Indian politics in later decades.

KEY CONCEPTS QUESTION

Significance: What was the significance of the government's commitment to unity and secularism in shaping its policies after independence?

Foreign crises

In international affairs, India opted for a policy of **non-alignment**, not allying itself with either the Western or Soviet blocs. Nehru became one of the leading proponents of the Non-Aligned Movement (NAM), which aimed to keep a balance between the two power blocs in the Cold War. India under Nehru also became a champion of anti-colonialism and anti-racism. India remained a member of the Commonwealth but, although Britain was a leading Western power in the Cold War, Nehru declared that India was not part of that conflict.

Non-alignment: a policy adopted by India and other developing countries that were unwilling to take sides during the Cold War. They declared themselves to be the 'Third World', not allied to either the First World (the West) or the Second World (the Soviet Bloc)

However, India faced two crises with neighbouring states, resulting in three wars with Pakistan over Kashmir, as well as war with China.

Kashmir was a large state, strategically placed in the northwest, and bordering on both India and Pakistan (see Figure 3.1). At the time of independence it had a Hindu prince ruling over a predominantly Muslim population. India and Pakistan fought a war for control of Kashmir between December 1947 and January 1949, before the United Nations arranged a ceasefire and divided Kashmir between the two, a result that satisfied neither side, nor the people of Kashmir. A UN peacekeeping mission remained in Kashmir to monitor the border between the two.

Since then, India and Pakistan have fought two more wars over Kashmir – in 1965 and 1999. As both states became nuclear powers in the 1990s, the ongoing conflict over Kashmir grew to be of grave concern to the international community. The dispute with

Pakistan over Kashmir remains unresolved, and the tensions between India and Pakistan remain high.

Historians Barbara and Thomas Metcalf explain the significance of Kashmir to Pakistan and India in **Source A**.

SOURCE A

Kashmir mattered not so much because it possessed rich mineral or other resources, nor because it was the original home of the Nehru family, but rather because for both sides it raised issues central to their self-definition as nations. For Pakistan, the critical fact was Kashmir's overwhelmingly Muslim population …

From the Indian perspective other issues were at stake. Nehru, and with him the Congress, although obliged to accept the creation of Pakistan, had never accepted the 'two nation' theory. India was not, in this view, a 'Hindustan' or land of Hindus. In a major defeat for Jinnah, Nehru maintained that his state was the legitimate successor of the British Raj …

In the view of the Congress, India was not only successor to the Raj, but also a secular state, in which Muslims, with all other minorities, stood, in principle, on equal footing with their Hindu fellow citizens. Millions of Muslims, remaining behind after partition by choice or necessity, already lived within India. The addition of the residents of Kashmir would only further testify to the inclusive nature of the new state.

B. Metcalf and T. Metcalf (2006), A Concise History of Modern India, *Cambridge: Cambridge University Press, pp. 224–5.*

QUESTION

Explain how the dispute over Kashmir was linked to the issues of religion and national identity in post-independence India.

Figure 3.10 The daily flag lowering ceremony at the Wagah border post in Punjab. Thousands of people on each side of the border gather to watch the ceremony, which demonstrates the ongoing tension between the Indian and Pakistani armies. The Indian soldiers are in khaki uniforms and the Pakistani army in black

India initially established a good working relationship with the People's Republic of China. The two countries shared similar problems of rural poverty and underdevelopment, and in 1957 they signed a treaty promoting trade and recognising each other's territorial rights.

However, there was competition between them to be the leading Asian nation in the developing world, as well as disputes over territory along their border. Relations grew strained when India granted **political asylum** to the Tibetan spiritual leader the **Dalai Lama**, who fled after Chinese troops occupied Tibet in 1959. In 1962, there was a short war between India and China when Chinese troops occupied a disputed area in northeast India. In a compromise agreement that ended the war, China retained control of Aksai Chin but withdrew from Arunachal Pradesh. These were the two border areas that it had occupied during the short war.

Political asylum: the right to live in a foreign country granted by the government to people who have been forced to flee their own country because of the threat of persecution

Dalai Lama: the spiritual leader of Tibetan Buddhism. The present Dalai Lama (Tenzin Gyatso) who was born in 1935 is the 14th Dalai Lama in a succession dating back to the 16th century. He established a government-in-exile in India after he fled from Tibet in 1959.

QUESTION

What factors influenced the evolution of democracy in India after independence?

3.5 How did the government respond to domestic crises?

In the first few years after independence, while it was taking steps to establish a firm basis for a stable democracy, the government also faced some significant challenges and domestic crises.

The women affected by partition

An immediate problem facing the new government was the issue of the 'abducted women'. During partition, thousands of women had been killed, raped, abandoned or forcibly married to their abductors. An estimated 75,000 Hindu, Muslim and Sikh women on both sides of the new borders had been forcibly taken from their communities. The Indian and Pakistani governments came to an agreement that the abducted women should be returned to their own communities. Nehru spoke out strongly in support of this, urging respect for the women and promising assistance.

By mid-1948, the Indian authorities had located 12,500 women and restored them to their families. Tragically, however, for many women the restoration programme was yet another ordeal. They awaited an uncertain reception and many were rejected by their own communities. The policy of forcible **repatriation** was abandoned in 1954.

Repatriation: returning people to their country of origin.

ACTIVITY

According to the historian Ramachandra Guha, women were the main victims of partition. When you read about what happened to many women, what does it suggest about prevailing attitudes towards women at the time? Is it justified to criticise the policy of forcible repatriation? How else could the Indian government have dealt with the issue?

The resettlement of refugees

Agriculture, in which more than 75 per cent of India's workforce was involved, was the sector of the economy most seriously affected by partition. The government had to deal urgently with the considerable disruption to existing patterns of farming, irrigation systems, roads and settlements in rural areas. The government also had to find a means of livelihood for the millions of refugees resulting from partition. The problem was most acute in Punjab, where Hindu and Sikh refugees had abandoned 2.7 million hectares (6.67 million acres) of farmland in West Punjab when it became part of Pakistan.

In Punjab, the government began a massive resettlement programme, using the land and villages abandoned by Muslim refugees after their flight into Pakistan. With government loans for seed and equipment, millions of refugees were resettled in villages where they could begin farming again. However, not all the refugees were farmers: there were also artisans, traders and workers. About half a million of them went to Delhi, where they initially lived in makeshift camps set up all over the city, until many of them were allocated land or houses in new townships and satellite towns built to accommodate them outside the city. In time, many of them came to play a dominant role in trade and commerce. By the early 1950s, most refugees in Punjab had found employment and homes.

The situation was more difficult for the over three million refugees who fled into West Bengal from East Pakistan, many of them to the city of Calcutta. Unlike the mass exodus of refugees who flooded into Punjab in the weeks after partition, the flow of refugees into West Bengal went on at a steady pace for years. It was difficult to provide them with work and shelter. Most of them had previously been involved in agriculture, but there was no land available on which to settle them, as there had been in Punjab. Some of them ended up living on the streets of Calcutta, while others formed informal settlements on vacant land, building their own houses and roads. Providing employment for such an influx of refugees proved to be an impossible task.

Threats posed by political extremism

Many of the challenges faced by the new government of India were linked to what historian Ramachandra Guha has called the 'axes of conflict' in Indian society: religion, language, caste, class and gender. Partition did not put an end to religious conflict, and independence did not solve the tensions over language and caste, nor end the inequalities resulting from class and gender.

Two issues in particular – religion and language – resulted at times in acts of political extremism and posed a threat to secular democracy in India. These issues involving religion and language sometimes overlapped with ethnicity as well, making them extremely complex and difficult to resolve.

One form of political extremism which created a crisis for the new government was right-wing Hindu nationalism, especially the threats posed by the Rashtriya Swayamsevak Sangh (RSS), a right-wing Hindu nationalist group. Its members were opposed to the creation of a secular state in India. They were openly anti-Muslim and portrayed Muslims as a hostile and alien element in Indian society. They had a vision of India as a land of, and for, Hindus. Although they claimed to be a cultural rather than a political organisation, they formed uniformed paramilitary cells. At the time of independence, they drew support from students, refugees and the urban lower middle classes. According to historian Ramachandra Guha, Nehru believed that they were responsible for much of the violence that accompanied partition. They were opposed to Gandhi's efforts to reduce communal violence and his conciliatory gestures towards Muslims. They promoted a campaign of hatred against Gandhi, accusing him of being a traitor.

In January 1948, less than six months after independence, Gandhi was assassinated by Nathuram Godse, an active supporter of the RSS, who was incensed by Gandhi's protection of the Muslim community in Delhi. For some months before his death, Gandhi had been in Delhi, trying to stop the communal violence there. The remaining local Muslim population was living in fear in strongholds and refugee camps, after the occupation of their homes by Hindu and Sikh refugees who had fled from Pakistan. Gandhi visited them in their camps, and had meetings with local Hindu, Sikh and Muslim leaders, trying to find a way of ending the violence. He also announced his intention of visiting Pakistan.

Figure 3.11 Mourners surround the body of Mahatma Gandhi as it lies in state after his assassination in January 1948

On 30 January 1948, Nehru broadcast the news of Gandhi's death to the shocked nation. An extract from the broadcast appears in **Source B**.

SOURCE B

The light has gone out of our lives and there is darkness everywhere. I do not know what to tell you and how to say it … A madman has put an end to [Gandhi's] life, for I can only call him mad who did it, and yet there has been enough of poison spread in this country during the past years and months, and this poison has had an effect on people's minds. We must face this poison, we must root out this poison…

We must hold together and all our petty troubles and difficulties and conflicts must be ended in the face of this great disaster. A great disaster is a symbol to us to remember all the big things of life and forget the small things of which we have thought too much. In his death he has reminded us of the big things of life, the living truth, and if we remember that, then it will be well with India.

J. Nehru (1965), Nehru: The First Sixty Years, Volume 2, *London: The Bodley Head, pp. 364–5.*

QUESTION

How effectively did the government respond to domestic crises?

After Gandhi's death, the government banned the RSS and arrested most of its leaders. It blamed them for their support for communalism and violence and generating an atmosphere of hatred towards Gandhi and secularism. However, the ban was lifted in July 1949, after the RSS renounced violence and secrecy, and agreed to restrict itself to cultural rather than political matters.

Hindutva, or the promotion of Hindu values and the creation of a state modelled on Hindu beliefs and culture, re-emerged in the 1980s as a powerful force in Indian politics. The main Hindu nationalist party was the Bharatiya Janata Party (BJP), which had close links to the RSS. The movement was stridently anti-Muslim and triggered communal violence in 1992, when Hindu extremists demolished a mosque in Ayodhya, claiming that it was built on one of the holiest Hindu sites. This action started a wave of violence between Hindus and Muslims in which more than 3,000 people were killed. In the 1998 general election, the Congress Party suffered its worst-ever defeat when the BJP emerged as the largest single party and ruled India as part of a coalition. Although the BJP was defeated by Congress in the 2004 election, it emerged again as the strongest party in the 2014 elections and its leader, Narendra Modi, became prime minister.

Historical debate:
After Gandhi's assassination, there was a reduction in the violence, and support for extremist Hindu nationalism declined. According to historian V.P. Kanitkar, 'right-wing Hindu organisations were discredited, and their political influence gradually diminished'. Public opinion against this kind of violence prevented the formation of other right-wing Hindu nationalist movements. This lasted until the 1980s when Hindu nationalism emerged once again, having, in the words of historians Barbara and Thomas Metcalf, finally been able 'to cast off the stigma of Gandhi's assassination'.

Fact: After his election as India's prime minister in 2014, one of the issues that Modi had to face was a campaign led by Mohan Bhagwat, the leader of the RSS, for the forcible conversion of Muslims and Christians to Hinduism. Crises such as these threatened the tradition of secular democracy in India.

3.6 How did the government react to protest movements?

As well as the crises which the government faced, it also had to cope with various protest movements, most notably those relating to language and ethnicity.

Protests about language

There were many hundreds of languages in India, and part of the colonial legacy was English as the language of government, the law courts and of higher education, as well as that of the middle and upper classes. The most widely used language was Hindi, spoken in the north, but it was used by only half of the people in India. The constitution recognised fourteen major languages, and made Hindi and English the official languages. However, it also allowed the Indian parliament to alter state boundaries, and this opened the way for different language speakers to press for changes to the borders.

The people of southern India were the first to campaign for the state boundaries to be redrawn along linguistic lines, so that their own languages could have official recognition within their states. Gandhi had supported the idea of separate states for different language groups, but the experience of partition made Nehru uneasy about further subdivisions. He had seen the country divided on grounds of religion; he did not want further divisions on grounds of language. Therefore he initially opposed all suggestions about redrawing boundaries. This resulted in violent opposition.

The Teluga-speaking Andhras were the first to campaign for a state of their own. In 1952, **Potti Sriramulu**, one of their leaders, fasted to death in protest against the government's refusal to create a province for Teluga-speakers. There were riots following his death and in 1953, a Teluga-speaking state, Andhra Pradesh, was created out of part of the state of Tamil Nadu, which at the same time was recognised as a Tamil-speaking state.

Potti Sriramulu (1901–52)

He was the Teluga-speaking Andhra leader whose death by fasting led to the creation of the state of Andhra Pradesh and, ultimately, to the redrawing of the map of India along linguistic lines.

The government also appointed a States Reorganisation Commission to investigate the whole issue. As a result of its recommendations, some state boundaries were reorganised in 1956, to create fourteen states on the basis of language. However, this did not satisfy every language group, so further changes were made later. There were violent riots in the state of Bombay over language issues, and in 1960 it was split into Gujarat and Maharashtra, to satisfy the demands of Gujarati and Marathi speakers respectively. Later Punjab too was divided on a linguistic basis, into Punjab and Haryana, with Punjabi and Hindi the official languages respectively.

Another linguistic issue was opposition to the use of Hindi as the sole official language. The constitution had made provision for the phasing out of English as an official language and for Hindi to become the main official language by 1965. Nehru was always aware of the importance of retaining English as an official language, partly as a means of satisfying the non-Hindi-speaking south, and also because of its value as an international language. After his death, Tamil-speakers in southern India protested violently against the use of Hindi, and several protesters burned themselves to death. As a result, English was retained not as an official language but as the main language of inter-regional communication, business and higher education. The continued use of English perpetuated another division in Indian society, between the small educated elite who spoke it and the rest of the population.

Theory of Knowledge

History and language:
There is a saying that 'language is power'. Why do people whose language is not officially recognised feel disempowered? What disadvantages do they suffer? What are the advantages and disadvantages to a country of having a large number of official languages?

Protests relating to ethnicity and separatism

Ethnicity in India was inextricably linked to issues of language and religion. Some of the people involved in struggles for the reorganisation of state boundaries along linguistic lines saw themselves as separate groups with their own history, culture and identity, as well as their own language.

QUESTION

Explain how issues relating to language, religion and ethnicity have sometimes been linked to political extremism in Indian politics.

The Sikhs were one such group, with a distinctive religion as well, and their own language, Punjabi. Before independence, there were about ten million Sikhs in India. Many of them resented the fact that, while Hindus and Muslims had been accommodated in the partition plan, Sikh demands for their own state were ignored. When partition came, millions of them left their farms and villages in West Punjab and went to India as refugees. By 1951, they formed one-third of the population of Indian Punjab, and held prominent positions in politics, business and the army.

The main Sikh political party was the Akali Dal (or 'Army of the Immortals'), which wanted more control for the Sikhs in Punjab. Some even wanted an independent Sikh state, to be called Khalistan, but Nehru was firmly opposed to the creation of any separate state based on religious grounds. In 1955 the Akali Dal held mass demonstrations demanding greater autonomy for the Sikhs. To stop the protests, the government ordered the army to invade the Golden Temple in Amritsar, the Sikhs' most sacred holy place, which the government believed was the centre of the protests.

Although Nehru refused Sikh demands, in 1965, a year after his death, the Indian government agreed to create a smaller Punjab state where Sikhs would be in the majority, after the Sikh leader Sant Fateh Singh threatened to fast to death unless the government recognised Sikh demands. Punjab was split into a new state called Haryana (which was mainly Hindu) and a smaller Punjab, where Sikhs formed slightly more than half of the population. The reorganisation of state borders was ostensibly made along linguistic rather than religious lines, with Hindi and Punjabi as the respective official languages.

Figure 3.12 The Golden Temple at Amritsar is the holiest site in the Sikh religion. There was a major confrontation there between the Indian army and Sikh separatists in 1984, when the government ordered the army to storm the temple

Fact: Political extremism took a heavy toll on India's leaders and particularly on Nehru's family. His daughter, Indira Gandhi (prime minister 1966–77 and 1980–4), was assassinated by her Sikh bodyguards after she had ordered troops to storm the Golden Temple at Amritsar in 1984 to arrest the leader of a militant Sikh separatist group, and in the process nearly 500 were killed. After her death, at least 2,000 Sikhs were murdered in anti-Sikh riots. She was succeeded by her son, Rajiv Gandhi (prime minister 1984–9). In 1991, he too was assassinated by a suicide bomber sympathetic to Sri Lanka's Tamil Tiger separatists and angered by his policies towards them.

However, the position of the Sikhs remained unresolved, and led to future problems for Nehru's successors. In the 1980s, a violent campaign for the creation of a separate Sikh state led to the assassination of the Indian prime minister Indira Gandhi.

Rural protests by tribal communities and peasant farmers

The 'tribal communities' made up about 7 per cent of India's population. Most of them lived in isolation in small communities, mainly in the hills and forest areas, and their culture, traditions and languages differed from those of surrounding communities. Some of them wanted greater autonomy and recognition of their language and culture. One such group were the half a million Naga people in the northeast. The 1950 constitution recognised the Naga Hills as part of the province of Assam, but the Nagas rejected this and declared their independence. When the Indian government refused to recognise it, Naga guerrilla fighters launched a campaign against the Indian army, which was sent in to crush resistance in 1955. After a long struggle, the Naga-speakers of the northeast became the separate state of Nagaland in 1963. However, the dissatisfaction of other 'tribal communities' remained unresolved, and later Indian governments faced violent acts of protest.

QUESTION

To what extent was the government's reaction to protest movements in keeping with democratic principles?

Another form of rural protest was a peasant uprising in the Telangana region of Hyderabad from 1947 to 1950. Large estates were seized from landlords and redistributed among the landless peasants, and the system of forced labour was abolished. The leaders of this rebellion were activists from the Communist Party of India, who hoped it would lead to a nationwide revolution. However, it was suppressed by the police and the army, and thousands were killed in the process.

End of unit activities

1 Go to www.bbc.co.uk/history/british/modern/partition1947_01.shtml and read the article called 'The Hidden Story of Partition and its Legacies' by historian Crispin Bates. Make brief notes on these issues: reasons for the hurried partition of India; the collapse of British control; problems with the new borders; the advantages that India had over Pakistan; unresolved issues from the time of partition.

2 Design a spider diagram to summarise the various challenges, crises and threats that the Indian government faced in the first decade after independence.

3 Read the news report published on the 50th anniversary of Gandhi's death at http://news.bbc.co.uk/2/hi/51468.stm. Evaluate the criticisms of Gandhi from left- and right-wing perspectives; assess whether he deserves the title of 'Father of the Nation'; and comment on the appropriateness of the title of this article ('The Lost Legacy of Mahatma Gandhi').

4 Explain the significance of each of these in the context of modern Indian history: political extremism; ethnic cleansing; repatriation; republic; ethnicity; separatism.

5 Draw up a table to summarise and evaluate the government's responses to the challenges posed by each of these issues. You can use this table as a model:

Issues	What was the underlying nature of the problem?	How successfully did the government deal with the issue?
Religion		
Unity and consolidation		
Political extremism		
Language		
Ethnicity		

The impact of democracy on Indian society

Unit 3

KEY QUESTIONS

- What economic and social policies did India implement?
- To what extent did the people of India benefit from these policies?
- What was the cultural impact of the establishment of democracy?

Overview

- Nehru's government introduced a series of Five-Year Plans to increase agricultural production, promote industrialisation and increase self-sufficiency. An underlying aim of the plans was to provide employment for millions of landless rural workers, by building factories and dams, and promoting labour-intensive small industries.
- With India's low literacy rate of 16 per cent, one of the biggest challenges facing the government was the need to increase the availability of education. Efforts to increase the number of children attending school had some success, but the aim of compulsory education for all was not achieved.
- There were impressive advances at the tertiary education level, and many new universities, institutes of technology and higher research establishments were established.
- Improvements in health care and medical training helped to lower the high death rates caused by disease. However, this resulted in rising population growth rates, which the government tried to control through family planning programmes.
- Social welfare was linked to rural development, and two different schemes were introduced at village level – the Community Development Programme and the Panchayati Raj. Neither succeeded in eradicating poverty and inequality in rural India.
- Major reforms of Hindu civil law improved the legal position of women, giving them greater equality in marriage, ownership of property and inheritance.
- Although the legal position of women improved, it was more difficult to change traditional attitudes and practices. Rural women were still vulnerable to abuse, and their educational opportunities remained limited.
- In 1947, the caste system and 'untouchability' dominated rural society. The 1950 constitution outlawed this practice, and the government

TIMELINE

1950 **Mar:** Indian Planning Commission established.

1951–6 First Five-Year Plan.

1952 **Oct:** Community Development Programme launched.

1955 **May:** Hindu Marriage Act.

1956 **Jun:** Hindu Succession Act.

1956–61 Second Five-Year Plan.

1959 **Oct:** First Panchayati Raj established.

1961–6 Third Five-Year Plan.

introduced programmes to raise the status of the 'scheduled castes and tribes', in an attempt to eradicate the inequality inherent in the system.

- Despite the government's efforts to remove poverty and inequality, they remained features of Indian society. There were wide gulfs between rural and urban areas, men and women, wealthier farmers and landless peasants, and between different regions.
- Culture in post-independence India was a combination of traditional and modern; the film industry flourished; radio reached all parts of the population; traditional music and dance thrived; and a free press was the main source of information and news to a wide audience.

Figure 3.13 Women keen to vote at the 1952 parliamentary elections receive their ballot papers at one of the booths in outer New Delhi

3.7 What economic and social policies did India implement?

The economic and social policies that followed after independence attempted to address some of the immense challenges facing the country. These included poverty, unemployment, landlessness and an unequal distribution of resources. Literacy levels and life expectancy were low, and there was discrimination based on gender and caste. The new government introduced policies to promote economic growth, extend education, improve health services, provide social welfare, improve the position of women and end the caste system. Underlying all of these was the desire to create a more equitable society and distribution of wealth.

Policies to promote economic growth

Nehru admired Stalin's achievement of rapid industrial growth in the Soviet Union, and he believed that a similar system of state involvement in the economy and centralised planning was essential for India's economic development. However, unlike the Soviet Union, India favoured a mixed economy, with some central planning, but also a large private sector outside direct government control. Development projects included state, private and joint ventures.

In 1950 the government set up the Indian Planning Commission, chaired by Nehru, to formulate plans to promote economic development and improve living standards. It was given wide powers and massive funding to implement a series of Five-Year Plans. The first Five-Year Plan (1951–6) focused on increasing agricultural production; the Second Five-Year Plan (1956–61) emphasised large-scale industrial development; and the Third Five-Year Plan (1961–6) aimed to make India self-sufficient in basic foodstuffs, increase industrial output and decrease dependence on imports. An underlying aim behind all three plans was to reduce unemployment.

The Second Five-Year Plan focused more specifically on the issue of unemployment. In 1950, only 12 per cent of India's workforce was employed in industry. Industrialisation, especially the building of factories and dams, was seen as the best way to reduce rural unemployment and population pressure on the land. Three giant steel mills were built, with the aid of foreign funding, as well as several large dams and irrigation schemes. In addition to heavy industry, labour-intensive small industries and labour-absorbing rural projects were set up as a means of providing employment. Labour legislation during this period recognised **collective bargaining** and gave workers the right to form trade unions and to strike. It also made provision for security of employment and for health and accident insurance.

The Five-Year Plans achieved a great deal. Agricultural production grew by 25 per cent during the first five years and a further 20 per cent in the second, and industrial production more than doubled between 1948 and 1964. Although much of the industrialisation was financed from abroad, Nehru was careful to limit foreign influence and avoid the dangers of **neo-colonialism** through high tariff barriers and government control of key industries.

The focus of economic policy from the late 1960s shifted from industry to agriculture in an attempt to make India self-sufficient in food production. This was the 'Green Revolution', which used high-yielding seed varieties, irrigation schemes and chemical fertilisers to increase agricultural output by impressive amounts. However, it intensified regional inequalities as well as social divisions. Certain regions were not suited to the new methods of agriculture, and wealthier farmers, with access to capital, larger farms and entrepreneurial skills, were the ones who benefitted.

Government controls over the economy were relaxed in the 1980s, as India sought to become part of the world capitalist system. Despite initial problems, the Indian economy has grown at an exponential rate since the 1990s, and India is fast becoming one of the key players in the world economy.

Policies to extend education

One of the biggest challenges facing the new government was the state of education. At the time of independence, only 16 per cent of the total population was literate.

Fact: Although industrial development during the Nehru period provided new employment opportunities in construction industries, steelworks and the building of infrastructure, the most important industries remained those based on agricultural raw materials, such as cotton, jute and tea. But, as India became more industrialised, new jobs became available in manufacturing industries, making products such as vehicles, railway carriages, machinery and electronic goods.

Fact: Although India has ten cities with more than three million inhabitants each, including Mumbai (twelve million) and Delhi (eleven million), the Indian population remains largely rural-based. According to the 2011 census, about 70 per cent of people still lived in rural areas.

Collective bargaining: a recognised system of negotiation between trade unions and their employers over working conditions and wages.

Neo-colonialism: literally, a new form of colonialism. It refers to the economic control that industrialised countries and international companies have over developing countries. The term was first used by the Ghanaian leader Kwame Nkrumah to refer to Africa's continuing economic dependence on Europe.

Fact: India is referred to as one of the BRICS countries, an acronym that covers the emerging economies of Brazil, Russia, India, China and South Africa. Some economists believe that these nations have the potential to form a powerful economic bloc to rival the current dominant economic powers by the middle of the 21st century.

The situation was worst in rural areas where on average only 6 per cent of people were literate, very few of them women. Many girls did not attend school at all. Nehru supported the extension of education because he believed that a literate electorate was essential for the survival of democracy. He also saw education as the means to bring about economic and social transformation.

The constitution committed the government to providing free and compulsory education for all children up to the age of fourteen, and set 1961 as the target date for this to be achieved, but this target was later extended many times.

The government allocated large sums of money for the extension of education at primary, secondary and technical level, and during Nehru's term of office there were impressive achievements. Between 1951 and 1961, the number of boys attending primary school doubled, and the number of girls trebled. There was even better progress in the numbers attending secondary school, and thousands of new schools were built.

There were impressive advances in the fields of tertiary and technical education. By 1964, forty-one new universities had been established, in which the number of female students enrolled rose to 22 per cent of the total. These included technical universities and higher research establishments, in which there was an emphasis on science and technology to sustain the economic policies of industrialisation and modernisation. However, from the late 1950s onwards there was a **brain drain** of scientists and other highly skilled personnel. Apart from the attraction of better pay and working conditions, this was partly due to the bureaucratic and hierarchical organisation of the institutes.

Brain drain: the loss of skilled and educated workers who migrate to countries where working conditions and salaries are better. This is a particular problem for developing countries, which spend scarce resources on education.

Policies to improve health services

In 1950, India had a population of 350 million, with an average life expectancy of thirty-two years. Millions of people died each year as a result of epidemics of smallpox, plague, cholera and malaria. Most towns had no modern sanitation, and only the wealthier parts of the big cities did. Health services were poor: in 1951, there were only 18,000 doctors and 113,000 hospital beds in the whole of India, and these were mainly in the cities. Polluted water, overcrowding, poverty and a lack of medicines to combat infection added to the problems.

At the same time, India had a high population growth rate. This was linked to the incidence of disease, as is made clear by the historian Godfrey Hodgson in **Source A**.

Theory of Knowledge

History, science and ethics: Read **Source A**. What evidence is there in this interview of the clash between science and traditional beliefs and attitudes in developing countries? How can governments in this type of situation solve the problem of high population growth rates? How do such questions concerning government policy, science and traditional beliefs highlight the issue of moral relativism?

SOURCE A

In Tegu Raghuvir's village in Uttar Pradesh, northern India, there was no hospital and no doctor. 'We used to go running to fetch a herbalist, but by the time we got back the patient would be dead,' he recalls. 'Smallpox, measles, cholera, plague, influenza – these were fatal diseases.' As many babies and children died, people tried to have large families, partly to help supplement the family income. Only six of Tegu Raghuvir's nine children survived. 'Some people had this fear that, "If I just have this one child, and if he dies, then my family will be finished". And some people kept having daughters, hoping they would have a son.'

G. Hodgson (1996), People's Century, Volume 2, *London: BBC Books, p. 137.*

The government allocated funding to improve health services, train more doctors and nurses and build hospitals and clinics. As a result, the number of hospital beds increased by 165 per cent during the Nehru period. With the help of the World Health Organization, the government also launched large-scale immunisation campaigns to tackle the spread of disease. Death rates began to decline as a result, but birth rates remained high, so population growth began to rise, putting more pressure on land and resources.

The government introduced family planning programmes to halt the rapid population growth, which threatened to undermine the progress that was being made in increasing food production and raising living standards. A government propaganda campaign encouraged people to have smaller families. However, this had limited success, in a country with high rates of illiteracy and where large families were a tradition. By the time Nehru died, the population had risen to nearly 500 million. Later Indian governments tried to slow down population growth by offering incentives for people to have smaller families and providing voluntary sterilisation programmes.

Fact: By 2014, India's population had tripled since the time of independence to nearly 1.26 billion people, the largest in the world after China. Population analysts predict that, by the middle of this century, India will have overtaken China, which has a lower population growth rate because of its strict 'one child per family' policy.

QUESTION

Explain how high rates of population growth affected plans for economic and social transformation.

Policies to provide social welfare

One of Nehru's aims was to create a welfare state, in order to raise the standard of living of millions, but he believed that improvements in social welfare could only be achieved through economic development. Economic development and social welfare were therefore closely linked. The government launched two major programmes in an attempt to lay the foundations of a welfare state at village level. The underlying aim was to improve the quality of life for the people of rural India, and at the same time promote rural development.

On the anniversary of Gandhi's birthday, on 2 October 1952, Nehru launched the first of these, the Community Development Programme. Its aims were to

Figure 3.14 The construction of this model fishing village, located south of Trivandrum, was sponsored by the Indian government in the mid-1950s

promote improvements in all aspects of rural life, such as agricultural methods, communications, education and health. Trained workers would advise farmers, but the emphasis was on self-help and self-reliance through popular participation at village level. Although it was initially received with enthusiasm and brought about some improvements, it did not achieve one of its fundamental goals, namely that of encouraging self-help. Instead it increased people's expectations of the government and the reliance of villagers on government officials, according to historian Bipan Chandra.

In 1959, a system of increased self-government in villages was introduced. This was called Panchayati Raj, and it was an experiment in democracy at grassroots level. Villagers would elect village councils to run the affairs of their village. These councils would draw up development plans for their area and allocate government funds for local projects in each community. In this way, villagers would be able to participate in making decisions and implementing development programmes. However, the system did not always work effectively because local councils came to be dominated by richer peasants and capitalist farmers, who directed the funds to benefit their own farms, while the poorer and landless peasants remained powerless. In addition, many state governments were not enthusiastic about the system, and the success of rural reform relied on state involvement.

QUESTION

How did the government try to transform India using a combination of massive industrial projects and simple village-based projects?

Policies to improve the position of women

Traditionally, Indian women in general had a subservient role in society. Male domination was the norm: a man could marry several wives, but a woman had no right to ask for a divorce. Daughters received a **dowry** when they married, but were excluded from any right of inheritance. As a result, women were always dependent on men and had no rights of their own. In rural areas, a woman moved into the home of her husband's family, where she was often subjected to oppression and control. Few women had access to education: in 1951 fewer than 8 per cent of women were literate, compared to 25 per cent of men.

Dowry: the money or property brought by a bride to her husband at the time of her marriage. An old tradition in South Asia, the dowry system was outlawed as it was often a reason for the abuse of women by their in-laws; but efforts to eliminate it altogether have proved unsuccessful.

After independence there were dramatic changes in the status of women. This owed much to Gandhi and Nehru, who had encouraged women's participation in the struggle for independence. Women were included among the first ministers and provincial governors. In the 1950 constitution, women were granted complete equality with men and the right to vote. Even so, Nehru, who was a strong supporter of advancing women's rights, knew that further measures were necessary to make equality a reality. In 1950 he and other reformists introduced the Hindu Code Bill to parliament, outlining reforms to the laws governing aspects such as marriage, divorce, inheritance and property rights. However, there was strong opposition from Hindu traditionalists, such as the BJS and other communalist groups, and also from conservative members of Congress, including influential leaders like Patel (home affairs minister and Nehru's deputy). Faced with this opposition, Nehru withdrew the bill, hoping to mobilise more support for reform. After Patel's death in 1950, Nehru was able to proceed with his reforms more easily. New legislation in the 1950s reformed Hindu law to improve the position of women in Indian society.

Historical debate: Muslim marriages continued to be governed by traditional Islamic law. The government did not want to be accused of tampering with the laws and traditions of a minority. As historians Hermann Kulke and Dietmar Rothermund note in *A History of India* (2004), critics pointed out that this exclusion was incompatible with the idea of a secular state in which a civil code should apply equally to all citizens, regardless of their religious affiliation.

The bill was later reintroduced and passed as a series of separate laws. The two most significant were the Hindu Succession Act, which gave women equal rights with men in the inheritance and ownership of property; and the Hindu Marriage Act, which

Figure 3.15 Jawaharlal Nehru, with his sister Vijaya Lakshmi Pandit and his daughter Indira Gandhi, being welcomed by the mayor of New York, William O'Dwyer at City Hall, 17 October, 1949

abolished **polygyny**, provided for maintenance for a wife if her husband divorced her, and gave women the right to sue for divorce. Another law gave women the right to adopt children. A further reform came in 1961, when the dowry system was outlawed. Nehru later stated that he considered his reform of Hindu law to improve the position of women to be his greatest achievement in Indian politics.

Polygyny: the practice of having more than one wife, which is accepted in some religions and traditions. Polyandry, where a wife has more than one husband, though less common, also exists in some societies. Polygamy is the generic term describing having more than one wife OR husband.

The extension of legal rights to Hindu women was an important step but, in practice, especially in rural areas, it was very difficult to change traditional attitudes. There was an improvement in the number of girls attending school, although educational opportunities for girls in rural areas lagged far behind those for boys. Even decades later, the literacy rate for women in India was significantly lower than that for men. However, women certainly became more active politically. By the time of the second general election in 1957, 94 per cent of women were registered as voters, although only about half of them actually exercised their right to vote: the percentage of women voting in the 1962 election was under 47 per cent.

Policies to protect the rights of minorities

The Indian government wanted to end the discrimination associated with the caste system as part of its plan to promote equality and civil rights. The caste system in India originated about 2,500 years ago. It divided society into a hierarchy of levels, called castes – high caste and low caste, 'touchable' and 'untouchable'. It is usually associated with Hindu tradition but, according to historian Mridula Mukherjee, it was prevalent among Sikhs, Christians and Muslims too, providing 'legitimation for the unequal access to resources, and to the exploitation and oppression of lower castes'.

B.R. Ambedkar (1891–1956)

He was a leading campaigner for the rights of Dalits ('Untouchables') and supported the principle of reserved seats in parliament for them. He served as law minister in the first government, and played a leading role in drawing up India's constitution. He was largely responsible for drawing up the Hindu Code Bill, and he resigned when the government withdrew it in the face of heated opposition.

The lowest caste, the 'Untouchables', were subjected to many forms of discrimination. They could not own land, enter temples or use common resources such as village wells or roads. They performed all the menial work, such as carrying water, tanning leather and working the land, usually as sharecroppers. The number of people regarded as 'untouchable' varied from area to area, with the highest numbers in the north, but, before independence, it probably included between 15 per cent and 20 per cent of the total population of India. Although there is evidence that some aspects of the system were beginning to change in urban areas, there were still social pressures, such as exclusion from hotels and restaurants. Some parts of India even instituted new restrictions in the 1930s, such as prohibiting literacy, and banning the use of certain clothing items, such as umbrellas, by 'Untouchables'. Gandhi had spoken out strongly on the issue of 'untouchability', and several movements were formed to fight the various forms of discrimination against the 'depressed classes', as they were termed in British India. **B.R. Ambedkar** emerged as their most respected leader. At the time of independence in 1947, the caste system still dominated rural society, and 'untouchability' remained a prominent feature.

Congress leaders who supported modernisation opposed the caste system as a source of division in Indian society. According to Nehru's biographer, Tariq Ali, Nehru saw it as an outdated practice. But there were others who held conservative views and saw the system as part of a tradition that should not be changed. The 1950 constitution gave equal rights to all, regardless of religion, race, gender, language or caste, and it specifically stated that 'untouchability' was abolished and its practice forbidden. It also reserved 20 per cent of the seats in parliament and in the state assemblies for the former 'Untouchables' and the forest tribes, another minority group. They were listed in a special schedule in the constitution, and became known from then on as the 'scheduled castes and scheduled tribes'.

Figure 3.16 In this 1946 photograph, a high-caste Hindu farm-owner fastidiously drops wrapped wages into the hands of his lowly Sudra caste workers, thus avoiding 'pollution'

The way lay open for the government to introduce reforms through a programme of social legislation. As well as having equality in law and as voters, the scheduled castes were now free to use the same shops, schools and places of worship as any other citizen. Special funding was set aside in the Five-Year Plans to improve their position by, for example, providing wells for them in villages where fellow villagers still refused to share water with them. They were also given special land allotments, as well as access to housing, health care and legal aid. To overcome their low rate of literacy, they were exempt from paying school fees, and given special access to hostel accommodation and scholarships. However, by the early 1960s their literacy rate was still only a third of the average for India as a whole.

In 1955, the practice of treating people as 'Untouchables' became a criminal offence, which could result in a fine or prison sentence. However, in reality, few people were prosecuted under this law and the scheduled castes were still frequently prevented from participating in ordinary community life.

Theory of Knowledge

History and ethics:
The policy of the Indian government towards the scheduled castes (or Dalits, as they prefer to be called) is a form of 'affirmative action'. What does this mean? How can a policy of affirmative action be justified? Does it conflict with the principle of equal opportunity?

KEY CONCEPTS ACTIVITY

Significance: Explain the significance of the caste system in India and the efforts to end it.

Policies to create a more equitable distribution of wealth

An important objective of all the Five-Year Plans, both during Nehru's time and afterwards, was the eradication of poverty and the improvement of living standards. According to historian Aditya Mukherjee, this was a legacy of the nationalist movement, which had always promoted equity and pro-poor policies. The Five-Year Plans emphasised growth with equity, and assumed that higher growth would make greater equity possible. In this way the emphasis on economic growth in the Five-Year Plans was believed to be the best means of solving the problem of poverty. Land reform was also a key factor, as well as greater access to education and health care, and eliminating the inequalities resulting from gender and caste.

Land reform measures freed most of the peasants from the domination of the major landholders. Legislation reduced the amount of land held by the *zamindari* (the landowners of large estates), who were often absentee landlords. However, it was usually the wealthier peasants who benefited most from these reforms. The position of poor peasants, such as sub-tenants and those who were landless, did not really change. Historians suggest that Congress did not want to alienate the richer peasants who were key supporters of the party. Similarly, it was the wealthier peasants who benefitted from rural development projects, such as the Panchayati Raj, by ensuring their election to the local councils and in this way dominating decision-making and the allocation of funding. In *A Concise History of Modern India* (2006), Barbara and Thomas Metcalf suggest that, because of these factors, the rural development schemes of the Nehru government did little to eradicate inequality or reduce poverty among the millions of landless villagers in India.

3.8 To what extent did the people of India benefit from these policies?

The economic and social policies resulted in substantial improvements in life expectancy, living standards and literacy rates for many Indians.

Fact: This table shows some of the improvements in living standards in the fifty years after independence. The number of people living below the poverty line decreased substantially, from 56 per cent in 1970 to 36 per cent in the 1990s.

	1950–1	1990s
Life expectancy	32 years	63 years
Literacy rate	16%	62%
Infant mortality	146 per 1,000	71 per 1,000

Historical debate:
In *India after Independence* (2000), historian Bipan Chandra suggests that there was a decline in educational standards because, apart from the technology sector, the education system was not reformed – the content of education remained largely unchanged from the colonial period. Pavan Varma, the director of the Nehru Institute in London, claims that the emphasis on institutes of higher learning was at the expense of primary and secondary education, resulting in substantial numbers of highly skilled engineers, scientists and technologists, but also the world's largest number of children not attending school. He concedes, however, that insufficient resources made it impossible to eradicate illiteracy and to invest in institutions of higher learning simultaneously.

Unemployment and regional inequality

However, although the Five-Year Plans increased agricultural and industrial production, and provided employment to more people in factories and workshops, the problem of unemployment remained critical. This was especially so for millions of landless peasants and for the increasing numbers of jobless people living in the streets, slums or informal settlements of large cities like Calcutta and Bombay.

Another problem was regional inequality. There were vast differences between the wealthier areas, such as Bombay and Punjab, and the poorer regions. Although the government recognised this and implemented plans to uplift the poorer areas, regional inequality remained a key feature of the economy. For example, there were huge regional differences in female literacy rates between the better-developed states such as Kerala, and the least developed such as Rajasthan, where even in the 1990s more than 80 per cent of girls in the state had never attended school.

Education

Despite impressive advances in the extension of primary and secondary schooling, the provision of schooling could not keep pace with the population growth, and by the mid-1960s only 61 per cent of all children, and 43 per cent of girls, were attending primary school. Although there were enough schools in the large cities, in some rural areas there were no schools at all and, even where they existed, the drop-out rates, especially among girls, were high. Rural schools and those in small towns lacked equipment and facilities, and 40 per cent of them had only one teacher to cope with several age groups at once. As a result, the literacy rate had risen to only 24 per cent by the time of Nehru's death in 1964.

Critics also believed that, although the government made progress in increasing the number of students attending school, there was insufficient reform of the education system as a whole. Therefore education failed to help raise the status of the majority of the population, namely the urban poor and those in rural areas.

The position of minorities

Another factor that contributed to continuing inequality was the caste system. Although the constitution put an end to discrimination and made provision to raise the status of the scheduled castes and scheduled tribes, there was no sustained campaign against the caste system. In *India after Independence* (2000), historian Bipan Chandra observes that, although discrimination based on caste was officially outlawed, the government made insufficient effort to eradicate the whole concept of the caste system as an ideology. The new laws and the special aid did not abolish social disadvantages and discrimination, and caste oppression was still common in rural areas, where acts of brutal violence against scheduled castes sometimes occurred. In some cases these attacks occurred partly because other people resented the preferential treatment the Dalits received as a result of government policies. In spite of government policies, progress in removing discrimination based on the caste system was slow.

The position of women

Although the legal position of women had improved with the passing of the Hindu Marriage Act and the Hindu Succession Act, it was very difficult to change traditional attitudes, especially in rural areas. For example, women were often reluctant to claim the rights of inheritance that the new laws gave them. And, although it had been officially outlawed, the dowry system continued. In *A Concise History of Modern India*, Barbara and Thomas Metcalf suggest that the new laws did little to change the position of women, because the lack of resources available to them and the constraints of traditional rural society made their application unlikely.

There was a significant improvement during the Nehru years in the number of girls attending school, but most of these improvements were in urban areas, and educational opportunities for girls in rural areas lagged far behind those for boys. Even decades later, the female literacy rate for India as a whole lagged far behind that for males.

In later decades, women's groups took up issues of violence against women, such as dowry deaths. These were the deaths of women who were tortured and murdered, or driven to suicide, when their husbands or in-laws tried to force their families to pay increased dowries. Other areas of concern to women's groups were attitudes towards rape and the declining proportion of females in the Indian population. This latter situation was linked to a 10 per cent higher infant mortality rate for girls than for boys, leading to strong suspicions of female infanticide, and the termination of pregnancies involving female babies.

In **Source B**, Robert Stern comments on the position of women in India forty years after the legal reforms were introduced:

SOURCE B

The position of Indian women in general still compares unfavourably with the condition of Indian men in general. The female literacy rate is little more than half the male rate, and in the countryside less than 20% of girls and women are literate. In secondary schools and universities, there are about two males enrolled for every female. Outside some areas of public sector employment, the proportion of women in the paid workforce has been declining over the years. This is the effect of a variety of causes. But among them, certainly, is the upward mobility of an increasing number of families, and their acceptance of the middle classes' usual preferences for women who are kept in housebound respectability and dependence on their men.

R.W. Stern (1993), Changing India, *Cambridge: Cambridge University Press, p. 44.*

KEY CONCEPTS ACTIVITY

Change and Continuity:
Explain how democracy brought both change and continuity for women in India.

Fact: Despite the efforts of the government, the courts and women's groups, dowry deaths have continued. In 2006, the Indian National Crime Records Bureau reported more than 7,000 dowry death cases in that year alone.

The distribution of wealth

Improvements resulting from economic and social policies were often offset by high population growth rates. As a result, efforts at land reform and rural development schemes had limited success in reducing inequality or poverty among the millions of landless villagers. However, although there were shortcomings in the attempts to bring about a more equitable distribution of wealth and resources, historians emphasise the importance of remembering that India's considerable achievements were made within a democratic framework. This was in marked contrast to the force used in totalitarian states such as the Soviet Union and China. In the words of historian Aditya Mukherjee: 'While persisting poverty has been the most important failure in India's post-independence development, the survival of the democratic structure has been its grandest success,' (in *India after Independence: 1947–2000*, 2000, p. 470).

ACTIVITY

Draw up a table to summarise the social and economic challenges facing India after independence, the policies the government implemented to address them and how successful these were. Use the example as a model.

Economic and social issues	What were the challenges?	What policies were implemented?	How successful were they?
Economic growth			
Education			
Health			
Social welfare			
Position of women			
Position of minorities			
Distribution of wealth			

3.9 What was the cultural impact of the establishment of democracy?

Culture in the new Indian democracy was a combination of modern and traditional. An example of the ultra-modern was Chandigarh, the newly built capital for the province of Punjab, which was built to replace the old capital, Lahore, which had been lost to Pakistan in the partition. Designed by the French architect Le Corbusier, it was a sprawling, starkly modernist city. Critics claimed that it disregarded India's architectural heritage and the realities of Indian life. But Barbara and Thomas Metcalf claim that this was precisely what Nehru intended: he wanted to 'use Le Corbusier's internationalist modernism as the vehicle for the creation of an India fit for the second half of the twentieth century' (*A Concise History of Modern India*, 2006, p. 237).

An important aspect of popular culture was the film industry, based in Bombay. Known as 'Bollywood', it later produced about a quarter of all films produced globally, making India the largest film-producing nation in the world. Commercial films were accessible to a wide audience and many of them were escapist romances. But others carried more serious messages, such as the ideals of nationalism, where stars placed 'nation' before 'self', or stressed the importance of tolerance and coexistence. Some films explored the challenges of modern Indian life, such as the exposure of rural peasants to the dangers of city life, or the reality of life for millions of poor living in the sprawling slums of the big cities. Stern comments that Indian films 'provide the foundation for an extraordinarily powerful and pervasive popular culture that is distinctly Indian' (Stern, *Changing India*, 1993, p. 13). Some films had a more explicit religious message and explored themes and

Figure 3.17 The High Court of Punjab and Haryana with its monumental buildings and bold colours is typical of the architectural style of Chandigarh

events from Hindu tradition. Art, posters and wallpapers displaying Hindu themes and characters also became immensely popular.

Stern also comments that Indian culture had not been 'colonized from abroad' and that, although there might be some features borrowed from Europe or the West, it remained distinctly Indian. Indian forms of music – folk, popular and classical – as well as Indian dance remained extremely popular.

Although Radio India only had six stations in 1947, the number grew substantially so that within a few decades they reached virtually 100 per cent of the population. After 1959, India built one of the largest television networks in the world.

Figure 3.18 A newspaper seller in Delhi, offering a range of daily newspapers. According to a 2009 BBC report, the World Association of Newspapers estimated that 109 million newspapers circulated daily in India

As literacy rates increased, newspapers became important sources of information for many people, and by the 1990s there were about 1,600 daily newspapers, some English, some Hindi, and many in local languages. Although freedom of the press was not specifically mentioned in the Indian constitution, freedom of speech and expression were, and it was

QUESTION

What was the cultural impact of the establishment of democracy in India?

KEY CONCEPTS ACTIVITY

Change and Continuity: Explain whether change or continuity was the key feature of Indian cultural life after independence.

generally accepted that freedom of the press was part of this and subject to the same restrictions, such as defamation and the security of the state. Later rulings by the Supreme Court ruled that press censorship posed restrictions on the right to freedom of speech and expression. Thus the press in India was substantially free although later legislation provided 'reasonable' censorship in times of emergency if it was in the public interest.

End of unit activities

1 Design a spider diagram to illustrate the economic and social problems arising from partition and how the government tackled them.

2 Divide into two groups: one group should work out an argument to support and the other group an argument to oppose the following statement: 'Considering the prevailing traditions and attitudes, Nehru's government did all that was possible at the time to improve the position of women in India.'

3 How successfully did later Indian governments tackle the issues of controlling population growth, eradicating illiteracy and promoting rural development?

4 The historian Bipan Chandra suggests that the shortcomings of the Nehru government were its failures to reform the education system, to eradicate communalism, and to implement meaningful land reform. Divide into two groups: one group should work out an argument in support of Chandra's view, and the other group an argument to oppose it.

5 **Either** find out about and make brief notes on the position of the Dalits in Indian society and politics since Nehru's time **or** find out what you can about the life of B.R. Ambedkar – the discrimination he faced as an 'Untouchable'; his distinguished academic career; his contribution to democracy in India; and his disillusion with the Congress Party and with Hinduism.

End of chapter activities

Paper 1 exam practice

Comprehension

What is the message conveyed by **Source A** about the impact of partition on India? [2 marks]

SOURCE A

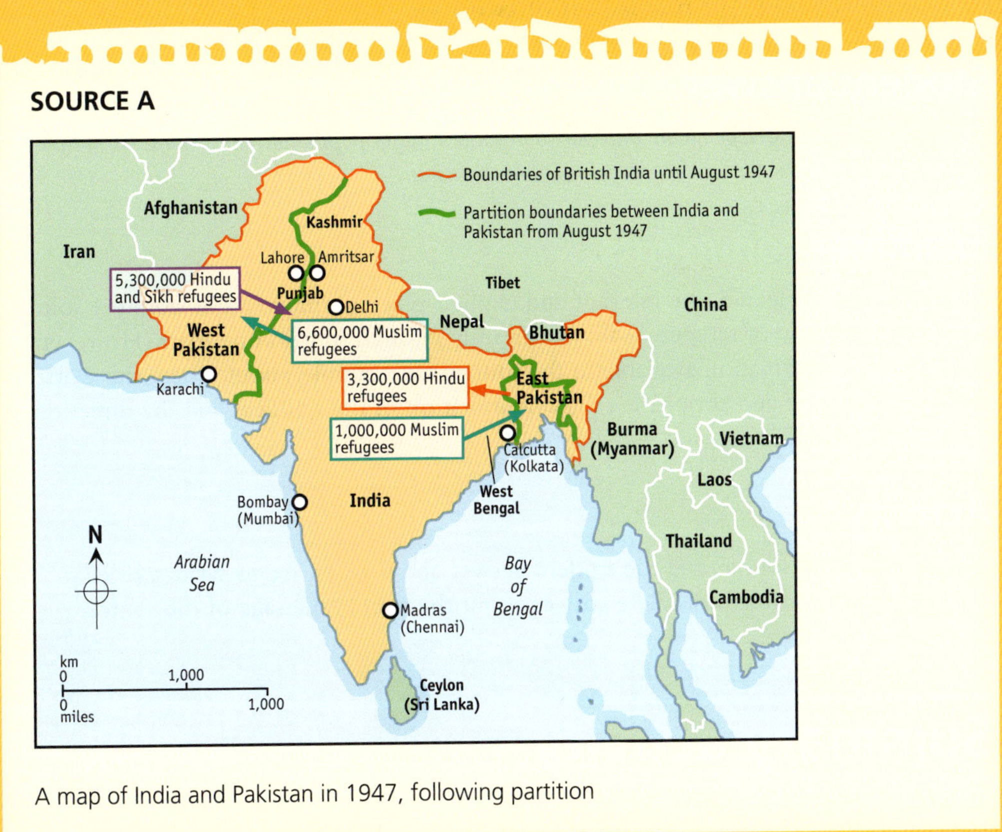

A map of India and Pakistan in 1947, following partition

Skill

Comprehension of the message of a source.

Examiner's tips

Comprehension questions are the most straightforward questions you will face in Paper 1 – they simply require you to understand the message presented by a source **and** to extract one or two relevant points that relate to the particular question and show/explain your understanding.

As only two marks are available for this question, make sure you don't waste valuable exam time that should be spent on the higher-scoring questions by writing a long answer here. All that's needed are just a couple of short sentences, giving the necessary information to show you've understood the main message of the source. Basically, try to give an overall view of the source, along with a couple of pieces of information to illustrate your points.

Common mistakes

When asked to show your comprehension/understanding of a particular source, make sure you don't just paraphrase or describe the source. What's needed are a couple of sentences that briefly point out the view/message of the source.

Simplified mark scheme

For each point/item of **relevant/correct understanding/information** identified, award one mark – up to a **maximum of two marks**.

Student answer

Source A shows that independence and partition caused major population movements as millions of refugees fled across the borders between India and Pakistan.

Examiner comments

The student has selected one relevant and explicit piece of information from the source, describing the flow of refugees – this is certainly enough to gain one mark. However, there is more information available in the source; for example, about where the worst affected areas were and about the religious affiliation of the refugees and the direction in which they were fleeing.

Activity

Look again at the source, and the student answer above. Now try to write a brief sentence to give a more complete answer about the overall message of the source.

Summary activity

Copy these three diagrams and, using the information in this chapter, make brief point form notes under each heading.

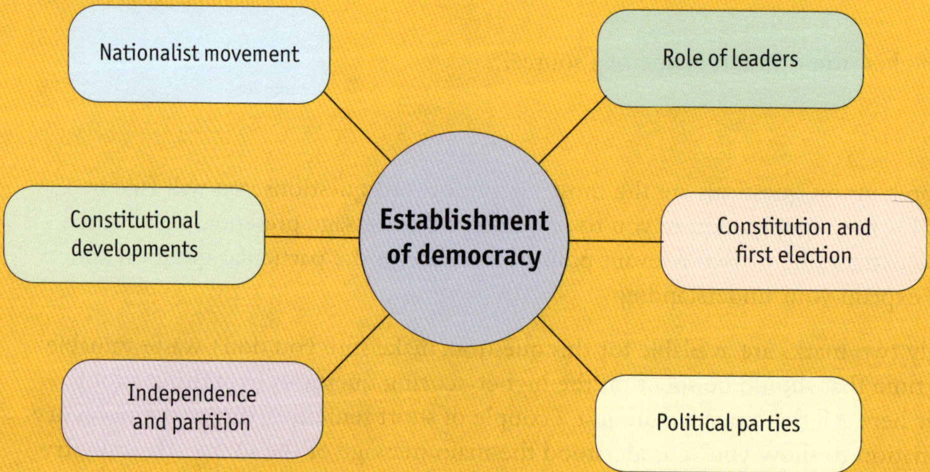

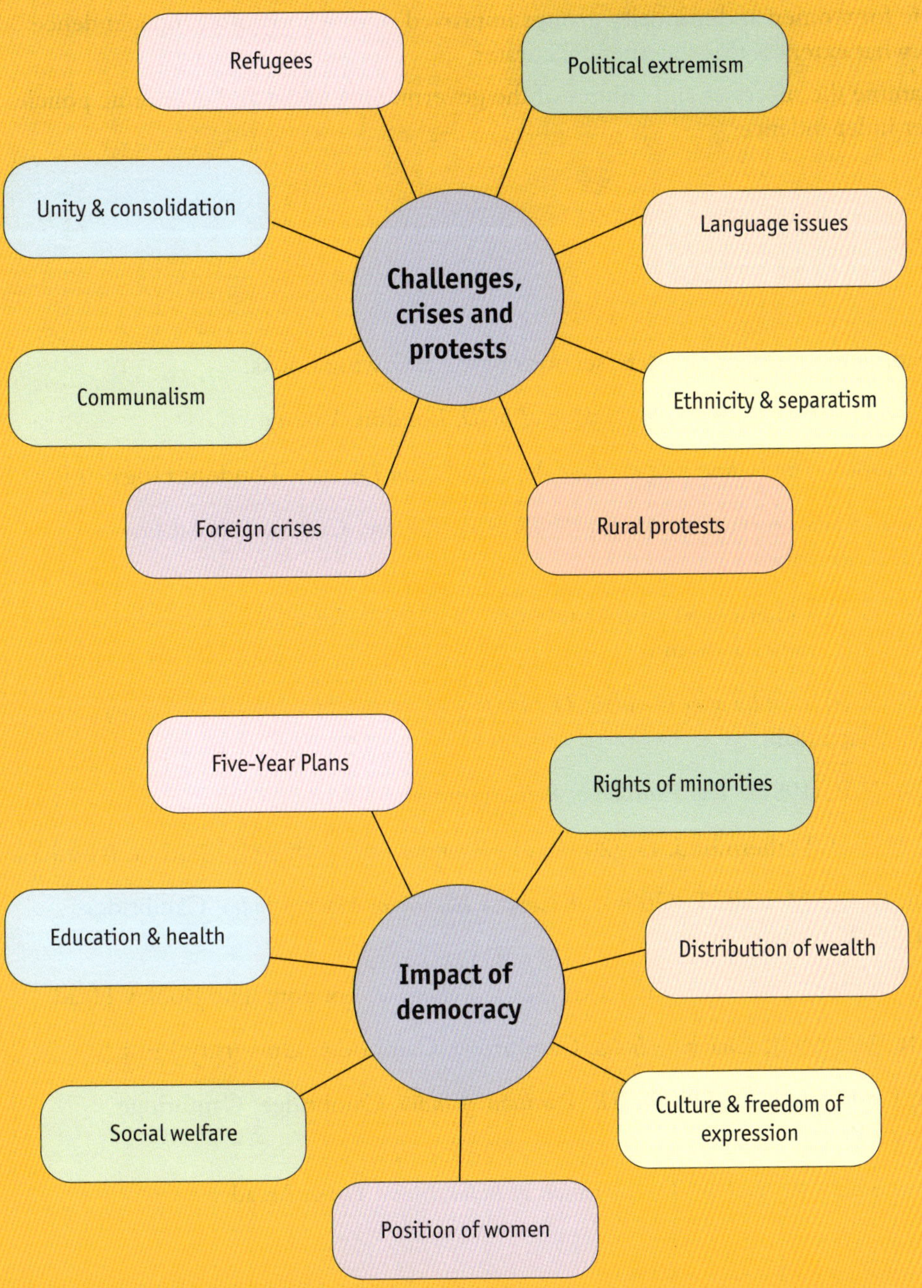

Paper 2 practice questions

1 Examine the factors that led to the independence and partition of India in 1947.
2 Evaluate the achievements of Nehru's government in its efforts to establish a secular, democratic republic in India.
3 Examine the challenges facing the government of newly independent India in 1947.
4 Examine the threats to democracy posed by political extremism and communalism.

3

5 'Life for women and minority groups improved significantly after independence.' To what extent is this statement accurate?

6 Examine the successes and failures of the government's social and economic policies after independence.

Further reading

Try reading the relevant chapters/sections of the following books:

Akbar, M.J. (1988), *Nehru: The Making of India*, London: Viking.

Ali, T. (1985), *The Nehrus and the Gandhis: An Indian Dynasty*, London: Hogarth Press.

Bose, S. and Jalal, A. (1998), *Modern South Asia: History, Culture, Political Economy*, London: Routledge.

Chandra, B., Mukherjee, M. and Mukherjee, A. (2000), *India after Independence: 1947–2000*, London: Penguin.

Guha, R. (2007), *India after Gandhi: The History of the World's Largest Democracy*, London: Macmillan.

Kanitkar, V.P. (1987), *The Partition of India*, London: Wayland.

Kulke, H. and Rothermund, D. (2004), *A History of India*, 4th edn, London: Routledge.

Metcalf, B. and Metcalf, T. (2006), *A Concise History of Modern India*, Cambridge: Cambridge University Press.

Nehru, J. (1965), *Nehru: the First Sixty Years, Volume 2*, London: The Bodley Head.

Stern, R.W. (1993), *Changing India*, Cambridge: Cambridge University Press.

Talbot, I. and Singh, G. (2009), *The Partition of India*, Cambridge: Cambridge University Press.

Tharoor, S. (2004), *Nehru: The Invention of India*, New York: Arcade.

USA 4

The emergence of democracy in the USA at key points in its history — Unit 1

KEY QUESTIONS

- What is the historical background of the USA up to 1890?
- How was the US constitution and its electoral system devised?
- How significant was the role of key leaders?
- How did democracy function?

Overview

- The USA faced social and political change in the late 19th and early 20th century; post-war social anxiety in the 1920s; the challenge of economic and social reform in the 1930s; and dealt with challenges in 1960s during a time of post-war prosperity.
- The US constitution provides the framework of government. Under it, power is divided into three main branches: the Executive (headed by the president), the Legislature/Congress (comprising the Senate and the House of Representatives) and the Judiciary (headed by the Supreme Court).
- The USA differs from other democracies in several ways, including the role of its political parties. Its two main parties are the Republicans and the Democrats; third parties have only occasionally gained significant support.
- A brief history of the USA from the time of the Civil War up to 1890 shows that as industrialisation and westward expansion both advanced rapidly in the period between 1870 and 1890, nonetheless some parts of the country were left behind.
- Politicians and thinkers began to look for ways of dealing with the problems caused by this transformation and the age of progressivism arrived.
- The progressive presidencies of Theodore Roosevelt, William Howard Taft and Woodrow Wilson enacted social reforms and afforded protection to ordinary people in an example of proactive federal responsibility.
- The 1920s brought a return to 'normalcy' where three Republican Presidents, Harding, Coolidge and Hoover managed the economy with policies of laissez-faire, non-intervention, tariffs and low taxation. It was also a period of great social tensions. A rapid economic boom then collapsed in 1929 with the Wall Street Crash.

TIMELINE

1890 Progressive Era begins.

1896 **Nov:** Election of William McKinley as US president.

1901 **Sep:** Assassination of McKinley – Theodore Roosevelt becomes president.

1908 **Nov:** William Taft elected president.

1912 **Nov:** Woodrow Wilson elected president.

1920 **Nov:** Warren Harding elected president.

1923 **Aug:** Warren Harding dies suddenly. Calvin Coolidge becomes president.

1928 **Nov:** Herbert Hoover elected president.

1929 **Oct:** Wall Street Crash – onset of Great Depression.

1932 **Nov:** Franklin D. Roosevelt elected US president.

1933 **Mar–Jul:** Hundred Days of FDR's New Deal legislation for relief, recovery and reform.

1961 **Jan:** John F. Kennedy assumes office as president.

1963 **Nov:** Kennedy assassinated – Lyndon Johnson becomes president.

1964 **May:** Johnson launches 'Great Society' at University of Michigan.

Jul: Enactment of 1964 Civil Rights Act.

1965 **Jul:** Medicaid and Medicare.

Aug: Voting Rights Act.

1965–73 US ground troop involvement in Vietnam.

1968 **Nov:** Richard Nixon elected president.

1972 **May:** Nixon wins landslide re-election.

1974 **Aug:** Nixon resigns over Watergate Scandal. Gerald Ford becomes US president.

- The New Deal of Franklin D. Roosevelt from 1933 to 1941 gave both the president and the Democratic Party almost unassailable power and huge popularity.
- Arguably Roosevelt saved democracy in the midst of an immense financial and political crisis in 1933.
- The 1960s brought the New Frontier and the Great Society as John F. Kennedy and especially Lyndon Johnson enacted some of the most significant liberal reforms since 1933. But Johnson's triumph was undermined by US involvement in Vietnam.
- The election of Richard Nixon in 1968 marked the end of a political coalition that had allowed 'New Deal style' politics to be conducted with a degree of consensus since the 1930s. Nixon's New Federalism brought conservative politics to the fore.
- Nixon's foreign policy triumphs ensured his landslide re-election in 1972, but he faced considerable economic problems and was finally disgraced by his role in the Watergate Scandal.
- As Gerald Ford took over in 1974, the Republican Party was tainted by Watergate, while the Democrats were looking for new figures and new blood, in the aftermath of Vietnam. It was an unsteady time for US democracy.

4.1 What is the historical background of the USA up to 1890?

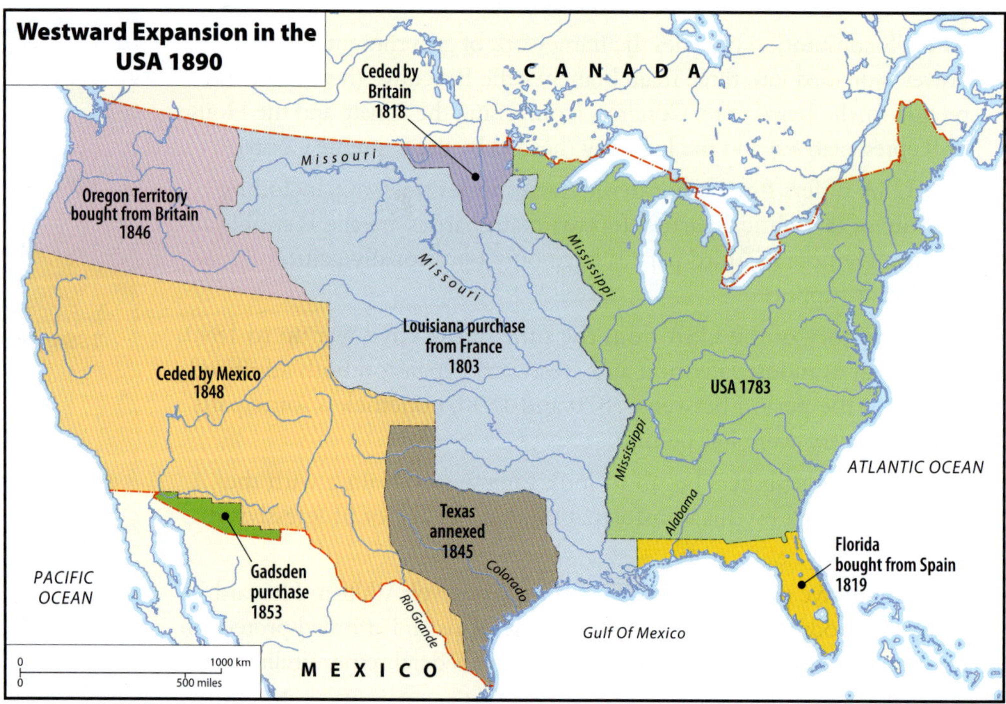

Figure 4.1 Map showing westward expansion in the USA up to 1890

The USA has always had a strong sense of individualism and self-reliance, since its Declaration of Independence in 1776. Most Americans have believed that their republican democracy was better and more egalitarian than the 'old order' of European empires from which they escaped.

The drafting of the US constitution in 1787 seemed to legalise the building of a God-fearing state, which early Americans hoped would be a political exemplar and endue them with the qualities needed for westward expansion.

By the 1870s, the USA had acquired all lands and territories south of Canada and north of Mexico between the Atlantic Ocean in the east and the Pacific Ocean in the west, chiefly through warfare and purchasing. Such settlement was so expansive that in the 1890 population census, no territory remained undeveloped for settlement.

But westward expansion brought conflict with the Native Americans, who were viewed as a hindrance and uncivilized, and in the 19th century they clashed with the US government, in the form of the American Indian Wars.

Figure 4.2 Gathering up of the dead for burial after the Massacre of Wounded Knee

By 1890, the spread of the railroad, disease, innovations such as the electric telegraph and the Winchester repeating rifle, and the attitude of white settlers and government had conspired against Native Americans. Tribes were broken down in an attempt to assimilate them, and the Dawes Act of 1887 eventually promised them full US citizenship if they gave up tribal customs. The US government then took ancestral Native American lands and broke up reservations into smaller areas, which then led to land-grabbing by whites. But this 'civilising' of Native Americans into white society, would backfire in the 20th century when they agitated for land and education.
The US Civil War of 1861–5 was a defining event in the 19th century. Westward expansion had exacerbated differences between the industrialised North and the more traditional, agrarian South, as the emergence of affluent new western states – especially

California – undermined a delicate political balance. The North's swift economic progress also worried many in a socially conservative South. But the principal divider between North and South was slavery.

Lincoln wished to readmit the Confederate states to the Union as swiftly as possible with minimal retribution, in a period of 'Reconstruction' after the war. In areas under Union military control, Reconstruction had begun as early as 1863.

But Lincoln faced radical Republicans in Congress who demanded total repentance from Confederates. Reconstruction was thus beset by problems. Lincoln was shot in the head on 14th April 1865, and died the following morning. Following this assassination, he was succeeded by vice-president Andrew Johnson, who was the only Southern senator to remain loyal to the Union during the Civil War; and because of such loyalty was invited by Lincoln to be his running mate in the 1864 election.

Johnson faced battles over Reconstruction, having to appease radical northern politicians who wanted to punish the South, yet trying to integrate Southerners who clung to their way of life. He pardoned most Southern whites, appointed provisional governors and introduced new state governments in the former Confederacy, saying each state could self-determine how it wanted African Americans to be treated. In the long-term, Southern states instituted laws or **Black Codes** that perpetuated white supremacy. Freed black slaves often found the post-war South identical to pre-1861. This infuriated Northerners, as did the return to power of former Confederate leaders.

In theory, slavery had ended with the 13th Amendment to the Constitution, ratified in December 1865. In 1868, the 14th Amendment declared that every state must offer equal protection under the law regardless of race; then the 15th Amendment of 1870 granted the right to vote to African American males. The pendulum of racial equality appeared to be swinging favourably, since Southern states had to agree to these amendments in their legislature, to be readmitted to the Union. But actually enforcing these laws was a different matter, and political turbulence still destabilised the South.

Some whites would not tolerate former slaves voting and holding office, and so the **Ku Klux Klan** was born, unleashing violence towards Republican leaders and blacks. Beatings and lynchings became features of clandestine nightlife in the South. But even the 1875 Civil Rights Act, a last measure to help Southern blacks, was merely an assertion of principle and had no impact in the former Confederate states.

By 1876 all the ex-Confederate states had returned to white Democratic rule. The new Republican president Rutherford Hayes reached a compromise in order to secure victory in a tied presidential election. Democrats accepted Hayes when he removed troops from the South and recognised Democrat governments in closely fought states. The South was now a law unto itself with political life in the grip of white **segregationists**, African Americans caught in a poverty trap and whites having unchallenged domination.

But more radical African Americans saw segregation as a statement of black community identity and, in the aftermath of Reconstruction, a small but influential number of black men became teachers, lawyers, doctors and entrepreneurs. They argued that at least the 14th and 15th Amendments were now firmly placed in the US constitution, to be invoked where necessary in the future.

Black Codes: laws passed across the South aimed at maintaining white supremacy. They restricted freedom of speech for blacks, as well as outlawing interracial marriages, unemployment, loitering, vagrancy, black legal rights and freedom of assembly. They were used by Southern whites to keep blacks in an inferior position for decades after the official abolition of slavery.

Ku Klux Klan: Born out of a desire to regain Southern white political ascendancy, the Klan, or KKK, targeted blacks in public office, black schools, churches and white sympathisers. Formed in December 1865 by ex-soldiers of the Confederate Army, it peaked around 1870. The Klan was suppressed by the Ku Klux Klan Act 1871 and the use of federal troops, but it would be reborn in 1915 with support from traditional white supremacists.

Segregationists: people who argue for the separation of different human races. In the USA around 1890, it meant keeping African Americans in inferior social, economic, political and cultural conditions.

QUESTION

Why did white Southerners resent Reconstruction and how did they try to undermine the process?

4.2 How was the US constitution and its electoral system devised?

In order to appreciate the significance of key leaders in the USA after 1890, and to judge how well democracy responded to the political circumstances of the time, it is necessary to summarise the key features of the US constitution and electoral system in place, and comment on their relevance.

The constitution

The constitution of the United States of America is its supreme law: the foundation and source of the legal authority underlying its federal system of government and overall existence. It was devised to provide the framework both for the organisation of the US government and the relationship of that **federal** government with the states, citizens and people. It also defines the three main branches of government: the **Legislature**, the **Executive** and the **Judiciary**.

Congress is **bicameral** because the Legislature consists of the House of Representatives and the upper house or Senate. Both houses have to agree on a law before it is passed. Each representative (congressman/woman) faces election every two years. The number of state representatives varies according to the size and population of the state. Balancing this is the Senate, with two senators representing each of the fifty states, regardless of size and serving a six-year term. There are one hundred senators (see section 4.3, The function of US political parties).

The Executive (or policymaking branch of government) is led by the president, who is elected every four years. He or she must be over thirty-five, have been born in the USA and – following the 22nd **Amendment** to the constitution in 1951 – if re-elected, cannot serve more than two terms of office. If the president dies in office or has to resign, the successor is the vice-president for the remainder of that four-year term. The next person in the line of succession is the speaker of the house.

The president can pass laws and run the country, but only with the approval of Congress. Congress can block laws proposed by the president if a majority votes against them; yet the president can veto any legislation from Congress deemed unacceptable. Congress therefore has the power to check or balance, but not overrule, presidential authority.

The Supreme Court heads the Judiciary, with nine judges or justices who, once appointed, hold office until they resign or die. In theory the Supreme Court is above the hurly-burly of politics and acts to uphold the constitution, guarding the interests and rights of the individual by protecting them against unconstitutional acts of government.

The nine judges ensure that neither Congress nor the president exceed their powers, and they have the final say on whether or not the actions of politicians are just and lawful. They can also overturn legislation from Congress. The president can appoint one of the nine Supreme Court justices should a vacancy occur, so the political complexion and balance of the court can change. Below the Supreme Court exists a network of federal courts throughout the USA.

Federal: the USA is a federal state, with power divided between a federal (or central) government in Washington, DC and its fifty states. Each state also has its own powers.

Legislature: the US Congress, which is divided into the House of Representatives and the Senate. Its job is to frame and construct the laws.

Executive: the policymaking and leadership branch of the US government, headed by the president.

Judiciary: the courts and judges, headed by the Supreme Court. Its job is to ensure that laws are legal and follow the principles of the constitution, as well as to make sure that neither Congress nor the president exceed their powers, as stated in the constitution.

Bicameral: the practice of having two legislative or parliamentary chambers. Thus, a bicameral parliament or bicameral legislature is a legislature that consists of two chambers or houses.

Amendments: additions and changes that have been made over time to the US constitution. For example, the 13th Amendment in 1865 officially abolished slavery, while the 26th Amendment in 1971 established voting rights for people over the age of eighteen.

QUESTION

What is meant by a 'system of checks and balances'?

The constitution specifies the powers and duties of each branch of government, and was devised to prevent any one branch becoming too powerful, highlighting the principles of 'separation of powers' and the 'system of checks and balances'.

Adopted in 1787, by the Constitutional Convention in Philadelphia, Pennsylvania, the constitution was ratified by conventions in each US state in the name of 'the people', providing the original model for modern **republican democracy**. The US constitution has been amended twenty-seven times, the first ten amendments being known as the Bill of Rights.

Republican democracy: a political system based on the concept of government by equal citizens, elected by the people. It rejects monarchy and elite systems.

Founding Fathers: the political leaders who signed the Declaration of Independence in 1776 and framed the United States constitution.

It is the shortest and oldest written constitution still in use by any nation in the world today. The handwritten original is displayed at the National Archives and Records Administration in Washington, DC. Over the years, politicians and academics have highlighted shortcomings in the constitution. Yet, despite the criticisms, it has proved a remarkably stable document.

The first ten amendments were in effect part of the original constitutional settlement drafted by the fifty-five **Founding Fathers** of the USA. Yet up to 2016, there have been only seventeen further amendments, the last one in 1992. Any proposed amendment must secure a two-thirds vote of members present in both houses. Then three-quarters of the state legislatures have to ratify the proposed change. It has been made very hard to amend!

To summarise, power is spread and counterbalanced between three different branches of federal government. The constitution deliberately grants members of those branches different terms of office. With the president serving four years, members of the Senate six, and members of the House of Representatives two years, the system puts a brake on rapid political change. However, the judges in the Supreme Court effectively serve for life.

The Founding Fathers clearly wished to create a system that was in sharp contrast to, and more democratic than, the monarchical system of absolute power in Britain at that time. However, the weakness of the American system is that government is slow, complicated and legalistic, whereas events unfold rapidly today and responses may be required quickly – unlike in 1787.

The electoral system

Unlike many countries, the USA has no strong minority parties, so coalition governments are not formed between several parties. Presidents usually come from either the Democratic Party or the Republican Party (or the Grand Old Party, as it is sometimes known). The reason for this seemingly predictable outcome lies in the structure of the system. Central to it is the electoral college system established in Article II of the constitution and amended by the 12th Amendment in 1804. Each state gets a number of electors equal to its number of members in the US House of Representatives, plus one for each of its two US senators. Each elector gets one vote. Thus, a state with eight electors would cast eight votes. There are currently 538 electors and the votes of a majority of them – 270 votes – are required to win.

The US presidential election is held every four years, on the Tuesday after the first Monday in November. When voting for a presidential candidate, an individual is actually instructing the electors from their state to vote for that candidate. For instance, those people who vote for the Democratic candidate are really instructing the state's electors to vote for the Democratic candidate. Electoral college representation is based on congressional representation. This means that states with more people get more electoral college votes. If none of the candidates win 270 electoral votes, the election is then decided by the House of Representatives. This has happened twice, in 1801 and 1825. The system occasionally makes it possible for a candidate to lose the nationwide popular vote, but still be elected president by the electoral college. This has happened three times, the last occasion being in 2000, when it brought the democratic basis of the US electoral system into focus and debate.

The idea of giving people the power to make important decisions is seen as a key democratic principle; consequently critics of the electoral college system consider it to be a strange and outdated apparatus, and a legacy from less technologically advanced times, created to prevent theoretical dangers. Advocates of a direct popular vote for the presidency see this method as truly democratic, as spreading voting power and influence equally among the fifty states, and controlling the advantage held by larger states, by ending the winner-takes-all electoral college voting.

The USA's founders divided power to protect less populated states from those with a bigger population. Supporters of the status quo argue that scrapping the electoral college changes the nature of campaigns and devalues democracy. They believe that grassroots campaigning would no longer serve as valuable a purpose; yet grassroots politics enthuses local people, who are then responsible for swinging highly contested states for one candidate or another. This influences the outcome of the electoral college significantly more with the winner-takes-all scenario; whereas in a direct election, local efforts might lose some relevance.

To many Americans, the US electoral college combines essential components of democracy, in holding a balance between the rights of the minority and the majority so that all voices are heard. Others still continue to press for reform, believing that a direct election would increase turnout and make every single vote count.

Several of the presidents covered in this book have found themselves in battles with different areas of the federal government. For example, the four progressive presidents between 1897 and 1921: Franklin D. Roosevelt in the mid-1930s, who faced strong opposition to his New Deal policies from the US Supreme Court; while Congress itself battled with John F. Kennedy and Richard Nixon, whose election wins, in 1960 and 1968 respectively, were wafer-thin.

They all had to 'do deals' in Congress and outwit opponents in order to pass legislation. They had to uphold the rights of individuals, as stated in the constitution, at key moments – for example in civil rights – and they had to appoint judges to the Supreme Court. They were, to a lesser or greater degree, kept in check by the system. But they had to fight many battles at party level, both within their own party and when facing the opposition. Managing Congress required political skill – and still does.

How democratic is the US political structure?

The US political system has almost always been dominated by the Democrats and the Republicans. They are old, very stable parties: the Democrats date to 1824 and the Republicans were founded in 1854. The main reason for this two-party dominance is that – like most other Anglo-Saxon countries (notably Britain) – the US electoral system

QUESTION

Explain the process by which Americans elect their president every four years.

Historical debate:
Richard Labunski faults the US constitution for enabling presidents to continue unpopular wars and for requiring them to be 'natural born citizens'. He calculated that if the twenty-six least populated states voted together, they would control the Senate, yet represent only 17 per cent of the national population. Sanford Levinson criticises the United States' inability to remove speedily an incompetent or ill president. Dana Nelson believes the presidency has become too powerful. In *Bad for Democracy*, she argues that US citizens vote for a president every four years, and then remain largely politically inactive. She condemns presidentialism (or worship of the president) and views the office as essentially undemocratic.

QUESTION

Why has there been a debate by historians about the US constitution? Explain three of its weaknesses as seen by constitutional historians.

Fact: In November 2000, Republican George W. Bush, with 50,456,002 popular votes, won 271 electoral votes. His Democrat opponent, Al Gore, won the popular vote with 50,999,897 votes, but won only 266 electoral votes. Bush became president. The election was controversial, especially over the awarding of the twenty-five electoral votes from Florida, where Bush's brother was governor. The result was hotly contested by the Democrats, with a subsequent recount [A]. The state canvassing board certified Bush the winner of Florida's electors by 537 votes. It was the closest election since 1876 and only the fourth election in which the electoral vote did not reflect the popular vote. [A] following the 'CHAD' fiasco which saw 70,000 ballots being rejected.

Economically interventionist: when a government takes action to influence its national economy, it is said to be economically interventionist. Such intervention can have varying aims, such as reducing inflation or increasing wages.

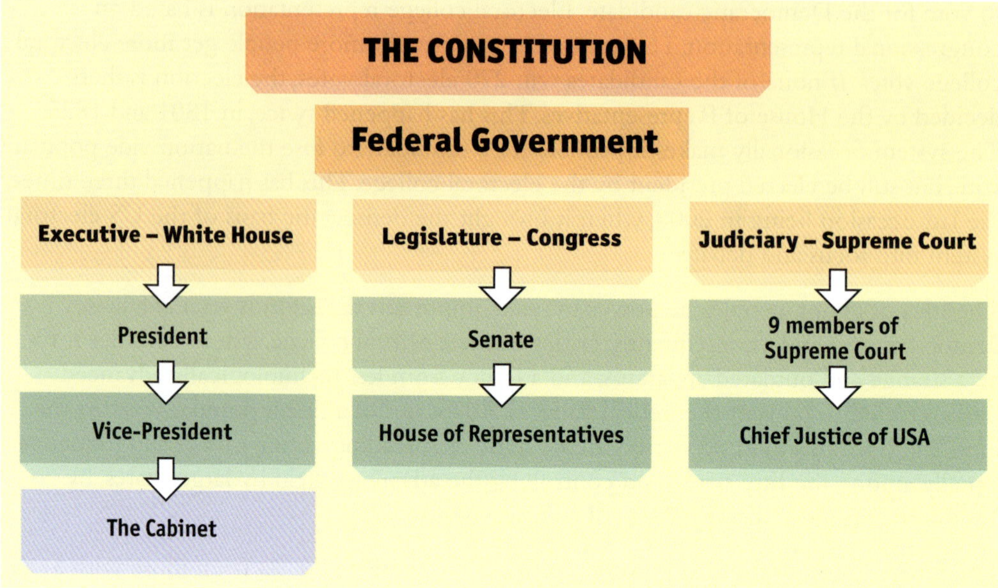

Figure 4.3 The US system of government

is 'first past the post' or simple majority. This, combined with the large voter size of the constituencies in the House and Senate, ensures that in practice only two parties can play.

Also important is the influence of money. Since a candidate can spend any amount of money on his or her campaign (unlike in many other countries) and can also buy broadcasting time (again not allowed in many countries, where limits are set on electoral expenditure), the US can only 'afford' two parties, with candidates from any other party facing a formidable financial barrier.

Some see the division between Democrats and Republicans as resembling that between Labour and Conservative in Britain, or between Germany's Social Democrats and Christian Democrats. These comparisons are valid in the sense that one party is characterised as centre-left and the other as centre-right, and one is more **economically interventionist** and socially radical than the other.

However, people who consider themselves 'centrist' in many Western European and Scandinavian countries might find the US 'centre' far to the right of what they believe in.

Factors apart from ideology influence individuals in the two main US parties. For instance, geography is more important in the USA than in many other democratic countries. After the 1861–5 Civil War and the 19th-century industrialisation of America, those living in the North and East of the country were exposed to rapid technological advances as well as to an influx of people of different nationalities.

Some Republicans living in these Northern, urban, industrialised states might therefore have more progressive values than many Southern Democrats in the generally poorer, less industrialised South. These conservative Democrats are known as 'blue dog' Democrats, or even DINOs (Democrats in Name Only) and President Kennedy faced considerable opposition from them when trying to pass legislation in 1961–3.

In the USA, divisions on issues such as abortion, gay and lesbian rights, capital punishment and race relations often follow party lines. By contrast, in Britain and Scandinavia such issues would be treated as matters for individual conscience. Religion generally features strongly in US politics, whereas Western European politicians generally 'don't do God'. The British prime minister from 1997 to 2007, Tony Blair, was sometimes criticised when he professed his Christian beliefs; yet local, regional and national candidates in the US are all expected to espouse very clear religious beliefs – and are seldom criticised. In 2012, the Republican presidential and vice-presidential candidates, Mitt Romney and Paul Ryan, spoke openly of their respective Mormon and Roman Catholic beliefs.

Another difference is that a US voter will register as a supporter of one of the major parties and subsequently vote in trial or primary elections, which then determine the party's candidate in the 'real' election. Moreover as discussed previously, the existence of the electoral college for the presidential election has divided opinion.

Finally, US political parties are less defined and slightly weaker than those in other democracies. US presidential and mid-term elections often place greater emphasis on the personalities of individual candidates, rather than promoting the party as a whole. This places a greater emphasis on the role of key leaders. Clearly the USA is different from other democracies and has been said to possess 'exceptionalism' (an ill-defined term), which nonetheless strikes a chord with the long-held belief in a Manifest Destiny. One major factor is the lack of a clear ideological division between the two major political parties. The USA has never developed a credible socialist or anti-capitalist party. There have been small third parties, such as the Socialist Party, the Progressives and the Prohibitionists, but they have rarely gained significant political influence.

The Libertarian Party (currently the third-largest party in America) was founded in 1971. Over the years, Libertarian candidates have been elected to state and local offices, but the two big parties have always massively dominated the political system. Whether in government or opposition, Democrats and Republicans remain centre stage, as they have done since the end of the Civil War in 1865.

The USA began with thirteen states and now has fifty. States were initially seen as the better protectors of individual rights against 'big' government in Washington, DC, which was seen as 'far away' to many people in a union almost 5,000 kilometres from east to west. Yet it was the disaster of the Depression and the powerful presidential response of Franklin D. Roosevelt in the 1930s that did much to end the inferiority and enhance the status of the federal government. Democracy functions only as well as the culture and hinterland within which the voters operate. The USA can, perhaps, be seen more accurately as a constitutional republic, designed to protect individual liberty from both the excesses of the state but also the excesses of the mobs and demagogues who might aim to supplant the existing system.

KEY CONCEPTS QUESTIONS

Causes and Consequences: What were the causes and consequences of the creation of the US constitution and electoral system? Why might some commentators consider it not to be fully democratic? Explain your answer carefully.

4.3 How significant was the role of key leaders?

Consideration will now be given to the role of some of the key leaders in the USA, within each of the four periods. These are from the 1920s with their underlying social conflict in the post-First World War world; the years between 1933 and 1941 encompassing the New Deal; and the post-Second World War years of 1961–74, where a

New Frontier and a Great Society gave way to political scandal, prior to the onset of the oil and energy crisis of the mid-1970s.

A society in conflict, 1920–9

Republican dominance in the 1920s

The period from 1920 to 1929 was one of great change, with underlying tension in society. It was a period of Republican dominance under the presidencies of Warren Harding and Calvin Coolidge. Herbert Hoover then succeeded Coolidge in March 1929 and continued Republican rule until 1933. A decade of outward prosperity and booming economy ended ignominiously with the **Wall Street Crash** of 1929.

Wall Street Crash: on 24 October 1929 almost thirteen million shares changed hands on the New York Stock Exchange. This sent financial shockwaves around the world, causing shares to collapse internationally. Many people lost money in the 'Crash' and it led to a decade of economic slump, bringing large levels of unemployment to almost all the industrialised countries in what became known as the Great Depression.

On one hand, this period has been called the roaring twenties, the jazz age and an era of affluence: conversely it has been seen as a time of major readjustment after the First World War, a retreat by the USA into international isolation and a time of suspicion and fear.

By the 1920s, the liberal ideals of the Progressive Era were replaced by intolerance, racial prejudice, the problems of prohibition and moral backlash. This will be examined in Unit 2. But for now, attention will focus on the significance of Harding and Coolidge, and their common themes during this difficult decade, which proved to be challenging for democracy in the USA.

Warren Harding (1865–1923)

Warren Harding grew up in a small town in Ohio, where he revived a moribund country newspaper, practising journalism. He later became a bank director, then the owner of a building society and also a timber company. After serving fourteen years in the Ohio State Senate, he became a US senator in 1914, where he missed more sessions of the Senate than he attended, being absent for key debates on issues such as women's suffrage and welfare!

But his dilatory and uncontroversial nature meant that he had few enemies, and he emerged as a compromise candidate for the presidency at the deadlocked Republican national convention in 1920. He went on to win the election running with the slogan 'A return to normalcy', defeating progressive Democrat James M. Cox in a landslide.

Harding's policies – as a self-made man and beneficiary of laissez-faire in the 1890s – rejected Wilson's progressive politics. Harding favoured low taxes on private income and business, more aid to farmers, higher import tariffs and the acceptance of fewer immigrants into the USA.

His hardline approach is evident in a 1921 bill that limited immigration to 3 per cent of the population of the respective ethnic groups resident in 1910. Similarly, in 1922, a Republican-dominated Congress passed the Fordney–McCumber Tariff, which raised import duties on chemicals, textiles, china, cutlery, farm products, guns and industrial machinery.

This was a distinct move towards **protectionism** and broke with progressivism. However, historians have noted Harding's approval of the Sheppard–Towner Maternity Aid Act, which gave federal aid to states to develop infant and maternity health programmes; also his pressurising of US steel to introduce a basic eight-hour working day.

Protectionism: the policy of protecting domestic industries against foreign competition by imposing tariffs or quotas. Republicans saw it as the reason for the USA's economic prosperity in the 1920s.

Figure 4.4 A cartoon from 1920 illustrating the growing isolation of the USA after the end of the First World War, leading to new immigration policies from Warren Harding

His rejection of the League of Nations (see section 4.3, The Democratic Party, 1890–1917), struck a chord with war-weary Americans, and this led Harding to construct a foreign policy that enabled the USA to participate in an international economic sphere, while maintaining a low profile and an open mind in political relations.

But Harding was not a natural, charismatic politician and he delegated much of his presidential authority to the heads of government departments. He died suddenly in August 1923, but not before his presidency was tainted with allegations of corruption and nepotism.

Harding was succeeded by his vice-president Calvin Coolidge who, in the first months of his presidency, endured the investigation of a number of Harding's ministers and advisors, several of whom resigned and were jailed for fraud and bribery. It culminated with the resignation of US attorney general Harry M. Daugherty, when it was proven that he had taken bribes to cover up the scandals, although he was the president's main law officer. Arguably Harding's greatest impact was dying in office and leaving a trail of corruption behind him!

Harding saw the role of president as largely ceremonial and was not a good role model for the office. But he was elected as an antidote to progressivism and active federal governance; so in this respect his reduction of its role, and his return to 'normalcy' were consistent! Perhaps this fitted the age of uncertainty in which the USA found itself.

Calvin Coolidge (1872–1933)

Calvin Coolidge was a competent but taciturn Republican governor of Massachusetts. He rose to fame in 1920, by sacking striking policemen in Boston. This secured him the vice-presidential nomination later that year.

He was conservative to the core and after he became president in 1923, Coolidge applied laissez-faire in the fullest sense of the term, by refusing to intervene and apply federal economic power, either to control the growing boom or to ease the depressed agricultural situation.

In December 1923 he told Congress that he wanted greater tax cuts and stricter immigration laws. His philosophy was simple; less government is good government: it should not interfere, but should help things to run themselves. He did argue for a minimum wage for women and he roundly condemned child labour, but such hints of progressivism were the exception rather than the norm.

Undamaged by scandals in Harding's administration and seen as a fundamentally decent man, Coolidge was elected president in his own right in 1924. He immediately introduced the Revenue Act of 1925. This reduced the maximum level of tax from 40 per cent to 20 per cent, halved death duties and abolished gift tax. This increased consumer spending and stimulated business investment.

Coolidge told US news editors in January 1925 that 'the chief business of the American people is business. They are profoundly concerned with buying, selling, investing and prospering in the world', adding that prosperity would be assured by allowing big business a free rein within a secure perimeter of tariffs and protection.

But the onset of the Great Depression in 1929–30 changed many things – not least Coolidge's reputation. Although he had retired in January 1929 and Herbert Hoover was now president, the nation's economic woes were now blamed by many on Coolidge. His reluctance to help the US agricultural sector was a particularly serious misjudgement.

More than 5,000 small rural banks in the South and the Midwest went bankrupt and thousands of farmers lost their land. Similarly – albeit with hindsight – it was seen that his tax cuts stimulated too rapid a boom, which then led to the overproduction of goods, excessive house-building, too much spending on credit, and an uneven distribution of wealth. Coolidge undoubtedly fed the frenzy of boom.

He was also one of the last presidents to write most of his own speeches and, significantly, he was the first to broadcast on radio in an era of growing communication. Through his cabinet members, Coolidge can be credited being at the helm during the implementation of the Dawes Plan, which helped delay total economic disaster in Germany, and for his continual support of disarmament and world peace.

When he was president, he seemed a dependable if dull navigator, but by the early 1930s he was judged differently and, along with Hoover, shouldered much of the blame for the Wall Street Crash – although by 1933 Hoover was deemed responsible for the even more dire economic downturn after 1930, by not ameliorating the effects of the Great Depression.

Coolidge's significance is that he was president during this decade of uncertainty between the two world wars, when the economic situation was thriving outwardly. However, the continuation of his and Harding's staunchly laissez-faire policies unwittingly laid the foundations for the economic disaster to follow. His approach to the presidency was also somewhat unusual, in that he did not see it as the president's role to be proactive. Some historians see him as a 19th-century style president in a 20th-century world, adhering to the notion that the role of the nation's top executive was simply to do the job of an executive. But he also presided over a period of greater social tension and prejudice.

Theory of Knowledge

History and economics:
Are economic needs the driving force of history? Ought President Coolidge to have intervened in order to help the distressed state of US agriculture, even though it ran against his economic thinking? What might this suggest more generally about the relationship between a government's economic policies and the needs of its citizens in a democratic state? Discuss this with a fellow student.

The age of the New Deal, 1933–41

Franklin Delano Roosevelt (1882–1945)

This seminal period in US history is synonymous with one man – Franklin Delano Roosevelt (FDR); 32nd president of the USA and chief executive for an unprecedented thirteen years. Roosevelt was the 1930s in the USA, and the USA was virtually his, with two landslide election victories in 1932 and 1936. He was both a key social reformer, an unquestioned democrat and, after 1941, the chief wartime leader.

FDR was born into a wealthy New York family. An only child, he went to a prestigious Massachusetts boarding school, then to Harvard and finally to law school. He married Eleanor in 1905 and afterwards entered politics. He ran successfully for the Democrats in the New York Senate election of 1910, and in 1913 Woodrow Wilson made him assistant secretary of the navy. In 1920, the party named him its vice-presidential candidate, although the Democrats lost to Warren Harding.

In 1921, Roosevelt contracted polio, and it devastated him physically, but he fought it and recovered sufficiently to resume public life. He ran successfully for governor of New York in 1928, which placed him in a favourable position to run for the White House. This he did in 1932, winning the Democratic Party presidential nomination and defeating Republican President Hoover convincingly.

At his inauguration in March 1933, FDR asked for powers equal to those a president might expect in time of war; such powers as would allow him to make decisions without too much scrutiny from Congress. He alarmed businessmen who considered his policies too regulatory and hostile towards them; he terrified right-wingers who saw his assumption of special powers as an attack on democracy; while those on the left wanted him to be much more socialist and less of tool to capitalism.

Roosevelt assumed office at the height of the Great Depression and his inheritance was unemployment at 25 per cent of the workforce and more than twelve million out of work. Economic conditions had deteriorated quickly in the transition period since his election in November 1932, with several key bank failures. Hoping to boost confidence in the minds of the electorate, FDR told them they had 'nothing to fear but fear itself'. Roosevelt had also promised them a 'New Deal' for all, which he delivered through a variety of daring and innovative policies. This period from 1933 up to the entry of the USA into the Second World War in 1941 is therefore rightly referred to by most historians as the age of the New Deal.

Immediately on assuming office, Congress passed Roosevelt's Emergency Banking Act, which closed insolvent banks and restructured others. In the first of his famous radio broadcasts or 'fireside chats' three days later, he urged Americans to put their savings back into the banks and by the end of March 1933, more than 70 per cent of them had reopened. Indeed, his first hundred days in office saw a raft of legislation passed, designed to bring relief, recovery and reform to the USA.

FDR ended Prohibition and he signed the Tennessee Valley Authority Act into law, enabling dam construction along the Tennessee River to generate cheap hydroelectric power for the inhabitants. Next, he introduced the National Industrial Recovery Act, which guaranteed workers the right to form labour unions and bargain collectively for higher wages and better conditions. He also suspended some anti-trust laws and set up a federally funded Public Works Administration. With further acts benefitting homeowners and farmers, and further legislation on banking, FDR's first hundred days pleased most and dismayed some, but it was beyond doubt that a vigorous reforming progressive president now occupied the White House.

In section 4.2 and section 4.3, further references will be made to other aspects of his New Deal legislation and opposition to it, but it is no exaggeration to suggest that in the long term, FDR's New Deal possibly saved democracy in the USA, whereas Germany had succumbed to Nazi dictatorship. FDR guided the USA from the brink of social, economic and possibly political breakdown, to a position by 1941 where the combined impact of all his reforms had alleviated the worst effects of the Depression on the most vulnerable, and had returned manufacturing production to its 1929 level.

Even more crucially in a democratic context, FDR's policies had endowed the US government with a sense of duty to look after the welfare of all its citizens, to regulate the excesses of capitalism and to ensure that all regions of the country were as economically viable as possible. His New Deal had continued the progressive ideals of order and regularity, for the good of the majority. Roosevelt had also tilted the country constitutionally, in that both economic regulation by the government and his decisive, powerful exercise of presidential authority were no longer seen as unconstitutional per se.

But Roosevelt's real influence – and perhaps his legacy – is found not just in the reality of his policy achievements but also in the changes he brought about in both the intellectual expectation and the governmental responsibilities that Americans now had of their president. Above all, he inspired confidence in people and was seen as a man of charisma and a figure of hope for a new start. The benign, ceremonial figurehead of a chief executive would no longer be tolerated.

But FDR was also important in foreign policy. He felt that the USA had an important world role to play, although throughout most of the 1930s economic problems and the existence of well-known isolationists in political and public life meant that Roosevelt had to suppress his internationalist views. He was sensitive to the constraints imposed by lack of political and public support. Significantly, between 1935 and 1939, Congress had passed a series of Neutrality Acts that made it impossible for FDR to give aid to any warring state, even if he had wanted to do so.

But with the advent of war both in Asia and then Europe, Roosevelt acted – albeit cautiously. In 1937, when Japan invaded China, he imposed an embargo on goods going to Japan; oil, iron and rubber. When war broke out in Europe with Nazi Germany's invasion of Poland in September 1939, FDR knew that the USA could not remain neutral for long. He scarcely hid the fact that he supported Britain and France against Hitler. In 1940, he passed the Selective Service Act, which allowed men to be conscripted in peacetime, and then got Congress to pass the Lend–Lease Act, which allowed Britain access to US weapons and supplies, despite their deteriorating financial situation and inability to pay.

Figure 4.5 Franklin and Eleanor Roosevelt riding from the White House to Congress, 1941

War eventually came to the USA, when Japan launched a surprise attack against the United States Pacific naval base at Pearl Harbor in Hawaii on 7 December 1941. Congress declared war the following day, and FDR became a wartime commander-in-chief as well as chief executive of the US government.

FDR was almost revolutionary in the way that his thirteen-year presidency changed the USA and its politics forever. When he died in office in April 1945, the USA was on the brink of victory in the Second World War. This made it an international power with economic clout, world influence and an atomic bomb. Not only did he strengthen and reshape the US presidency following a period of inertia after the departure of Woodrow Wilson in 1921; but Roosevelt created modern America, expanding the political and constitutional powers of the executive office. He also helped the Democratic Party to capture and maintain a power base that subsequently gave them electoral dominance until the 1970s. The esteem in which he was held is evident in **Source A**.

SOURCE A

Franklin Roosevelt was a man of power and vision. He was a master politician who took command with absolute authority; he knew….that he could save the country and that no one else could … Thanks to Franklin Roosevelt, in short, six years (1933 to 1938) transformed America from a country which had been laid low by troubles which its own incompetence had brought on it, and which it was quite unable to cope with, to a country, as it proved, superbly equipped to meet the worst shocks the modern world could hurl at it. It was enough.

H. Brogan (1985), History of the United States of America, *London: Longman, p. 546.*

QUESTION

Why do you think FDR is described in **Source A** as a 'master politician'? What do you think is meant by 'the worst shocks the modern world could hurl at it'? Explain your answers carefully.

From the New Frontier to Watergate, 1961–74

Fact: The USA wanted to prevent a North Vietnamese communist takeover of South Vietnam as part of their wider strategy of containment, and they became involved in a war in Vietnam. US military advisers arrived in Vietnam, beginning modestly in 1950, in growing numbers after 1955 and tripling by 1962. US combat units were deployed in Vietnam from 1965. Operations spanned borders, and Laos and Cambodia were heavily bombed. US involvement peaked in 1968. After this, US ground forces were withdrawn, as part of a Vietnamisation policy. The Paris Peace Accords were signed by all parties in January 1973 and US forces left by March 1973. Nevertheless, fighting continued until the fall of Saigon in April 1975.

Watergate Scandal: this began when five men were arrested for breaking into the Democratic Party's national committee headquarters in Washington, DC at the Watergate complex on 17 June 1972. Payments to the burglars were linked to members of President Nixon's staff, and some incriminating tape recordings revealed that the president himself had tried to cover up the break-in.

The period from 1961 to 1974 saw the role of the US government expand greatly in domestic affairs, against a background of rising national and international disapproval of the USA's role in South Vietnam. There was also a noticeable shift in gender roles, with the increasing activity of women's movements; together with major legislation in civil rights.

The reforming years of John F. Kennedy's New Frontier and Lyndon Johnson's Great Society programmes were followed by the contradictory presidency of Richard Nixon. Section 4.2 will look more closely at their social and economic responses during this period, but the three presidents in office at this momentous time were of immense significance, with each administration facing a potentially troublesome threat during its period in office.

Kennedy attempted social reform and faced increasing demands from African American civil rights campaigners (viewed as dangerous by those who opposed them), while Johnson became the most pro-active president since Roosevelt in 1933.

Johnson's Great Society reforming legislation emphasised a 'war on poverty' – but war in Vietnam severely harmed his reform programme and led him not to seek re-election in 1968. The civil rights movement also became more vocal and at times extreme in its message, during his presidency. Nonetheless, the short, tragic presidency of Kennedy and the dynamic but flawed administration of his successor Johnson can be seen as the high point of post-war US economic and social reform.

Richard Nixon's victory in the 1968 presidential election saw a change in economic and social policy. Nixon continued with some welfare and supported federal programmes that did not sharpen class politics, yet he wanted to limit dependence on welfare agencies. His presidency also coincided with the onset of a major international economic downturn and ended with his resignation in August 1974 over the shameful abuse of personal power represented by the **Watergate Scandal**.

Also, both Johnson and Nixon were challenged by forces on the left, with specific grievances relating to Vietnam, Black Power and women's rights.

Certainly, the period from 1961 to 1973 appears to have been coloured by political extremism, at times having the potential to greatly undermine democracy. However, some historians have argued that the 1960s, the so-called 'hotbed of extremism', was not that different from other eras – the only real difference was that increasingly advanced mass media made the public more aware of the discontent. Certainly each of these three presidents was undoubtedly under exceptional media scrutiny.

John F. Kennedy (1917–1963)

John F. Kennedy (JFK) was the son of Joseph Kennedy, former US ambassador to the UK. JFK graduated from Harvard in 1940, joined the navy and became the skipper of a boat that was sunk by a Japanese destroyer (he swam to safety, towing an injured man). After a short period as a journalist, he entered politics, serving in the US House of Representatives from 1947 to 1953 and then as a senator for his home state of Massachusetts. Kennedy won the Democratic presidential nomination in 1960. He then narrowly defeated the incumbent Republican vice-president Richard Nixon in the closest election of the 20th century. In

January 1961 he was inaugurated as the first Roman Catholic president, and the youngest person elected to that office. Kennedy had the dynamic idea of a 'New Frontier' approach in dealing with problems at home, abroad and in space. But he faced problems with Congress. With the Democratic majority in Congress razor-thin and many Southerners in his own party suspicious of JFK and his affluent northeastern background, Kennedy was repeatedly forced to compromise on his legislative programme.

His proposals for medical care for the aged and aid to education were defeated, but on the minimum wage, trade legislation and other measures, he won important victories. Kennedy also proposed civil rights legislation, but most of this had to be carried through by his vice-president Lyndon Johnson, for JFK was assassinated in Dallas, Texas, on 22 November 1963, allegedly by Lee Harvey Oswald. Perhaps most controversially, Kennedy involved the USA in the military defence of South Vietnam.

The short duration of his presidency makes in-depth assessment difficult, but JFK's accession to office played a significant role in modernising US politics. By 1961, television had a real impact on the electorate, with style becoming as essential as substance. With a highly educated, cultured and attractive First Lady – Jacqueline (Jackie) – and two adorable young children, the Kennedy family projected vitality, youth and normality. Even today, Kennedy is still viewed by many as a charismatic, articulate, handsome and progressive leader, during a period of growing challenges to society. Above all, he was the symbol of the new changes many Americans wished to see, and his untimely death leaves many having a 'what if …?' perspective, about a promising presidency, cruelled wiped out.

Fact: Various scandals relating to JFK have emerged over the years, which have tarnished his public image. These include his dependency on certain drugs; his numerous affairs; and, most controversially, his possible involvement in the death of film actress Marilyn Monroe, with whom both he and his brother, Robert Kennedy, were having affairs.

Figure 4.6 President Kennedy and his family on holiday in Hyannis Port, Massachusetts, August 1962

Lyndon Johnson (1908–1973)

When John F. Kennedy was assassinated in Dallas on 22 November 1963, Lyndon B. Johnson (LBJ) assumed the presidency. He lacked the personal charisma of JFK and was deficient in charm and tact, but he had steely determination. LBJ was determined to build on Kennedy's legislative beginnings and sought to use the power of federal government to improve the lives of millions. A blunt Texan from a modest small-town background, Johnson first became a teacher, then Texas administrator for Roosevelt's National Youth Administration. In 1937 he was elected to Congress as a supporter of Roosevelt. He served in the Pacific Navy and entered the Senate in 1948. Although the opposite of JFK in personality and background, LBJ was still a clever political operator and a brilliant politician. He rose to become the acknowledged leader of the United States Senate and its Democratic Party leader in 1953. He lost the 1960 Democratic nomination to Kennedy, becoming vice-president before succeeding him in 1963.

As president from 1963 to 1969, Johnson got the backing of Congress to wage an all-out 'war on poverty'. He won a landslide election victory in his own right in 1964, and introduced some of the most important welfare and civil rights reform in US history, yet he quit office four years later as one of the least popular presidents of all time. At first sight, this is hard to comprehend, since LBJ's legislative record was phenomenal.

Under his umbrella term of the 'Great Society', the ex-teacher introduced the Elementary and Secondary Education Act to benefit poor states, improve resources and help fund disabled and disadvantaged children. The Higher Education Act gave students loans to pay for university and granted federal scholarships for less well-off undergraduates. Headstart provided preschool classes for children and money was allocated to cities to develop public transport networks.

Then the 1964 Civil Rights Act and the 1965 Voting Rights Act abolished laws that had made African Americans second-class citizens in the South, and in 1965 the Medicare Act and Medicaid Act were passed. These provided health care for the poor, the elderly and the disabled – to be paid for from taxation and federal funds. Then the Omnibus Housing Act allocated money to build cheap housing and provide rent aid for the poor. These are only some of the measures passed under LBJ – a depth of progressive and socially democratic reform unheard of since Roosevelt's New Deal.

But Johnson's increased commitment to Vietnam was undoubtedly the catalyst in his downturn. The Vietnam War was one of the most divisive events since the Civil War, as it truly polarised the USA. It diverted funds from LBJ's social and welfare reforms, and gave rise to serious military, political and moral debates. When communist guerrillas in Vietnam mounted an uprising in 1968 at the Tet Festival and were seen across the world's media in the compound of the US embassy, it highlighted the failings of the US military campaign and suggested that the war was unwinnable. LBJ faced strong opposition to his re-nomination as Democratic candidate, notably from JFK's brother, senator Robert Kennedy. Johnson thus declined to seek a second term.

Historian Paul Boyer says that Johnson's actions made the United States 'a more caring and just nation', while LBJ's domestic affairs advisor Joseph Califano said that it was no longer acceptable in a 20th-century democracy to 'accept poverty, ignorance and hunger as intractable, permanent features of American society'. Critics have argued that the outbreak of riots in many of the USA's cities in the late 1960s proved that LBJ's Great Society had failed. But his presidency did benefit millions with its emphasis on education, health care and civil rights, and it made the USA more democratic. Balancing its cost against the growing cost of an unwinnable and unpopular campaign in Vietnam was the insoluble problem.

Figure 4.7 Retiring President Lyndon Johnson, right, confers with president-elect Richard Nixon in the White House in Washington, January 1969

QUESTION

Why do you think President Johnson's popularity collapsed so drastically between 1964 and 1968?

Richard Nixon (1913–1994)

Republican Richard Nixon very narrowly defeated US vice-president Hubert Humphrey to win the 1968 election. A lower-middle-class boy from small-town California, Nixon excelled at acting, public speaking and debating in school. After graduation, Nixon worked as a lawyer for five years. He joined the US Navy in 1942 and became a lieutenant commander. He was elected as a congressman for Southern California in 1946 and made his name by sitting on the House Un-American Activities Committee, where he rose to national stardom during the investigation of Alger Hiss, a senior official in the US State Department, who was discovered to have leaked information to the USSR. Nixon was elected to the Senate in 1950 and was then approached by General Dwight Eisenhower to be Republican vice-presidential candidate in the 1952 election. Eisenhower and Nixon won in 1952 and 1956 and, although Nixon lost narrowly to Kennedy in 1960, he returned to win in 1968.

Nixon was only as conservative as he could be, and only as liberal as he had to be. He appealed to what he called the 'silent majority' by promising law and order, and – more importantly – he partly won the 1968 election by promising to end the war in Vietnam and unite Americans at home. He kept both of these promises, in so much as he withdrew US troops from South Vietnam and by 1973 he had united Americans at home – but against him! Eighteen months after a landslide re-election victory, national condemnation forced him to resign the presidency, following the abuse of his presidential power after the Watergate burglary.

He was the first US president to visit China, which he did in 1972, and along with Soviet leader Brezhnev, Nixon signed treaties to control nuclear arms. The agreements in May 1972 – a Strategic Arms Limitation Treaty (SALT) and an Anti-Ballistic Missile treaty – significantly smoothed the way for future agreements that aimed to reduce and eliminate arms. Nixon also signed agreements with the USSR on trade, cultural exchanges, science and space. Most significantly of all, he brought US troops home from Vietnam. All this had enhanced his international prestige greatly, so his political fall over a burglary was very surprising, given his major successes in foreign affairs.

Nixon took office after eight years of Democratic rule and he embraced politics, but often appeared ill at ease and aloof. Although Nixon subscribed to the Republican emphasis on financial responsibility, he also recognised the need for an expanded role for the government and accepted the basic outline of the welfare state as advocated by the Democrats. However, he wanted to manage the government's welfare programmes better. Nixon had to face a series of economic problems during his presidency. By 1973, the inflation rate was 9 per cent and the Dow-Jones average of industrial stocks fell 36 per cent between November 1968 and May 1970. Significantly, the unemployment rate had reached 6.6 per cent by the end of 1970. Nixon imposed wage-price controls in 1971 in order to ease the situation, but they made little difference.

Budget deficit: when a country or organisation spends more money than it earns through taxation or tariffs.

By the end of 1972, unemployment stood at 5.6 per cent. Soon he was presiding over the 'Nixon recession' of 1971–4. Some of this was due to a huge **budget deficit** from both the Vietnam War and the expensive Great Society policies brought in by Johnson. Japan, West Germany and South Korea were also increasingly challenging the USA in world markets. Furthermore, the US Central Bank, the Federal Reserve, had raised interest rates, making borrowing more expensive. Although Nixon enjoyed a temporary boom in 1972, which was enough to get him re-elected, this suddenly changed.

QUESTION

How did events outside the USA conspire to undermine Nixon's economic policies? What were the consequences of this by 1973–4?

Nixon's economic policies were first undermined and then totally thrown off course by external factors. In autumn 1973, Israel fought off Egypt and Syria in the Yom Kippur War. Having supported Israel in this conflict, the USA was affected by an oil embargo introduced by Saudi Arabia. The Saudis wielded great influence over the Organization of the Petroleum Exporting Countries (OPEC), which proceeded to quadruple its oil prices. Americans endured petrol shortages and rapidly rising consumer prices. The threat of 'stagflation' (economic recession combined with inflation) now loomed over Nixon. Although the embargo ended the following year, by the end of Nixon's presidency in 1974 there was 12 per cent inflation and even higher unemployment. The USA's seemingly unstoppable post-Second World War economic boom was definitely over.

Theory of Knowledge

History and ethics:
The 19th-century British politician Thomas Macaulay wrote that '*the measure of a man's character is what he would do if he knew he never would be found out*'. Consider Richard Nixon. Do you think that all political leaders should conduct themselves as if all their actions could be made public? Will all leaders have things they wish to hide? How far does an election promise made by a leader in a run-up to an election matter when he/she takes office?

Nixon also restructured the US government. He felt that the New Deal and Great Society style of federal bureaucracy was outdated and stifled enterprise, creating an over reliance on the state. He called instead for a 'New Federalism', a system that directed resources away from federal bureaucracy and handed back financial decision-making to the states, in what he specifically called 'revenue sharing'. This marked a major shift in the role of the state. It also coincided with a growing concentration of power within the White House, as Nixon was accused of creating an 'imperial presidency', where there were more unchecked powers and growing evidence of decisions made without following constitutional procedures (see section 4.4).

Nixon's presidency is seen, therefore, as pivotal. Not only was he the first president to resign from office, but he moved the country to the political right, while seeking to bolster the role and powers of the chief executive. But ultimately Nixon was to bestow upon young Americans a generation of mistrust and cynicism about their political leaders, following his arrogant misconduct and his blurring of image and reality.

4.4 How did democracy function?

The function of US political parties

US political parties have a key role in the organisation and running of democratic government. They bring together individuals from all the states who share their viewpoints and interests. Parties are an arena in which to formulate policies, provide training for would-be candidates, act as a force for persuasion and to organise voters to elect their particular candidate to office. They are also a repository of experience and expertise for the next generation of politicians.

But although they are fundamental in the operation of government at all levels, political parties are not the government itself, and the US constitution of 1787 makes no reference to them, as there were no parties in the nation. In fact, few if any nations in the world had voter-based political parties at that time, and it was the growing need to consolidate popular support for the new democratic republic while accommodating differing viewpoints that led to the emergence of voter-based political parties by the early 19th century.

Their basic purpose was – and is – to nominate candidates for public office and get as many as possible elected. Then, once elected, these officials hope to achieve the goals of their party by making laws, creating policy initiatives and passing legislation.

Ideally, apart from showing party loyalty, they must perform to their highest level of personal integrity and ability in the public interest; and hope that they might also attract new supporters from within their district or state – some of whom, being ambitious recruits, may in time decide to run for office themselves.

As well as representing individuals, political parties often represent interest groups with specific concerns, so they may represent the interests of the medical profession, teachers, urban African Americans, environmentalists, or specific industries such as agricultural or mining – any groups who might cooperate to express a specific agenda.

In the USA most politicians – representatives (congressmen/women), senators and the president – usually come from either the Republican Party or the Democratic Party. These two major political parties dominate the scene and always have done.

The Republican Party is now known for its firm associations to business and commerce. Republicans tend to favour 'less government' and more individualism, while adopting more conservative positions on social issues.

The Democrats have increasingly supported labour unions, workers' rights and have shown greater interest in advancing the rights of minorities. They have also advocated that the federal government ought to be proactive and involved in solving many of society's problems. Certainly since 1932, the Democrats have positioned themselves firmly as a liberal party on domestic and social issues.

Both parties state their aims or philosophy in a general manner, so that the electorate can get a broad overview without having to focus microscopically on every policy detail. The changing role and performance of these main parties will now be considered with respect to the functioning of democracy in the USA.

QUESTION

What is the main function of a political party?

The Democratic Party

The US Democratic Party dates back to the presidency of Andrew Jackson (1829–37) and is currently the oldest political party in the world that is still in existence. It came to be an upholder of states' rights and defend the views of the slave-holding Southern states, while the federal government was increasingly likely to ban slavery throughout the Union. The party split apart over slavery in 1860 at its presidential convention in Charleston, South Carolina.

Northern Democrats nominated Stephen Douglas as their presidential candidate, while Democrats in the South nominated a pro-slavery candidate, John C. Breckinridge. Abraham Lincoln and the recently formed Republican Party won the poll, and after the defeat of the Confederacy in the US Civil War (see section 4.1), the Democrats lost the political initiative, with Republicans entering a fifty-year period of dominance.

Most white Southerners opposed the more radical Republican elements of Reconstruction, detesting its support of African American civil rights and preferring to maintain white supremacy. The Democratic party of the late 19th century was not especially 'democratic' and was a far cry from its members today; a diverse group of people who espouse the need to promote social, economic and political opportunities for all citizens, and support individual human rights.

The Democratic Party was seen as the white people's party and by the end of Reconstruction in 1877, once more dominated the South. The legacy of this was that the US South became highly 'undemocratic' in as much as that it almost became a fiefdom for the highly prejudiced Southern Democrats, who were elected almost automatically to every congressional or senatorial election.

The South remained a Democrat stronghold until the 1960s, but this in itself created problems for Republicans and more liberal Northern Democrats. With the structure of the US Congress paying great attention and respect to seniority, the continually re-elected Southern politicians – often through the same family – were able to control most of the committees in both houses.

This meant that any socially contentious or liberal legislation – especially connected to civil rights – could easily be crushed. Even Democrat presidents such as FDR and JFK had to watch the Southern flank of their own parties when promoting bills. For example when an anti-lynching bill was brought to Congress by FDR on several occasions in the 1930s, Southern senators repeatedly **filibustered** it.

Filibuster: a procedure where a debate is extended, often for hours, allowing politicians to delay or completely prevent a vote taking place on some (usually divisive) issue. It can be referred to as 'talking a bill to death', but is really a legal way of obstructing the passage of legislation.

1920–9

During the 1920s, the Democrats were again out of the White House and the party experienced internal struggles and a real lack of dynamic leadership. A resolution denouncing the Ku Klux Klan failed by just a single vote at the 1924 Democratic Convention; and a growing divide over social and cultural issues such as Prohibition, permissiveness and immigration ensured Republican dominance. The dominance of the pro-business Republicans contrasted with the Democratic Party. In the 1920s, their chief supporters were an eclectic mix of Southern-born white Protestants, liberal academics and Northern Catholics, Jews or Italians. Their presidential campaigns in the 1920s were disastrous. In 1924, the Democrats nominated an unpopular and obscure Wall Street lawyer, John W. Davis; then in 1928 they put forward New York governor Al Smith, the first Catholic presidential candidate, who was the first Democrat since 1864 to lose multiple states of the old Confederacy in the South. But also in 1928, Franklin D. Roosevelt's election as governor of New York in succession to Al Smith brought a new leader to the fore.

1933–41

With the onset of the Great Depression following the 1929 Wall Street Crash, Democrat nominee Franklin D. Roosevelt won an overwhelming victory in the 1932 election against the incumbent Republican president, Herbert Hoover. He had campaigned promising 'relief, recovery and reform', and FDR's 'New Deal' was subsequently a high point in the legislative history of the US Democratic Party. The Democrats gained substantial majorities in both houses of Congress and among state governors, and FDR won re-election handsomely in 1936 and comfortably in 1940.

In contrast to their post-Civil War outlook, the Democrats became democratic! The Democratic Party of small government and 'the white man' in the 1890s now functioned as the party of proactive, federal government; championing the ordinary man and civil rights. FDR moved them towards an ideology of economic regulation and insurance against hardship. Levine and Papasotiriou recognise this in **Source B**.

SOURCE B

Franklin Roosevelt actually shaped postwar American politics because he succeeded in transforming what might have only been a temporary Democratic victory in 1932, into a lasting party alignment. His New Deal coalition dominated American politics until 1968.

P. Levine and H. Papasotiriou (2005), America Since 1945, *Basingstoke: Palgrave Macmillan, p. 12.*

1961–74

After losing the presidency in 1952 to Dwight D. Eisenhower, the Democrats became the governing presidential party again following the narrow election victory of John F. Kennedy in 1960. The Democrats maintained what by this time had become their 'traditional' power base of organised labour, urban voters and immigrants, and even during their period of opposition in the 1950s, the Democratic Party had taken more 'big government' positions, advocating a larger role for the federal government in regulating business. By the 1960s, the Democrats were advocating extensive governmental involvement in social issues such as education, urban renewal and the minimum wage. Moreover, the Democratic Party associated itself very early with the growing Civil Rights Movement, and championed the Civil Rights Act and the Voting Rights Act.

Kennedy had read Michael Harrington's controversial book *The Other America*, which identified a subculture revolving round low-income, dead-end jobs and poor health care and schooling. Kennedy established the Area Redevelopment Administration (ARA), but this spread itself too thinly, trying to help too many communities. Then Lyndon Johnson – who declared 'unconditional war on poverty in America' in his first major presidential address – launched his anti-poverty programme in March 1964, submitting the Economic Opportunity Act to Congress.

Johnson battled to get welfare reforms past groups with vested interests, such as unions, corporations and some professions. Despite the obstacles, Johnson did make progress and the overall poverty rate was halved, declining from 22.4 per cent in 1959 to 12.1 per cent in 1969.

But with Johnson's increased involvement in Vietnam proving ever-more costly, and with increased demands for more money for social programmes by religious leaders and labour unions, the longstanding coalition of support for the Democrats began to crack – not least with the growing demands for civil rights, which angered the conservative Southern Democrats who were the base of the party outside the urban industrialised North and West.

When LBJ withdrew from the presidential race for re-election, it marked the end of the New Dealers in the Democratic Party only three years after its greatest and most liberal post-war triumph in legislation. Richard Nixon captured the presidency for the Republicans in 1968 and the Democrats would never again win support from its supporting coalition of blue-collared workers, academics, Catholics, Jews, African Americans, Southern whites and Northern liberals. The high point of federal involvement in social and welfare issues would also be eclipsed. The Democratic Party would never be quite the same again, or function in quite the same way; and apart from the difficult and turbulent one-term presidency of Democrat Jimmy Carter from 1977 to 1981, Nixon's victory in 1968 saw the Republicans control the White House until 1993.

SOURCE C

President Lyndon B. Johnson speaking to an adviser about the unrest during his time in office:

I tried to make it possible for every child of every colour to grow up in a nice house, eat a solid breakfast, attend a decent school, and get to a good and lasting job. I asked so little in return, just a little thanks. Just a little appreciation. That's all. But look at what I got instead. Riots in 175 cities. Looting. Burning, shooting ... Young people by the thousand leaving the university, marching in the streets, chanting that horrible song about how many kids I had killed that day ... it ruined everything.

W. Chafe (1999), The Unfinished Journey, *Oxford: Oxford University Press, pp. 338–9.*

QUESTION

How far is **Source C** an accurate comment on the presidency of Lyndon Johnson and the success of the Democratic Party from 1963 to 1969?

The Republican Party

The Republican Party or GOP (Grand Old Party) was founded by anti-slavery campaigners and modernisers in 1854. In the period between 1861 and 1933, it dominated US politics, having a strong base in the North and West and providing twelve of the fifteen different presidents to hold office during that time.

The Republican Party initially came to power with the election of Abraham Lincoln in 1860. They oversaw the defeat of the Confederate states in the Civil War and the preservation of the Union. Thereafter, one of their key features was the end of slavery, the granting of equal rights to all men – regardless of which side they had fought on in the Civil War – and the Reconstruction of the South.

The party gathered its support from businessmen, small business owners, many factory workers, the self-employed, farmers and African Americans. It was pro-business and banking, advocating high import tariffs to promote economic growth and protect US industry. By the 1880s – with the economies of the North, the Midwest and California booming with heavy and light industry, railroad expansion, mines, expanding cities and prosperous agriculture – the Republican party reaped the electoral rewards and promoted policies to sustain the fast growth.

But the party was also conflicted by virtue of the rapid and aggressive industrial expansion; and by 1890 the GOP had agreed to the Sherman Anti-Trust Act and the Interstate Commerce Commission in response to small businesses and farmers, who had complained that they were being squeezed by the large corporations. Such early hints at more progressive and less *laissez-faire* legislation were to come to the fore after the election of William McKinley in 1896.

1920–9

The 1920s saw the comfortable election of three Republican presidents: Warren Harding in 1920, Calvin Coolidge in 1924 and Herbert Hoover in 1928. The pro-business policies of the decade seemed to produce an unprecedented prosperity until the Wall Street Crash of 1929 heralded the Great Depression.

Harding sensed that the American people after the war wanted neither more international involvement nor the level of government intervention in social and economy matters as pursued by Woodrow Wilson. He campaigned on the simple promise of a 'return to normalcy', which meant a government that was supportive of business, anti-tax, and against government regulation.

After Harding's sudden death in 1923, Coolidge continued this theme, and the pro-business, free-market economic outlook of the Republican Party would define the USA for the rest of the decade. But GOP dominance would eventually collapse following the crash in the American economy between1929 and 1932.

1933–41

FDR's New Deal policies, his Democratic Party coalition and the reaction to laissez-faire Republican policies in the 1920s would all keep the Republicans out of the White House until 1952. In this period there were only two presidents, since FDR ignored the two-term tradition and ran for an unprecedented four terms, all of which he won. Following Roosevelt's death in April 1945, vice-president Harry S. Truman became president and he was elected in his own right in 1948. It was not until the mid-term elections in 1946, that the Republicans won a majority in both the Senate and the House.

They needed to rebuild, to examine themselves, to be proactive and have fresh ideas; and at the same time, the GOP had to recognise its role in a democratic state and challenge the Democrats, who appeared particularly unassailable at times under FDR. It was not easy. In the 1934 mid-term election, ten Republican senators went down to defeat, leaving them with twenty-five against seventy-one Democrat senators. The House of Representatives was similarly disadvantaged against them.

Then in 1936 there was a temporary split within the party, into a conservative faction that was dominant in the West and Midwest, and a northeastern liberal faction. There also still remained progressives in the party. It was a long and difficult period of opposition for the Republicans. Part of this change involved trying to create a greater political role for women; so the party decided that the Republican National Committee (RNC) chair and co-chair should be of the opposite sex. In 1937, Marion Martin became the first assistant chair of the RNC, then in 1940 the GOP became the first major political party to endorse an equal rights amendment for women in its platform.

Politically, the Republicans were able to make something of a comeback by 1940, when a recession in 1938 temporarily dented FDR's legislative campaign and his popularity. This was made possible by them winning 50 per cent of the vote outside the South in the mid-term elections. They felt they had a strong base for the 1940 presidential election, but had not reckoned on Roosevelt running for a third term.

As a minority or opposition party, the Republicans always had two wings – the left wing supported some of the New Deal policies while opposing the running of it and its extravagance. The right wing did not support any aspects of FDR's legislation and opposed it from the start. Indeed, this group later managed to repeal sections of it during the 1940s with help from ultra-conservative Southern Democrats. But undoubtedly, the period from 1933 to 1941 was one of the toughest in the history of the Republican Party, many of whose members felt they were observers in a one-party state.

1961–74

The 1960 presidential election brought eight years of Republican government under Dwight D. Eisenhower to a close. Most of the period under his governance had been a time of consumer and cultural confidence and – at least outwardly – a period of self-contentment. It is necessary to put this into context, in light of the momentous events of the 1960s and 1970s.

Post-war America saw industry switched from war production to the manufacture of consumer goods. More houses were built, town suburbs developed and homeownership increased rapidly. By the mid-1950s – during Eisenhower's presidency – America had a continually rising per capita income, employment and inflation. Innovation in transport and air travel created jobs in the service and travel industries. The expansion of technology, space exploration and the media (especially television) created totally new careers and greater disposable income.

This period also witnessed the rapid growth of car ownership and credit availability. It is estimated that well over 50 per cent of the population enjoyed a 'middle-class' lifestyle and shared in a consumer boom that was even greater than that of the 1920s. But poverty was still fairly widespread, and poor people got insufficient attention – it was easier to celebrate the abundance of a booming consumer economy. Moreover, even people who had lived through the Great Depression of the 1930s and had been poor emphasised the relative economic security of the 1950s. It was not until the 1960s that affluent Americans rediscovered poverty amid the prosperity.

Eisenhower had advocated a balanced budget, sought a low rate of inflation and wanted a rate of growth that was sustainable over the long term. 'Under conditions of high peacetime prosperity,' he said, 'we can never justify going further into debt to give ourselves a tax cut at the expense of our children.' Many Republican congressmen disagreed and felt that Eisenhower was not rigorous or conservative enough. They believed that tax cuts and laissez-faire policies were needed, and that Eisenhower's approach was too liberal. They saw it as too much of a consensus, a 'middle way', influenced by Democrat New Deal politics.

Although vice-president Richard Nixon only lost the 1960 election to John F. Kennedy by the narrowest of margins, the Republicans faced calls for more conservatism to balance the New Frontier and Great Society of Kennedy and Johnson, and this was reflected in the selection of right-wing Arizona senator Barry Goldwater as the 1964 presidential nominee. Goldwater was strongly opposed to the New Deal and to the United Nations and called for a stridently anti-communist foreign policy. But he and many Republicans were heavily defeated, as the country voted in a landslide for Lyndon Johnson and his Great Society. It seemed that the GOP was again at a low ebb in the political tide. Indeed, between 1964 and 1968, the Republicans were looking for a leader, without having an obvious candidate. Yet Vietnam, social unrest and inner-city racial tensions strained the relationship between the US electorate and President Johnson, whose popularity plummeted and who was forced not to seek re-election in 1968.

Figure 4.8 The 1968 Republican Party Convention

Eventually Nixon, who had withdrawn from political life after losing the election in 1962 to become governor of California, announced he would run again. Ultimately the Republicans nominated him as their candidate, as he represented a link with more peaceful and prosperous times. He narrowly won the election (see section 4.3). Opposition to the war in Vietnam and to growing federal social programmes had 'converted' some Southern Democrats and led them to vote Republican in increasing numbers. Nixon had also campaigned very cleverly on a small-government, anti-war platform as a defender of the 'silent majority'. He also advocated a policy of cutting back federal power and returning power to the states, in what he called 'New Federalism'.

Nixon was soon riding high internationally and his expertise in foreign affairs brought him much success. He firmly believed – and stated – that the USA had a better form of republican democracy than any other country and that they ought to export this by playing a more proactive role internationally. Certainly his visits to China and the USSR, his weapons treaties with the Soviets and his ending of the Vietnam War guaranteed him a stunning re-election victory in 1972, carrying forty-nine states.

Yet within two years he had resigned in disgrace over the Watergate affair and vice-president Gerald Ford had to pick up the pieces, not only of the presidency, but also the demoralised Republican Party. Any thoughts of long-term rule were now dashed, especially since President Ford gave Nixon a full pardon and in doing so, almost split the Republican Party. Unsurprisingly, it gave the Democrats a weapon they readily used to make major congressional gains in the 1974 mid-term elections. Ford adopted a humbler approach to the office as president and he did halt the decline of the office of president in the eyes of many. But he was rejected by the electorate when he ran for president in 1976.

Gerald Ford had taken over as president when the Republican Party was tainted by the disgrace of Watergate; while the Democrats were looking for new ideas and politicians, 'clean' personalities and new recruits, in the aftermath of Johnson's humiliation in Vietnam. With an international oil crisis and inflation about to hit the major Western economies, it was an unsteady time for US democracy.

QUESTION

To what extent were the Democrat and Republican Parties' policies from 1920 to 1974 in keeping with democratic principles? Reread the text and carry out some research using the library and the internet.

End of unit activities

1. Using the text and your own research, explain the significance of each of these in relation to democracy in the USA: electoral college, Reconstruction, trusts, Platt Amendment, New Freedom, Voting Rights Act 1965, Watergate scandal.
2. Design two parallel spider diagrams to illustrate the differences/similarities between the Democratic and Republican Parties in the USA. Colour-code it as appropriate, and also note how the parties have changed through time.
3. Use the information in this unit as well as additional information from books or websites to write an obituary for Lyndon Johnson, evaluating his contribution to democracy in the USA.
4. Draw a spider diagram or chart outlining the checks, balances and forms of opposition or pressure placed on the Executive under the US constitution.
5. Find out what you can about the 1968 presidential election. Look for information on the effects it had on or how it was affected by **three** of the following: Democrat Party; Republican Party; Vietnam War; African Americans; Southern Democrats; US big business corporations; Lyndon Johnson; Richard Nixon.

The development of a democratic state in the USA

Unit 2

KEY QUESTIONS

- What factors influenced the development of democracy in the USA?
- How did the government respond to domestic crises?
- How did the government react to protest movements?

Overview

- There were several key factors influencing the evolution of the USA between 1890 and 1975, with respect to immigration, economic forces and foreign influences.
- The period of mass migration from 1880 to 1924 is considered alongside the post-1965 era of immigration following the liberalisation of tough immigration laws enacted in the 1920s.
- The impact of economic forces and their ideology are seen through three contrasting periods encompassing progressivism, laissez-faire and the New Deals of the 1930s and 1960s.
- The anxieties about 'alien culture' and revolution being imported into the USA precipitated the Red Scare of the 1920s. This is examined alongside the impact of the Vietnam War in the 1960s, as examples of foreign influences on the USA.
- Consideration is given to US government response to key domestic crises. The banking crisis and depression of 1893, Roosevelt's handling of the 1933 bank collapse and the ruined country he inherited, plus the response of government and people to the Watergate scandal from 1972 to 1974 are all examples of how greater calamities – and threats to the democratic structure – were avoided.
- Finally a study is made of key protest movements and how they were managed by the government. Attention is focused on populist protest in the 1890s, the movement for women's suffrage and emancipation in the early 20th century and the anti-war movement of the 1960s.

Introduction

Since independence, the USA has been a successful state in an ideological sense, given that the American Revolution and the US constitution created a relatively democratic, constitutional republic. The USA has never had a single dictator – although the powers assumed

TIMELINE

1894 Immigration Restriction League founded.

1896 **Nov:** William McKinley elected president.

1901 **Sep:** Assassination of McKinley, Theodore Roosevelt becomes president.

1908 **Nov:** William Taft elected president.

1912 **Nov:** Woodrow Wilson elected president.

1918 **Jan:** Sedition Act and Alien Act.

1920 **Aug:** 19th Amendment gives women the vote.

Nov: Warren Harding elected president.

1921 Quota Act limits immigration.

1923 **Aug:** Warren Harding dies suddenly, Calvin Coolidge become president.

1924 Immigration Act.

1928 **Nov:** Herbert Hoover elected president.

1929 **Oct:** Wall Street Crash.

1932 **Nov:** Franklin D. Roosevelt elected US president.

1933 **Mar–Jul:** One hundred days of FDR's New Deal legislation.

1960 **Nov:** John F. Kennedy elected president.

1962 **Jun:** Students for a Democratic Society (SDS) formed – New Left.

1963 **Nov:** Kennedy assassinated, Lyndon Johnson becomes president.

1964 **May:** Johnson launches 'Great Society' at University of Michigan.

1965 Immigration and Nationality Act (Hart–Celler Act).

1968 **Nov:** Richard Nixon elected president.

1970 **May:** Shootings at Kent State University.

1972 **Jun:** Burglary at Watergate Building.

1974 **Aug:** Nixon resigns over Watergate scandal, Gerald Ford becomes president.

or the sweeping legislation adopted by certain presidents has occasionally led to such accusations.

Ideally, democratisation must ensure that all citizens have a right to vote and a voice in their political system. In this respect, it must be noted that slavery was only abolished after the American Civil War of 1861–5 – and then sometimes in theory only – while civil rights and full voting rights were only given to African Americans in the 1960s.

In-between there were periods of prejudice towards immigrants and some religions, and times of great deprivation and poverty that inevitably locked many people out of society in general. So the USA – although fundamentally democratic – was still very much 'a work in progress' and arguably remains so today.

Factors such as immigration, economic forces and foreign influences, have been important in the ongoing development of the democratic ideal between 1870 and 1975.

Figure 4.9 Irish immigrants arrive in the USA, 1902

4.5 What factors influenced the development of democracy in the USA?

The impact of immigration on the USA

1890–1941

The impact of immigration has been phenomenal. As sociologist Oscar Handlin commented, 'immigrants were American history'. The US economy and its democracy cannot be separated from immigration, which has occurred throughout its existence. But the most significant period was the Age of Mass Migration from 1880 to 1924. Statistics reveal that between 1880 and 1890, more than 5.2 million immigrants entered the USA. In 1890, 80 per cent of New Yorkers had been born outside the USA, and the city had more Irish than Dublin and more Italians than Naples! Other Irish settled in Boston, Scandinavians in the Great Lakes region, while Chicago had large numbers of Poles and Irish living there.

Over this forty-year period, immigration patterns changed greatly in nature. Prior to the 1880s, immigrants were mainly North and West European, although many Chinese labourers arrived on the West Coast in the mid-19th century to help build the transcontinental railways.

But by the early 1900s – when more than one million immigrants were arriving annually – there were now many Southern and Eastern Europeans. Persecution – notably against Jews and ethnic minorities in the Russian Empire – had changed immigration patterns.

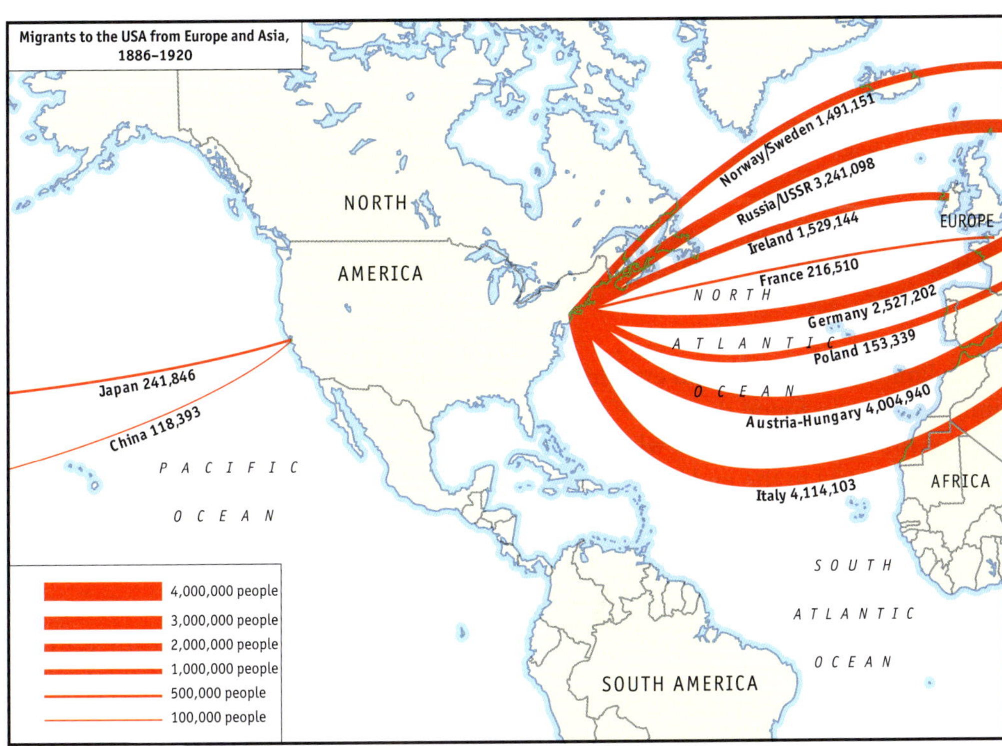

Figure 4.10 From 1880 to 1920, more than twenty million people settled in the USA from Europe and Asia

The newcomers were Russians, Hungarians, Czechs, Slovaks, Greeks, Serbs, Croats and Romanians. They brought with them new languages and religious practices. Judaism and the Eastern Orthodox religion were added to the mix, while a major increase in Poles and Italians entering the USA augmented the existing number of Roman Catholics

They chose the USA because of its industrial revolution and its reputation as a land of opportunity. With visible economic expansion and westward settlement, there seemed to be room for all, as well as a demand for cheap, unskilled labour, which most new immigrants could provide. The wages offered appeared derisory to Americans, but were attractive to those fleeing poverty, persecution and **subsistence agriculture**. By 1900, a third of the residents of the major US cities were foreign-born, and their arrival led to fundamental change.

Subsistence agriculture: the production of food solely for the survival of those that produce it, and not for sale on the open market.

A Frenchman in New York, Jean de Crévecoeur, spoke of America's 'melting pot', believing that people of any ethnicity might arrive in the USA and be transformed into Americans by virtue of their adaptation to a new life. By the 1920s this 'melting pot' still remained illusory.

Most immigrants clung to their native language and culture, living and working in localised urban districts, like a 'mosaic'. Their tendency to concentrate was determined by economics and proximity to work, while some racist city-dwellers used high rents and pressure to exclude them from areas dominated by whites.

SOURCE A

Every major city had its share of rundown, overcrowded slum neighbourhood. Generally clustered within walking distance of manufacturing districts, slums developed when landlords subdivided long, narrow buildings with few windows, called tenement and packed in too many renters. The poorer the renters, the worse the slum. Slums became ghettoes when laws, prejudice and community pressure prevented the tenement inhabitants from renting elsewhere. During the 1890s Italians in New York, blacks in Philadelphia ... and Chinese in San Francisco increasingly became locked in segregated ghettoes.

P. Boyer, C. Clark, J. Kett, N. Salisbury, H. Sitkoff and N. Woloch (2006), The Enduring Vision: A History of the American People – Volume II: Since 1865, *Boston: Houghton Mifflin Company, p. 571.*

QUESTION

What does **Source A** reveal about the living conditions of immigrants in the USA? How might resident Americans view this situation?

With limited integration, and even less possibility of assimilation into American society, immigrants soon found themselves encountering hostility; not least between newly arrived immigrants and those who had settled earlier. For example, the majority of those who had arrived in the mid-19th century were North European Protestants, while the immigrants of the 1900s were mostly Catholics or Jews.

There was also hostility by resident Americans. Immigrants were seen as threatening their job opportunities or depressing wage levels by working for rates that locals would not accept. Working-class resentment of these 'gate-crashers' was strong, as many feared the loss of privileges and status that were associated with their white skin colour. Only gradually did Jews, Slavs and Italians come to be considered 'white'.

Living in ethnic neighbourhoods, immigrants were targeted by local city bosses who exploited the demographics and dominated some districts, building networks of loyal voters in return for assistance. Politically, the immigrants were largely attracted to the Democratic Party.

This upset many Americans who believed in the **Jeffersonian ideal** of the individual carefully using his given right to vote, but casting it judiciously for the good of the whole. It led to accusations of nepotism and civic corruption. Worries arose as many of these immigrants were Catholic. Might they place loyalty to the Pope and the Vatican, or their parish priest above that of patriotism to the USA?

Jeffersonian ideal: the belief that society should be made up of independent small-scale farms and businesses.

These new immigrants were conspicuous and soon they were blamed for everything unsatisfactory in US society. Labour violence often began in immigrant-dominated slum areas, while restlessness among urban workers was largely blamed on East European immigrants. General health concerns grew as crowded living conditions in the tenements led to high child mortality rates. In one strongly immigrant ward in Chicago, more than 20 per cent of infants born in 1900 died in their first year of life.

The immigrants undoubtedly became scapegoats, but many people felt that – with the unrest and the political machinations – they genuinely posed a threat to democracy. In 1891, the government opened a Bureau of Immigration established under the Treasury Department. Then in 1892, the Ellis Island immigration reception centre opened in New York Bay to screen immigrants entering on the East Coast; with Angel Island in San Francisco Bay screening those on the West Coast. After 1924, Ellis Island became a detention and deportation processing station, in view of the increasingly tough anti-immigration laws passed throughout this period.

The Chinese Exclusion Act (1882) halted Chinese immigration for ten years and prevented those Chinese living in the USA from obtaining citizenship. A head tax was also placed on immigrants, which was renewed indefinitely in 1902. In many respects, this was the hinge on which US immigration policy turned and a symbol of the unfriendly climate toward minorities that would prevail for decades.

The Dillingham Commission 1907 was established by Congress to investigate social problems due to lack of assimilation. The American Federation of Labour (AFL) and other unions pressurised the Commission to restrict the flow of cheap immigrant labour, but both Republicans and Democrats were opposed to this in the Progressive Era.

Attitudes changed during the First World War and immigration halted during the conflict. Yet there was continual suspicion about the loyalty of 'enemy aliens' from Germany, Austria and Hungary living in the USA. There also existed a growing fear of a communist revolution after 1917, when the communists took over Russia and attempted takeovers in Berlin and Munich. So in 1917 the Literacy Test was brought in, requiring all immigrants into the USA to be able to speak English.

Many Americans also worried that subversives would infiltrate the USA through these East European immigrants. This led to the Sedition Act and the Alien Act in 1918, both of which fuelled anti-immigration feeling. The Sedition Act attempted to clamp down on the expression of anti-American ideas and views. The Alien Act gave the government powers to deport anybody who had been a 'member of any anarchist organisation'.

Some Justice Department officials disliked the laws and privately thought that they were undemocratic. But they also hoped that, even if there were few prosecutions, their existence would satisfy the public who urged more government action. This fuelled the first Red Scare of 1919–20, which was a reactionary impulse to foreign influences and a wish to recreate an old-fashioned America of culturally homogeneous people.

The Emergency Quota Act (1921) reduced immigration from Eastern Europe, stipulating an annual maximum of 3 per cent of people from any country who were living in the USA at the time of the 1910 census. It also applied to Italians and Poles (Catholics) and Russian Jews.

The Act aimed at restricting immigration to 350,000 people per year; half from Northern Europe and half from Southern and Eastern Europe. There were exemptions for certain professions, such as nurses, doctors, lecturers and actors. This basically prohibited the unskilled and illiterate. The Republican administrations of Harding and Coolidge, as well as the US Congress in the 1920s, were filled with **restrictionists**.

Fact: The Immigration Restriction League was founded in 1894 by Harvard-educated Bostonians who believed that the new immigrants from Southern and Eastern Europe were racially and culturally inferior to Anglo-Saxons, and that they would bring in poverty, disease, organised crime and revolution. The League opened branches in New York, Chicago and San Francisco, gathering support from writers, academics and philanthropists. They advocated a literacy test to slow the tide of immigration, which was producing an 'alarming number of illiterates, paupers, criminals, and madmen who endangered American character and citizenship'. The League employed lobbyists in Washington in the mid-1900s and aimed to build an anti-immigrant coalition consisting of farmers' associations, patriotic clubs, politicians in the South and in New England, plus others who supported its viewpoint.

ACTIVITY

Using the library and the internet, undertake some more research on the Sedition Act and the Alien Act. Why do you think these were introduced?

Restrictionists: those in Congress who wanted to drastically cut down the flow of immigration or halt it altogether.

The National Origins Act (1924) toughened the 1921 act by reducing the Eastern European quota to 2 per cent as at the 1890 census. The Act also excluded Chinese and Japanese immigrants altogether. President Coolidge signed the bill into law commenting, 'America must be kept American'. In 1929, Congress changed the base year for determining quotas from 1890 to 1920, and this formula then stood until 1965. The legislation indicated a strong conservative backlash by native-born US Protestants. Immigration fell from 1.2 million in 1914 to under 300,000 by 1929.

The law had no limits on Latin America. Political instability and poverty in Mexico, plus its proximity to the USA, meant that thousands of Mexicans moved northwards. But the Great Depression hit them badly with unemployment, and the US government forcibly sent back nearly 400,000 Mexicans and Mexican-Americans.

Figure 4.11 A black family from the South arrives in Chicago, 1919

African American migration northwards had begun in the 1890s with the expansion of industries in the North, and peaked in the war years, when 500,000 African Americans moved to cities such as New York, Chicago, Detroit, Cleveland, St Louis, Philadelphia and Boston. This so-called Great Migration, was the largest internal migration in US history.

The chance of urban work proved alluring especially when wartime munitions factories created jobs not only for women but for immigrant workers. But it added to the existing racial tensions between blacks and whites. Their arrival into cities resulted in serious housing shortages that affected the white population, meaning that black workers were stigmatised in the same way as the Eastern European immigrants had been.

Immigration control was highly restricted in the period 1924–65, although the onset of the Great Depression after 1930 did much in itself to control the flow of immigrants. The high unemployment and dire state of the US economy was evident for all to see internationally.

During the period from 1933 to 1941, the US political landscape shifted. The Democratic Party had forged a coalition of urban lower-income groups, African Americans, members of labour unions and those ethnic and religious minorities from recent immigrant groups. Franklin Roosevelt could also now add the Southern states. They all became part of a New Deal Democrat constituency and, importantly, many of the newer immigrants now felt they had a say in the affairs of their adopted country, rather than being seen as inferior.

The New Deal had brought them to the Democratic Party. Roosevelt appointed Jews and Catholics to important positions in his administration, not just Anglo-Saxon Protestants. This pleased the immigrant newcomers, who felt that FDR was their president and that he watched after their interests. By 1940, it was not uncommon for Roosevelt's picture to hang in a favoured spot in an immigrant's home or at their business. He had democratised their life and given them a stake-hold in the affairs of state as they struggled to assimilate into society and still faced opposition. Their vote counted and their opinion mattered. They and their children would vote Democrat for the next generation.

1961–74

The next significant wave of immigration followed the passing of the Immigration and Nationality Act of 1965, also known as the Hart–Celler Act. Its purpose was to increase immigration to the USA, especially from Latin America and Asia. It was a hugely significant piece of legislation enacted by Lyndon Johnson.

The admission criteria were family reunification and scarce occupational skills. The new preference system allowed highly skilled professionals – primarily doctors, nurses and engineers from Asian countries – to immigrate and eventually to sponsor their families. It shifted immigration from Europe towards Asia and Latin America, removing selection based on country of origin.

Inner cities and heavily industrialised areas of the North and East remained the likely destination for new immigrants. However, in sunbelt states such as California, Florida, Georgia and the Carolinas, there was discontent among suburban homeowners. The affluent and (often retired) white middle classes still supported segregation.

The right wing – especially those on the Christian right – continued to resist the Democrats' progressive immigration policies. But at the height of the Civil Rights Movement of the 1960s the old law was seen as an embarrassment by Kennedy, who called the quota system of the time 'nearly intolerable'. After Kennedy's assassination, President Lyndon Johnson signed the bill at the foot of the Statue of Liberty as a symbolic gesture.

The 1965 legislation transformed the USA racially and ethnically, in abolishing the quotas from the 1920s. In 1960, Asian-Americans were less than 1 per cent of the population, but would be nearly 5 per cent in 2000. Similarly, the Hispanic population would increase from 4.5 per cent in 1970, to nearly 12 per cent in 2000. The USA was now set on the road to greater population diversity and the many benefits – be they cultural, social, linguistic, musical, artistic, religious or culinary – this would bring. Immigrants to the USA and their descendants thus played a major role in broadening and enhancing US social democracy.

> **KEY CONCEPTS ACTIVITY**
>
> **Significance:** Explain the significance of the huge influx of immigrants into the USA between 1890 and 1924 and the efforts to control it.

The impact of economic forces on the USA

There are several factors or driving forces behind any economy, the existence or absence of which usually determines its success or failure. A strong labour force is crucial. Natural resources in abundance are advantageous, as is good organisation in manufacturing, so the right equipment and tools are produced. Good transportation is essential in ensuring that resources and products are carried to the places they are needed. Credit is also vital because an economy needs credit available for those buying goods, and the people selling them, so that they don't have to wait to buy what they need. A demand for products and services is essential in order for anyone to make money, and profit for the companies selling a product or service is crucial in order to keep companies in operation. The USA has seldom if ever been deficient in any of these factors.

1890–1917

Initially, the USA's economic structure meant money was made with minimal government interference: by 1890 the USA was poised to overtake Britain and Germany. A number of economic forces had precipitated its expansion: the abundance of cheap natural resources, the availability of cheap immigrant labour, a big increase in markets and a growing demand for supplies, goods and services in an expanding continent.

Technological innovations increased mechanisation: the steel plough, the refrigerated transport container and railway expansion from East to West. There was a growth in meat production for home and abroad; the opening up of the Great Plains enabled the cultivation of fertile land and inevitably led to huge surpluses, while high import tariffs kept out foreign goods.

By the 1890s, businessmen were moving from trade to manufacturing, where exceptional profits existed. Similarly, US banks now offered extended credit to the new manufacturing businesses and invested money in them. This was typified by the emergence of major industrial companies such as the Carnegie Steel Corporation, the Standard Oil Company and the Bethlehem Steel Corporation. Banking and finance sectors also adapted and expanded rapidly, as new types of financiers like J.P. Morgan emerged to bankroll this industrialisation.

Many companies merged and formed huge enterprises cutting across manufacturing, shipping and rail transportation. Inventors such as Henry Ford and Thomas Edison linked their technical creativity with their business skill and controlled all the processes for their product, such as raw materials, production and marketing. This **vertical integration** accelerated the development of trusts and monopolies. Smaller companies could not compete and when this was combined with occasional unexpected downturns in what was a largely uncontrolled economy, small businesses, farmers and their workers were often ruined. DuPont controlled nearly 90 per cent of the chemical industry and US Steel became the world's first billion-dollar corporation: it was created when Carnegie Steel Corporation was sold to J.P. Morgan in 1901.

Vertical integration: where one firm controls all the stages in the production and marketing of a product.

This had a major impact on politics, with some historians suggesting that there were undemocratic undertones, where unelected powerful industrialists were effectively running the USA in the absence of any dynamic politicians. This may be an exaggeration, but industrialisation had made the USA into an urban society, dominated both by a powerful elite and by the northeast, where most banks were centred and where businesses quickly accessed money and credit. It also gave these men direct political access and influence, especially with the Republican Party.

QUESTION

Did the American development of industry in the late 19th and early 20th century pose a threat to democracy?

SOURCE B

There was confusion about the role of government. It was clearly responsible for supporting business and industry for the good of the nation, but could the government at the same time, protect those used and abused by the realities of rapid industrial growth?

J. de Pennington (2005), Modern America: USA 1865 to the Present, *London: Hodder Murray, p. 47.*

New ideas were now discussed in the mass labour force, and workers organised into trade unions. It was also the era of the progressives, who believed in appropriate government intervention to encourage reforms and efficiency. Above all, they wanted to protect people's rights against corruption and excesses of industrialisation.

Progressive President Theodore Roosevelt established his reputation as a 'trust buster' when he acted against the Northern Securities Company, a powerful railroad trust, in 1904, and the US Supreme Court, supported him (see section 4.3). Further progressive success came when the Supreme Court ordered the dissolution of the Standard Oil Company, while President Woodrow Wilson brought in banking reform, new anti-trust laws and introduced federal income tax in 1913. This tax legislation proved to be a major economic driving force, which kick-started a process of converting the tax system from a regressive consumption-based system that hit the poorest, to a more democratic system that levied taxes based on the ability to pay. It took only a few years for federal income tax to replace revenues from tariffs as the government's chief source of income. It also facilitated a rapid expansion of the tax system after 1917, when existing taxes proved inadequate in wartime.

1920–9

Between 1920 and 1929, the USA experienced widespread prosperity, with average wage levels rising steadily. Consumers could now purchase a wider variety of goods, now available through mass production. The growing use of moving assembly lines in manufacturing also brought a sharp rise in the productivity of labour and capital.

The Republican presidents of the 1920s believed in minimal government – laissez-faire – yet wanted to create a prosperous economic and business climate to benefit all Americans.

The Ford–McCumber Tariff Act of 1922 placed import duties on farm products, chemicals, textiles, china, cutlery, farm products, guns and industrial machinery. It gave many domestic producers a guaranteed market and reduced the level of foreign trade throughout the 1920s. Then the secretary of the Treasury, Andrew Mellon, cut the tax of the rich from 50 per cent to 20 per cent. This encouraged the development of large businesses. As the *Wall Street Journal* reported in the mid-1920s: 'Never before, here or anywhere else, has the government been so completely fused with business.'

Figure 4.12 African Americans – like many people in the 1920s – could see the prosperity, but they couldn't share in it

But prosperity bypassed many: the urban poor, small farmers, African Americans, the unemployed. The economic focus of the 1920s was for affluence and the development of the free market. But as Hugh Brogan commented, 'at every stage the story displays the devastating consequences of a bland unawareness of economic and political essentials', while Doug and Susan Willoughby note, 'the continuing existence of poverty experienced by so many different groups of Americans, and the failure of anyone to deal with it, limits the extent to which the period can be judged to be an age of prosperity … it was a fragile prosperity as the Crash of 1929 clearly demonstrated'.

Laissez-faire had brought a level of prosperity across a far wider social spectrum of the USA than ever before. Nor must it be forgotten that the capitalist system survived the dreadful financial collapse of 1929–30 virtually intact. But strengths were outweighed by weaknesses: production exceeded buying power, too many large profits, high earnings and low taxes allowed huge sums of money to accumulate with individuals who failed to invest the money well.

1933–41

The economic policies of Franklin D. Roosevelt proved to be a seminal moment in US history, and while details of his New Deal will be discussed when we consider social and economic policies and reforms in Unit 3, it is no exaggeration to suggest that FDR possibly saved democracy, or at least underpinned it with the authority of the federal government – something sadly deficient in Germany in 1933.

GNP: gross national product; an economic statistic that states the market value of all finished goods and services produced by the citizens of a country in one year.

The years 1932 and 1933 were the worst of the world depression. In the USA, industrial stocks lost 80 per cent of their value since 1930. Ten thousand banks failed, **GNP** had fallen 31 per cent since 1929 and more than thirteen million people lost their jobs between 1929 and 1932. In 1933, unemployment stood at almost 25 per cent.

The Roosevelt administration acted partly on the economic ideas of **John Maynard Keynes** in an effort to revive the USA. FDR's 'New Deal' introduced some of Keynes' fiscal features that produced government deficits. The income tax system, the social security system and the unemployment insurance scheme were devised so that government revenues dropped while government expenditures increased in a period of depression.

Roosevelt then began modest deficit spending that arrested the economic downturn and resulted in respectable growth. When 1936 produced 14 per cent growth, FDR eased back on the deficit spending, against Keynes' advice, as he was worried about balancing the budget. But this caused the economy to regress into a temporary recession in 1938, and unemployment rose. The USA gradually emerged from this recession when FDR borrowed $1 billion for rearmament and, as the Second World War broke out in Europe, US munitions industries building weaponry helped to boost US finances, giving people work.

John Maynard Keynes (1883–1946)

He was a British economist whose reputation was made as a key adviser at the 1919 Paris Peace Conference. Keynes challenged orthodox economic thinking, advising government intervention to maintain economic stability. Keynesianism – as it became known – had 'deficit spending' at its core. Governments spent during a recession to prevent markets from drying up. After depression ends and prosperity returns, deficit spending must be reversed. Keynesian economists believed governments must avoid extremes in the economic system during prosperity. This meant that the money supply must not be permitted to increase in a runaway fashion. Keynesian economics thus advocated a mixed economy – chiefly private sector, but with a role for government intervention during recessions.

1961–74

America of the 1950s is often described as being 'complacent'. Indeed, when John F. Kennedy became president in 1961, he took office during a recession at the end of Eisenhower's eight-year Republican government, which he felt had been 'coasting along'. By contrast, the 1960s and 1970s held great change, as established countries – especially in Asia – became economic powerhouses, challenging the USA. Economic forces and relationships now became predominant at a time when politicians and economists began to appreciate that military might was not the only means of growth, expansion and influence in the global arena.

During the 1960s, the USA experienced its longest uninterrupted period of economic expansion, and the federal government again became the principal driving economic force. Its role in the economy grew throughout the decade; indeed, it fulfilled several economic roles: consumer, employer, regulator and – particularly under Johnson's Great Society – social welfare agency.

As a consumer, it supported scientific research, bought military equipment and built roads. By doing so, billions of dollars were injected into the US economy. As an employer, the federal government provided many civilian and military jobs. As a regulator, it kept a close watch on business in general, to manage the economy and shape the business environment.

In 1961, business bankruptcies had reached their highest level since 1932, farm incomes had decreased 25 per cent since 1951 and six million were unemployed. Many families had overstretched themselves with debt through hire-purchase schemes and freely available credit. JFK acted immediately by targeting unemployment. His response was a series of policies which are considered in **Unit 4.3**, but they were designed to lower taxes, protect the unemployed, increase the minimum wage, and focus on the business and housing sectors to stimulate the economy, thereby creating jobs and reducing unemployment.

Partly as a result of pumping money into domestic and military spending, the recession had eased by late 1961 and unemployment fell. Kennedy cut tariffs to encourage trade and stimulate industry and gave businesses $1 billion in tax credits for new equipment and investment, while the Manpower Development and Training Act of 1962 provided job training for poorly educated people in the more than forty states that had applied for funding.

Kennedy's assassination in November 1963 meant that vice-president Lyndon Johnson took over the work on reducing unemployment and poverty, and his presidency saw even greater expansion in the role of the government as an economic force. Johnson laid out his vision at the University of Michigan where he asked Americans to move toward a 'Great Society'.

Johnson believed that federal government had to set policies, establish minimum commitments for state governments to meet and provide additional funding to meet these goals. He sought high employment, improved employment rights and greater equality of opportunity in employment. These aims overlapped with his policies on health, education and social welfare (for details see Unit 4.3).

Consequently, in August 1964, Johnson signed the Economic Opportunity Act, which established the Office of Economic Opportunity to direct and coordinate a variety of educational, employment and training programmes – the foundation of Johnson's 'war on poverty'. He saw the money spent on helping the unemployed – especially the young unemployed – as a 'hand up' rather than a 'hand out'.

Johnson had an unflinching belief in the power of government to change lives and to improve the lives of the poorest in society. Jobs and work training programmes were established for 10,000 youths: nearly 250,000 homes were built, and support was given to depressed country areas. Unemployment dropped by 5 per cent.

LBJ introduced Kennedy's tax reduction bills, which boosted consumer spending, while military spending on the Vietnam War brought jobs in munitions and defence, and boosted army recruitment. But the Vietnam War and its cost would impact on Johnson's plans, proving that economic forces in any country can sometimes become hostage to external influences.

When Richard Nixon became president in 1969, his term coincided with the onset of inflation and a gradual end to the decade of unprecedented prosperity in the USA. Big-spending federal government programmes were questioned, and with rises in crime and racial conflicts, many Americans wondered if the Great Society reforms had been misguided.

When Nixon spoke of 'local control' and 'self-help', many feared he would dismantle Johnson's liberal reforms, but although he emphasised individual fiscal responsibility, Nixon recognised the need for a government role, and accepted the basic outline of the welfare state as advocated by the Democrats. He was concerned by what he saw as an inflated welfare system, which provided money and encouraged a culture of dependence and low self-esteem. Nixon argued that welfare also contributed to the breakdown of families by providing assistance only to households not headed by a working male.

Nixon created the Family Assistance Plan (FAP), which gave direct cash payments to those in need. Conservatives disliked the idea of a guaranteed income for people who didn't work, while liberals and trade unions saw the proposal as a threat to the minimum wage, fearing that many jobs would be eliminated. The FAP was dropped by Nixon prior to the 1972 election.

By the time of his re-election, unemployment stood at 5.6 per cent and he was presiding over the 'Nixon recession' of 1971–4. With the downturn in world affairs precipitated by the oil crisis, by the end of Nixon's presidency in 1974 there was 12 per cent inflation and even higher unemployment. Nixon's economic 'halfway-house' of New Deal government intervention and Republican individualism was undone by the aftermath of a war in the Middle East, the legacy of Vietnam and the deep public crisis of confidence in US institutions following the Watergate scandal.

KEY CONCEPTS QUESTION

Causes and Consequences: What were the causes and consequences of the decision by President Kennedy to build housing, lower taxes and increase the minimum wage after becoming president in 1961?

QUESTION

What evidence is there that Kennedy's and Johnson's proactive administrations were the driving economic forces in the USA during the 1960s?

The impact of foreign influences on the USA

Immigration, prohibition and 'alien culture'

Today the USA is viewed – for good or bad – as the world's policeman, exerting global influence. American culture has permeated the planet, with corporate icons such as Coca-Cola, McDonald's, Kellogg's, Ford and Microsoft. The USA has influenced or forced the hand of many nations. But there have been a few occasions when the USA has itself been influenced by outside factors.

In the early 19th century, many Americans were concerned about immigrants; especially those later arrivals from Eastern and Southern Europe, whom they felt did not embrace American culture and imported unsettling political ideas such as **anarchism** and **communism**. This became a particularly worry when President McKinley was assassinated in September 1901 by Leon Czolgosz, an American anarchist of Polish immigrant descent. After McKinley's death, the new President Theodore Roosevelt declared: 'When compared with the suppression of anarchy, every other question sinks into insignificance.' Similarly, Russian immigrants came under scrutiny after the 1917 Russian Revolution when communists toppled the royal family and the entire structure of government. By the end of the First World War in 1918, these foreign influences had impacted on US domestic life.

Another major issue was **Prohibition**, introduced under the 1919 Volstead Act. Alcohol was seen by many as un-American, and by the time Prohibition was made law across all the USA, 75 per cent of states had already approved it. It also had religious implications, as most new immigrants were Catholic or Eastern Orthodox. Many of them originated from cultures where social drinking, especially by men, was a central part of everyday life; for example, wine drunk with meals in Mediterranean countries, or vodka in Poland and Russia.

Members of the middle-class Protestant Anti Saloon League were critical of the behaviour of wine-drinking immigrants in crime-ridden cities such as Chicago. There

CHIEF EXECUTIVE THE VICTIM OF MOST COWARDLY ANARCHIST

JOYOUS THRONG SHOCKED

Many Witness the Assault on Guest.

President Strives to Calm Enraged People.

When Serious Nature of Wounds Appear an Uproar Ensues.

SHOOTER PROMPTLY ARRESTED.

Saved From the Enraged Populace.

Attempt Is Made to Lynch Fiendish Assassin.

Officers of the Law Lose No Time in Jailing the Prisoner.

Figure 4.13 Front page of a newspaper reports the shooting of President McKinley in September 1901 and demonstrates the fear of anarchism in the country at the time

Anarchism: a political theory with the idea that all forms of government are oppressive and undesirable and should be abolished. Anarchism aims to create a society within which individuals freely cooperate together as equals. Control by the state or by capitalism is seen as harmful to the individual and their individuality, as well as unnecessary.

Communism: a social and economic system in which all key components of a country's economy are owned and managed socially; either by the state, by local communities or by cooperatives. As opposed to capitalist countries, where land, industries and banks are privately owned, social ownership is intended to result in a classless society.

Prohibition: the campaign to ban the selling or consumption of alcoholic drinks, which was successfully implemented in law by the National Prohibition Act or the Volstead Act in 1919. It defined liquor as drink containing 0.5 per cent of alcohol and prescribed penalties for breaking the law. It remained in place until 1933, when Frankline Roosevelt repealed the Act.

was also pressure from groups such as the Women's Christian Temperance Union, which campaigned for Prohibition in the hope that it would reduce family neglect and improve the health of Americans. Small-town America was worried about 'alien culture' undermining traditional values. Some industrialists also exerted pressure, claiming that drinking alcohol reduced productivity and industrial efficiency.

Also, many brewers were German and as the USA had just been at war with Germany, people did not want to buy or drink their alcohol. Anti-German feeling, combined with suspicion of East Europeans, was very strong at the time the legislation went before Congress.

But Prohibition led to a massive increase in organised crime and corruption. Gangsters controlled towns and cities using bribery and violence to protect their moneymaking businesses. One Chicago mobster ran all the illegal drinking saloons or 'speakeasies' in the area, accumulating $30 million before he retired. Worryingly, the amount gangsters acquired meant that politicians could be controlled or bribed, as could the poorly paid law enforcement agents.

By 1930, there were 32,000 speakeasies in New York – twice the number of its legal saloons before Prohibition. Prohibition ended in March 1933 as Franklin Roosevelt became president, because of a massive shift in public opinion. Millions of Americans became convinced that Prohibition was pointless and the 21st Amendment cancelled the Volstead Act. Prohibition was dead and its enduring success was the huge growth of the soft drinks manufacturers, notably Coca-Cola!

The Red Scare and intolerance in the 1920s

Liberal America retreated in the 1920s, as reaction, suspicion and intolerance were visibly asserted. US participation in the First World War and the activities of communists in Russia and Germany both acted as catalysts that generated reaction and racism. Congress had already passed two acts predicated on a fear of foreigners, radicals and revolutionaries: the Sedition Act and the Alien Act, but the reaction continued.

Following a series of bombings by anarchists in 1919 – one of which almost killed US attorney Mitchell Palmer – the Justice Department ordered raids on magazine offices, union headquarters and private houses. They rounded up 6,000 'aliens' who were detained in prison without a hearing, and deported hundreds. Many of the immigrants arrested were peaceful people and they were eventually released.

Palmer organised this purge, having fuelled a Red Scare by alleging that there were around 150,000 communists in the USA working to spread communism. Some state governments tried to expel elected socialists from their seats and there were many bad prosecutions undertaken in an atmosphere of hysteria. Largely, the Palmer Raids were a response to imaginary threats. One example was the case of Nicola Sacco and Bartolomeo Vanzetti.

Sacco and Vanzetti were Italian immigrants and known anarchists who had opposed the war, evaded army service and supported strikes. Following a series of robberies in Massachusetts that involved fatal shootings, Sacco and Vanzetti were arrested and charged in May 1920. They had anti-government booklets in their car when apprehended and were unable to prove their whereabouts on the day of the crimes.

Public opinion was critical of them both because they were immigrants and because of their politics. Sixty witnesses said they had seen them, but their defence lawyer had 107 witnesses confirming that they had been elsewhere when the crimes were committed. The judge was prejudiced against them, and on circumstantial evidence they were convicted and sentenced to death.

Another man then admitted that he had committed the crimes, but Sacco and Vanzetti lost an appeal and in August 1927 they were both executed by electrocution. The trial became an international '**cause celebre**'.

In another famous example, John Scopes, a biology teacher in Dayton, Tennessee, was arrested and charged for teaching Charles Darwin's theory of evolution to his classes in 1925. In the early 1920s, Christian fundamentalists had succeeded in passing the Butler Act, banning the teaching of anything contradictory to the literal version of the creation story as described in Genesis. Six southern states (including Tennessee) had implemented this law.

The American Civil Liberties Union (ACLU) offered to defend anyone who wished to test the law. The Scopes or 'Monkey' Trial – as it became known – commenced. A momentous courtroom battle between ACLU lawyer Clarence Darrow and fundamentalist politician and ex-Republican candidate William Jennings Bryan, led to Scopes being found guilty of breaking a state law and fined $100. But Bryan was belittled in court and his **fundamentalism** was ridiculed by the press. The Butler Act remained in force until 1967.

Both the Sacco and Vanzetti Case and the Scopes Trial reveal the gulf in US society at this time and the widespread existence of bigotry, fear of immigrants and modernity, suspicion of foreign influences and the clash between big-city liberals and small-town traditionalists.

Cause celebre: an issue or test case, attracting great discussion across a wide area – often internationally. With respect to Sacco and Vanzetti, it gravitated into something much bigger. They were immigrants and victims of racial discrimination. The trial was prejudiced by fear of subversion and other foreign influences. Moreover, the defendants held political views that, however unpalatable, they had a right to hold in a democracy. They were victims of the mood of the day.

Fundamentalism: the firm belief that events in the Bible are literally true and correct.

The domestic impact of the Vietnam War in the 1960s

President Johnson was concerned about the impact of the Vietnam War on his domestic policies – not least upon his democratic reforms; the Great Society. He had every right to be. By March 1965, he had made the war in Vietnam a fully American war by commencing strategic air strikes on North Vietnam and committing the first ground forces, two battalions of US Marines.

Protests grew over this commitment and in November 1965, 40,000 protesters, led by several student activist groups, surrounded the White House, calling for an end to the war. They then marched to the Washington Monument. On the same day, Johnson announced a troop increase in Vietnam from 120,000 to 400,000.

The draft system was a particularly hated aspect of the war. In 1964, only 16 per cent of those drafted were killed, but by 1968 it was 60 per cent. The draft also drew unfairly on the population, and hit African Americans and white working-class men hardest, with 80 per cent of enlisted men coming from such backgrounds. Many questioned why they should fight in Vietnam when they still faced discrimination, poverty and lack of opportunity at home. This impacted upon domestic stability in the USA.

By 1968, US forces numbered 540,000, replacing the South Vietnamese army in fighting the Vietcong. But the Vietcong was aided by equipment from suppliers in North Vietnam, who in turn received equipment from the Soviets. The unfamiliar jungle terrain and climate proved hazardous to US soldiers facing a Vietcong experienced in guerrilla warfare. Booby-traps and ambushes frequently thwarted disheartened US troops.

US bombers also hit few real targets, although between 1965 and 1968, more US bombs were dropped on North Vietnam alone than upon Nazi Germany, Italy and Japan combined during the Second World War. But all this cost the US taxpayer $30 billion a year, while 300 soldiers' bodies were being repatriated weekly in 1968. This aroused huge anti-war sentiment.

As early as December 1965, Johnson's economic advisers urged a tax increase to help pay for the increasingly expensive war and to hold down inflation. For political reasons,

ACTIVITY

Try to watch the 1960 Hollywood film *Inherit the Wind* about the Scopes Trial, featuring Spencer Tracy as Clarence Darrow and Frederic March as William Jennings Bryan.

QUESTION

What evidence is there that the USA in the 1920s was marked by a reaction to modernity?

Fact: Vietnam was seized by France in the 19th century. In 1930, Vietnamese nationalist Ho Chi Minh formed the Indo-Chinese Communist Party or Vietminh to fight for independence. During the Second World War the Vietminh fought against Japan, so it expected the USA to help it to gain independence. But the USA feared communism and supported France's efforts to contain communism in Indo-China. A war of independence was fought between France and the Vietminh. France lost, and a peace conference in Geneva divided Vietnam between a pro-US South and a communist North. By 1958, South Vietnamese communists (Vietcong) were fighting a guerrilla war against the South Vietnamese government and Ho Chi Minh announced his intention to reunite Vietnam. By 1963, the USA had sent 16,000 military advisors to support South Vietnam, but 35 per cent of South Vietnam was in Vietcong hands, so more troops were required. An opportunity arose with the Gulf of Tonkin incident in August 1964, when the US destroyer *Maddox* – on an intelligence information-gathering exercise – was fired on by North Vietnamese patrol boats. President Johnson got Congress to pass the Gulf of Tonkin Resolution, which gave him authority to 'take all necessary steps including the use of armed force' to protect South Vietnam and basically prosecute war without making a formal declaration. In 1965, Johnson sent in ground troops.

Figure 4.14 Map of Vietnam, 1965

Johnson ignored their advice until 1968, when he introduced a 10 per cent income tax surcharge, which was too little too late. In fact, a growingly strident Congress got tough with Johnson and actually refused the 1968 tax surcharge until he agreed to cut $6 billion from non-defence programmes.

There is no doubt that Johnson would have spent more on his Great Society domestic reform policies had he not had to pay for Vietnam. It appalled liberals that social reforms were being shelved and economic plans distorted by a Democrat government running a $150 million war that was being lost by soldiers who were no longer willing to fight.

Things came to a head when an offensive was launched by the North Vietnamese and Vietcong during the Tet religious festival in January 1968. Towns and US bases across the south were attacked, including the US embassy in Saigon. By April, the US had regained nearly all land and bases lost, killing 50,000 communist troops, but the fact that this could happen to a supposed superpower had a huge impact, not least by igniting the growing anti-war movement in the US.

Consequently in March 1968, Johnson quit the presidential race, began peace talks with North Vietnam in Paris and scaled down the bombing. The price Johnson paid was his presidency, so his successor Richard Nixon knew that his fortunes likewise hinged on forces beyond US shores. Nixon took office at a time when universities and colleges were bubbling with discontent, as war still raged in Vietnam, as Robert D. Schulzinger discusses in **Source C**.

SOURCE C

Nixon had no secret plan for ending the war in Vietnam, but he knew what he did not like. The war had wrecked Johnson's ability to act freely in foreign affairs and the new president wanted to restore the authority of the White House.

R.D. Schulzinger (2002), US Diplomacy Since 1900, *5th edn, Oxford: Oxford University Press, p. 289.*

But the price ordinary people paid was in the Great Society not fulfilling its real potential. Johnson, distracted by Vietnam, found it hard to provide the robust legislative leadership necessary for implementing further reforms. Millions benefitted from his education and health care programmes, but his zeal of 1964–5 could not be maintained.

The impact of Vietnam on US domestic politics between 1964 and 1969 was enormous. It influenced future events on the home front dramatically by dragging the USA into an all-consuming foreign policy. It diverted much-needed funds for further social reform and it brought the downfall of a president while dramatically altering the way future presidents thought about military interventions. Few periods in domestic, legislative history were more shaped by foreign influences than the USA in the mid-1960s.

Fact: For more than fifty years, the draft system provided back-up personnel for the US Armed Forces. Between 1948 and 1973, men were drafted into the armed forces to fill vacancies. As US troop strength in Vietnam increased, more men were drafted, yet many at home sought ways of avoiding it. For those seeking a safer alternative to the army, navy or air force, the coast guard was an option. Since only a handful of national guard and reserve units were sent to Vietnam, enlisting in the guard or the reserves became a favoured tactic. In 1973, the draft ended and the US converted to an all-volunteer military.

4.6 How did the government respond to domestic crises?

Since 1890, the US government has faced many challenges, international conflicts and several wars. But it has also had to respond to a number of specific major domestic crises that had the potential either to threaten democracy itself, or precipitate massive upheaval in the economic, political or legislative system. Three of these will now be summarised, each of which invite further student research in themselves.

Democracy and capitalism in crisis: the depression of 1893–7

President **Grover Cleveland** had to face a major domestic crisis – the most severe depression the nation had suffered to that point – in his second term as president from 1893 to 1897. The panic of 1893 was a spectacular financial crisis that contributed to a major economic recession and threatened domestic stability.

During the 1880s, railway companies had acted spontaneously in a time of economic boom by issuing more stock and promising investors higher dividends than they ought.

Grover Cleveland (1837–1908)

He was the only US president to serve two non-consecutive terms of office – 1885–9 and 1893–7 – and was the first Democrat elected after the Civil War. A lawyer and former governor of New York, Cleveland believed in self-sufficiency, personal integrity and fiscal conservatism. He believed that the presidency was a check on abuses by Congress and he vetoed 414 bills in his first term. His second term coincided with a major financial depression and time of domestic crisis.

Growth slowed in 1890 and, just as Cleveland took office for the second time in 1893, the Philadelphia & Reading Railroad, a major eastern line, failed.

This collapse triggered a panic as alarmed investors converted stock holdings to gold. Stock prices dropped dramatically in May and June and gold reserves sank. By the end of 1894, seventy-four railroads and almost 600 banks had failed, while businesses dependent upon the Philadelphia & Reading and other railroads had also crashed. Fearing further collapses, European investors had withdrawn funds, but the crisis eventually reached Europe. A full scale depression – hitherto unknown in magnitude – hit the USA. This was magnified by an ongoing agricultural depression in the West and South, which continued to deepen, with farm prices falling 20 per cent over the next three years.

In 1894, the USA had an 18 per cent unemployment rate, which then soared. Eventually, more than 30 per cent of the wage earners in manufacturing and 25 per cent of urban workers stood idle: they were also discontent as the crisis exacted a heavy human toll.

Newly arrived immigrants faced disaster, while resident Americans had no money to heat their homes or feed their families. Two exceptionally harsh winters on the East Coast in 1894 and 1895, overwhelmed relief services in places such as New York, Boston and Philadelphia. Still President Cleveland did little, believing that the business cycle was a natural phenomenon that would correct itself. But unrest grew across the country.

In Ohio, Jacob Coxey, a self-taught monetary expert, suggested to Cleveland a $500m public works programme funded with paper money – not backed by gold, but simply called 'legal tender' as per today. With gathering support for his scheme, he organised Coxey's Army – a band of Midwest unemployed workers – to march to Washington, DC. Thousands joined and 500 reached Washington in April 1894. The US press covered the march widely, but Coxey's efforts failed since Cleveland was unmoved and believed that government should not sponsor work projects to alleviate the depression. Cleveland then had Coxey and several hundred of his supporters arrested. At the time, Coxey was viewed as a dangerous eccentric by the Washington establishment, yet his requests closely resembled government programmes later adopted in the 1930s.

Then 150,000 railroad workers from all over the USA went on strike in sympathy with the Pullman Car Workers' strike near Chicago. The governor of Illinois implored Cleveland not to send in federal troops to break the strike, but the president did. He crushed the revolt and arrested the leaders. Unsurprisingly, some Americans blamed the tense atmosphere and growing violence on the strikers and marchers, but others sympathised with the plight of the underpaid and unemployed. In a polarised situation, many feared that the USA was either facing anarchy or the end of democracy and the beginning of presidential tyranny.

Cleveland's handling of the strike alienated many Northern workers from the Democratic Party and sparked great general criticism. The series of failures and bankruptcies led to an upsurge in business consolidation and the growth of trusts, with poorer people and immigrants believed they had been neglected. Cleveland was viewed by many as an unsympathetic bully, only concerned about protecting his presidential power. His responses reveal how oblivious he was to many aspects of this situation.

Cleveland blamed all the economic problems on the **Sherman Silver Purchasing Act** passed during the previous Republican administration. He tried to repeal the act, which split the Democratic Party. His heavy-handedness and abject failure to deal with a serious depression brought a huge Republican victory in the 1894 mid-term elections and

Sherman Silver Purchasing Act: an 1890 law that required the US Treasury to purchase 4.5 million ounces of silver a month for coinage as silver dollars. The purchased silver would also allow the government to issue notes to the public that could be redeemed for silver or gold. In consequence, silver production increased while gold supply fell, making gold more expensive. By 1893, the gold value of the silver dollar fell to sixty cents.

virtually gifted the White House to Republican William McKinley in 1896. Cleveland left the presidency an embittered but defiant man, believing he was misunderstood.

Historians see Cleveland's presidency as strengthening the power of the executive branch in relation to Congress and taking a step towards the emergence of the modern presidency that truly began with Theodore Roosevelt in 1901; although the negative side of this is that Cleveland distanced himself from reality and wider advisors in the party machine. He insisted that the president had a 'special relationship' with the people that superseded any obligation to party workers. It was almost monarchical in tone; yet he remained oblivious to the deprivations of 'his people'.

Overall, the 1890s depression was akin to the Great Depression of the 1930s. It was a very serious domestic crisis that threatened both the entire financial system and the greater US stability. Cleveland made no attempts to pass laws or grant aid to end the chaos. Instead he reacted harshly to the revolts and protests of angry, hungry and unsatisfied citizens. In doing so, he fuelled a disastrous depression that would last for nearly five years, and alienated many people from both the economy and the entire political process.

Theory of Knowledge

History and ideology:
President Cleveland believed firmly in self-sufficiency, persona integrity and fiscal conservatism. Does awareness of his viewpoint help the historian to understand or justify his inaction on the welfare front towards ordinary people during a time of severe crisis?

The banking crisis of 1932–3

Snow or rain;
Temp.—Max. 36; Min. 28

PRICE—THREE CENTS

BANKS OF ENTIRE NATION ARE CLOSED FOR BRIEF HOLIDAY

Federal Government To Provide Temporary Medium of Exchange

Washington, March 6.—(U.P.)—The nation began a four-day emergency bank holiday today with assurance from the federal government that a ... for payrolls and other essential needs would be pro- ... Thursday for corrective

Figure 4.15 News headlines covering the announcement of FDR's bank holiday, March 1933

When Franklin Roosevelt was inaugurated as US president on 4 March 1933, he faced an immediate domestic and fiscal crisis of major proportions, and a demoralised, impoverished nation.

In the four months since his election in November 1932, unemployment had reached fifteen million and those in work had seen their wages cut. Strikes had spread, and buses and trains stopped running in many towns and cities as transport companies went bankrupt; even gas and electric supplies were cut off. Daily life was severely threatened, as was the democratic system. In Germany, similar traumas had brought the death of democracy under the Nazi Party.

Roosevelt had no illusions about the gravity of his inheritance and the need to act quickly, tackling high unemployment, widespread poverty and economic mismanagement. But underpinning all of this was an inherited banking crisis, as the governors of thirty-four states had closed their states' banks. Roosevelt's response to this most precarious element of the entire crisis situation would be critical.

In the weeks prior to his inauguration, Roosevelt and his economic team had met frequently and concluded that the banking situation nationally was so serious that only swift and drastic measures could save the banks from closure. Borrowers defaulted repaying their banks, householders missed mortgage payments and increasing queues of depositors withdrew their funds in gold or gold certificates. A proposal was even made to give the Treasury the authority to deposit government funds directly in any bank looking likely to collapse, but even the Treasury itself did not have sufficient funds to deposit. Thousands of banks had failed since October 1932, when the governor of Nevada had declared a twelve-day bank holiday to stop a run on the banks in his state. But alarm spread from coast to coast, and in February 1933 there was a run on banks in Detroit. It was evident a major domestic crisis was gathering speed and magnitude.

Also, under the US constitution, the new president could not take office until March, despite being elected in November. This produced a state of limbo between the outgoing free-market, non-interventionist administration of President Hoover and the intentions of the incoming Roosevelt. Mimicking this political situation, US banking likewise ground to a halt in the last week of February 1933. So when FDR became president on 4 March 1933, the whole financial structure of the USA – and perhaps the capitalist system – was at stake.

Roosevelt leapt into action by ordering all banks to close on his second day in office, Monday 6 March (see Figure 4.15). He then created the Emergency Banking Act on 9 March, which imposed a four-day bank holiday. The accounts of all US banks were to be inspected and then only those with a surplus of cash and properly managed accounts would be permitted to reopen, under careful supervision.

So for an entire week, Americans had no access to banks or banking services. They could not withdraw or transfer their money, nor could they make deposits. The night before the end of the banking holiday, FDR gave his first radio fireside chat to the US public, in order to restore confidence. He told Americans that their money would now be safe in the banks and to stop withdrawing. His message worked and the following day deposits exceeded withdrawals.

So within the first hundred days of his presidency – when FDR brought in a huge amount of legislation – he brought in another banking act. The Glass–Steagall Act of June 1933 judiciously prevented commercial high street banks from indulging in investment banking; a major cause of the 1929 Wall Street Crash. FDR also set up the Federal Deposit Insurance Corporation (FDIC), which guaranteed small bank deposits up to a maximum of $5,000.

While some banking sector differences persisted – for example, in the division between federal and state-organised institutions – FDR's reforms stabilised banking. He boosted security further by introducing the Federal Securities Act, which monitored the Stock Exchange by requiring the disclosure of certain types of information to investors. In June

1934 he extended government supervision further by introducing the Securities and Exchange Commission to help regulate the Stock Exchange further. By 1936, no banks at all had collapsed in the USA for the first time in sixty years.

Roosevelt's proactive response to the banking crisis of 1932–3 was in contrast to Cleveland's in 1893. Both responses to these major domestic crises – laissez-faire and New Deal – were within the constraints of the fundamental structure of the capitalist system, but that is about all they have in common. Roosevelt realised that he had inherited a society that had lost faith in many of its own institutions, and democracy or rule of law might be next. During his election campaign he commented that 'the country needs and, unless I mistake its temper, the country demands bold persistent experimentation'. FDR provided it with strong responses, but not as in Germany or Italy under the banners of fascism, but under the flag of democracy, saving the economic system of the USA.

QUESTION

How effectively did Roosevelt respond to the domestic banking crisis?

The Watergate scandal 1972–4

In 1972, President Nixon had just visited Beijing and Moscow. It was an election year, and the Republican president was arguably at the height of his prestige in international affairs and was unopposed as the Republican Party candidate for re-election that year.

At dawn on 17 June, police in Washington, DC were called to the office of the Democratic Party National Committee (DNC), located in the Watergate Building. The five prowlers who were arrested inside turned out to be linked to Nixon's re-election campaign, and they were caught trying to steal secret documents and set up listening devices in the offices.

Over the next two years, 'Watergate' would unravel and reveal the greatest abuse of presidential power and criminality by the US Executive. The arrest of those five men was the first step toward unearthing numerous misdeeds by the Nixon administration. It was to conceal these other crimes that Nixon and his team instigated the cover-up; the investigation of which in turn unravelled the illegal conduct. Two investigative reporters with the *Washington Post*, Bob Woodward and Carl Bernstein, played a major role in linking Nixon with the Watergate break-in.

The scandal caused a major crisis of government for the USA, yet by virtue of the very investigations and enquiries that ultimately led to Nixon's resignation, Watergate also became a case study in the operation and triumph of the American constitution and its democratic, political values.

While historians today are still unsure whether or not Nixon knew about the Watergate operation before it happened, what later emerged with certainty was that he took steps immediately to cover it up. Nixon raised 'hush money' for the burglars, and obstructed the Federal Bureau of Investigation (FBI) from investigating this incident by getting evidence destroyed and by sacking uncooperative members of his personal staff and administration. On 9 August 1974, facing **impeachment** by Congress after his role in the Watergate conspiracy had been fully exposed, Nixon resigned. His successor, **Gerald Ford**, immediately pardoned Nixon. In the eyes of many, Ford dealt badly with this aspect of the crisis, but he argued that in pardoning Nixon he was trying to move forward, put the past behind them for everybody's sake and put an end to Nixon's torment.

Nixon later explained to British television interviewer Sir David Frost, that he was not the first US president to use the FBI or the Central Intelligence Agency (CIA) to

Impeachment: to accuse a public official before an appropriate tribunal of misconduct in office. In the USA this would occur in Congress with charges made in the lower house (House of Representatives) and trial to take place before the upper house (Senate).

Gerald Ford (1913–2006)

He was a former lawyer who entered the House of Representatives as a Republican in 1948. He became vice-president in 1973 and succeeded Nixon as US president in 1974. He lost to Democrat Jimmy Carter in the 1976 presidential election.

monitor political opponents. But Nixon's constant covering up and lying diminished his position even more in the eyes of the US public.

Figure 4.16 President Richard Nixon, right, and his wife Pat, second from right, leave the White House in Washington for the last time following his resignation, escorted by vice-president Gerald Ford and his wife Betty, 9 August 1974

> **ACTIVITY**
> Using the library and the internet, research further into Watergate. Create a timeline of the unfolding events from June 1972 to August 1974. Look for mini-biographies of Nixon's advisers and the members of his cabinet. Consider also the role of the press and especially Woodward and Bernstein. Then make a bullet-point list to answer whether or not you consider Watergate to be a crisis point in US constitutional politics.

Although Nixon was never prosecuted, Watergate changed American politics forever, causing the public to question their president and political leaders. It also demonstrated the strengths of the US system. Nixon was forced from office because of the public outcry: democracy in action. It also served notice to future presidents that deceit would not be tolerated.

But an inherent weakness was demonstrated, in that the system itself neither guarded against Nixon's excesses of presidential power, nor detected them when they first happened. Watergate was appropriately described by President Gerald Ford as a 'constitutional nightmare and domestic crisis', but the USA survived it with its constitution and form of government intact.

4.7 How did the government react to protest movements?

US governments had to cope with various protest movements; most notably those relating to popular protests such as the Populist Movement in the 1890s, women's suffrage and emancipation in the 1920s and the Vietnam anti-war movement in the 1960s.

The Populist Movement

The Populist Movement of the late 19th century was the largest, indigenous, democratic mass protest movement in US history. It sprang from an agrarian revolt in the South and Midwest against both political parties for appearing disinterested in their problems.

Many felt that basic democratic, economic tenets of their society were working against them. Millions of farmers felt abandoned to the excesses of industrialisation, as proven by the events in their lives: drought, crop failure, falling prices – especially for Southern cotton – and poor credit facilities. Farmers increasingly felt a sense of isolation.

The entrepreneurial success and growing affluence of those involved in manufacturing and in business corporations was resented. Many railroad owners, money-lenders and others with whom farmers did business had given their agrarian counterparts a hard time and driven a hard bargain, often patronisingly.

During the 1880s, two organisations formed: the segregated National Farmers' Alliance and the Coloured Farmers' Alliance. They won important regional victories and carried out protests, but many knew that a national party was needed in order to progress.

The seminal moment was the adoption of the 1890 McKinley Tariff, crippling those farmers who sold their harvests on unprotected markets yet had to purchase expensive manufactured goods. So to protest against the tariff, thousands of farmers united to vote the Republicans out of the House of Representatives in the 1890 congressional elections. This success motivated many to move from mass protesting towards political organising. By 1892 they had formed the Populist, or People's Party.

It had a radical agenda for its day that shook both the Democrats and Republicans. Its significance as a protest movement was that the People's Party challenged the corporate state and the ideology it put forward.

Meeting in Nebraska at their convention in 1892, the Populists issued the Omaha Platform, a manifesto almost revolutionary for its day, denouncing laissez-faire economics and government. They demanded that the federal government helped to buffer economic depressions and regulate the stock exchange, banks and massive corporations. They sought the 'free and unlimited coinage of silver and gold', an increase in the money supply and realistic help for farmers suffering hardship.

Among many other demands in the Platform were some particularly far-seeing ones, such as:

- Progressive income tax – there was no income tax in 1892 and the government received its income from tariffs on goods and the sale of public lands.
- National ownership of transportation and communication – seen by both main parties as socialist, too radical and a threat to private enterprise and capitalism. Populists demanded that the railroad, telephone and telegraph systems were so important that they should be owned by the people.
- Privatisation of land held by corporations 'in excess of their actual needs' and reclamation of the 'land owned by aliens'.
- The direct election of United States senators – in 1892, legislators chose senators. But this was a weakness in the democratic chain, since state legislators were susceptible to special interests. Populists argued that letting people vote directly for senators would ultimately reduce nepotism and produce a government that was more accountable to the people.

- The regular use of the referendum – having a referendum on crucial matters would give voters power to approve or reject legislation.
- A one-term limit on presidents – at that time there was no limit, although no president had served more than two four-year terms.

The Populist Party contested the presidential election in 1892, with the two main parties being alarmed by this party of protest. Feeling threatened by the 'crazy' Populists, they agreed to run a relatively uncontroversial campaign. The Republicans nominated incumbent Benjamin Harrison while the Democrats nominated New Yorker Grover Cleveland for a second, non-consecutive term. The Democrats held on to their power base in Southern states, by appealing to white supremacy and using some intimidation. Many refused to risk white supremacy by voting against them.

Although they did not win, the Populists gained more than one million votes and carried four states – Colorado, Idaho, Nevada and Kansas. Presidential candidate James Weaver saw several members of his party elected to Congress, three governors and hundreds of minor officials and legislators, nearly all in the Midwest.

In the South, the Populists challenged white supremacy by forming coalitions with black farmers. These coalitions then worked hard between 1892 and 1896 and eventually won several elections in different states. They also controlled the legislature in South Carolina. But the big breakthrough never materialised.

Having won the 1892 election, Cleveland and the Democrats were severely weakened by the crisis of 1893–4. Some Populists, called 'fusionists', urged Weaver and other officials to seize control of the Democratic Party away from its more conservative leaders. But others wanted to maintain a separate third party. Other factions felt in 1896 that the focus should be on running well-organised campaigns. This indecision proved costly and the Populists missed their chance to break the two-party dominance.

By 1896, the Populists had largely fused with the Democratic Party, although with the Republican domination of elections thereafter until 1912, the Populists slowly diminished as a political force. But as economists, they were considerably more thoughtful and realistic than their contemporary rivals in both major parties; and as organisers of a huge democratic movement, Populists were far more advanced than most Americans, then or since. They were also revolutionary.

SOURCE D

As a cultural movement of radical agrarian protest, populism effectively rejected the re-definition of America as an urban, industrial and corporatist state.

A. Munslow (1992), Discourse and Culture: the Creation of America 1870–1920, *London: Routledge, p. 14.*

QUESTION

What changes did the Populists hope to make to the political and economic system?

They undoubtedly helped set the goals of the progressive movement and by 1920, the USA had direct election of senators, income tax, railroad regulation and referendum.

FDR's New Deal, was undoubtedly indebted to some of the more radical points expressed in the Omaha Platform. An agrarian protest movement had turned political and eventually caused future governments to acknowledge many of its precepts.

Women's suffrage and emancipation

The US campaign for women's suffrage began in the 1820s, when the first articles written by women appeared in publications. They advocated the vote for women, but also promoted topics such as education, birth control, divorce laws, career opportunities for women and the abolition of slavery.

The organised movement for women's rights originated when the Seneca Falls Convention was held in 1848 to discuss 'the social, civil and religious rights of women'. From then until the Civil War began in 1860, annual conventions were held and soon there were two suffrage groups in existence: the National Woman Suffrage Association (NWSA) and the American Woman Suffrage Association (AWSA). The campaign had its first success in 1869 when the territory of Wyoming gave women the vote.

But it became apparent that success was going to be slow. Utah territory gave women the vote in 1870, Colorado in 1893 and Idaho in 1896. By 1914, eight more states had made amendments to state constitutions conferring full suffrage to women, including the important state of California in 1911. But the more industrial Eastern states resisted. Despite 600,000 signatures, a petition for women's suffrage was ignored by New York state officials in 1894, while an amendment to the US constitution regarding full voting rights for women across all states was put before every Congress after 1878 but never succeeded in passing.

It was obvious that more concerted effort was needed, so in 1890 the two suffrage groups united as the National American Woman Suffrage Association (NAWSA). Over the next thirty years, a large number of women in the USA subsequently became involved in the protests and campaigns for women's rights. There was greater solidarity than before, although women's groups still focused on a range of issues, rather than uniting fully behind political rights. Consequently, between 1890 and 1920, protests and campaigns were stepped up, usually to the dismay of the authorities.

Associations of Jewish and coloured women were formed and by 1920, women were accepted as fully qualified doctors and lawyers.

In 1912, Theodore Roosevelt's Progressive Party included women's suffrage in their presidential election manifesto and in 1913, on the eve of President Woodrow Wilson's inauguration, women's suffrage campaigners marched in parade in Washington, DC. They were attacked by a mob and hundreds of women were injured, several seriously, but no arrests were made.

In 1916, a more radical group broke from the NAWSA and form the National Women's Party (NWP). Led by **Alice Paul**, the NWA began a more aggressive campaign. They helped to secure the election of a woman to Congress and in 1917 picketed the White House in winter weather, enduring public abuse and ridicule.

Later that year, sixty-eight women – many of them NWA members – became the USA's first political prisoners when they were arrested for peaceful picketing. They were imprisoned, but staged hunger strikes and were force-fed. Some of the women also alleged abuse by prison guards. President Wilson now knew that this was becoming a serious issue, distracting attention from the war and proving to be an international embarrassment. So in January, 1918 he announced that women's **suffrage** was urgently needed as a 'war measure'.

Alice Paul (1885–1977)

She was armed with a PhD from the University of Pennsylvania. She visited the UK in 1906 and became involved in militant suffragette activity. In 1909, she returned to the USA and became active, as the main leader and strategist of the campaign for the 19th Amendment to the US constitution.

Suffrage: the right to vote.

19th Amendment: this prevented sex discrimination in voting and also empowered the US Congress to enforce this by law.

Feminists: women who believed in women's rights and freedoms, and in sex equality. They campaigned and worked actively for political, economic and social recognition. This campaigning included the recognition of women's rights in legal matters such as suffrage, marriage, divorce and property ownership.

Jane Addams (1860–1935)

She was active in promoting both social issues and women's rights. Educated in the USA and Europe, she was a pacifist and became president of the Women's International League for Peace and Freedom. She spoke at many international conferences in the 1920s, advocating the end of war, reducing armaments and prohibiting the use of poison gas in warfare; although in the USA of the 1920s she was accused of being communist. She helped make Americans think of issues of concern to mothers, such as the needs of children, local public health and birth control. In 1932 she became the first American woman to be awarded the Nobel Peace Prize and is recognised as the founder of the social work profession in the USA.

The House of Representatives then passed the federal woman suffrage amendment by 274 to 136; but the Senate did not, although Wilson himself had attended the Senate to urge senators to pass this amendment. Another attempt in February 1919 also ended in failure in the Senate by one vote. The amendment was finally passed by the Senate on 4 June 1919, by sixty-six to thirty. In August 1920 the **19th Amendment** was certified by the secretary of state, when all states had finally ratified it, and made it legal. In the 1920 presidential election of that year, women voted for the first time. But in southern states, African American women experienced the same discrimination as men when they attempted to vote; a scenario that would continue until 1965.

In 1916 the first birth-control clinic was opened in the USA by Margaret Sanger in New York. Although the clinic was shut down only ten days later and Sanger was arrested for distributing 'obscene literature on contraception', her trial allowed her to appeal eloquently and passionately. It also generated controversy.

Sanger felt that in order for women to have a more equal footing in society, they needed to be able to decide when to have children. She also wanted to prevent unsafe abortions, so-called 'back-alley abortions', which were widespread at the time as abortion was illegal. Sanger eventually won support through the courts and opened another clinic in 1923, fully staffed by women – the first in the USA.

By 1924, Wyoming state had elected a female governor and in 1926 the city of Seattle elected its first female mayor. At a more grassroots level, public acceptance of wage-earning jobs for young unmarried women was now growing. American women in the 1920s were now working in offices, shops and department stores, with their career opportunities no longer being confined to domestic service or menial labour in mills or factories. It also became acceptable for working girls to live away from their families. A few young married women worked until they had children, but they were generally unable to resolve the conflict between work and home.

Working for wages certainly gave women independence and prior to the onset of the Great Depression in 1930, about one in four women had a job, although the industrial workforce remained overwhelmingly male. Discrimination in wages also persisted, as did the opinion that women only worked until they married – or, at the very best, until they became pregnant. Right to vote or not, the idea of women combining home, job and family would not take off permanently until the 1960s.

Feminist activists in the 1920s like **Jane Addams** now put their efforts into other areas of social reform such as the abolition of child labour and the reduction of weapons internationally. Others still pursued equal rights in employment, earnings and promotion.

In this sense, the different feminist organisations had equally noble but slightly different themes and objectives. Their work continued, but with philosophical differences and a lack of cohesion. The first wave of women's protest and feminism is considered by many to have succeeded with that victory over suffrage, when Wilson finally reacted and accepted the inevitable. But it was still felt that many social and sexual issues were unresolved. It would take the second wave of feminism in the early 1960s to reignite the movement fully.

The anti-war movement of the 1960s

The anti-war movement of the 1960s, activated by involvement in Vietnam, was arguably the most politically significant and socially divisive protest movement of modern times in the USA.

QUESTION

How far had suffrage for women enabled them to improve their status in the USA by 1930?

SOURCE E

The Vietnam war divided the USA along the lines of political party, age, class and family. Opinion polls showed that support for the war was stronger in the middle class than in the working class. However, the opposite was true of young people from 20 to 29 years, who displayed greater support for the war than any other age group – but included the bulk of the antiwar movement in the universities. Given that many antiwar students came from middle-class families supportive of the war, the result was a fierce generational confrontation. Even high-ranking members of the Johnson and Nixon administrations had children who opposed the war. Moreover, the privileged antiwar students who benefitted from draft deferment, were much despised by the patriotic majority of America's young that was drafted and served in Vietnam.

P. Levine and H. Papasotiriou (2005), America Since 1945, *New York: Palgrave Macmillan, p. 114.*

Its diverse membership contained both staff and students from colleges and university campuses as well as trade unionists, feminists, families from middle-class suburbs, black civil rights activists, film and TV stars, writers, sports celebrities and even members of government institutions.

When US involvement in Vietnam grew significantly after 1964 (see section 4.5, The domestic impact of the Vietnam War in the 1960s), many Americans believed that protecting South Vietnam from communist aggression was worthwhile, as non-intervention would send a message of weakness and possibly encourage conflict elsewhere. But as the war dragged on and became increasingly unwinnable, increasing numbers of Americans became angered by mounting casualties, by the growing numbers being taken in the draft to replace the dead and injured, and by the escalating costs.

The anti-war movement had several independent interest groups, united only in opposition to the Vietnam War, but they grew into a major force, revealing a genuinely deep schism within US society. This grew after 1965 and lasted into the 1970s, but probably peaked in 1968. It strangled Lyndon Johnson's presidency and shackled his successor Richard Nixon into leaving Vietnam. It also presented the US government with its largest and most serious protests, pressurising leaders into totally reviewing US strategy. How it coalesced is very significant.

Students for a Democratic Society (SDS), was a student activist group founded in 1962. It objected to the institutions running America – politicians, the military, banking and big business corporations; they named themselves the 'New Left' and focused initially on domestic concerns such as civil rights, and on actively supporting Johnson in his 1964 presidential campaign.

Another link within the New Left was the Free Speech Movement (FSM) at the University of California at Berkeley. Formed in December 1964, they believed students could bring change through organisation, having sent fieldworkers to help with black voter registration in Mississippi prior to the election.

The New Left rejected the idea that the working classes were the agents of social change, and focused on the spiritual crisis of an opulent society rather than on widespread economic misery. The SDS thus became the organisational focus of the New Left.

By early 1965, an anti-Vietnam war movement base had coalesced on US campuses and now lacked only a 'smoking gun' to bring wider support to its position. This came when LBJ ordered the bombing of North Vietnam. The pace of protest quickened and its scope widened.

With the SDS coordinating opposition to the war, they organised marches to the main military bases where troops departed for Asia. Then faculty members at the University of Michigan held a series of 'teach-ins', designed to make the student population aware about both the moral and political foundations of the USA's involvement. This teach-in format spread across the USA and so brought faculty members into active anti-war participation.

On 17 April 1965, almost 25,000 people gathered in Washington to protest – a turnout that surprised even the organisers and greatly alarmed Johnson. In November 1965, 40,000 protesters surrounded the White House, calling for an end to the war. On the same day, President Johnson announced an increase of troops in Vietnam from 120,000 to 400,000 and extended the draft.

The draft system was hated and unfairly tilted towards working-class and black men. In 1964, only 16 per cent of those drafted were killed, but by 1968 it was 60 per cent. This further galvanised movement leaders – still mainly students – who restructured their protest methods and gained new supporters. Campus editors formed networks to share information on effective protest methods; the Underground Press Syndicate (1966) and the Liberation News Service (1967) being two of the most effective and productive in spreading information.

In June 1967, more than 1,000 theological college students and trainee priests from across the USA wrote to the secretary of defense stating moral objections to the draft; while throughout that summer, the anti-war movement placed adverts in the major newspapers calling for 'negotiation now', which proposed a halt to bombing and a general ceasefire.

A two-day march on the Pentagon in October 1967 attracted nationwide media attention, while leaders of the war resistance called for young men to turn in their draft cards. The movement spread to the military itself, with dissenters refusing to fly to Vietnam. Draft evaders escaped to Canada or Sweden, with churches providing sanctuary for those attempting to avoid conscription.

The world of sport even found itself at the centre of the protest movement when in April 1967 the world heavyweight boxing champion Muhammad Ali refused his draft into the army and was stripped of his title. He was convicted of draft evasion, fined $10,000 and sentenced to five years in prison, but was not jailed as his case went to the court of appeal and was eventually overturned. But perhaps even worse for an internationally famous sportsman aged only twenty-five, fit and in his prime, he was banned from boxing for three years.

Political issues had now turned into very personal issues and the New Left had truly become a revolutionary youth movement, with its own counterculture. Black civil rights and anti-Vietnam War and student movements challenged the US government and radicalised a generation. Students, wearing army fatigues, blue jeans, long hair, beads and flowers called for personal liberation through music, meditation, sex and experimenting with drugs. The Haight-Ashbury district of San Francisco (known for its many musicians, writers, artists and hippies) captured the mood of the 'Summer of Love' in 1967 with the slogan 'Make love, not war'.

But such images also presented problems, and the anti-war movement was not without its internal divisions and doubters. Some liberal protestors distrusted the motives of the SDS and the far left, fearing that close personal association with them might damage their own credibility. Then there was a divide between those who called for negotiations with North Vietnam while others believed all the Vietnamese had the right to determine their own future. But what is undeniable is how disparate groups had exerted such pressure on the US government and exerted a strong agenda-setting force on both government and society.

By 1968, some on the left in the Democratic Party were vocally critical that social reforms were sacrificed to an unwinnable $150 million war. Demonstrators taunted Johnson with the now infamous anti-war chant, 'Hey hey hey, LBJ, how many kids did you kill today?' Yet in fairness, Johnson had still pursued his Great Society reforms, and had not ceased because of the distractions of Vietnam. More than 200 laws were passed from 1965 to 1968, but the potential for further legislation was curtailed by the need to divert money for war.

Johnson quit the election race when he was challenged for the presidential nomination by candidates in his own party, disillusioned by what he saw as betrayal and ingratitude, as shown in **Source F** in Unit 4.1.

Some believed that by supporting Republican Richard Nixon in the 1968 presidential election, they had voted to end the war, but Nixon launched a massive new bombing campaign and then advocated Vietnamisation: cutting American troops and giving South Vietnam greater responsibility for fighting the war, while still giving financial aid. US troops dropped from 539,000 in 1969 to just over 157,000 by 1971.

Nixon then sent troops to destroy communist supply bases in neighbouring Cambodia in April 1970, appeasing critics and marking time; attempting to stem the flow of North Vietnamese soldiers and supplies into South Vietnam. But violation of Cambodian neutrality provoked anti-war protests and at a demonstration at Ohio Kent State University, national guardsmen killed four protesters, leading to another huge anti-war demonstration in Washington.

Peace negotiations began and dragged on through 'backchannels' to Beijing and Moscow, before a ceasefire was agreed in January 1973 whereby the armies of North and South Vietnam retained the areas under their respective control when fighting stopped. This favoured North Vietnam, who held large parts of the South, but the North accepted South Vietnam's existence – a major concession given that their aim was to unite Vietnam. The US withdrew and prisoners of war were released. But by April 1975, the North had taken over all of Vietnam anyway. Two million Vietnamese and 55,000 US soldiers had died.

Americans were now less supportive of global intervention yet ever-more ready to protest. It might be about government policy, as over Vietnam, or an outcry about the conduct of those leading them, as shown over Nixon and Watergate.

But the 1960s anti-war movement – albeit divisive – made all Americans 'think' and re-evaluate their democracy. When protest had set such an agenda and changed both the national mindset and the nature of presidency, it could not have failed to have had such a seminal impact.

QUESTION

Look at **Source F** in Unit 4.1 and reread this section on the anti-war movement. To what extent did political protest undermine government in the 1960s?

End of unit activities

1 Use the information in this unit, as well as additional information from books or websites, to write a brief outline of the life of **two** of the following: Grover Cleveland, Jane Addams, Alice Paul, Muhammad Ali, John Maynard Keynes. Make sure that you focus on and explain their influence – direct or indirect – on the evolution of democracy in the USA, and how their role helped or hindered this.

2 Design a mind map to summarise some of the crises influencing the USA during the period from 1890 to 1975. These should include fear of revolution and anarchy; economic collapse; popular protest; problems with the presidency.

3 Explain the significance of each of these in the context of US history: the Jeffersonian Ideal; 1924 National Origins Act; laissez-faire; populism; New Left: Hart–Celler Act; Prohibition; the draft: Sacco and Vanzetti; the SDS.

4 Carry out further research into the Populist Party. What do you regard as the most important reason for the rise of populism? To what extent was it a failure?

5 Draw up a table to summarise and evaluate the government's responses to the challenges posed by each of these issues in the period studied. You can use this table as a model:

Issues	What was the underlying nature of the problem?	How successfully did the government deal with the issue?
Immigration		
Women's suffrage		
Political extremism		
Economic forces		
Conflicts with the presidency		

KEY QUESTIONS

- To what extent did the economic and social policies implemented benefit US citizens?
- What has been the cultural impact of democracy within the USA?

Overview

- A number of social and economic policies and reforms benefitted US citizens between 1890 and 1975.
- Policies on education and social welfare and policies towards women and minorities are considered, as well as attempts to confront issues surrounding the distribution of wealth.
- The reforms of the Progressive Era are contrasted with the laissez-faire government of the Republicans in the 1920s, then the federal involvement of Roosevelt's New Deal and Johnson's Great Society are evaluated.
- The impact of policies towards women and minorities are seen through three particularly contrasting periods covering the late 19th century, the 1920s and 1930s, and finally the turbulent years of the 1960s with its backdrop of war in Vietnam and the struggle for civil rights.
- Finally a study is made of key moments and decisive changes in US culture from 1890 to 1975. Consideration is given to how democracy has impacted on freedom of expression in the arts, media and the wider arena of leisure and sport. The structural changes in US society are linked to the rise of a counterculture of the 1960s, where dissatisfaction with the political and social elites in the USA grew as military involvement in Vietnam escalated, and was then followed by the Watergate Scandal.

4.8 To what extent did the economic and social policies implemented benefit US citizens?

The various economic and social policies implemented in the USA during the period 1890–1975 attempted to redress key challenges facing the country. Different administrations – be they Democrat or

TIMELINE

1920 **Nov:** Warren Harding elected president.

1922 Ford–McCumber Tariff.

1923 **Aug:** Warren Harding dies suddenly. Calvin Coolidge becomes president.

1924 Indian Citizenship Act.

1926 Revenue Act.

NBC begins broadcasting.

1928 **Nov:** Herbert hoover elected president. Franklin D. Roosevelt becomes governor of New York.

1932 **Nov:** Franklin D. Roosevelt elected US president.

1933 **Mar–Jul:** Hundred days of FDR's New Deal legislation.

1934 Indian Reorganisation Act.

1939–45 Second World War.

1960 **Nov:** John F. Kennedy elected president.

1962 Trade Expansion Act.

1963 Equal Pay Act.

Higher Education Facilities Act.

Nov: Kennedy assassinated. Lyndon Johnson becomes president.

1964 **May:** Johnson launches 'Great Society' at University of Michigan.

Aug: Economic Opportunity Act.

Nov: Johnson elected in landslide over republican Barry Goldwater.

1965 Omnibus Housing Act; Appalachian Regional Development Act; Elementary and Secondary Education Act; Immigration and Nationality Act (Hart–Celler Act); Higher Education Act.

1966 National Organisation for Women (NOW).

1967 Public Broadcasting Act.

1968 American Indian Movement formed.

Nov: Richard Nixon elected president.

1969 **Aug:** Woodstock Festival, New York.

1970 **Aug:** 'Strike for Equality' march.

1974 The Equal Credit Opportunity Act.

Republican – sought to promote economic growth, according to their way of thinking. Other policy aspects – such as developing education, improving health, providing better social welfare, improving the position of women and trying to create a more equitable society and distribution of wealth – were not always pursued as consistently and were often determined by the ideology or emphasis of the political party in the White House. Consequently they benefitted US citizens to a lesser or greater extent, not least due to the ethnicity and financial status of many.

Policies to promote economic growth

Economic growth and performance were influenced by new technologies, the change in size of economic sectors and the consequences of legislation and specific government policy.

1920–9

The election of Republican Warren Harding in 1920 marked a turn away from the regulatory state and its progressive politics, and instead it brought a revival in free enterprise and corporate capitalism. The next decade was associated with growing prosperity. Some economists have claimed that the low unemployment and low inflation of the 1920s was the best economic performance of any decade in US history. Certainly there was easier access to new consumer goods and their markets; lower prices, lower taxes, higher **real wages** and very strong big business – stimulated by wartime industrial production and buoyed by favourable pro-business policies.

Real wages: the value of wages after inflation has been taken into consideration.

Harding wanted to lower unemployment and further boost US industry. In 1922, Congress passed the Ford–McCumber Tariff, which raised import duties on numerous items such as chemicals, textiles, china, cutlery, farm products, guns and industrial machinery. This was a move towards protectionism. Harding also created the US Budget Bureau to monitor, streamline and reform US government spending, with a focus on cutting wastefulness and providing value for money. The federal debt was reduced by about a third from 1920 to 1930, and the nation's rate of unemployment dropped markedly during Harding's short presidency.

Calvin Coolidge became president when Harding died in 1923. He oversaw rapid economic growth. His stance on taxation, including the passage of the **Revenue Acts of 1924 and 1926** decreased income tax rates in line with significant reductions in federal expenditure. Coolidge's commerce secretary, Herbert Hoover, was popular and well-respected by business leaders, and he would succeed to the presidency in March 1929 with the same promises of low taxation and minimum regulation or anti-trust actions.

Revenue Acts of 1924 and 1926: the Revenue Act of 1924 cut federal tax rates. The top rate of tax was slashed from 50 per cent to 20 per cent, and all income taxation was eliminated for two million people. The Revenue Act of 1926 reduced inheritance and personal income taxes, removed many excise duties and prohibited public access to federal tax returns.

The Wall Street Crash of October 1929 then brought an end to the Republican boom years, with its dire consequences of massive unemployment and rapid economic stagnation. Economic policies thereafter – such as they were – brought minimal relief and benefitted few US citizens. It was not until several years into the Roosevelt presidency that economic growth was revived.

Somewhat ironically, the US government in the 1920s presided over major economic growth without necessarily implementing many policies to promote these conditions – although important tax concessions were significant. The laissez-faire approach of 'staying out' worked, but only for so long; and the Republicans created a strong business ambience. Yet there were a number of factors often disconnected to government policy that underpinned this boom and from which the Republicans benefitted.

The US economy had outstripped its international rivals before 1914. Industrialisation and the exploitation of excellent natural resources were boosted by greater technology and better communications. The First World War had boosted production, especially munitions and food supply; also it had caused far greater industrial dislocation in Europe, while US industry had little or no recovery to make. So export and banking markets serviced previously by Germany and Britain were now opened up and the USA soon became the world's main creditor.

The US economy in general recovered more quickly than its rivals, and an abundance of cheap capital and credit encouraged new businesses, boosted domestic consumer spending and encouraged widespread speculation on the Stock Exchange – this time by ordinary Americans, not just the giants of big business. It appeared as though the boom would eventually benefit many US citizens.

In 1921 the US Federal Reserve had extended $45 billion in credit: by 1929 it was $73 billion. The 1920s witnessed huge oilfield expansion, extension of the electricity supply; and the development of the industrial assembly line by **Henry Ford** at the Ford Motor Company, which revolutionised the means and rate of production. An absence of foreign competition, together with high import tariffs and continued innovation in US industry, guaranteed high sales of home-produced goods. This in turn stimulated manufacturing – and so the circle went round.

US economic growth in the 1920s was phenomenal, and the policies of the governments cannot be dismissed. But while recognising the impact of key tax and fiscal legislation introduced, in general the roots of this economic growth were in place by 1920. A business climate and corporate ambience existed, perhaps suited to minimalist government policies.

Yet for all those swept up in the benefits of industrialisation, many did not share in the prosperity. Older staple industries such as wool and cotton textiles, railways, shoe-making and timber were getting left behind as new growth industries such as oil, concrete and artificial textiles developed. Worse still was the plight of many in farming, for whom government policies had little benefit.

The 1920s were a decade of agricultural depression, where Republican governments focused on industry while social commentators and journalists reported the exciting lives of urban classes, the Hollywood stars and the mega-rich in their New England summer palaces. The 1920s perpetuated the noticeable divide between the rural communities and the urban-dwellers.

During the First World War from 1914 to 1918, agricultural exports to Europe soared, and corn, wheat, and cotton hit high prices. Farmers expanded their business, tried new growing, and significantly, borrowed much more. When prices collapsed in the 1920s, the rural financial collapse was inevitable. But all eyes were on the industrial manufacturing centres. The laissez-faire policies of Harding, Coolidge and Hoover bypassed the men and women of the rural interior. The welfare net for them was the church and their community of family, friends and neighbours. Several families now had to share the same house or to take in lodgers. But in an era of depressed food and cotton prices, the outcome was frequently a life of disillusion, foreclosure and deep poverty.

Henry Ford (1863–1947)

He was the founder of the Ford Motor Company and the chief sponsor of the prototype assembly line technique of mass production. Ford changed the lifestyle of millions by developing and manufacturing the first car affordable to many ordinary Americans: the Model T Ford. He became one of the world's richest and well-known men. He believed in the mass production of inexpensive goods coupled with high wages for workers, claiming that international consumerism was the key to world peace. He was also a renowned inventor and was awarded 161 US patents during his life. Ford's political views earned him some derision, notably his objection to the USA's entry into the First World War in 1917. In the 1930s he expressed admiration for Hitler's Germany, and in 1938 accepted the Nazi regime's highest medal for non-Germans – the Grand Cross of the German Eagle.

KEY CONCEPTS ACTIVITY

Significance: Undertake some further research into the life and career of Henry Ford. Then explain the significance of Ford and his pioneering of the assembly line and mass production.

1932–41

When Franklin D. Roosevelt was elected president in November 1932, it was in the middle of the Great Depression – a watershed moment in the social, political and economic life of the USA. Along with his team of brilliant but eclectic advisors, they formulated plans for relief, recovery, reform and regulation in a socio-economic package known as the New Deal. The laissez-faire politics of the Republican Party that had created the economic boom of the 1920s was no longer appropriate.

He took office in March 1933, inheriting a critical banking crisis that had the potential to destroy the entire economic system and threaten democracy itself. But his emergency action – the Emergency Banking Act – bought time, helped restore confidence and arguably, pulled the USA back from the precipice of economic destruction. Later legislation such as the Glass-Steagall Act and the Federal Securities Act helped Roosevelt to implement reforms to the Stock Exchange and the banking system. He sought to repair the economic damage caused by the Wall Street Crash, while ending the practices of cheap credit from banks and irresponsible share trading on the Stock Exchange. The next part of his economic policy was designed to stimulate consumer demand and revive manufacturing.

FDR ended Prohibition, and then established a series of agencies to help vulnerable sectors of the economy – such as agriculture – and provide employment. They became known as **Alphabet Agencies**. The first raft of legislation – primarily focusing on business needs and with the aim to promote economic growth – has become known as the First New Deal.

But by 1935, more progressive members on the left felt that the New Deal didn't go far enough, while some business interests in the Democratic Party actually found themselves agreeing with the Republicans who believed that FDR was managing a government takeover of the economy. The American Liberty League was formed by financiers and business leaders who claimed that FDR was 'Sovietising America' with his federal intervention, in spite of having pulled the USA back from the brink. A number of conservative judges then began to pass injunctions to block measures. Indeed the greatest opposition to FDR's handling of the economy came from the US Supreme Court.

In 1935, the court ruled that if Congress were permitted to make laws like the National Industrial Recovery Act (NIRA) – which asserted the federal right to regulate economic activity in individual US states – then there might be no limits to the power of the federal state. Roosevelt moved swiftly and aggressively in response after the court's decision, introducing what became known as the Second New Deal – a phrase used by contemporary observers and adopted by historians since.

This second stage of FDR's legislative programme, introduced to Congress in January 1935, specified several major targets: to provide security against old age, illness and unemployment; to establish a national welfare programme (the Works Progress Administration) to replace state relief efforts, to make better use of the USA's natural resources and to undertake major slum clearance.

Economically, FDR had halted a downward spiral, and fostered some of the most rapid output, employment and corporate profitability gains in US history. But some of the early vigour of the New Deal later evaporated. There was a mini-recession and an unemployment rise in 1938 when FDR eased back on deficit spending, against the advice of John Maynard Keynes (see section 4.5, The impact of economic forces on the USA; 1933–41). The USA gradually emerged from this when FDR borrowed

Theory of Knowledge

History and personal prejudice:
To what extent is our perception of the USA in the 1920s coloured by our own social, economic and political prejudices? Is it important to try to empathise with the Republican presidents of the 1920s as they concentrated on trying to strengthen the USA financially after the First World War, in order to understand their policies and actions?

Alphabet Agencies
These agencies were created to stimulate economic recovery, to channel subsidies to people in need, and to create work for the unemployed. The main schemes were:

The National Industrial Recovery Act 1933 (NIRA): this promoted recovery and reform by setting up the **National Recovery Administration** and **Public Works Administration.** It was declared an unconstitutional act by the Supreme Court in 1935.

National Recovery Administration 1933 (NRA): this tried to help industry and factory workers by increasing wages and improving hours and conditions. It also regulated fair competition between businesses, banned child labour and gave workers the rights to organise trade unions.

Public Works Administration 1933 (PWA): this programme financed 34,000 federal, state and local projects costing $6 billion and created jobs for unemployed people to build schools, roads and dams. It proved a large source of employment.

$1 billion for rearmament. But the Great Depression didn't fully end until the outbreak of war in Europe in 1939 boosted munitions and galvanised US finances.

Nonetheless, the New Deal initiatives and agencies created a framework for a welfare state that has since served as the template for public policy in the USA. It also set a precedent for the federal government to play a key interventionist role in the economic and social affairs of the nation, if the private sector was unable to guarantee either economic security or financial opportunity.

SOURCE A

Figure 4.17 Cartoon from 1934 about Roosevelt's New Deal

1961–74

Kennedy's short presidency and the dynamic but flawed administration of his successor Johnson were the high point of post-war US economic and social reform, as Kennedy attempted reform in his 'New Frontier' programme while Johnson became the most proactive president since Roosevelt in 1933 with his 'Great Society' legislation emphasising a 'war on poverty' and economic advancement for all.

Federal Emergency Relief Administration 1933 (FERA): this provided $500 million to state and local groups to help the poor in a number of basic ways, such as giving clothing grants, making relief payments and setting up food kitchens.

Agricultural Adjustment Act 1933 (AAA): this provided farmers with federal subsidies to compensate them for controlling their farm production. It helped to stabilise prices, and aimed to end overproduction and raise agricultural prices to profitable levels.

Civilian Conservation Corps 1933 (CCC): similar to the PWA, this agency provided work camps for large numbers of young men working in conservation schemes in the countryside.

Tennessee Valley Authority 1934 (TVA): this was a massive agency and it provided major regeneration schemes across seven states in the entire Tennessee River valley. It brought hydroelectric power to seven states in one of the worst affected areas of the USA, and built dams and power stations, thus creating many jobs.

Federal Housing Authority 1934 (FHA): this provided government funding to help people to keep up mortgage payments.

QUESTION

Look at **Source A.** Was it drawn by a supporter or opponent of FDR? How do we know? Explain your answer carefully. What is this cartoon saying about Roosevelt's economic policy?

America experienced its longest uninterrupted period of economic expansion in the 1960s, with federal government being the driving economic force. But the cost of the Vietnam War eventually constrained them, and Nixon's 1968 election victory heralded changes, as his presidency coincided with the onset of a major international economic downturn, prior to his resignation over the Watergate scandal (see section 4.6, The Watergate scandal 1972–4).

When Kennedy took office in 1961, the economy had shrunk by 4.2 per cent with business bankruptcies at their highest level since 1932, and six million unemployed. He responded with policies to lower taxes, protect the unemployed, promote job creation, increase the minimum wage and stimulate the economy.

Kennedy injected billions of dollars into the US economy, especially domestic and military spending. By late 1961, unemployment began to fall and the recession had eased. The 1962 Trade Expansion Act cut tariffs to encourage trade and stimulate industry and the Revenue Act gave businesses $1 billion in tax credits for new equipment and investment. Kennedy and his advisers believed that this would 'fine-tune' the economy and precipitate a decade-long boom.

Between 1961 and 1963, Kennedy added $23 billion to the US national debt. This was an 8 per cent increase to the $289 billion debt level at the end of 1960. His deficit spending ended the recession and contributed to an economic expansion that lasted until 1970, under which Johnson funded his Great Society.

Following Kennedy's assassination in November 1963, Johnson served his remaining term before winning an election in his own right in the presidential election of November 1964. Gaining 61 per cent of the votes and the largest popular margin in history, it enabled him to expand the role of Federal government and drive through his economic policies.

Johnson's Economic Opportunity Act established the Office of Economic Opportunity and coordinated educational, employment and training programmes that stimulated the economy. He also provided for the construction of nearly 250,000 homes in the Omnibus Housing Act 1965. This boosted the building industry and provided more employment. Likewise, support to depressed country areas was aided by loans to rural and small businesses. The Appalachian Regional Development Act of 1965 continued support to the area originally targeted by Kennedy. With the economy expanding, unemployment dropped by 5 per cent. Johnson then pushed through Kennedy's tax reduction bills, which increased consumer spending. This was raised further by general international economic growth, and specifically helped in the USA by Johnson's work programmes.

Military spending on the war in Vietnam also brought jobs in munitions and defence, boosting both employment and army recruitment. However, growing US involvement in Vietnam affected domestic spending and the economic programme began to stall.

Nixon, who became president in January 1969, had a traditional Republican emphasis on fiscal responsibility and efficiency; but he also recognised the need for the government's expanded role and accepted Democrat ideology for the welfare state, albeit wanting to run welfare programmes more economically.

Nixon preferred foreign policy to domestic but being the consummate politician that he was, he realised that economic improvement was key to domestic popularity. In 1969, inflation was at 4.7 per cent, its highest rate since the early 1950s. LBJ's Great Society and the costs of the Vietnam War had racked up significant budget deficits. Unemployment was low, but interest rates were approaching their highest in a century. Nixon's policies were thus determined by this economic climate.

He introduced temporary wage and price controls in August 1971 in an attempt to reduce inflation and strengthen the US economy. Nixon's apparent decisiveness increased his popularity. Inflation was halted temporarily and then appeared to slow down when he created the Pay Board and the Price Commission in November 1971. They monitored compliance with the guidelines for wages and price increases, although in 1973, restraint on pay and price increases was again made voluntary.

In August 1971, the USA abandoned the fixed exchange rate system established at the end of the Second World War. This aimed to create stability in international trading. The US dollar was its lynchpin. But in the difficult economic climate, the USA could no longer underpin it. The Smithsonian Agreement of 1972 brought a formal end to fixed exchange rates across Western capitalist economies. Consequently, the US dollar was devalued, making exports cheaper and imports dearer. Nixon placed a tariff on imported Japanese cars to protect the US motor industry.

Together with more tax cuts, this produced a brief economic upturn – enough to get Nixon re-elected in 1972. But in Nixon's second term, price controls became increasingly unpopular, and the threat of 'stagflation' (economic recession combined with inflation) perplexed Nixon. By the end of his presidency in 1974, inflation was 12 per cent, following the Middle East war and its subsequent oil crisis. It marked the onset of a decade of price instability, increasing inflation rates and a poorer standard of living for much of middle America.

The US economy would undergo even further restructuring. US citizens by the mid-1970s were not in an advantageous position any longer. They were poised to face even more difficult social and economic problems. Arguably the interventionist policies of Kennedy, Johnson and Nixon – undermined and stymied by conflict in Vietnam and by an international downturn – had run out of steam.

Policies to extend education

Prior to 1920

The public (meaning state/federal as opposed to private) education system in the USA is mainly run by individual states and school districts, having developed formally in the 19th century. Until the 1840s it was highly localised and available mainly to the children of wealthy people.

But during the 19th century, reformers campaigned for better educational facilities and argued that schooling for every child would create better citizens, benefit the economy and help to alleviate crime and poverty. By 1870, all states had free elementary schools, and private academies opened in many towns. In more rural areas there were few schools prior to the 1890s, but by the end of the century, free public education became available for all US children. Massachusetts and New York had made school attendance compulsory as early as the 1850s. By 1918, all US states had passed laws compelling children to attend elementary school.

During the period of the progressive presidents, education was high on the policy agenda, with educationalists and advisors claiming that the US public needed a good education to help create successful leaders. Education was reformed by introducing compulsory elementary school laws, by standardised testing and emphasising the professional role of teachers and school administrators.

The first public secondary or high school in the USA was founded in Boston in 1635, where Harvard was the first university. At first, high schools were seen more as preparatory academies for colleges and universities, but by 1910 they were a fundamental core part of the US education system, with more than 6,000. By 1920, education had been transformed and far more young US citizens were starting to benefit, even though this was very much a 'work in progress'.

SOURCE B

The demand for higher learning drove the college student population up from 52,000 in 1867 to 157,000 in 1890 and to 600,000 in 1920 ... women's access to higher education improved markedly in the late nineteenth century. Before the Civil War, a few colleges had already gone coeducational, and state universities in the West were commonly open to women from the start. But colleges in the South and East fell in line very slowly ... in 1875 two more excellent women's colleges appeared in Massachusetts: Wellesley and Smith, the latter being the first to set the same admission requirements as men's colleges. Thereafter the older women's colleges rushed to upgrade their standards in the same way.

G.B. Tindall and D.E. Shi (2004), America: A Narrative History, *New York: W.W. Norton & Company, p. 700.*

Progressive educationalist **John Dewey** was largely responsible for the growth of elementary and secondary schools in this period and an enrolment boom in schools. Only 4.5 per cent of children aged between fifteen and nineteen were enrolled in secondary schools in 1890. By 1930, this had increased to more than 40 per cent.

The Morrill Acts of 1862 and 1890 provided federal financial support to state universities and in particular, the 1890 Act required each state to show that race was not an admissions criterion, or else to provide a separate institution for 'persons of colour'. Under the Act, more than seventy colleges and universities were created, many of them forming the basis of the **Historically Black Colleges and Universities (HBCUs)** of the USA.

1920–41

Between 1920 and 1941, US education was increasingly influenced by government policies. The Republican dominance of the 1920s contrasted greatly with the New Deal Democratic presidency of Franklin D. Roosevelt after 1933. Education was differentiated likewise, and a sense of double standards prevailed. In the 1920s, the US business community wanted the government to encourage education, especially in the public high schools, from where much of the skilled labour necessary for industry, originated.

SOURCE C

We endorse the principle of Federal aid to the States for the purpose of vocational and agricultural training. Wherever Federal money is devoted to education, such education must be so directed as to awaken in the youth the spirit of America and a sense of patriotic duty to the United States. A thorough system of physical education for all children up to the age of 19, including adequate health supervision and instruction, would remedy conditions revealed by the draft and would add to the economic and industrial strength of the nation. National leadership and stimulation will be necessary to induce the States to adopt a wise system of physical training.

From the Republican Party Platform, 8 June 1920, www.presidency.ucsb.edu/ws/?pid=29635.

John Dewey (1859–1952)

He was a psychologist, philosopher, educator, social critic and political activist. He travelled as an educational consultant, visiting Turkey in 1924 to recommend education policy. He also visited schools in the USSR in 1928. He believed strongly in progressive educational reform and felt that education should be based on the principle of learning through doing. Dewey believed that US democracy was strained by industrialisation, which had brought great wealth for the few, rather than benefitting society as a whole. He saw the major political parties as servants of business corporations.

Historically Black Colleges and Universities (HBCUs): US institutions of higher education established before the Civil Rights Act of 1964 to educate the black community, usually set up in the decades after the end of the Civil War. Historically, they admitted students of all races. There are 106 HBCUs including public and private institutions, medical schools and law colleges. Most are located in the former slave states of the Confederacy.

QUESTION

What does **Source C** tell us about the Republican Party beliefs in 1920 regarding education? Does it reveal any other aspects of Republican ideology? Explain your answer carefully.

But after the onset of the Depression in the 1930s, skilled people were less in demand. Suddenly many in the business world objected to government funding of education. It would come from taxation, yet entrepreneurs now needed tax breaks and regretted money going towards education.

FDR soon realised that schools, teachers and students had suffered enormously. Almost 25 per cent of all students in New York city had malnutrition. Even in affluent areas, there were big cuts in education budgets, which meant major cuts in teaching staff, and reductions in subjects being offered. Georgia closed almost all schools in the state, making teachers redundant. Rural pupils and schools across the USA were badly hit.

As part of Roosevelt's crisis response, he allocated $20 million of federal money to provide immediate relief and help secure schools in danger of closure. The National Educational Association (NEA) applauded his action and assumed that this would now be the new direction: continual aid with direct federal support for state and local schools. But future money came primarily through agencies such as the National Youth Administration (NYA), the Civilian Conservation Corps (CCC) and the Works Progress Administration (WPA), and provided relief to individuals rather than organisations.

The New Deal tendency to target individuals revealed major failings in the US education system, with much illiteracy and a shortage of key skills discovered. When the CCC began in 1933, a critical need for technical training and basic literacy was woefully apparent.

Classrooms were opened where CCC employees could voluntarily take remedial classes in key areas such as literacy and numeracy and soon different lessons were added in subjects such as geography and history. This necessitated more teachers. It also led to more thorough basic technical and vocational training. By 1939, more than 90 per cent of CCC workers were studying subjects in classes. Meanwhile, in just over seven years, the WPA built almost 6,000 schools, while the NYA – encouraging education and providing part-time student jobs – set up an NYA division for Negro Affairs, to ensure that African Americans also benefitted from NYA and WPA schemes.

Before Roosevelt, the government interpreted having an equal opportunity in education as meaning that they provided basic education, after which individuals could go to whatever establishment they could get in to, or afford – if they wanted to go at all. Those such as African Americans, immigrants, the children of rural famers and most minorities were hugely disadvantaged, and the existing system was not beneficial to this constituency of citizens, but FDR's New Deal agencies began to rectify this education gap.

1961–74

On becoming president in 1961, John F. Kennedy submitted the School Assistance Bill to Congress, seeking $2.3 billion to help build new schools and to improve the pay and classroom conditions of teachers. However, since the First Amendment of the US constitution kept the Church separate from the state, Catholic schools and schools of other religious denominations did not qualify. Being a Roman Catholic himself, Kennedy knew that the bill did not cover Catholic schools.

Not surprisingly, the Roman Catholic Church and supporters from other faiths opposed it and got sufficient support to defeat it in Congress. Kennedy did manage to push through the 1963 Higher Education Facilities Act, which allocated nearly $150 million for graduate schools in languages, science and engineering. However, this was seen as less about educational reform and more a response to the perceived growth in the power of the Soviet Union.

Figure 4.18 Lyndon B. Johnson with his first pupils at the Welhausen School in Cotulla, Texas in 1928. He is seated middle row, fifth from left

President Lyndon Johnson was a schoolteacher in Texas in the late 1920s, and education topped his policy list. He passed the Economic Opportunity Act that established the Office of Economic Opportunity (OEO). This coordinated schemes including Headstart, where children went to preschool classes. The OEO also established Community Action Programs (CAPs), which set up clinics.

One of Johnson's top priorities was to broaden educational opportunities across the social spectrum. He wanted to improve the quality of education offered from preschool through to university. So after his 1964 landslide brought in many supportive congressmen, he introduced the Elementary and Secondary Education Act (ESEA), which was passed in 1965.

Education was now subject to full federal responsibility for the first time with large sums – more than $1 billion – going to state schools. In practice, ESEA meant helping all school districts, with more money going to districts with a large proportion of students from poor families (all the big cities). However, private schools (mostly Catholic schools in the inner cities) also received services, such as library funding, comprising about 12 per cent of the ESEA budget. Johnson's second major bill was the Higher Education Act of 1965, which funded lower-income students, including grants, work–study money and government loans. This benefitted 25 per cent of all American students.

LBJ also extended education in other ways by creating the National Endowment for the Humanities and the National Endowment for the Arts, supporting writers and artists; and in 1967 the Public Broadcasting Act created educational television programmes to supplement the broadcast networks. But although Johnson's support among teachers' unions was strong, neither the Higher Education Act nor the Endowments appeased those increasingly unhappy with events in Vietnam.

President Nixon had strong Quaker beliefs and valued learning. He had also declared that existence of racism was the greatest moral failure of the USA. He married the two issues by embarking on the first large-scale racial integration of schools in the South, but he had to tread a middle path between segregationists and liberal Democrats, and stated 'I am convinced that while legal segregation is totally wrong, forced integration of housing or education is just as wrong'. Some have interpreted this to mean that Nixon was merely following the order of the courts – desegregation – but disagreed with bussing children to schools in different areas. Nevertheless, desegregation did take place.

In 1968, 68 per cent of black children in the South were attending all-black schools. By late 1970, two million black children were enrolled in newly created, unitary, fully integrated school districts. This meant that only 18 per cent of Southern black children now attended all-black schools. By 1974, that number had fallen still further, to 8 per cent.

Policies to improve health and provide social welfare

1890–1920

During this period, largely dominated by progressive presidents, there were specific responses to the social problems arising from urbanisation and industrialization.

Settlement houses were set up in heavily populated, low-income, urban communities. They provided key community services to alleviate social problems exacerbated by the severe economic depression of 1893 and tried to bridge the growing gap between social classes. The settlement movement became effective and influential.

Settlement houses: also known as social settlements, these were neighbourhood centres for social services and social reform activities.

US reformer Jane Addams brought the idea from a visit to Britain in the 1880s. The first settlement was in New York City in 1886. The movement quickly spread throughout US urban centres and by 1910, there were approximately 400 nationally. But these were not government schemes, although they were supported and extolled by presidents including Theodore Roosevelt. He believed that strong corporations were good for US prosperity, but felt that their behaviour must also be monitored to ensure that corporate greed did not get out of hand; similarly that the workers they employed had better provision in their daily lives.

The governments of this period brought in important legislation to help improve health and social welfare. Much of this was prompted by the publication of a book called *The Jungle*. It criticised aspects of urbanisation, highlighting unsanitary conditions in the meatpacking industry. This led to a public campaign for government inspection of meatpacking plants, and closer monitoring of food production. The Department of Agriculture then disclosed the dangers of chemical additives in canned foods, while a muckraking journalist reported about misleading and fraudulent claims in non-prescription drugs.

To improve health and safeguard food consumption, Roosevelt introduced the Meat Inspection Act of 1906, which set levels of health and sanitation in the food packing industry, and the Pure Food and Drug Act 1906, which outlawed the adulteration or false labelling of food and drugs. These acts were significant, being among the first pieces of federal health legislation of their kind. President Wilson then established the Department of Labour in 1913, 'to foster, promote and develop the welfare of working people, to improve their working conditions, and to enhance their opportunities for profitable employment'.

Throughout this era, individual states passed legislation and established agencies related to child welfare, workplace safety, minimum wages, housing, sanitation and workers' sickness.

For example, in 1903, Illinois passed a law authorising special pensions for the blind; while in Pennsylvania, the Pittsburgh Associated Charities was formed in 1908 in response to the ongoing need for a single, short-term, combined appeal for food, shelter and medical supplies. Then in 1912, the first division of child hygiene was established in a State Department of Health in Louisiana. But these were not nationally implemented federal laws.

In 1909, the first White House Conference on Children brought together child welfare officials to discuss reform, focusing on dependent and neglected children. By 1920, most US state governments had established public pensions for widows with dependent children, while the US Children's Bureau had been established, headed by social workers and members of the settlement house movement.

1920–9

The 1920s were notable for a relative lack of legislation and government initiatives in health and social welfare. It was basically 'as you were', given that laissez-faire self-reliance was prevalent in US politics. By 1933, the USA lagged far behind both Germany and Britain when it came to social security schemes. Only twenty-seven states had introduced old-age pensions, and only one state – Wisconsin – had an unemployment insurance scheme.

Yet there were initiatives – in the early 1920s, the Women's Bureau, a division of the US Labour Department, was formed to safeguard women's working conditions while the Association of Training Schools of Professional Social Work was formed, which would later become the Council on Social Work Education.

The key piece of legislation in this decade was the Sheppard–Towner Maternity and Infancy Act of 1921. This distributed federal grants to states for prenatal and child health clinics, midwife training and visiting nurses for pregnant women and new mothers. It also promoted information on nutrition and hygiene; as such, it became the first federally funded social welfare measure in the USA.

Regrettably, this law was allowed to expire in 1929 so the facility was not available when the help was needed most, with the onset of the Great Depression. Government policies seemed inconsistent in being beneficial to US citizens.

QUESTION

Look at **Source D** and reread the section on 1920–9. What evidence is there to suggest that the administrations of the 1920s were complacent? Or is there evidence to suggest that there was progress?

SOURCE D

During the 1920s complacency became an article of faith among many comfortable Americans. Things were as they should be, business was good, America was strong and God was in His heaven. Republican presidents explained the logic of contentment that appealed to many voters. Beneath the gaze of the satisfied, however, other Americans felt disorientated and dissatisfied by the economic, political and racial status quo. For them, complacency was a problem, rather than a result of all the problems being solved.

M. Johnson (2002), Reading the American Past, Vol II, *2nd edn, Boston: Bedford/St Martin's, p. 119.*

1933–41

With Franklin D. Roosevelt's inauguration as president in 1933 came his First New Deal legislation with its Alphabet Agencies and legislation to provide immediate recovery and reform. In 1935–6, came the Second New Deal with provisions to improve health, and to provide social welfare and security against illness, old age and unemployment. Also a national welfare programme was developed to replace state relief efforts.

The Works Progress Administration (WPA) became the most important work relief agency. Until it wound up in 1943, it spent more than $11 billion on relief work and employed eight million Americans. As Michael Parrish comments: 'In seven years, they built 2,500 hospitals, 5,900 schools, 350 airports, 570,000 miles of rural roads and 8,000 parks.' The WPA dealt with the immediate problem of giving relief to the unemployed, but FDR also tackled long-term permanent assistance with the Social Security Act of 1935.

The Act is of significance as it introduced a compulsory federal system of old age pensions, plus a joint federal-state scheme for unemployment benefit. This was financed by contributions from both employers and workers, with a payroll tax of 3 per cent. There was also survivors' benefits for the victims of industrial accidents and aid for disabled persons and dependent mothers with children. It had the potential to benefit many ordinary people, and it did.

Its downside was the lack of sickness benefits, and no publicly funded health care programme. Roosevelt actually removed these provisions from the bill in order to get its other features passed by Congress. Many doctors and medical interests wanted to maintain private health care. Indeed, such caution was exercised by different governments towards organised medicine's opposition to universal health care for many years. Also the pensions and benefits did not include the self-employed, farm labourers, domestic servants and casual labour – often the most vulnerable of all.

But the Social Security Act was the greatest attempt by any US government to date to promote better social welfare and health. It was the first occasion that help for the aged and unemployed was provided for by the federal government. It marked the birth of something potentially better for all citizens – the US federal welfare state system. It firmly established the principle of national responsibility for health and social welfare.

1961–74

Health and social welfare in the period 1961–74 was determined by the personality of the president or the circumstances in which he attained office. Kennedy's ambitious plan for health reform was restricted by the narrowness of his electoral victory in 1960, in consequence of which he faced stern opposition in Congress. Not until Johnson's landslide in 1964 and his 'Great Society' programme did health and welfare reform really gather pace. It continued, albeit more slowly, with the election of Nixon in 1968.

In 1961, Kennedy set up a Taskforce on Health and Social Security for the American People. It recommended hospital insurance, as well as other welfare measures. Kennedy looked ahead to the mid-term elections in 1962 for better opportunities to build the congressional majority for his programme. Accordingly the decision was made to postpone Medicare until 1962, when he hoped that Congress might be more responsive to public pressure. But under Kennedy came an improved Minimum Wages Law, which brought about a gradual increase in the minimum hourly wage, from $1 to $1.25. Higher social security benefit was also granted.

Kennedy had been deeply influenced by reading Michael Harrington's book *The Other America*, which stated that forty million Americans were living in poverty. Poverty was defined as a family of four living on less than $3,000 per annum. His 1961 Housing Act thus provided $5 billion to fund housing projects for the poor. But it was after 1964 that social welfare policies expanded under Johnson's Great Society programme.

Figure 4.19 Children waiting to receive social welfare relief in 1963

Johnson's landslide victory in November 1964 enabled the passage of more than sixty pieces of groundbreaking legislation, including ten health measures. Millions of elderly people were aided by the 1965 Medicare amendment to the Social Security Act, providing free health care for the elderly and paid out of social security taxes. Johnson then went further with the Medicaid Act, which provided for welfare recipients in the same way that Medicare provided for the elderly. Medicaid thus offered free health care for certain groups (those on low incomes, and unemployed or disabled people) under the Medicare age of sixty-five. The Medicare Act overcame opposition from private insurance companies and the doctors' lobbying group, the American Medical Association, who believed that the Act would reduce earnings among private health groups benefitting from their many elderly clients.

Johnson compromised to get the legislation through Congress and felt that it was not as far-reaching as he would have wished. In total, nearly $7 billion was spent and the Medicare Act provided health care access for people who were previously unable to afford it. However, it did not cover prescriptions and, in the long term, Medicare/Medicaid proved very costly. Nonetheless Johnson's health reforms were of major benefit to US citizens in a country with no previous government health insurance scheme. Compared to what had existed previously, the Medicare Act was a big advance. Johnson's aide Jack Valenti stated 'Of course we made mistakes but … we were doing things!'

Johnson also identified deteriorating urban life as an urgent welfare problem. The Demonstration Cities and Metropolitan Development Act of 1966 aimed to improve the welfare of people living in blighted inner cities and slums, by means of comprehensive building and reconstruction projects. The government offered local authorities 80 per cent grants to deal with health care, housing improvement, crime prevention, job creation and the improvement of recreational facilities.

His 1968 Housing Act proposed a huge federal housing initiative – the building of twenty-six million homes over ten years, at affordable prices to buy or to rent. There were fixed limits on the profits of builders and investors, but many developers were sceptical and, consequently, both quantity and quality suffered. However, under Kennedy and Johnson, the number of families living in poverty decreased from forty million in 1960 to twenty-five million by the time of the 1970 census. While a thriving economy may partly explain this, the social welfare policies enacted by Democrat presidents also had a significant impact and were of incalculable benefit to hundreds of thousands.

Nixon was concerned by what he saw as an inflated welfare system, and argued that it hastened the breakdown of families by providing assistance only to households not headed by a working male. Nixon created the Family Assistance Plan (FAP), replacing programmes such as Food Stamps and Medicaid with direct cash payments to those in need.

Those in work but on poor wages would also now qualify for financial aid and support would not be limited to single-parent families. The FAP also stated that all recipients (except mothers of preschool-age children) would have to work or undertake training for employment.

Heavy criticism followed. Welfare advocates declared the income level Nixon proposed ($1,600 per year for a family of four) insufficient. Conservatives disliked the idea of a guaranteed annual income for people who didn't work. Liberals and trade unions saw the proposal as a threat to the minimum wage, fearing that many jobs would be eliminated. A disappointed Nixon pressed for the bill's passage until the election season of 1972. However, Nixon knew a difficult campaign issue when he saw one and he let FAP expire.

Yet strangely, Nixon's term of office saw the amount spent on social programmes exceed defence spending for the first time. Under a Republican president who specialised in foreign policy, such a shift seems extraordinary. Yet, by the time Nixon left the White House, social spending accounted for 40 per cent of the budget, with an allocation of $132 billion in 1975. When Lyndon Johnson had left office in 1969, it was only 28 per cent.

The Model Cities Programme and the Department of Housing and Urban Development – both key features of the Democrats' Great Society concept – continued under Nixon; and he supported some of the major spending policies (such as automatic cost-of-living increases for social security recipients) that later caused problems for his successors Gerald Ford and Jimmy Carter.

However Nixon was unhappy when Congress increased social security benefits by linking increases to the rate of inflation, as well as increasing the funding for food stamps given to the unemployed instead of money.

By 1975 America was a country firmly wedded to the concept of a mixed economy – combining federal programmes and private incentives – in social and economic policies. In this respect – and despite variations in emphasis – the policies to improve health and provide social welfare between 1961 and 1975 were of the utmost significance, central to an industrialised society; and now a prime concern of modern government.

Historical debate

Johnson's 'Great Society' health and social welfare reforms:
Throughout Johnson's programme, it was alleged that some recipients of welfare felt shamed and believed the federal state was intruding, while conservatives resented the federal government moving into areas of people's lives. Also the growing cost of US involvement in Vietnam meant that Johnson could not carry out all he wanted to. Historian William Chafe says that the war on poverty remained a disappointment for the president 'when measured by the expectations set forth by Johnson'. But that did not mean the reforms were a failure. Historians Alan Farmer and Vivienne Sanders note that critics of LBJ cite the outbreak of urban riots in many USA cities in the late 1960s as proof that the Great Society did not deliver, but they suggest that millions benefitted from its health care programmes and that maybe the problem was 'it aroused expectations which it was then unable to deliver' in a short period of time. Historian Allen J. Matsuow suggests that even with the Great Society, the 'war on poverty' could not be won. The only real solution being a radical redistribution of wealth through taxation, while the Medical Care Act merely ended up paying doctors for services that they had previously given for free, and historian Alonzo L. Harmby says that Johnson 'in his striving for hyper-accomplishment ... simply tried to do too much'. But LBJ's biographer Robert Caro explains this speed of reform by saying that 'Johnson had always cared deeply about the injustice being done to blacks, to Mexicans, to the poor and downtrodden, but had never had the chance to show how much he cared. When he got that chance, he took it.' Historian Joanne de Pennington says that his health and welfare programme, 'put poverty, justice and access into the centre of politics ... it proved that big government was sometimes necessary for national change and benefits', while historian Paul Boyer sums up the debate elegantly when he comments that the USA under Johnson's Great Society became 'a more caring and just nation'.

Policies to improve the position of women

1890–1933

In 1917, the first woman was elected to Congress and finally, in 1919, President Woodrow Wilson initiated the legislation that became the 19th Amendment in August 1920. This gave women the vote.

But a distinctive women's movement never materialised. By 1929, the League of Women's Voters could show that 145 women had won seats in thirty-five state legislatures and two had become governors, but the political arena remained male-orientated and government policies likewise, in spite of the more independent lifestyle of many women and the 1920s stereotype of the '**flapper**'.

Flapper: the nickname given to the supposedly sophisticated, pleasure-seeking, fashionable young women of 1920s America, who were unconventional and wild. Older generations of women saw them as brazen and lacking morals.

But women had influenced government in other ways, through organisations such as the Young Women's Christian Association, the National Consumers' League, labour unions and professional associations. Women secured minimum wage and maximum hours laws for female workers; they also successfully pushed for better public health for pregnant women and babies, plus greater educational opportunities for children and adults.

They even succeeded in securing the creation of the Children's Bureau in 1912 and then the Women's Bureau in 1920, in the federal Department of Labour. But in spite of such policies, with wage discrimination and the dominance of the opinion that women only worked until they married, the notion of a woman combining home and family duties with proper employment was frowned upon.

1933–41

Upon becoming president in 1933, Roosevelt appointed Frances Perkins as secretary of labour, the first female in US Cabinet history, who remained in office throughout FDR's entire presidency until 1945.

He then appointed Ohio judge Florence Ellinwood Allen, to be the first woman on the federal Court of Appeals. But this did not necessarily mean that women's rights were going to advance. Even Perkins urged married women to stay out of the labour market so more men could work. In 1939 women teachers earned nearly 20 per cent less than male teachers with comparable experience. When FDR brought in a statutory national minimum wage and a forty-hour week as part of the Fair Labour Standards Act of 1938 (FLSA); many women workers were not covered by it, including the more than two million who worked for wages in private households.

But women benefitted from special programmes instituted under all three of the main relief agencies to provide work for the skilled and professional worker. Sometimes this benefitted the community by providing education, medical care and advice. Women also found employment through the WPA, yet when they did, it was invariably in lower-paid jobs such as caring for the elderly, sewing or supervising lunch and play-time in nursery schools. Moreover, only 14 per cent of people in the WPA scheme were women. FDR's administration had a mixed view towards women. Significantly, New Deal legislation took for granted the idea that women were paid a lower rate than men, while relief schemes were aimed mainly at the provision of support for families and had an emphasis on the provision of relief to men.

Whilst women's rights did not necessarily regress, nor were policies promoted that helped women to benefit in the manner they ought, given the reforming zeal present in the Roosevelt administration.

ACTIVITY

Using the library and the internet, do some more research on Frances Perkins (1880–1965) – her life, her career, her beliefs and her policies. What was significant about her role in the Roosevelt administration?

1961–74

In the 1960s, gender issues really came to the fore. Despite making up 50 per cent of the nation's voters, women's professional and political participation was still very limited. There were no female Supreme Court judges, federal Appeal Court justices, governors or ambassadors, and only two out of one hundred senators were women. Women were also underrepresented at the higher levels of industry and commerce, and their pay usually averaged 60 per cent less than men's. Fewer than 2 per cent of leading American business executives were female, and more than 95 per cent of lawyers were still male. Many women worked in the service industries, as secretaries, waitresses and beauticians. In several Southern states, women could not sit on juries, while other states restricted their right to make contracts, wills, sell property and negotiate in business. Married women even had limited control over their own earnings.

Kennedy set up the Commission on the Status of Women in December 1961. It was the first presidential committee ever to look specifically at such gender issues. Its creation sent out a signal that the status of women was now a national issue. Its finding in 1963 criticised many of the legal restrictions placed on women, including obstacles to them owning property, entering into business or making contracts. It also recommended equal employment opportunities and emphasised the need for more childcare.

In 1963, Kennedy introduced the Equal Pay Act, which required equal pay for men and women working in the same jobs under the same conditions. It was the first federal law to specifically prohibit gender-based discrimination.

Congress also struck a blow in the fight against sex discrimination. Johnson's 1964 Civil Rights Act prohibited employment discrimination based on colour, race, ethnicity, religion or gender by private employers and unions. This was especially relevant when it came to promotion and hiring or firing. When it was passed in the House of Representatives, a female voice shouted from the gallery: 'We made it! God bless America!'

The Equal Employment Opportunity Commission (EEOC) was also set up, and in order to pressure it, **Betty Friedan** and 300 other women formed the National Organization for Women (NOW) in 1966. NOW pledged 'to take action to bring women into full participation in the mainstream of American society now, exercising all the privileges and responsibilities thereof in truly equal partnership with men'. It filed a suit against the EEOC 'to force it to comply with its own government rules' and sued America's 1,300 largest corporations for sex discrimination, and it also challenged airlines' insistence that stewardesses should retire upon marriage or on reaching the age of thirty-two. In consequence of much lobbying, the EEOC then ruled that separate job advertisements for men and women violated the 1964 Civil Rights Act.

Betty Friedan (1921–2006)

She was an eminent US writer, feminist and political activist. A leading figure in the US women's movement, Friedan was the catalyst for the second wave of American feminism in the 20th century. She founded the National Organization for Women (NOW) in 1966 and was its first leader. NOW aimed to bring all women into the mainstream of US society in equal partnership with men.

In November 1967, NOW drew up a Bill of Rights for women. It urged adoption of an Equal Rights Amendment (ERA) to the constitution, prohibiting sex discrimination, ensuring equal educational, training and housing opportunities for women, and calling for the repeal of laws limiting access to contraceptive devices and abortion. Membership grew rapidly, reaching 40,000 by 1974. The organisation constantly lobbied and protested.

Nixon's election in 1968 was opposed by feminists, but after initially ignoring women's rights, he then acknowledged the movement – although he used the CIA and FBI to infiltrate protest groups. Nonetheless, the feminist movement was at its height. In August 1970, the women's movement demonstrated its strength by mounting a national 'Strike for Equality' march. In New York, 50,000 women marched down Fifth Avenue. In Chicago, 3,000 women took to the streets. About 400 members of a group called the New York Radical Women demonstrated outside the Atlantic City Convention Hall during the Miss America beauty pageant. The protestors provided a 'freedom trash can' for women to dispose of 'old bras, girdles, high-heeled shoes, women's magazines, curlers and other instruments of torture to women'. But contrary to the legend that later grew up, no women actually burned their bras.

Figure 4.20 A women's liberation march up Fifth Avenue in New York, August 1970

In 1971, commerce secretary Barbara Hackman Franklin was instructed by Nixon to recruit qualified women for positions in the administration. This was the first time a US president had specifically tried to promote women's rights within his administration, and it was well-received. Yet he then angered women by vetoing the Comprehensive Child Development Bill of 1972 (universal day-care); but then he supported the Equal Rights Amendment and signed the Education Amendments of 1972, ending sex discrimination in schools and athletics. The Equal Credit Opportunity Act of 1974 meant that women were now legally entitled to receive credit facilities from banks on the same terms as men. Nixon established another commission on women and appointed more women to positions of power. In a national address in 1972, Nixon stated on television: 'While every woman may not want a career outside the home, every woman should have the freedom to choose whatever career she wishes, and an equal chance to pursue it.' That was quite an innovative statement by a politician of that time. Nixon's administration was more of a champion for women than it might first appear. His administration's policies had proven more beneficial to women in the US than might have been anticipated.

Theory of Knowledge

History and language:
There is a saying that 'language is power'. To what extent do you feel that the writings of Betty Friedan and the type of language used by feminists during the 1960s and 1970s to describe both the situation of women and their treatment by men helped them to feel empowered? What do you think the general reaction in America would have been to such language?

Policies to protect the rights of minorities

When the USA was founded in 1776 it was based on the concept that the equality of all its citizens was 'self-evident' and that key human rights were inalienable, such as 'life, liberty and the pursuit of happiness'. The constitution does provide for equal access to a wide range of civil rights and liberties, while the 13th Amendment prohibits slavery and the 14th entrenches the due process of law and equal protection for all.

But until the 20th century, many of these rights were absent or misinterpreted in order to suit the social and political climate. This meant that many minority groups were disenfranchised; Native Americans removed from land; official racial segregation permitted; and unequal access to public services allowed to continue. Even the Supreme Court repeatedly condoned practices by interpreting them as legal and acceptable in certain circumstances. Indeed, looking at the actions of the federal government over time reveals that there was never a really consistent 'minorities' policy, nor in fact was there a consistent policy toward any particular group.

From 1890 to the Second World War

Between 1887 and 1924, the US government tried to control Native American travel beyond the reservations. Since they did not get full citizenship until 1924, they were deemed wards of the state and so were denied various rights, such as freedom to travel. The government-managed Bureau of Indian Affairs (BIA) even discouraged natural off-reservation activities, including the right to hunt, fish, or visit other tribes, and introduced a 'pass system' designed to limit their movement, whereby they had to obtain a pass before they could leave their designated reservation.

Partly in recognition of the thousands of Native Americans who served in the armed forces during the First World War, the Snyder Act of 1921 authorised the federal government to provide special services to Native Americans. It culminated, in 1924, in the Indian Citizenship Act, which gave full citizenship to almost half of the 300,000 US indigenous people. Those not included had already become citizens by being in the armed forces or by fully assimilating into mainstream US life.

Under Roosevelt's New Deal, Congress subsequently passed the Indian Reorganisation Act of 1934, which reinstated tribal governments that could have their own legal systems, police and constitution. Despite these changes, seventy-five of the 245 Native American tribes opposed the Act, including the largest group – the Navajo of New Mexico and Arizona. But it was now possible to be a tribal citizen as well as a US citizen. In addition, Roosevelt authorised the federal government to contract with state and local governments to provide services to Native Americans. A major outcome of this policy was that Native American children and students in many areas became integrated into white schools long before African Americans and Hispanic Americans.

But many Native Americans still did not have voting rights until 1948, due to opposition in some US states. But while Native Americans were being integrated – or rather assimilated – into US society, African Americans were given a 'separate but equal' status.

By the early 20th century, many African Americans moved to industrial cities in the north in the Great Migration, while the majority still lived in the Deep South under Jim Crow Laws. Yet even into the 1930s, interracial violence and hostility was still commonplace.

But during the Depression of the 1930s, black workers in the North and the South began to join trade unions. These provided a platform for their grievances and led to an increased awareness of their predicament. The quest for civil rights would be boosted by African American participation in the Second World War, with almost one million being drafted to fight. By the time Kennedy and Johnson dominated the US political scene in the 1960s, US African American rights were at the forefront of the domestic political agenda.

Up to 1941, the US government had implemented little in the way of specific policies to improve the lives of African Americans – or, indeed, the other minorities. Two decades on, this would be significantly different.

Fact: In the 1880s, governments in the southern states passed anti African American laws, known as 'Jim Crow Laws' after the name of a typical 1830s black minstrel show character. These were discriminatory laws forbidding African Americans from using public facilities such as restaurants, theatres, cinemas, hotels, transport and swimming pools. Schooling was segregated according to colour and in many states, marriages between whites and African Americans were illegal. African Americans effectively had second-class citizenship, although these laws claimed to provide 'separate but equal' facilities to both whites and blacks. In reality, black facilities were poorer and in worse locations.

Fact: In the Great Migration of 1910–40, more than two million blacks migrated from the rural South to the large industrial cities of the North, to escape rural poverty and social oppression. New York, Chicago, Philadelphia and the car-manufacturing centre of Detroit were the main areas of settlement. The African American population of New York rose from 91,000 to 328,000 during this period.

Sharecropping: when landowners divided up their land into small tenancies of thirty to fifty acres. Poorer white farmers and black free men could then rent their own farms by giving half of their crops to the landowner as rent. This was beneficial to former slaves and their families, who could now work together on the land as a family.

SOURCE E

By the time of America's entry into the Second World War, almost three-quarters of the country's black population still lived in the south, in spite of the large-scale migrations that had taken place during the First World War and in response to the Great Depression of the 1930s. Here they were almost all excluded from voting and from serving on juries. They were refused access to white hospitals, universities, public parks and swimming pools. In urban areas, they were condemned to work in lowly, unskilled occupations. In rural areas, they struggled to survive as **sharecroppers**, tenant farmers or labourers. Their life expectancy was at least ten years less than that of white people. In the north they were subjected to racist violence and discrimination in the workplace and in housing. Unemployment rates, especially during the Depression, were significantly higher than those of white workers.

D. Paterson, D. Willoughby and S. Willoughby (2001), Civil Rights in the USA 1863–1980, *Oxford: Heinemann, p. 246.*

1961–75

In the period between 1961 and 1975, federal government actions and legislation radically influenced the status of minority groups. The major civil rights legislation implemented applied not only to African Americans, but also to Native Americans and

Hispanic Americans. The Civil Rights Act of 1964, the Voting Rights Act of 1965 and the Fair Housing Act of 1968 were all designed to ensure that race and ethnicity did prohibit people from having the basic rights guaranteed to all US citizens.

Pre-Second World War Mexican agricultural labour had been largely seasonal and migratory. Many labourers had returned to Mexico for the winter. But with the outbreak of war in 1941, labour shortages were evident in all areas of the US economy with many workers being in the military and industrial priorities shifting towards munitions. The labour shortage forced Roosevelt into changing US policy on immigration and the institution of Bracero Programme (also known as the Mexican Farm Labour Programme) with Mexico. This led to contract workers being supplied to the USA between 1942 and 1964, and authorised more than four million border crossings of guest workers from Mexico into the USA. Meanwhile, Hispanic immigrants from Cuba had arrived in the USA in substantial numbers after 1959, following the communist takeover.

When President Kennedy took office in 1961, he had been supported by the Mexican American Political Association, which had run an unprecedented voter registration drive in Hispanic communities, and Mexican-Americans in Texas, New Mexico, California, Arizona, Illinois and Indiana had helped Kennedy win critical votes in the closely fought 1960 election. Johnson also enjoyed support from Hispanics who campaigned for him during his landslide victory in 1964 and 'Latinos' now came to be acknowledged as an important voting bloc.

Although the Civil Rights Act of 1964 is seen predominantly in terms of the African American community that pushed for the passage of legislation, Mexican-Americans had a leader who worked with Johnson and the black leadership. Hector P. Garcia was a Texas physician and community activist, and was appointed by LBJ to serve on the US Civil Rights Commission – the first Hispanic to do so. President Johnson also formed a new Cabinet Committee on Mexican-American Affairs – a major innovation – and appointed Texan Vicente T. Ximenes as chairman.

This was major progress, and the influence of this ethnic group was further demonstrated in 1966 when Hispanics staged a three-day march from Albuquerque to Santa Fe in New Mexico, demanding that land taken by the USA in 1848 be returned to local Mexicans. Hispanic grape-pickers led by trade union activist **Cesar Chavez**, went on strike in California in 1965 demanding union recognition for Hispanics. Nixon granted this in 1970 and during his five-year presidency he appointed more Hispanics than any preceding president, including Kennedy and Johnson. In 1974, shortly before he resigned as president over the Watergate scandal, Nixon passed the Equal Opportunity Act, which resulted in more bilingual teaching and examination in public schools. This policy was especially beneficial to Hispanics in education.

Native Americans underwent considerable change after 1945. With 44,000 of them serving in the US wartime armed forces between 1941 and 1945, most did not want to return to the poverty of the reservation. Many obtained good jobs in US cities and, by the 1960s, the US Native American urban population had doubled to around 60,000. But with many still preferring to live separately on reservations and in spite of the huge social reforms of the 1960s under Johnson's Great Society, they still faced poverty, unemployment and alcohol and drug abuse. In 1944, they had formed the National Congress of American Indians (NCAI) to help all Native American tribes, and in the 1950s, they had used their influence to stop the US government from ending Indian rights on reservations.

QUESTION

What does **Source E** suggest to us about the lives of African Americans during the socially reforming years of Roosevelt's New Deal?

Cesar Chavez (1927–1993)

He was a prominent labour union organiser born in Arizona to Mexican-American immigrant farm workers. He forced agricultural producers to agree to trade union contracts after national boycotts of grapes, avocados and lettuce in the 1960s and 1970s.

On the back of the black civil rights movement, 1968 witnessed the formation of the American Indian Movement (AIM) to fight much more proactively for their rights. Using the courts and by direct actions, Native Americans began to gain civil and social equality as the 1970s progressed. In 1969, fourteen AIM activists occupied the derelict Alcatraz jail in San Francisco Bay. In 1972, AIM militants occupied the famous Wounded Knee battle site in South Dakota, then later that year the Supreme Court made a landmark decision in *Passamquaddy v Morton*. The Passamquaddy tribe from Maine received compensation from the US government for land seized from them in 1790 in a broken agreement. Finally in 1974, the US government passed the Indian Self-Determination Act, granting all tribes control over federal aid programmes on their reservations, as well as control of their own schools.

The African American struggle in many respects was the main campaign, as it attracted worldwide attention, so by 1961, African American civil rights had moved towards the top of the political agenda. In 1954, the US Supreme Court had made a landmark ruling in the *Brown v Topeka Board of Education* case, declaring that the existence of separate public schools for white pupils and black pupils was wholly unconstitutional. In doing so, the Supreme Court had overturned its own *Plessy v Ferguson* ruling from 1896, which had legalised and advocated such segregation, on the merits of 'separate but equal'.

The legal basis for segregation was removed. This had the potential to change radically the lives of many black children and students and it was a potential nail in the coffin of racial segregation, which all blacks faced from nursery school to the grave. This case was broadened by later rulings extending desegregation into other areas and requiring the US government to take a proactive stance in integrating racial and ethnic groups and providing equal opportunity.

In 1964, LBJ passed the Civil Rights Act, which outlawed discrimination on the basis of race, colour and creed in voting, employment, federal programmes and public facilities. This was then followed by the Voting Rights Act of 1965 to prohibit attempts – mainly in Southern states – to deprive minorities from suffrage. Johnson's Great Society policies also greatly helped African Americans, with laws regarding equal employment opportunity, fair housing, poverty alleviation and beneficial social welfare schemes.

Richard Nixon made minority business enterprise a key theme of his administration, and whether motivated by political, practical or philosophical factors, his often overlooked policies towards minorities – not least African Americans – were beneficial to the black community and subsequently influenced federal policies towards minority-owned businesses for many years.

On his accession to the presidency, Nixon increased the US budget for civil rights programmes, and between 1969 and 1972 it rose from $75 million to $600 million. He also created an Office of Minority Business Enterprise in the Department of Commerce, which helped African Americans launch business ventures and acquire patents for many products. However, critics would point out that Nixon's administration, in offering help to would-be entrepreneurs from minorities, were gearing themselves too much towards people like themselves – middle-class and upwardly mobile – the benefits of such policies, therefore, might then be reaped only across a limited social spectrum.

Regarding the education of African Americans and indeed all ethnicities, Nixon affirmed that racism was a moral failing in the USA and that the law must be colour-blind. In this manner, he embarked on the first large-scale racial integration of schools in the South.

Between 1969 and 1973, federal aid to predominantly black colleges and universities doubled as a result of the desire to level the playing field between historically black colleges and other major US colleges. Undoubtedly Nixon's policies towards African Americans had a benefit – they provided the nucleus of a growing, aspirational black middle-class who would mature in business, commerce politics, professions and academia over the next two decades. But it cannot be said that all African American US citizens reaped the harvest.

Policies to create a more equitable distribution of wealth

The usual definition of wealth is the value of everything owned by an individual or their immediate family, minus any debts. However, economists and sociologists only see wealth in terms of marketable assets, such as property and stocks. They discount consumer durables, such as refrigerators, hi-fi equipment and furniture, as the value of such items is derived from their intrinsic usefulness, rather than the amount of money realised by reselling them. Sociologist G. William Domhoff observes that since the value of all marketable assets is determined, debts such as mortgages and credit card debts should be subtracted. The figure left is a person's net worth. We also need to differentiate wealth from income. People earn income from wages, dividends and interest. Indeed, some very wealthy individuals may or may not have high incomes, depending on the returns received from their wealth. But, realistically, the wealthiest members of society usually have the highest income.

With the Republican presidents of the 1920s, the inequality persisted. The boom of the 1920s had virtually passed the South and West by, and the geographical variations in industrial development meant that wages varied according to where the industry was based or what type of industry it was.

For example, in 1929 the average per capita age in the northeast – as in states like Michigan, or Pennsylvania – was just over $900, whereas in the southeast it was $365 per year per capita. It also varied within regions according to the type of work. In South Carolina and Georgia it was just over $400 for non-farm workers, yet only $130 per year for farmers. By 1929, many struggled to reach the minimum annual amount calculated by the Federal Bureau of Labour as the basic income necessary for an acceptable living. Women fared even worse, working for lower pay than men, with African Americans, Native Americans and Hispanics at the bottom of the pile. Unsurprisingly, by 1930 the bottom 90 per cent of the population held just 16 per cent of America's wealth, in itself much less than that held by the top 0.1 per cent, which had controlled a quarter of total wealth prior to the 1929 Crash. The 1920s brought no wealth redistribution.

Between 1930 and 1945, the share of total wealth among the middle classes rose. This was due less to government policy – even under Roosevelt's New Deal – and rather more to collapsing wealth among affluent households. This is not to suggest that Roosevelt was lax, as he supported a broader distribution of wealth but he cautiously avoided demanding wholesale redistribution. FDR vowed to break up 'concentrated' wealth, which he believed threatened the social, economic and political harmony of the USA, as well as compromising the effectiveness of democracy.

In 1935 at the time of the Second New Deal he particularly criticised US revenue laws as having functioned 'in many ways to the unfair advantage of the few and …

have done little to prevent an unjust concentration of wealth and economic power'. Such eloquence helped him to pass the Revenue Act of 1935 through Congress. This increased federal income tax on higher income levels, by introducing a 'Wealth Tax'. It was a progressive tax that took up to 75 per cent of the very highest incomes. But no great redistribution occurred during the Roosevelt years.

In the post-war decade after 1945, the US economy reached heights unattained since the 1920s, with a major consumer boom and a population increase of twenty-one million between 1953 and 1961. But prosperity was unevenly spread. In 1953 the median income for a white family was $4,392, but only $2,461 for non-whites. By 1960, the gap was $2,600. In 1960, 22 per cent of the population lived below the poverty line, and rural areas and inner cities were especially depressed.

By the early 1960s, Kennedy was battling to pass legislation designed to increase the minimum wage and provide funds for urban renewal. Kennedy had read Michael Harrington's controversial book *The Other America*, which identified a subculture revolving round low-income, dead-end jobs, poor health care and inadequate schooling. Kennedy established the Area Redevelopment Administration (ARA), but this spread itself too thinly, trying to help too many communities.

It was Johnson who declared 'unconditional war on poverty in America' in his first State of the Union Address. He launched his anti-poverty programme in March 1964, submitting the Economic Opportunity Act to Congress. Poverty was highest among African Americans, but there was uneven income distribution among whites and poverty was most common among the sick, poorly educated and female single-parent families. Johnson battled to get welfare reforms past groups with vested interests, such as unions, corporations and some professions. Despite the obstacles, Johnson did make progress. While in 1965, almost 66 per cent of black children lived below the poverty line, Johnson's policies cut that figure to 39.6 per cent by 1969 – a tremendous achievement. The overall poverty rate was halved, declining from 22.4 per cent in 1959 to 12.1 per cent in 1969. However, this still did not lead to a major redistribution of income, in the sense that the amazingly rich still remained very rich. Although their taxation bills might have been higher, the top 1 per cent of the US population still controlled 31 per cent of the nation's wealth in 1969, even after the great social reforming years of Democrats Kennedy and Johnson.

Nixon steered America into the 1970s against a backdrop of rising crime, urban ghetto violence and drug abuse. He questioned the policy of huge public spending to alleviate poverty and social problems, observing that the crime rate had surged immediately after Johnson's Great Society reforms. Nixon used the presidential veto to halt incomplete Democrat initiatives in health, education and welfare benefits, preferring financial assistance to be more means-tested. Interestingly, the 1970s also witnessed a population move from the North to the South. The industrial North became known as the 'rust belt', with its outdated, declining industries, whereas the South and West now attracted newer growth industries. The end of racial segregation in the South had resulted in near normalisation of race relations. Benefitting from lower taxes and less crime, the South now became less isolated from the rest of the USA and income rose. Nevertheless, international economic problems and unemployment rising to 5.6 per cent by 1972 made for a difficult decade.

In spite of the progressive presidents, a 1920s boom, a New Deal and a Great Society – all played out against the USA's international economic mastery – those with fewest resources were still hardest hit. Inequitable distribution of wealth and resources continued as President Gerald Ford and the USA celebrated the bicentenary of American independence in 1976.

4.9 What has been the cultural impact of democracy within the USA?

1890–1941

By the 1890s, the dominance of cities and larger towns had eclipsed the farming communities so pivotal in the early everyday life of the USA. Initially, America was an importer of culture, especially music and literature, with its own composers and writers being sometimes judged inferior to European artists. Publishers' demands focused on short popular fiction and items using regional language and songs or tales about folklore, which were supplied by regional artists.

But as the USA reached the 20th century, its artistic reputation had blossomed, with a growing homogeneous culture evident in the output of writers and poets such as Henry James, Emily Dickinson, Mark Twain and Walt Whitman. A vigorous tradition of home-grown classical music now developed, especially in Connecticut and Massachusetts.

The composers of the so-named Second New England School included such figures as George Whitefield Chadwick, Amy Beach and Horatio Parker who, while at Yale University, taught Charles Ives (1874–1954) – later one of the first American composers of international renown. They were responsible for the first significant body of concert music by US composers, having served their musical apprenticeship in Britain and Germany. They returned home to teach and nurture young music students and to compose distinctly American music.

From 1883 to 1930, one of the most significant cultural advances in the USA was the creation of Carnegie libraries, built with the proceeds of capitalism and industrialisation, from money donated by Scottish-American multimillionaire businessman and philanthropist **Andrew Carnegie**.

Carnegie libraries brought prestige, learning and employment to people and communities, offering jobs to a growing number of female librarians and providing a much-needed educational touchstone for children and adults – frequently immigrants – who came to borrow books.

Carnegie had a 'formula' for deciding which towns got the libraries. He required proof of financial commitment from the community that received the donation. Carnegie insisted on public support rather than making an endowment because 'an endowed institution is liable to become the prey of a clique'. Money was not handed out all at once but disbursed gradually as the project proceeded; and for each application submitted, Carnegie required potential recipients to prove the local need for a public library, to provide a site, to contribute annually 10 per cent of the cost of the library's construction to support its operation and – above all else – to ensure that it provided free services to everyone. They were culturally important as they were run in a democratic,

ACTIVITY

Choose a writer *and* a musician from the following lists:

WRITER: Henry James; Emily Dickinson; Walt Whitman; Mark Twain.

MUSICIAN: George Whitefield Chadwick; Amy Beach; Horatio Parker; Charles Ives.

Now using the library or the internet, find out about their life, career and their contribution to the development of American culture at the turn of the 20th century. Make notes sufficient to give a brief biographical résumé to your class.

Andrew Carnegie (1835–1919)

He was a Scottish born self-made steel tycoon and one of the wealthiest USA entrepreneurs in the 19th century. After emigrating to the USA, he first worked in railroads and made some shrewd investments, particularly in oil. His substantial share profits eventually led to him developing the Carnegie Steel Corporation, later the largest of its kind in the world. With new technology revolutionising his methods of steel production, he became one of the dominant figures in US public life. He sold

Carnegie Steel in 1901 to financier J.P. Morgan, and used his 'retirement' to do philanthropic work, establishing the Carnegie-Mellon University in 1904. An avid reader, he donated $5 million to the New York Public Library so that it could open several branches. With other donations elsewhere in the USA, more than 1,600 Carnegie libraries were opened across the nation with his support. Including libraries funded to open outside the USA, a total of 2,509 were built between 1883 and 1929 in places such as Canada, Australia, New Zealand, Malaysia, the Caribbean, Ireland and the UK. In the early 20th century, a Carnegie library was often the most imposing structure in most small US communities.

open manner, having open book stacks that encouraged people to browse and ultimately choose for themselves the books they wished to read. Carnegie's libraries addressed the aims of the progressive era and of the Democrats and they also appealed to the Republicans of the 1920s as evidence of what wealth and philanthropy could bestow on a nation energised by business and corporate capitalism.

While hundreds of the US Carnegie library buildings are now used as community centres, museums, or private residences, more than 50 per cent remain as valuable community libraries and centres of learning, especially in low-income neighbourhoods.

Cultural change developed apace in the 1920s or the 'Jazz Age'. This was an era of innovation with music coming directly from African American culture. Reflecting the Great Migration northwards, Chicago and Harlem in New York became centres for jazz. Jazz influenced new dance styles, so out went the Waltz, and in came the Charleston and the Black Bottom! But more conservative areas of the USA disliked this new music and its 'decadent' dance styles. Small-town and white working-class America – especially in the South and West still listened to country and western music.

With the expansion of mass periodicals, sensationalist tabloid magazines and the growing adoration of the film industry based in Hollywood, California, Americans sought to escape boredom from the daily routine. When 'talking pictures' arrived in 1927, the Hollywood film industry grew astronomically in popularity, influence and prestige. Literature and art also enjoyed their greatest boom since the 1890s as Scott Fitzgerald, Ernest Hemingway, William Faulkner, Eugene O'Neill and Sinclair Lewis dazzled readers and theatre audiences alike with their output.

America in the 1930s was unified by the same songs, news and films. Local radio had started in 1921, and grew quickly so that the first US national radio network, NBC began broadcasting in 1926, with CBS the following year. Radio sales soared from $12 million in 1921 to $366 million by 1929. By 1940, more than 80 per cent of all US citizens had access to a radio and a wide choice of channels. Radio carried political content, as when Franklin D. Roosevelt enhanced his credibility by addressing the US public regularly through his radio 'fireside chats' on a Sunday evening. But his opponents also had the democratic freedom of expression to counter his ideas on air. Radio's credibility and cultural power was so significant that when Orson Welles broadcast H.G. Wells' *War of the Worlds* at Halloween in 1938, many panicked and fled their homes believing that a Martian invasion of earth was being reported by radio stations.

Spectator sport also became a major attraction for families who could now watch games together and enjoy sport, even if the demands of the working day in urban centres meant they had little time to participate in it personally.

Mass spectator sport and radio came together most effectively in baseball and professional boxing. Baseball was the most popular professional sport and attendance doubled in the 1920s. 'Babe' Ruth was a major baseball hero, while the boxing ring provided an arena of achievement for African Americans. Joe Louis was dominant, holding the world heavyweight title from 1935 to 1947. Sport thus became a big part of US culture as it benefitted from better venues, equipment and radio coverage.

People now watched and read about the same sports stars, danced the same dances and bought the same consumer goods. Regional traits existed, but to a much lesser degree. The years 1920–41 transformed the USA culturally and homogenised American culture, permitting a democratic flourish of expression in the arts and media. Its intellectual creativity and imaginative entertainment proved globally influential.

Figure 4.21 An American family sit in their comfortable living room watching a family entertainment programme in the late 1950s

KEY CONCEPTS QUESTION

Change and Continuity: Explain to what extent American cultural life had changed between 1890 and 1941. Were there any elements of continuity?

1961–75

The Second World War was a turning point in American cultural life.

SOURCE F

Something had changed profoundly with the conclusion of World War II. The United Sates had entered the war a wounded economic giant and emerged from it as the dominant superpower in the world. By the end of the war, America and Europe had changed places ... modern American culture represented a revival of the democratic creativeness which presided at the birth of the Republic and flourished up to the Civil War.

P. Levine and H. Papasotiriou (2005), America Since 1945, *Basingstoke: Palgrave Macmillan, p. 33.*

By the late 1950s, many – although not all – US citizens enjoyed prosperity and became enthused with the concept of the **American Dream**. Some 140 million people (7 per cent of the world's population) controlled half of the world's manufacturing output, with a per capita income that was more than double that of any other country.

Public policies had accelerated housing, the development of suburbs, and the rapid growth of car ownership and credit availability. By 1960 well over 50 per cent of the population enjoyed a 'middle-class' lifestyle, sharing in a consumer boom greater than the 1920s. Television was the dominant medium, heralding global communications. The presidential elections of 1952, 1956 and 1960 had used television fully, and families now saw news footage of world events unfolding in their own homes.

American Dream: a national ideal where citizens are recognised by others for what they are and in which democracy and a free society provide the opportunity for success, prosperity and upward social mobility achieved by hard work and honesty. Originally it was not meant to be determined merely by high wages, the latest television sets, fridge-freezers or cars, but the 1960s consumer culture had added a new measurement by which people realised the American Dream.

Culturally, many people abandoned traditional pre-war practices. Central to this was the rise of the suburbs, loosening the social fabric that had once tied communities. Daily life now revolved around the immediate family gathered round the dinner table, the television set or the record player. Extensive car ownership also meant that people could leave their suburbs and visit friends beyond their locality.

Stanley Kurtz in *Culture and Values in the 1960s* comments that neighbourhood friendships and local civic organisations never fully disappeared, but people's social lives and friendships, were shaped increasingly by choice and sharing common beliefs, as opposed to proximity or accident of birth; 'so in the 1960s … we got movements of individuals who banded together in order to protect the freedoms cherished by all Americans. So movements began to coalesce around the theme of resistance to oppression.'

With democratic freedom of expression existing in the arts, media and on the streets; a 'counterculture' soon evolved. It was fuelled by opposition to the Vietnam War, to the injustice of racial discrimination and to the increasing demands for equal opportunity. San Francisco captured the mood in the 1967 'Summer of Love' (see section 4.7, The anti-war movement of the 1960s).

In *America Since 1945*, Levine and Papasotiriou speak of the 'imaginative crisis of the 1960s' when writers and filmmakers challenged liberal assumptions about America's affluent society. The country had elected its youngest president and then seen him shot. His successor Johnson won the largest electoral victory to date in 1964, implementing major social reforms, yet had to withdraw from re-election.

Patterson, Willoughby and Willoughby in *Civil Rights in the USA 1863–1980* note the flourishing of black literature, music, fashion and theatre, giving the black community cultural pride and a sense of identity, and it was a changing and turbulent time socially and culturally. Illegal drug usage grew as the mid-1960s witnessed the Beatles, the Rolling Stones, the Who and other British groups transforming American music. Rock and Roll morphed into something more edgy and anti-establishment and 'hard rock' came to the fore, while songs with a political or social commentary became commonplace. Singer-songwriter Bob Dylan found that his songs became anthems of the anti-war and civil rights movements. Jim Morrison, lead vocalist of the American rock group the Doors, became one of the most influential front-men in rock music history, establishing himself as popular culture's most rebellious and oft-displayed icon, symbolising the generation gap and youth counterculture, before his death in 1971.

During Nixon's first year in office, the three-day Woodstock Festival was held in August 1969. This famous musical gathering in rural New York state, epitomised American counterculture and the desire to 'turn on, tune in, drop out' as proposed by Harvard professor and poet, Timothy Leary. In total, 400,000 people congregated to experiment with a new way of life focused on drugs, sex and rock music, and the festival – immortalised on film and through record albums – gave its name to the Woodstock generation.

The US film industry in the late 1960s and 1970s blossomed with this newfound artistic freedom. A daring and talented new generation of filmmakers – the New Hollywood generation – brought values representative of the counterculture, and introduced previously prohibited subject matter. They spoke for a generation disillusioned by war and angry with the political elite. They were culturally significant in helping nourish modern independent American cinema and capturing the human drama of everyday life. By not filming glamorous romances, farces, fantasy musicals or other well-established genres, the film fan had access to the likes of *Rosemary's Baby*, *Bonnie and Clyde*, *The Graduate*, *Midnight Cowboy* and *Easy Rider*: trail blazing and grittier movies in an era of cultural disquiet and uncertainty.

The USA underwent significant cultural change from Kennedy's presidency through to Nixon's Watergate resignation. But US democracy made that change – that rebellion – possible; something unimaginable in Hitler's Germany, Stalin's Russia or the North Korea of today. Arts and media in the 1960s and 1970s were more politicised than ever, and US culture more diverse than before. But since democracy is arguably not what we have but what we do, the turbulent artistic changes in these decades are living proof of the true impact of democracy on culture.

QUESTION

In what ways did counterculture shape US culture in the period 1961–74?

End of unit activities

1. Design a spider diagram to illustrate how the US government addressed economic and social problems arising either in the period 1890–1920 or 1961–74.
2. Divide into two groups: one group is to prepare an argument to support, and the other oppose this statement: 'Considering the prevailing attitudes and the economic situation, the administrations between 1920 and 1941 did as much as they could to improve the position of American women.'
3. How successful was Betty Friedan in bringing women's rights to the fore of the US political and social agenda in the 1960s?
4. Using the library and the internet, carry out some further research into the counterculture of the 1960s and 1970s. Who do you regard as the key figures? To what extent had it become overtly political?

End of chapter activities

Paper 1 exam practice

Question

Compare and contrast what **Sources A** and **B** reveal about the apparent reasons for student unrest in 1968 and 1970. **[6 marks]**

SOURCE A

President Lyndon B. Johnson speaking to an adviser about the unrest during his time in office:

I tried to make it possible for every child of every colour to grow up in a nice house, eat a solid breakfast, attend a decent school, and get to a good and lasting job. I asked so little in return, just a little thanks. Just a little appreciation. That's all. But look at what I got instead. Riots in 175 cities. Looting. Burning, shooting … Young people by the thousand leaving the university, marching in the streets, chanting that horrible song about how many kids I had killed that day … it ruined everything.

W. Chafe (1999), The Unfinished Journey, *Oxford: Oxford University Press, pp. 338–9.*

SOURCE B

Nixon had announced that he had a secret plan for ending the war, but as it turned out the war, or at least America's involvement in it, lasted longer under him than it had under Johnson … His attack on Cambodia led in 1970 to further widespread student disturbances … four students were shot and killed by the National Guard. There was universal outrage on the campuses of America: students, faculty and administrators at last came together to express their indignation.

H. Brogan (1999), The Penguin History of the United States, *London: Penguin Books, pp. 661–2.*

Skill

Cross-referencing.

Examiner's tips

Here you are being asked to cross-reference and therefore compare and contrast the information/content/nature of the sources. Make sure you don't just comment on one source or you won't get higher than Band 4. Before you write your answer, draw a rough diagram to show similarities and differences between the sources. Also, make sure that you are commenting on the correct source.

Simplified mark scheme

Band Marks		
1	Both sources **linked**, with **detailed references** to the two sources, identifying BOTH **similarities and differences**.	6
2	Both sources **linked**, with **detailed references** to the two sources, identifying EITHER **similarities or differences**.	4–5
3	**Limited consideration/comments** on origins and purpose or value and limitations. Possibly only one/the wrong source(s) addressed.	3
4	Discusses/comments on **just one source**.	0–2

Student answer

Source A shows that students in America were angered by the thought of people their age being killed in Vietnam. They blame Johnson personally and the source refers to a popular chant of the time 'hey hey hey LBJ, how many kids did you kill today?' It surprises and hurts Johnson. After all, he had improved social conditions for young and old alike: the source refers to him giving all children 'a solid breakfast … a decent school … a lasting job'. But with riots in 175 cities and the president being blamed personally, the cause is not his social achievements. It is Vietnam, attacked loudest by the draftees. Johnson can't grasp this.

Source B from 1999 looks back at the killing of four students at Kent State University in 1970. The source speaks of the problem being Nixon's attack on Cambodia which led to 'student disturbances' and 'universal outrage on the campuses' when people were shocked that Nixon's plan to end the conflict in Vietnam meant attacking another country.

Comparing these sources, I can see that they are similar in that they are both 'attacking' a decision by a president – although Source B is much more specific (Cambodia) than Source A, which appears to feature more general disturbances, although the reference to 'kids' being killed clearly points at Vietnam. Source A expresses Johnson's opinion in a tone of dismay from the time and is written in the first person; while B is a secondary source and is more factual, speaking also of academics protesting not just students of draft age – so there is some difference. Also one source deals with fatalities at a particular venue whereas the other is more general.

Nonetheless both sources reveal the criticism and abuse US presidents faced over Vietnam, especially from the student generation; although Source A might suggest issues of race and social deprivation are behind some of the problems – 175 cities with looting and rioting is a lot.

Examiner's comments

The candidate has understood **Sources A** and **B** well, and stated the fundamental similarities and differences between them, thereby linking both sources in the last paragraph. The candidate appeared to have 'bolted on' a last comment about **Source A** and this would have been better dealt with in the first part of the answer on A. However, the candidate would still gain six marks here.

Summary activity

Draw a spider diagram or chart outlining examples of crises faced by the administrations in our period of study. Make brief notes under these **suggested headings**: banking and financial crises; immigration; anti-war movement; Watergate.

Paper 2 practice questions

1 'Government policies in the USA barely affected the distribution of wealth.' To what extent do you agree with this statement?

2 Examine the extent to which the US government was the prisoner of big business corporations between 1890 and 1920.

3 'Republican presidents of the 1920s were indifferent to the needy and motivated only by business.' To what extent do you agree with this statement?

4 Evaluate the success of Roosevelt's New Deal policies in lifting the USA out of economic depression during the period 1933–41.

5 Evaluate the role of Lyndon Johnson in the campaign to implement social and economic reform in the USA between 1963 and 1969.

6 Examine the reasons for the explosion of political unrest in America in the period 1967–70.

Further reading

Try reading the relevant chapters/sections of the following books/websites:

Brogan, H. (2001), *The Penguin History of the United States*, London: Penguin Books.

Dallek, R. (2003), *Kennedy: An Unfinished Life 1917–63*, London: Allen Lane.

Degler, C. (1977), *The Age of the Economic Revolution 1876–1900*, Illinois: Scott, Foresman and Co.

Farmer, A. and Sanders, V. (2002), *An Introduction to American History 1860–1990*, London: Hodder Education.

Levine, P. and Papasotiriou, H. (2005), *America Since 1945*, New York: Palgrave Macmillan.

Munslow, A. (1992), *Discourse and Culture: The Creation of America 1870–1920*, London: Routledge.

Murphy, D. (2004), *Flagship Historymakers – JFK and LBJ*, London: Collins Educational.

Murphy, D., Cooper, K. and Waldron, M. (2001), *Flagship History – United States 1776–1992*, London: Collins Educational.

Paterson, D., Willoughby, D. and Willoughby, S. (2001), *Civil Rights in the USA 1863–1980*, Oxford: Heinemann.

Sanders, E. (1999), *Roots of Reform: Farmers, Workers and the American State 1877–1917*, Chicago: University of Chicago Press.

Sanders, V. (2006), *Race Relations in the USA 1863–1980*, London: Hodder Education.

Tindall, G.B. and Shi, D.E. (2004), *America: A Narrative History*, New York: W.W. Norton & Company.

Traynor, J. (2001), *Mastering Modern United States History*, Basingstoke: Palgrave Macmillan.

Venn, F. (1998), *The New Deal*, Edinburgh: Edinburgh University Press.

South Africa 5

From apartheid to democracy: the emergence of a democratic state in South Africa Unit 1

KEY QUESTIONS

- What conditions led to the establishment of democracy in South Africa?
- Why did these changes happen when they did?
- What role did political parties and leaders play?
- How did democracy function in the new South Africa?

Overview

- In the 1990s, South Africa was transformed into a democratic state after centuries of discrimination and segregation.
- The roots of segregation lay in years of colonial rule stretching back to the 17th century; systems of government varied in different regions, but a common factor was a weak democratic tradition in most parts.
- When the regions united to form the Union of South Africa in 1910, political and economic power lay in the hands of the white minority.
- For the next eighty years, white domination was enforced, first by segregation laws and from 1948 by a strict system of apartheid implemented by a National Party government.
- Under the system of apartheid, black people had no political rights, opposition parties such as the African National Congress (ANC) were banned and their leaders were in prison or exile.
- During the 1980s, sustained protests, guerrilla attacks, international pressure and economic decline weakened the apartheid state.
- By the end of 1989, a combination of these factors, as well as the fall of the Berlin Wall and the collapse of communist governments in Eastern Europe, led to change in South Africa as well.
- In 1990 the government lifted the ban on the ANC and other opposition parties, released the ANC leader, Nelson Mandela, and announced that the government was willing to negotiate with the ANC.
- Talks between the government and the ANC started off in a spirit of compromise and cooperation, and South Africans were filled with optimism and hope; but there were many obstacles to the process of reform, and the talks broke down on several occasions.

TIMELINE

1854 Cape Colony gets representative government with non-racial franchise.

1899–1902 South African War.

1910 **May:** Formation of the Union of South Africa.

1948 **May:** National Party government comes to power and introduces apartheid.

1955 **Jun:** African National Congress (ANC) and other resistance groups adopt Freedom Charter.

1960 **Mar:** Sharpeville shootings.

Apr: Banning of ANC.

1976 **Jun:** Soweto uprising.

1983 **Aug:** Formation of United Democratic Front.

1989 **Aug:** Mass Democratic Movement begins its defiance campaign.

1990 **Feb:** De Klerk announces reforms; Mandela released from prison.

1991 **Dec:** Convention for a Democratic South Africa (CODESA) talks begin.

1992 **May:** Breakdown of CODESA talks.

Jun: Boipatong Massacre.

Sept: Bisho Massacre; Record of Understanding – agreement to resume talks.

1993 **Apr:** Chris Hani assassinated; Multi-Party Negotiating Forum resumes talks.

Nov: Agreement on interim constitution.

1994 **Mar:** AWB invasion of Bophuthatswana.

Apr: Inkatha agrees to participate in election; South Africa's first democratic election.

May: Nelson Mandela inaugurated as president; establishment of the Constitutional Assembly.

1995 **Feb:** Constitutional Court officially opens.

1996 **May:** New constitution adopted; break-up of the Government of National Unity.

1999 **Jun:** Second democratic election; Mbeki succeeds Mandela as president of South Africa.

- Extremist political groups tried to sabotage the negotiations by boycotting talks, killing civilians, assassinating leaders and staging violent disruptions; thousands of people died in politically related violence before a settlement was reached, an interim constitution drawn up and elections held.
- The ANC won the first democratic election in South Africa's history in April 1994, a peaceful event that was deemed to be 'free and fair' by international observers; the ANC formed a coalition government with the National Party and Inkatha. This Government of National Unity set about transforming South Africa into a working democracy.
- The unit also examines the significance of the roles played by the National Party, the ANC and other political parties, as well as the dominant role of some of their leaders.
- Parliament formed a Constitutional Assembly, which drew up a new democratic constitution, including a progressive Bill of Rights, which made it one of the most liberal constitutions in the world.
- The Government of National Unity broke up when the National Party withdrew in 1996. After this, the ANC became progressively more dominant, with an increased majority in the 1999 election.
- Opposition parties were small and fragmented. In 1999, the Democratic Party became the official opposition, but won less than 10 per cent of the vote, compared to nearly 67 per cent for the ANC. Support for other opposition parties declined.

Figure 5.1 When South Africa became a democratic state in 1994, Nelson Mandela voted for the first time in his life at the age of seventy-five, after twenty-seven years as a political prisoner of the apartheid government

5.1 What conditions led to the establishment of democracy in South Africa?

The history of South Africa for most of the 20th century is associated with racism, discrimination and segregation. Until 1994, the country was ruled by a white minority government, which preserved white power and privilege under a strictly enforced system of **segregation** called **apartheid**. It was certainly not a democratic state. However, in a remarkable few years between 1990 and 1994, this continuity was disrupted and a dramatic change occurred. A settlement was negotiated that put an end to white domination and established a constitutional multiparty democracy.

Segregation: a system of laws to separate people, based on race.

Apartheid: the strictly enforced system of racial segregation introduced by the National Party government in South Africa after 1948.

The roots of white domination

Discrimination based on race did not start with apartheid in 1948. It had been present right from the early days of colonialism, when the Cape was colonised by the Dutch in the 17th century. After Britain took over the Cape during the Napoleonic Wars, many of the descendants of the early Dutch settlers moved into the interior to escape British control. In the process they conquered the African tribes already living there and established two independent Boer Republics. ('Boer' means farmer in Afrikaans, the language they spoke.) Britain later added the colony of Natal to its possessions in southern South Africa. So by the middle of the 19th century, there were two British colonies – the Cape Colony and Natal – and two Boer Republics – the South African Republic (or Transvaal) and the Orange Free State – as well as large areas still under the control of independent African kingdoms.

There were differing systems of government and democratic traditions in the different regions of southern Africa. The Cape Colony was granted representative government by Britain in 1854. This gave colonists the right to elect representatives to a legislative assembly, which was a step towards becoming a self-governing colony. The vote was given to all adult males, regardless of race, who owned property worth £25 or who earned an annual income of at least £50. Although in practice few African or coloured males qualified to vote, they were not barred from doing so by race and, over the years, more of them gained the necessary property or income to exercise this right. Although the franchise qualifications were later raised and a literacy test was added, this 'non-racial' franchise was maintained and was referred to as the Cape 'liberal tradition'.

The British colony of Natal also had a non-racial franchise in theory, but the qualifications were so stringent that by 1909 only six Africans had qualified to vote. In the Boer Republics, only white males had any political rights. The 1858 constitution of the Transvaal actually stated that 'the people desire to permit no equality between coloured people and the white inhabitants, either in Church or State' (Oates, 1992, *Illustrated History of South Africa*, p. 129).

The discovery of diamonds (in 1867) and then gold (in 1886) led to significant changes in Southern Africa, both economically and politically. Economically it led to an industrial revolution in the region and the potential for rapid economic growth. But it also laid the foundations for a formal system of segregation, by introducing strict systems

Theory of Knowledge

Terminology and bias: Although South Africa today is a non-racial democracy, it is impossible to understand its recent history without reference to race. Hence terms such as 'coloured', which most people today would avoid using, are used in this text. The term 'black' had two uses: it was sometimes used to refer specifically to 'Africans' but was also used to refer collectively to anyone who was not white. How can terminology be considered controversial? How can terminology be linked to bias in history?

Migrant labour: male workers from rural areas who signed contracts to work on the mines for a fixed period and then returned home again; their families remained at home. They came from all over Southern Africa, and during the 20th century Mozambique, Lesotho and Malawi became major sources of migrant labour for the gold mines in South Africa.

Fact: The Indian nationalist leader Mahatma Gandhi spent twenty-one years in South Africa, where he was involved in organising protests for democratic rights for Indians living in South Africa. When the South African War broke out in October 1899 he persuaded the Indian community that, if they were demanding rights as British citizens, it was their duty to support Britain in the war. He organised an Indian Ambulance Corps in which 1,100 Indian volunteers helped wounded British soldiers, mainly as stretcher-bearers. Gandhi himself served in the unit.

of control over black mineworkers. Under the system of **migrant labour**, black workers from rural areas did the manual labour on the mines for low wages. Their movement to the mines was strictly controlled by a system of 'passes'. This system formed the basis for much of the segregation and apartheid legislation during the 20th century.

The political results of the mineral discoveries were equally far-reaching. They led to renewed British interest in the region and Britain subsequently defeated and annexed the remaining independent African kingdoms. The vast gold deposits in the Transvaal led to war between Britain and the Boer Republics for control of the gold mines. This was the South African War (or Anglo–Boer War) of 1899–1902, during which Britain defeated and annexed the two Boer Republics as British colonies – the Transvaal and the Orange River Colony. During the war, most black South Africans supported Britain, hoping that a British victory in the war would bring political change, with an extension of the vote and other democratic rights. However, their hopes were dashed when British promises of a better deal after the war came to nothing.

British actions during the war (especially a scorched earth policy and concentration camps for Boer civilians) left a legacy of bitterness among Afrikaners, and so Britain was keen to conciliate them by making concessions. In the Treaty of Vereeniging, which ended the war, Britain undertook to restore self-government as soon as possible and, crucially, agreed that the decision about franchise rights for blacks would only be decided after this had happened. As everyone had anticipated, both colonies opted for a whites-only franchise when self-government was established within five years of the end of the war. Historian John Pampallis observes that 'White solidarity against blacks thus outweighed Anglo-Boer rivalries, and Britain abandoned its war-time promise to protect the rights of black people' (*Foundations of the New South Africa*, p. 47). Many blacks were bitterly disappointed by what they perceived as a British betrayal. They formed political organisations to put pressure on the colonial administrations and the British government to extend democratic rights more widely.

Discrimination in the Union of South Africa

Having annexed all of southern Africa, Britain pushed for a union of the separate colonies, and invited representatives from all four colonies to discuss the issues involved at a national convention, to which no black representatives were invited. There were heated debates at the convention about many aspects of the new constitution, notably the issue of franchise rights. The former Boer Republics refused to join any proposed union in which blacks were granted political rights, while the Cape refused to give up its long tradition of a non-racial franchise. Ultimately, a compromise was reached: each colony would retain its existing system. The Cape franchise was to be an 'entrenched' clause in the constitution (which could only be changed by a two-thirds majority in a joint sitting of both houses of parliament). As a result, African and coloured males in the Cape continued to qualify to vote. But at the same time, the vote was given to all white adult males without qualification criteria. A further clause that impeded the development of democratic institutions was the stipulation that only whites were to be allowed in parliament.

The Union of South Africa was created by a British Act of Parliament in 1910, as a self-governing dominion within the British Empire. Right from the start, political and economic power was firmly in the hands of white South Africans, who at that stage formed 21 per cent of the population. From 1910, a succession of Union governments introduced segregation laws that protected white privilege and discriminated against

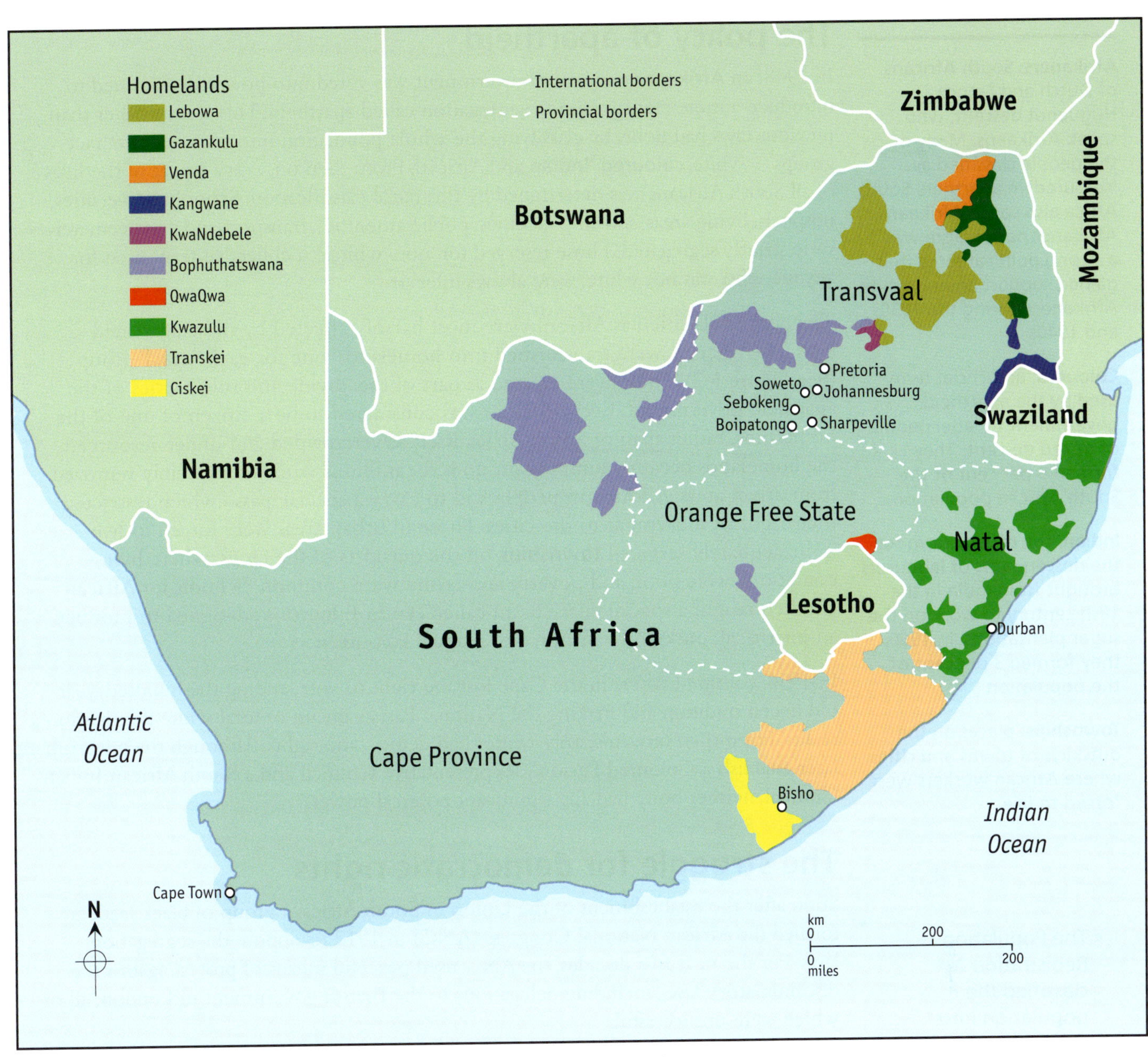

Figure 5.2 A map of pre-1994 South Africa, showing the so-called homelands

anyone who was not white. The most significant of these laws, and one that laid the basis for much of the poverty and inequality in contemporary South Africa, was the 1913 Land Act. This act restricted African land ownership to the **reserves**, which covered less than 10 per cent of the total land area of South Africa.

Reserves: the only areas where Africans could own land. By the 1950s, the reserves formed 13 per cent of the land area and became the basis for the homeland system under apartheid.

Among the discriminatory legislation passed by later Union governments was a law granting the vote to white women in 1933, but this right was not extended to African and coloured women, even in the Cape. Then, in 1936, in a major blow to democratic development, the entrenched clause supposedly safeguarding the non-racial Cape franchise was changed, and Africans in the Cape lost the right to vote in general elections. As a sop to democratic formalities, the government established an elected Natives Representative Council, which had advisory powers only and, as a result, had minimal power or credibility.

The policy of apartheid

Afrikaners: South Africans of Dutch and French Huguenot descent, who speak Afrikaans. Many of the people classified as 'coloured' in apartheid South Africa also speak Afrikaans. Afrikaner nationalism was a strong political force that gained support among white Afrikaners during the 1930s and 1940s.

Coloured: an official term used by the apartheid government to label people of mixed descent. They formed 9 per cent of the South African population.

Indian: the official term for the descendants of labourers brought from India in the 19th century to work on the sugar plantations. In 1960, they formed 3 per cent of the population.

Townships: places on the outskirts of towns and cities, where African workers were forced to live.

In 1948, an **Afrikaner** nationalist government was voted into power, determined to introduce a more rigid system of segregation called apartheid. This went further than previous laws had done, by classifying the whole population into four separate 'race groups' – white, **coloured, Indian** and African. From then on, every aspect of the lives of all South Africans was determined by this racial classification. Schools, universities, hospitals, living areas, sporting facilities, public amenities, transport and even cemeteries were strictly segregated. Those reserved for 'non-whites', a collective term used for anyone who was not white, were always inferior.

The people classified as African were most harshly affected by these apartheid laws. The reserves were transformed into homelands, one for each 'tribal' group (See Figure 5.2). These were created as part of the 'divide and rule' tactics of the apartheid government. Every African was considered to be a citizen of one of the homelands, rather than of South Africa itself. Overcrowded and under-resourced, the homelands became dumping grounds for millions who were forcibly removed from urban areas. All African people had to carry a special 'pass', which restricted their right of movement to the cities. Those in urban areas were forced to live in inadequately serviced **townships** on the outskirts of the cities, where living conditions were poor, and poverty and crime were common. Schools for African children taught a special curriculum called Bantu Education, designed to produce an uncritical, unskilled workforce of manual labourers.

In 1956, coloured voters in the Cape lost the right to vote, ending the hundred-year-old liberal tradition and making the National Party's dream of total white domination a reality. From then onwards, only whites had democratic rights. Although the government later establish a Coloured Person's Representative Council and a South African Indian Council, neither body had any significant political power.

KEY APARTHEID LAWS

- The Population Registration Act classified the population into different race groups; everyone had to have an identity card stating their racial classification.
- The Mixed Marriages Act outlawed marriages between those classified as white and other race groups.
- The Immorality Act outlawed sexual relations between those classified as

The struggle for democratic rights

Soon after the establishment of the Union of South Africa, a group of black leaders formed the African National Congress (ANC) in 1912 to oppose the segregation laws. For the next five decades, the ANC used peaceful means of protest against the discriminatory laws, including delegations to the British government in London, all of which were unsuccessful.

After the Second World War, the ANC and other opposition organisations became more assertive in their demands. The 1950s were a decade of sustained but non-violent protest actions. A significant development in 1955 was the drawing up of a Freedom Charter by the ANC and allied organisations in which they outlined their vision of a future democratic South Africa, based on equality and non-racialism. This document became a blueprint for the kind of democratic constitution that the resistance movements hoped to create.

However, non-violent protests against apartheid laws were unsuccessful in their aim of forcing the government to change its policies. The era of peaceful protest ended in 1960, when police opened fire on a group of protesters against the **pass laws**, in Sharpeville, a township south of Johannesburg. A total of sixty-nine people were killed and more than one hundred injured. After Sharpeville, the government banned the ANC and used increasing force to crush resistance. As a result, the ANC set up its headquarters in exile and formed an armed wing, Umkhonto we Sizwe or MK ('Spear of the Nation'), to carry on underground resistance against the apartheid government. It was at this stage that Nelson Mandela and other MK leaders were arrested, found guilty of trying to overthrow the government and sentenced to life imprisonment.

By the mid-1960s, the apartheid government appeared to be firmly in control. However, a new generation of black youth, led by **Steve Biko**, formed the Black Consciousness Movement, asserting their belief in black identity and power. Inspired by these ideas, students in Soweto protested against the inferior system of Bantu Education. This was the 1976 Soweto uprising, in which an estimated 1,000 people died. After the uprising, thousands of young people left the country to train as guerrilla fighters in MK camps in neighbouring countries. Many historians see the Soweto uprising as a crucial turning point (see **Source B**), after which the apartheid government never recovered full control.

SOURCE A

Figure 5.3 Antoinette Sithole, sister of twelve-year-old Hector Pieterson, the first victim of police shooting in the Soweto uprising, poses alongside the famous image of her dying brother; the original photograph shocked people around the world and created greater awareness of the violent nature of the apartheid state

SOURCE B

The uprisings forever changed the balance of power in South Africa. Minority rule in South Africa entered a deep-seated structural crisis. Existing institutions could no longer resolve the strains and contradictions within South African society. The Soweto uprisings shattered the myth of white invincibility and made it impossible for the white minority to continue to rule in the old way. Putting down the revolt could not hide the crisis.

A. Odendaal (2004), 'The Liberation Struggle in South Africa, 1948–1994', in Y.N. Seleti (ed.), Africa Since 1990, *Cape Town: New Africa Education, p. 177.*

white and other race groups.

- The Group Areas Act set aside different residential areas for each race group; thousands of people were forced to leave their homes.
- The Separate Amenities Act specified separate services, facilities and amenities for 'whites' and 'non-whites'.
- The Bantu Education Act specified a separate curriculum for African schools, focusing on manual skills; far less money was allocated for these schools.
- The Separate Universities Act provided for separate universities for each race group.

Pass laws: these prohibited the free movement of African people out of the reserves. Failure to carry a pass would result in a prison sentence.

Steve Biko (1946–77)

He developed the philosophy of Black Consciousness, which promoted pride in black culture, identity and heritage. It stressed the use of the word 'black' as a direct challenge to the apartheid term 'non-white'. These ideas influenced the students of Soweto to reject the system of Bantu Education in 1976. Biko was murdered by police while in prison in South Africa in 1977.

The changing nature of the struggle after 1976

After Soweto there was a complete clampdown by the state in its efforts to crush opposition. It banned the Black Consciousness organisations and gave the police the power to imprison suspects for indefinite periods without trial. Huge sums of money were spent on armaments for the police and army, and all young white men were conscripted to do two years of compulsory military service.

At the same time, the government introduced limited reforms in an effort to win support for its policies. The most significant of these was the introduction of a new constitution in 1983. This gave some degree of representation in parliament to coloureds and Indians, in separate houses of a three-chamber or 'tricameral' parliament, but the white parliament maintained most of the power. The government hoped the new constitution would win support from coloureds and Indians, but instead it sparked off mass countrywide protests. A number of organisations joined together to form the United Democratic Front (UDF), a non-racial organisation that soon had a membership of about three million. The UDF urged people to reject the new constitution and, as a result, fewer than 20 per cent of coloured and Indian voters took part in the first tricameral election in 1984. Many new black trade unions joined the UDF and they worked with civic organisations to organise boycotts and stayaways. In 1985 smaller unions joined together to form the Congress of South African Trade Unions (COSATU), which played an important role in the ongoing resistance.

Theory of Knowledge

History and emotion: Photographs such as the one shown in **Source A** create a powerful emotional response in the viewer. Why does a visual source often have a more emotive impact than a written source? What limitations do photographs have as historical evidence?

QUESTION

What was the significance of the Soweto uprising? In what ways was Sharpeville also a turning point?

State of emergency: this gave the police and army unrestrained powers to crush resistance, and indemnity from prosecution for their actions; they could detain and interrogate protesters, search buildings, stop meetings and censor news.

The new constitution totally excluded Africans and so created intense anger in the townships, leading to a sustained uprising from 1984 onwards. The government declared a **state of emergency**, and sent in the army to patrol the townships. Although thousands were killed in clashes with the police and army, the violent repression failed to crush the ongoing protests. For most of the 1980s, South Africa was in a state of virtual civil war.

In 1989, the UDF and COSATU formed the Mass Democratic Movement (MDM), which launched a nationwide defiance campaign to put more pressure on the government. There was huge support for the campaign and the mood of defiance grew. People ignored banning orders, forced previously segregated facilities to be opened to all and openly flew the flag of the banned ANC. The MDM organised huge 'Freedom Marches' in the major cities. The government had previously used force to crush such protests but now it took no action. It seemed that the stage was set for major change in South Africa.

This change started on 2 February 1990, when the leader of the National Party and president of South Africa, F.W. de Klerk announced the unbanning of the ANC and other opposition parties, the unconditional release of political prisoners, the suspension of the death penalty and the willingness of the government to negotiate with the ANC and other political groups to create a democratic constitution for South Africa. This was a dramatic moment, which set in motion a transition to democracy. Shortly afterwards, Nelson Mandela was released from prison, opposition leaders returned from exile and negotiations between the government and the ANC began.

A tentative start to change

Although the breakthrough had been made, it was by no means certain that a peaceful transition to democracy would follow. It took four years of negotiations about the nature

Figure 5.4 A march organised by the Mass Democratic Movement in Cape Town in September 1989

of constitutional change, and 15,000 deaths in political violence, before a settlement was reached.

The ANC and the government had fundamental differences and conflicting visions of the future. While the ANC wanted majority rule, the government wanted some form of power-sharing that would protect 'minority interests'. In addition, the ANC wanted a new constitution to be drawn up by a democratically elected constituent assembly, but the government wanted the National Party to play a leading role in the decisions about a new constitution. However, both sides showed a willingness to compromise and talks soon got underway.

Initial talks between the ANC and the government began in Cape Town in May 1990. They discussed obstacles to negotiations, such as the state of emergency, the ongoing violence, political prisoners, the continuation of the armed struggle, economic sanctions and the return of exiles, including the president of the ANC, Oliver Tambo, who was still in Lusaka in Zambia. They announced their agreement on many issues and their commitment to further negotiations in the 'Groote Schuur Minute'. Further progress was made in the 'Pretoria Minute' of August 1990, when the ANC agreed to suspend the armed struggle and the government lifted the state of emergency. Although these meetings took place in an atmosphere of mutual suspicion, they resulted in significant agreements that made the later negotiated settlement possible. The process of change and reform was underway.

In December 1991, formal negotiations between the government and the liberation movements finally began, at a multiparty conference called the Convention for a Democratic South Africa (CODESA), which met at the World Trade Centre at Kempton Park, outside Johannesburg. Nearly 300 delegates representing nineteen political groupings attended, but the ANC and the National Party dominated the talks. Parties on the extremes of the political spectrum, such as the Pan Africanist Congress (PAC) on the left and the Conservative Party on the right, boycotted the meetings, hoping to wreck the negotiations.

Inkatha: this was originally formed as a Zulu cultural organisation, but became a political party, the Inkatha Freedom Party (IFP). It promoted a distinct Zulu nationalism, and members carried 'traditional' weapons, such as spears and knobkerries. Most of its support was in Kwazulu-Natal, and among Zulu migrant workers in the townships around Johannesburg. Fierce rivalry between Inkatha and the ANC contributed to much of the violence during this period.

Third Force: a suspected group of military and police personnel who were thought to be secretly stirring up violence between Inkatha and ANC supporters. Later investigations proved that there was indeed such a force.

CODESA reached a compromise agreement: the drawing up of the constitution would be a two-stage process. A multiparty conference would draw up an interim constitution, and the first elected parliament would use this as a basis for drafting the final constitution.

The threats posed by continuing violence

But the negotiations broke down on several occasions. The economic situation in the country added to the problems. Poverty and unemployment had reached serious levels, especially in the townships. After nearly a decade of militant protest, many people were impatient for change, and ongoing violence threatened the whole process.

- Violent conflicts between supporters of the ANC and **Inkatha** caused concern, especially in rural Kwazulu-Natal and in the townships around Johannesburg, where Zulu migrant workers living in hostels clashed with township residents. Many people began to suspect that a sinister '**Third Force**' of security personnel was provoking the violence. When evidence emerged that members of the government were secretly supplying funds, military training and weapons to Inkatha in this conflict, many began to doubt the government's commitment to a negotiated settlement.

Figure 5.5 Members of the Zulu-based Inkatha carry their 'traditional weapons'. Violence between Inkatha and ANC supporters threatened the negotiations and claimed the lives of thousands of people between 1990 and 1994

- The first talks, planned for April 1990, were called off by the ANC, after protesters in the township of Sebokeng were shot by the police. The government was forced to make concessions before talks could begin. These included the appointment of a judicial commission to investigate the Sebokeng killings.
- During 1992, a breakdown in the negotiations and several incidents of extreme violence made many people fear that a bloody civil war was inevitable. In May, the ANC broke off negotiations with the government. In June, in Boipatong, south of Johannesburg, Inkatha supporters, helped by the police, attacked ANC members

attending a funeral. Dozens of people were killed, mainly women and children. The ANC demanded a full investigation into the massacre, and police involvement in it. In response, the government appointed a commission to investigate the causes of the violence. The Goldstone Report later confirmed suspicions about the involvement of the police and the existence of a sinister 'Third Force' of security personnel who were trying to sabotage the negotiations.

- After this, the ANC, South African Communist Party (SACP) and COSATU launched a campaign of 'rolling mass action' involving strikes and protest demonstrations. Another massacre happened in September 1992 in Bisho, the capital of the Ciskei homeland, when soldiers fired on a group of unarmed protesters, killing several people and injuring 200 more.

The ANC and other parties voiced their concerns about the ongoing violence and accused the government of deliberately stirring up conflict so that the National Party could benefit. The initial spirit of cooperation and compromise was replaced by an atmosphere of anger and suspicion.

Sources C and **D** examine the impact of the challenges facing South Africa at the start of the negotiations:

SOURCE C

Millions of blacks are caught in a spiral of landlessness, homelessness, unemployment and poverty. Add to that a clash between modern political structures and traditional tribal ones. Mix in a struggle for hegemony (power) in the region between major political players. Stir in the security forces in all their guises … Add faceless, apparently trained killers such as the 'third force' … Sprinkle all that with ancient and recent political and social grudges and you get a deadly brew.

Rich Mkhondo, a Reuters journalist, describes some of the problems facing South Africa in the early 1990s. Quoted in D. Oates (ed.) (1992), Illustrated History of South Africa, *Cape Town: Readers' Digest, p. 511.*

SOURCE D

It seemed that the unbanning of the political organisations and the release of Mandela and the others had lit a fire under South Africa. A huge pot was beginning to cook, and it looked like it might boil over. There were a lot of ingredients in the pot – moderate white people who were worried about losing their comfortable lifestyle, right-wing white nationalists who were determined not to accept majority rule, black radicals who thought that the only way to gain freedom was to drive white people out of the country, Zulu nationalists who were set on having power in their own part of the country and many others.

Whenever there was a bit of progress in the negotiations, there seemed to be another riot or massacre somewhere in the country. Often, there were reports that the police or the army were either helping the violence to happen, or not doing anything about it when they could. The pot got hotter.

K. Pampallis (2000), Mandela, *Cape Town: Maskew Miller Longman, p. 61.*

ACTIVITY

Compare and contrast the factors that contributed to the tensions and violence, as expressed in **Sources C and D.**

The start of change

As the situation in the country deteriorated, Western governments put pressure on the government and the ANC to resume talks, and the United Nations sent observers to investigate the violence. After the Bisho massacre, both sides realised that it was crucial for the negotiations to reopen. In September, their leaders signed a 'Record of Understanding', paving the way for the work of CODESA to continue.

Both sides agreed to concessions to make this possible. The government agreed to release more political prisoners and to ban the use of 'traditional weapons' (axes, spears, knobkerries and sharpened metal sticks) at Inkatha rallies. The ANC agreed to a government of 'national unity', which would include the National Party, for the first five years, and to honour the existing contracts of members of the civil service, judiciary, police and defence force. These concessions, which were referred to as 'sunset clauses', were proposed by Joe Slovo, the leader of the SACP. They provided the crucial breakthrough in the negotiations.

Violent attempts to prevent change

However, during 1993 and 1994 more violent attempts to prevent a peaceful settlement threatened to derail the negotiations once more:

Chris Hani (1942–93)

He left South Africa in 1962 to go into exile. He received military training in the Soviet Union and became chief of staff of MK in 1987. He returned to South Africa in 1990 and succeeded Joe Slovo as head of the SACP. He supported the suspension of the armed struggle and was a leading member of the ANC negotiating team.

- In April 1993, the most serious obstacle to a peaceful settlement occurred when **Chris Hani**, a popular MK, ANC and SACP leader, who had played a critical role in persuading more militant members of the ANC to accept the negotiation process, was assassinated. His assassin was an anti-communist Polish immigrant, Janusz Walus, with a gun supplied by a member of the Conservative Party. Hani's death led to angry demonstrations and an increase in racial tensions. It was only Mandela's appeal for calm that prevented the country descending into anarchy.

SOURCE E

An extract from Nelson Mandela's televised speech to the nation on 10 April 1993, the night that Chris Hani was assassinated by a Polish immigrant, who was arrested shortly afterwards when an eyewitness alerted the police:

Today, an unforgivable crime has been committed. The calculated, cold-blooded murder of Chris Hani is not just a crime against a dearly beloved son of our soil. It is a crime against all the people of our country. A man of passion, of unsurpassed courage, has been cut down in the prime of his life. During that time he served the cause of liberation with distinction, earning the respect and love of millions in the country. His death demands that we pursue that cause with even greater determination … This killing must stop.

Tonight I am reaching out to every South African, black and white … from the very depths of my being. A white man, full of prejudice and hate, came to our country and committed a deed so foul that our whole nation now teeters on the brink of disaster. A white woman, of Afrikaner origin, risked her life so that we may know, and bring to justice, this assassin … Now is the time for all South Africans to stand together against those who, from any quarter, wish to destroy what Chris Hani gave his life for – the freedom of all of us.

- There were violent attempts by the Afrikaner right-wing to prevent a power-sharing agreement between the government and the liberation groups. Historians Hermann

Giliomee and Bernard Mbenga believe that in 1993 there were as many as 200 paramilitary or fundamentalist white groups determined to wreck any negotiations. The most prominent of these was the *Afrikaner Weerstandsbeweging* (AWB) or Afrikaner Resistance Movement. It wanted to maintain white supremacy and carried out acts of violence to promote its agenda. In August 1991, the AWB confronted police in the small town of Ventersdorp, where F.W. de Klerk was defending his policy of reform at a public meeting. Four people were killed in the incident. In June 1993, hundreds of AWB members stormed the World Trade Centre in Johannesburg in an armoured car and assaulted delegates, in an attempt to stop the negotiations of the Multi-Party Negotiating Forum. Although this failed, right-wing Afrikaners continued their attempts to halt negotiations. Bomb blasts targeted political party offices and voting venues. In a bizarre incident shortly before the election, 5,000 armed AWB members invaded the homeland of Bophuthatswana, shooting at black civilians in the streets. Even on election day itself, right-wing plotters exploded a powerful bomb at Johannesburg International Airport.

- There were also violent attacks by the Azanian People's Liberation Army (APLA), the extremist armed wing of the Pan Africanist Congress (PAC). They attacked civilians with guns and hand-grenades, including the congregation at a service at St James's Church in a Cape Town suburb, where twelve people died and fifty-six were injured. The PAC only formally suspended its armed struggle at the end of 1993.
- Buthelezi, the leader of Inkatha, refused to have anything to do with the negotiations, and threatened to boycott the election. He wanted a virtually independent Kwazulu, under Inkatha control. A month before the election, a clash between ANC and Inkatha supporters on the streets of central Johannesburg left fifty-three people dead and many others wounded. Tensions mounted, with bloody clashes a regular occurrence.

Despite the violence and the attempts to disrupt the negotiations, the Multi-Party Negotiating Forum made progress. It set a date for the first democratic election in which all South Africans over the age of eighteen could vote for a new government and, in November 1993, agreed on an interim constitution, which was also approved by the existing tricameral parliament. A Transitional Executive Council, with representatives from all the major parties, was established to oversee the process leading to the election.

ACTIVITY

Look at **Source E.** What techniques does Mandela use in this speech to promote peace and unity? Compare Mandela's speech here with the speech made by Nehru after the assassination of Gandhi in India in 1948 (see section 3.5, **Source B**). What are the similarities and what are the differences?

The first democratic election

In spite of their opposition to the reform process, many right-wing Afrikaners decided to participate in the election and formed a new political party, the 'Freedom Front'. The ANC formed a tripartite (or three-party) alliance with the SACP and COSATU, the biggest trade union federation. Several ANC leaders were also members of the SACP, and links between the two parties went back a long way, although the ANC had not formally adopted communist policies. One week before the election, after an emergency meeting between Mandela, De Klerk and Buthelezi, Inkatha agreed to take part, to the relief of millions who had predicted even more bloodshed in Kwazulu-Natal if Inkatha had not been part of the election process.

From 27 to 29 April, nearly twenty million people, most of whom had never voted before, participated in South Africa's first democratic election based on universal suffrage. After all the violence and opposition, the process was remarkably peaceful. Foreign observers declared the elections to be 'free and fair', although there were some doubts about the voting procedures in parts of Kwazulu-Natal.

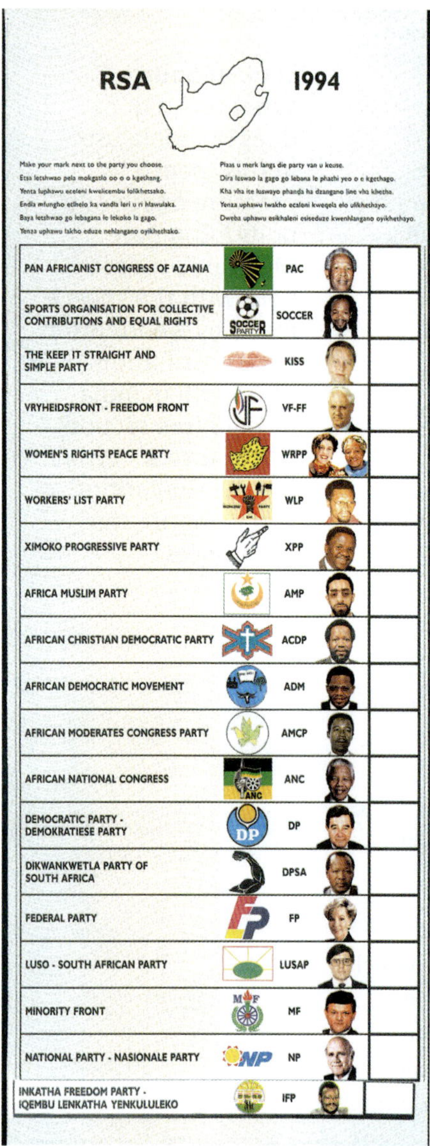

Figure 5.6 In the first post-apartheid election in South Africa, in April 1994, the ballot paper featured the colours and logo of each party, as well as the photographs of their leaders, to help illiterate voters make their choice

The ANC with its alliance partners gained nearly 63 per cent of the votes cast and won a majority in seven of the nine provinces, with the National Party winning in the Western Cape, and Inkatha gaining a narrow majority in Kwazulu-Natal. All other parties received minimal support. At last South Africa was a democracy, and the nature and structure of the state was about to change fundamentally.

Table 5.1 The results of the 1994 election. All other parties received less than 1 per cent of the votes cast

Party	Number of votes	% of votes
ANC	12,237,655	62.65
NP	3,983,690	20.39
IFP	2,058,294	10.54
FF	424,555	2.17
DP	338,426	1.73
PAC	243,478	1.25

5.2 Why did these changes happen when they did?

Historians debate the relative importance of the factors leading to the dramatic changes that brought about a negotiated settlement. However, most of them agree that it was a combination of several factors.

The ANC and the armed struggle

The ANC – and its armed wing, MK – had intensified the armed struggle, focusing guerrilla attacks on high-profile targets inside the country, including the oil refinery at Sasolburg, the Koeberg Nuclear Power Station outside Cape Town, the air force headquarters in Pretoria and the naval dockyard at Durban (see Figure 5.7). By the mid-1980s, MK had units and support structures throughout the country and had stepped up its attacks on police stations and other targets.

The ANC and MK received support from the 'frontline states', such as Angola, Mozambique, Zimbabwe and Zambia. South African Defence Force (SADF) raids into these neighbouring states, and the assassination of opposition leaders in exile, failed to halt the attacks by MK operatives.

The influence of external factors

South Africa had become increasingly isolated from the rest of the world after it withdrew from the Commonwealth in 1961, was expelled from the Olympic Movement and international groups such as the International Labour Organisation, and was suspended from the General Assembly sessions of the United Nations (UN). There was growing overseas support for the international anti-apartheid movement's call for sporting, academic and cultural boycotts of South Africa, as well as economic sanctions.

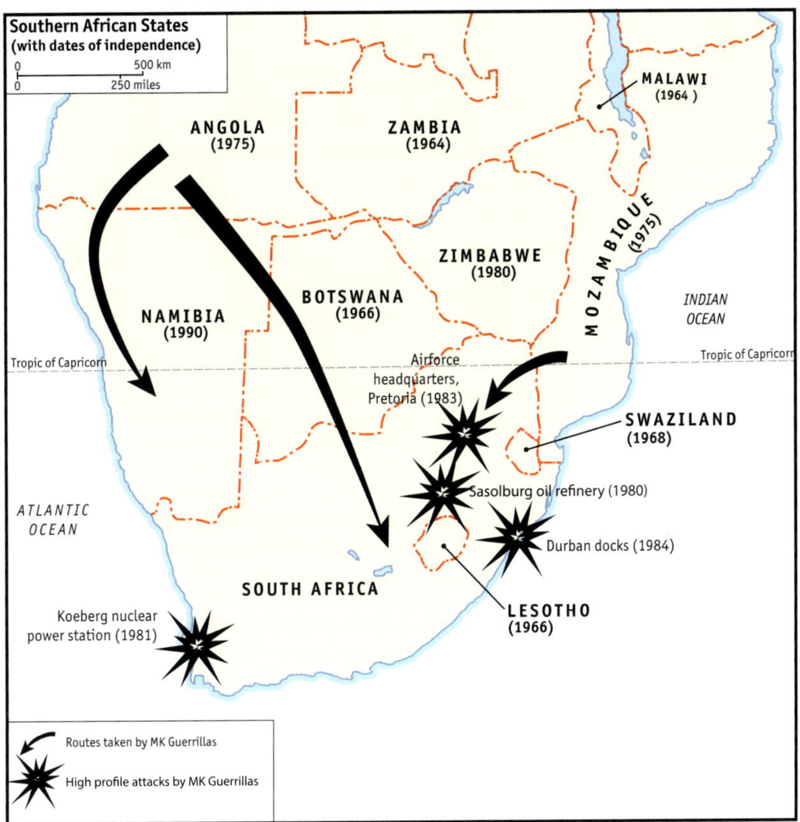

Figure 5.7 Southern Africa, with the dates of independence of each state. This shows how it became easier for MK guerrillas to launch attacks into South Africa after 1975, when Angola and Mozambique became independent

For many years, the SADF had been involved in a civil war in Angola, to defend South Africa's occupation of Namibia. The defeat of South African forces in Angola by Cuban forces in 1988, at Cuito Cuanavale, forced the government to reassess its military capabilities. As a result, it accepted a UN settlement plan for the independence of Namibia, which went ahead in 1990.

The collapse of communism in Eastern Europe and the Soviet Union was a significant factor, affecting both the government and the ANC. The South African regime could no longer rely on support from Western leaders, notably Margaret Thatcher in Britain and Ronald Reagan in the United States, both of whom had been reluctant to implement sanctions against a government that they perceived to be a valuable anti-communist ally. At the same time, the ANC lost the backing of its strongest supporter, the USSR, and its MK bases in Angola were closed, as part of the settlement plan over Namibia. The National Party's fear of a communist-controlled ANC also diminished, as communism lost ground in Eastern Europe. Historian Nigel Worden suggests therefore that the fall of the Berlin Wall was the critical factor in the timing of De Klerk's announcement of major reforms. Hermann Giliomee contends that the collapse of the USSR deprived the ANC of its major source of funding, making it more willing to negotiate with the government, and suggests that this was the 'decisive factor in the ANC's abandonment of the revolutionary struggle' (1995, 'Democratization in South Africa', *Political Science Quarterly*, 110(1), p. 92). Francis Wilson, however, suggests that the end of the Cold War was something which "facilitated the process of change in South Africa, but which did not cause it' (2009, *Dinosaurs, Diamonds and Democracy*, p. 107).

Fact: For a long time the British prime minister Margaret Thatcher (in power 1979–90) and the American president Ronald Reagan (in power 1980–8) were firmly opposed to sanctions despite pressure from the public in both countries. Although they did not support apartheid, they saw the National Party government as an ally against the advance of communism in Africa. They were also suspicious of the ANC's links with the Soviet Union. It was only once the Cold War started to thaw that they changed their stance.

Economic forces

The economy had been in decline since a financial crisis in 1985, when overseas banks cancelled loans and the rand (South Africa's currency) had collapsed. Growing support in the United States, Europe and the Commonwealth for stricter economic sanctions and disinvestment hastened the economic decline. A critical step was the passing of the Comprehensive Anti-Apartheid Act by the US Congress in 1986, which banned all new investments and loans to South Africa and barred South African Airways planes from landing at US airports. In response to student protests, American institutions such as universities started selling off their investments in companies that had South African connections. As a result of these measures, about two-thirds of US companies with investments in South Africa closed down or sold off their operations there. These included large corporations such as IBM, Coca-Cola, Kodak, General Motors, Mobil and General Electric.

Added to the effects of sanctions and disinvestment was the high cost of implementing and defending apartheid. By the end of the 1980s, sanctions, disinvestments and boycotts were having a significant effect on the South African economy and adding to the growing sense of isolation among National Party supporters. Some historians believe that these economic factors played a crucial role in convincing the government to accept that change was necessary.

Sustained civic protests

The government was unable to suppress the sustained protests by township residents, students, workers and many others. The United Democratic Front, formed in 1983 to oppose the tricameral constitution, played a leading role in the protests, which culminated in a nationwide defiance campaign by the MDM in 1989. Other organisations that played prominent roles in the resistance were COSATU, the South African Council of Churches and the National Education Crisis Committee.

The township revolt involved various forms of protest: rent boycotts by township residents, nationwide stayaways by workers, a boycott of local elections and consumer boycotts of products made in factories where workers were underpaid. Education was severely disrupted as students stayed out of school demanding 'liberation before education'. Township residents formed 'civic organisations' to act as pressure groups on the authorities to improve services in the townships. They formed street and area committees and in many places they replaced the township administration with a form of 'people's power'.

Opposition from church leaders played an important role in these civic protests. Notable among them was Archbishop Desmond Tutu, who was an outspoken critic of the policies and actions of the apartheid government. He was also a strong supporter of economic sanctions as a means of putting pressure on the government.

Historian Chris Saunders believes that the mass uprising of the 1980s was the most significant factor in putting pressure on the government to negotiate.

KEY CONCEPTS ACTIVITY

Causation: Compare the perspectives of these historians on the reasons for the radical change that began in 1989/90: Nigel Worden, Hermann Giliomee, Francis Wilson, Chris Saunders, Leonard Thompson and Martin Meredith.

The situation by 1989

Historian Leonard Thompson believes that by 1989 both sides had come to accept that a military solution was unlikely, so they were ready to negotiate a political solution. The government had been unable to halt the protests and to stop MK attacks, and the liberation movements had been unable to topple the government.

By 1989, even members of the National Party could see the need for a change of policy. F.W. de Klerk, who became president in 1989, was more open to reform than his predecessor, P.W. Botha, had been. The National Party believed that it could control the negotiation process and continue to play a key role in government. It also believed that the ANC had been weakened after thirty years in exile. In *The State of Africa*, Martin Meredith suggests that De Klerk believed that the government had such a firm hold on power that it would be able to control the negotiations.

Some historians argue that the change was not dramatic or unexpected. The government had moved Mandela from Robben Island to a mainland prison in 1982, and there had been secret talks between Mandela and the government since 1985. In 1988 he was moved to a house in the grounds of a prison outside Cape Town, and had held secret meetings with P.W. Botha in 1989 and F.W. de Klerk in 1990 before his release.

The government had also previously offered to release Nelson Mandela on condition that he renounced the use of violence as a political weapon. Mandela, however, rejected any form of release with conditions attached (see **Source F**).

SOURCE F

I am in prison as the representative of the people and of your organisation, the African National Congress, which was banned …

What freedom am I being offered when the organisation of the people remains banned? What freedom am I being offered when I may be arrested on a pass offence? … What freedom am I being offered when I must ask for permission to live in an urban area? What freedom am I being offered when I need a stamp on my pass book to seek work? What freedom am I being offered when my very South African citizenship is not respected? … Only free men can negotiate … I cannot and will not give any undertaking at a time when I and you, the people, are not free. Your freedom and mine cannot be separated. I will return.

A statement by Nelson Mandela, read by his daughter Zinzi Mandela to a mass meeting in Jabulani Stadium, Soweto, 10 February 1985. At the time Mandela had been in prison for 21 years but had been moved from Robben Island to a prison on the mainland. Quoted in B. Nasson (ed.) (2004), Turning Points in History: People, Places and Apartheid, *Johannesburg: STE Publishers, p. 13.*

There had also been meetings between ANC leaders in exile with white business leaders in Lusaka (1985) and with a delegation of prominent Afrikaners in Dakar, Senegal (1987). In 1989, the ANC confirmed its conditional support for negotiations with the government, in the Harare Declaration.

5.3 What role did political parties and leaders play?

The National Party and F.W. de Klerk

Since 1948, the National Party had been committed to maintaining white domination and enforcing apartheid. It had brutally suppressed all movements for democratic change

KEY CONCEPTS QUESTION

Cause and Consequence: What were the causes and consequences of each of these as an agent of change in South Africa during the 1980s: the armed struggle; international pressure; economic forces; the end of the Cold War; the independence of Namibia; popular protest; changes within the National Party itself?

Fact: Organisations that played important roles in South Africa's transition to democracy were:

- The African National Congress (ANC) was formed in 1912 and banned in 1960, after which it went into exile and took up an armed struggle against the apartheid government. The ban was lifted in 1990 and the ANC played a dominant role in negotiations for democratic change.
- The Pan Africanist Congress (PAC) was formed in 1959, under the leadership of Robert Sobukwe, by members of the ANC who disagreed with the non-racial policies of the ANC and favoured an Africanist approach. Like the ANC, it was banned in 1960, took up an armed struggle and was unbanned in 1990.

since it came to power. Yet it was changes within the National Party that helped to break the deadlock that South Africa had reached by the end of the 1980s. Its leader, F.W. de Klerk, played a key part in this.

Frederik Willem de Klerk (b. 1936) replaced P.W. Botha as leader of the National Party and then as president of South Africa in September 1989, when Botha stepped down on account of ill-health. De Klerk was more open to reform than Botha had been and he realised the urgency of the situation. However, his announcement on 2 February 1990 was unexpected. He later said that the timing of this move was influenced by the fall of the Berlin Wall and the end of the Cold War, and the impact of these developments on the situation in South Africa.

- The South African Communist Party (SACP) was formed in 1921 as the Communist Party of South Africa, and banned in 1950, after which it changed its name to the SACP. It was unbanned in 1990, and formed the Tripartite Alliance with the ANC and the Congress of South African Trade Unions (COSATU).
- The United Democratic Front (UDF) was formed in 1983 to oppose the tricameral elections. It quickly drew a membership of several million. It formed the core of resistance during the 1980s when the liberation movements were still banned or in exile. It dissolved itself in 1990 after the unbanning of the ANC and other parties.
- In the 1980s, black trade unions played an important role in the protests, after their legalisation in 1979. In 1985, several unions united to form COSATU, which emerged as a powerful pressure group.

SOURCE G

The impact was enormous. At home, there was a mixture of trauma, exhilaration, and disbelief as different groups struggled to come to terms with a change so profound. Abroad, there was a sense of wonderment and relief. Here, so soon after Gorbachev's perestroika revolution, was another miracle of reform: at a stroke South Africa and all it symbolized were transformed. The February 2 speech was to race relations everywhere what the collapse of the Berlin Wall was to communism …

Just as Gorbachev could not have known that his restructuring of the Soviet system would lead to the loss of his eastern European empire, the collapse of communism, and the dismemberment of the Soviet Union itself, so too De Klerk did not expect his reforms to lead to black majority rule and the end of Afrikaner nationalism before the end of the decade.

Writer and journalist, Allister Sparks, analyses the significance of F.W. de Klerk's announcement to parliament on 2 February 1990, in A. Sparks (1994), Tomorrow is Another Country, *Johannesburg: Struik, pp. 9–10, 12.*

De Klerk's speech took many people by surprise, including members of his own party, and not all of them supported his bold initiative. Some thought that the National Party should form an alliance with the conservative Inkatha Freedom Party (IFP), led by Mangosuthu Buthelezi, and in this way retain some power. During 1991 there was growing opposition to De Klerk's reforms from more conservative members of the party. They were concerned about the repeal of several key apartheid laws, the return of political exiles and the influence of the SACP on the negotiation process. They were losing faith in the ability of the National Party to uphold their interests, and many of them turned to the right-wing Conservative Party and the militaristic AWB, which was willing to use violence to oppose change. Many observers began to fear that members of the police and army with right-wing sympathies would use force to prevent any negotiated settlement.

ACTIVITY

Explain the comparisons that Sparks makes in **Source G** between events in eastern Europe and South Africa, and between the Soviet leader Mikael Gorbachev and F.W. de Klerk.

In 1992, De Klerk decided to meet this challenge by holding a referendum among white voters to gauge support. The result was a triumph for him, with 69 per cent of the white electorate voting in favour of continuing the reform process. This gave the National Party greater confidence in the negotiation process, and it adopted a tougher position when the CODESA talks resumed, demanding special protection for minority rights and a coalition government.

The CODESA talks were dominated by the ANC and the National Party, through their chief negotiators, Cyril Ramaphosa and Roelf Meyer respectively. But De Klerk continued to play a key role in the negotiations. During these years, the remaining apartheid laws (such as the Group Areas Act, the Population Registration Act and the Separate Amenities Act) were repealed by De Klerk's government. Many people respected him for breaking with National Party tradition and facing up to opposition from conservative Afrikaners. However, some critics accused his government of secretly funding a 'Third Force' of security personnel to promote violence between the ANC and Inkatha.

De Klerk and Mandela were jointly awarded the 1993 Nobel Peace Prize for their efforts to end apartheid and bring about a peaceful settlement. After 1994, De Klerk served as a deputy president under Mandela, until 1997 when he resigned as leader of the National Party and retired from politics. After this, the National Party split up and the party that had enforced apartheid and dominated South African politics for so many years no longer existed.

Historical debate:
Historians have different opinions about the point at which the National Party lost the initiative in its negotiations with the ANC. Leonard Thompson believes that the signing of the Record of Understanding, when the government conceded to several of the ANC's demands, was the moment when the government lost control of the transition process and Mandela gained ascendancy over De Klerk. Hermann Giliomee and Bernard Mbenga, on the other hand, believe that Boipatong was the turning point. Before then, they argue, the two sides had been evenly balanced, but afterwards the ANC had the upper hand.

The ANC, Nelson Mandela and other key leaders

The ANC had been unable to operate as a legal political organisation inside South Africa since its banning by the National Party government in 1960. Many of its leaders, including Mandela, were imprisoned, after the underground armed wing of the ANC (Umkhonto we Sizwe or MK) was uncovered by police. Other leaders went into exile, from where **Oliver Tambo** led the movement, first from London and then from Lusaka, Zambia. He slowly built up international support for the organisation and the anti-apartheid struggle. At the same time, the ANC trained MK guerrillas to operate underground inside South Africa.

After it was unbanned in 1990, the ANC had to transform itself from an exiled liberation movement and build up party structures inside the country. There were differences of opinion about policy and tactics between leaders who had spent many years in exile, and those who had remained in the country, some in prison and others as leaders of the United Democratic Front. Not all ANC members supported the idea of a peaceful settlement, believing that they should continue the armed struggle and seize power. They mistrusted Mandela because of his willingness to negotiate with the government.

In the eyes of the world and of most South Africans, Nelson Mandela was the key player in the negotiations. After his release from prison, he visited the leaders of the ANC in Lusaka. They confirmed that the ANC was willing to negotiate with the government to end apartheid. Mandela also visited thirteen African, European and North American countries a few months later, where he was welcomed as a hero wherever he went. In 1991, he became president of the ANC in place of Oliver Tambo.

After his release, Mandela called for the continuation of sanctions and the armed struggle until he was sure that the National Party was really prepared to negotiate. But after that, he strongly supported a negotiated settlement and argued against those in the ANC who wanted to continue the armed struggle. However, he was prepared to act forcefully against the National Party by suspending negotiations after police involvement in township violence in Boipatong. His powerful influence on events was demonstrated after the assassination of Chris Hani when it was Mandela's appeal for calm in a televised address that diffused the situation. After 1994, Mandela focussed on reconciliation between the races after the deep rifts caused by apartheid.

QUESTION

Reread the earlier text, and suggest why historians have selected the Record of Understanding and Boipatong as turning points in relations between the two negotiating teams.

Oliver Tambo (1917–93)

He was a founder member of the ANC Youth League in 1944. After the banning of the ANC in 1960 he went into exile, where he led the movement for many years, before returning to South Africa in December 1990. A severe stroke prevented him from playing any further active role in politics, and he was replaced as ANC president in 1991 by Nelson Mandela.

The ANC, SACP and COSATU formed the Tripartite Alliance for the negotiation process and for the first election, and delegates from all three organisations worked together at CODESA. Cyril Ramaphosa was the chief negotiator for the ANC and Tripartite Alliance. He had been leader of one of the largest trade unions, the National Union of Mineworkers, and had played a key role in the formation of COSATU in 1985. At CODESA, he proved to be an extremely skilled negotiator and formed a close working relationship with the chief government negotiator, Roelf Meyer.

Another key negotiator on the ANC team was Joe Slovo, the secretary-general of the SACP and a leader in MK. Many in the government negotiating team were suspicious of him, partly because he was a communist, and also because they saw him as a traitor because he was white. However they came to respect his willingness to compromise and his skill as a negotiator. It was his suggestion of a 'Government of National Unity' (which would include the National Party) to rule for the first five years, that provided a breakthrough when the negotiations had reached a deadlock. After 1994, he served briefly as a minister in the first democratic government before his death from cancer in 1995.

Inkatha and Mangosuthu Buthelezi

Buthelezi was the leader of Inkatha, which had started off as a Zulu cultural organisation, but later became a political party, the Inkatha Freedom Party (IFP). From 1972 he had been the chief minister of the homeland of Kwazulu, but he refused to accept the government's offer of 'independence', despite pressure from the government. He was critical of the ANC for its use of guerrilla warfare and its support for economic sanctions. He was criticised by other black leaders for his willingness to work within the homeland system, and also for his promotion of a distinct Zulu nationalism.

Figure 5.8 Mangosuthu Buthelezi, F.W. de Klerk and Nelson Mandela at a press conference in April 1994, after the last-minute agreement that Inkatha would participate in the election

Tensions between Inkatha and other political groups led to violent confrontations between their supporters in the mid-1980s and early 1990s, especially in Kwazulu-Natal. There were also violent clashes in the townships around Johannesburg, where Inkatha-supporting Zulu migrant workers living in hostels clashed with ANC-supporting township residents. This violence threatened to disrupt the negotiations on several occasions. Buthelezi played an unpredictable role in the negotiations and threatened to boycott the election itself. The crisis was averted by a last-minute emergency meeting between Buthelezi, Mandela and De Klerk one week before the election. Buthelezi agreed that Inkatha would take part in the election, thus averting the prospect of even more violence in Kwazulu-Natal if Inkatha refused to take part.

After the election, Buthelezi served as part of the coalition Government of National Unity, and the violence between Inkatha and ANC followers subsided.

KEY CONCEPTS ACTIVITY

Significance: Compare the significance of the roles played by Nelson Mandela and F.W de Klerk in the transition to democracy in South Africa, as well as the roles played by the ANC and National Party in the process.

5.4 How did democracy function in the new South Africa?

The ANC had won a clear majority in the first election in April 1994, but in terms of a pre-election agreement – the 'sunset clause' – all parties gaining at least 5 per cent of the votes would form a coalition government (the Government of National Unity) for the first five years.

The Government of National Unity

This Government of National Unity included twelve representatives from the ANC, six from the National Party and three from the IFP. The National Party leader, F.W. de Klerk, served as a deputy president, along with Thabo Mbeki of the ANC. The Inkatha leader, Mangosuthu Buthelezi, was the minister of home affairs.

The fundamental task facing the new government was to transform South Africa into a working democracy after centuries of white domination and minority rule. This involved major changes. The former homelands were incorporated into nine new provinces; new local, provincial and national government structures were established; and the civil service and police force were restructured. A new national defence force had to integrate MK and APLA guerrilla fighters and the homeland armies into the apartheid-era army.

The ANC and the National Party had agreed that the drafting of a new constitution would be a two-part process: an interim constitution would be drafted before the election, and the final one would be drawn up by the first elected parliament. The elected members of parliament (the 400 members of the National Assembly and the ninety members of the Senate) together formed a Constitutional Assembly to implement the second stage of the process. It was chaired by Cyril Ramaphosa, the ANC's chief negotiator in the run-up to the election. The members of the assembly were assisted by a large team of legal advisers.

The 1996 constitution

The Constitutional Assembly met from May 1994 until May 1996. It made efforts to ensure that the views of ordinary people were taken into account in the process. Public meetings and workshops were held around the country, and a massive media campaign encouraged people to send in their ideas. Altogether 1.7 million written submissions were made, on issues ranging from abortion and the death penalty to animal rights and environmental concerns. In the constitutional negotiations, the National Party and Inkatha tried unsuccessfully to gain greater powers for the provinces.

The Constitutional Assembly adopted the final constitution in May 1996. It made provision for a two-house parliament: a National Assembly of 400 members; and a National Council of Provinces (replacing the Senate), with ten representatives from each province. Provincial governments were given limited powers, but their decisions could be overridden by the National Assembly, and most of their funding was allocated by the central government.

Elections, by secret ballot, were to be held every five years, after which parliament would elect a president as head of state. The president's term of office was limited to two terms. Any amendments to the constitution would require a two-thirds majority of a joint sitting of the two houses of parliament. Elections would use a system of proportional representation, based on lists drawn up by each party before the election. Historian Tom Lodge has suggested that the list system weakened the workings of parliamentary democracy, as ANC parliamentarians were often reluctant to question government policies because their places on party lists, and therefore their positions as members of parliament, were determined by the party leadership.

Under the apartheid government there had been no culture of human rights in South Africa. Instead there was a long history of discrimination and oppression. In an effort to build a culture of human rights and an awareness of constitutional democracy, millions of copies of the constitution were distributed, in all eleven official languages. The new constitution included a comprehensive Bill of Rights, which listed economic as well as civil and political rights. For example, it listed 'access' to housing, health care, water and social security as the basic rights of all citizens, although these rights would be difficult to enforce by law. Many of the rights included in the Bill of Rights echoed the words of the Freedom Charter, which had served as an inspiration and a basis for ANC policies since 1955.

Fact: Several structures to protect democracy were put in place:

- A Human Rights Commission
- A Commission for Gender Equality
- An Independent Electoral Commission
- An Independent Broadcasting Authority
- A Public Protector
- An Auditor General
- A Commission for the Promotion and Protection of the Rights of Cultural, Religious and Linguistic Communities

The Constitutional Court

The constitution established a Constitutional Court to protect and uphold the constitution. The court had the power to decide whether parliament had passed a law that was unconstitutional, or whether the government was acting against the constitution. In its first case, the court ruled that the death penalty was unconstitutional.

Individuals or communities could appeal to the court if they believed that their constitutional rights were threatened. In 1999, after such an appeal, the court ruled that prisoners serving a sentence had the right to vote in an election. A later ruling by the Constitutional Court ordered the government to provide free antiretroviral medicines free of charge to HIV-positive pregnant women, after an AIDS activist organisation had taken the issue to the court to force the government to change its policy regarding AIDS. Another ruling ordered the government to introduce legislation to legalise same-sex marriages.

Apart from the Constitutional Court, there were additional structures to protect democracy and ensure that the rule of law was followed.

By adopting the new constitution and establishing structures such as these, the Government of National Unity achieved its major goal of establishing a firm basis for constitutional democracy in South Africa.

Opposition parties

A key feature of a democratic state is the role played by opposition parties and, although there were no restrictions on their freedom, opposition parties were small and fragmented. Shortly after the new constitution was adopted, the Government of National Unity broke up. In May 1996, the National Party withdrew, claiming that, as a minority party in the coalition, it had little influence on decisions, and that it intended instead to form a strong parliamentary opposition. De Klerk stepped down from his position as deputy president, and the other National Party ministers resigned from the government.

After leaving the Government of National Unity, the National Party began to disintegrate. Several leaders, including De Klerk, retired from party politics. The National Party re-formed itself into the New National Party, but struggled to attract support. It subsequently split up and disbanded itself in 2005.

With the collapse of the National Party and dwindling support for the Freedom Front, the ideology of Afrikaner nationalism, which had dominated South African history for much of the 20th century, was no longer a significant factor.

The Democratic Party became the official opposition after the 1999 elections. Many former National Party members switched their support to it and together they formed the Democratic Alliance (DA). However, the DA did not attract significant support from black voters, except in the Western Cape and Kwazulu-Natal, where many coloured and Indian voters supported it. Conservative whites continued to support the Freedom Front. Party politics therefore remained largely split along racial lines, with relatively few white voters supporting the ANC.

Inkatha remained a part of the Government of National Unity when the National Party resigned. Even after new elections were held in 1999, Buthelezi remained a cabinet minister. The ANC's inclusion of Inkatha in the government reduced the violence between supporters of the two parties in Kwazulu-Natal. As relations between the ANC and Inkatha improved, there were even talks of a merger, although the differences between them were too fundamental to make this a reality. Other political organisations, such as the PAC, failed to draw significant support and provided no real alternative to the ANC, which remained the dominant party, although a small group of supporters broke away in 1997 to form the United Democratic Movement (UDM).

Historical debate:
Historians suggest different explanations for the withdrawal and demise of the National Party. Leonard Thompson believes that the new constitution was the final straw for the National Party, because it made no provision for power-sharing beyond the 1999 election. Nigel Worden suggests that the party's collapse was due to a miscalculation by De Klerk: 'De Klerk's gamble in 1990 that the NP would be able to position itself as a viable opposition to an Africanist and socialist government was defeated by the ANC's adoption of multiracial and free market policies.' Hermann Giliomee attributes the collapse to the revelations made at the Truth and Reconciliation Commission hearings (which you will read about in Unit 5.2), which he thinks 'probably destroyed' the National Party.

KEY CONCEPTS QUESTION

Cause and Significance: What were the causes and the significance of the collapse of the National Party?

The 1999 election

Nelson Mandela had always said that he would not serve longer than one term as president, and in 1997 Thabo Mbeki had taken over the leadership of the ANC, a position that ensured he would be the next president of South Africa. In the 1999 election, support for the ANC increased. Its closest rival was the Democratic Party, which won less than 10 per cent of the votes.

QUESTION

How do the results shown in Table 5.2 illustrate the advantages and disadvantages of the system of proportional representation?

Table 5.2 The 1999 election results show why South Africa was referred to as a 'one-party democracy' – the remaining eight seats in the National Assembly were held by another five parties, all of them new to parliament

Party	% of votes	Number of seats
ANC	66.36	266
DP	9.55	38
IFP	8.59	34
NNP	6.87	28
UDM	3.42	14
ACDP	1.43	6
FF	0.8	3
PAC	0.71	3

When Mbeki succeeded Mandela as president in 1999, the focus of government shifted from reconciliation to transformation, and Mbeki himself spoke out against the reluctance of whites to give up their privileges and accept transformation. As a result, some white South Africans regarded his attitude as hostile and racist. At the same time, Mbeki's strong support for capitalist economic policies antagonised COSATU and SACP leaders, as did his failure to involve them in policy decision-making. Others criticised Mbeki for his intolerance of criticism, his centralisation of power within the ANC, and the appointment of ANC nominees to key positions in state institutions. He was also criticised for his policy towards the dictatorship of Robert Mugabe in neighbouring Zimbabwe, and his government's response to the AIDS crisis.

Although historian Leonard Thompson voices some concerns about the power of the ANC by calling South Africa a 'one-party democracy', he also points out that there were strong checks on the abuse of power, such as a free press, a vigorous civil society and powerful business organisations and trade unions. Political scientist David Welsh, writing in *The Rise and Fall of Apartheid* (2009, p. 578), notes that although a single party dominant system seemed to have become entrenched, democratic constitutional forms had been maintained: 'Democracy has survived, and even if it is democracy of a poor quality, South Africa is nevertheless a vastly better society than it was under apartheid.'

QUESTION

To what extent did the changes after 1994 provide a firm foundation for democracy in South Africa?

After 1994, South Africa was transformed from an authoritarian state, in which 90 per cent of the population had no political rights, to a democracy with one of the most liberal constitutions in the world, and powerful mechanisms to uphold it. However, as you will see in Unit 5.2, the government faced challenges in maintaining and extending democratic practices.

End of unit activities

1 Write a brief report to explain why there was a lack of liberal democratic traditions and institutions in South Africa before 1994.

2 Draw up a table to summarise the background and role of each of these organisations or movements, using the headings suggested in the example below:

Organisation	Circumstances leading to its formation	Aims/Vision	Significance
ANC			
MK			
Black Consciousness			
UDF			
COSATU			

3 Go to http://news.bbc.co.uk/onthisday/hi/dates/stories/february/2/newsid_2524000/2524997.stm and read the news report and play the video clip showing reactions to President de Klerk's announcement of the start of reform on 2 February 1990. Analyse the different reactions to the announcement, explaining why some people were sceptical about the reforms.

4 Design a spider diagram to illustrate the process of political transformation between 1990 and 1994, using the following headings: negotiations; setbacks; compromises; settlement.

5 Divide into two groups to discuss the contribution of Mandela and De Klerk to the peace process in South Africa. Each group should prepare an argument for a class debate. One group should support the view that Mandela and De Klerk deserved to be joint winners of the 1993 Nobel Peace Prize; the other that De Klerk, as the leader of the political party responsible for enforcing apartheid and imprisoning Mandela, did not deserve equal recognition.

6 **Either** investigate the role of the 'frontline states' in supporting the liberation movement in South Africa, showing how these states paid a heavy price for their support **or** investigate and make brief notes on the activities of the international anti-apartheid movement in Britain, the United States, the Commonwealth and other European countries.

2 Unit The development of a democratic state in South Africa

TIMELINE

1994 **May:** UN lifts arms embargo; South Africa joins Organisation of African Unity (OAU).

Jun: South Africa rejoins Commonwealth.

Aug: South Africa joins Southern African Development Community (SADC).

Nov: Restitution of Land Rights Act.

1995 **Dec:** Formation of PAGAD.

1996 **Apr:** First session of the Truth and Reconciliation Commission (TRC).

1998 **May:** Thabo Mbeki's 'Two Nations' speech.

1998–2002 Urban terror campaign in Cape Town.

1998 **Oct:** Report of the TRC.

Dec: Formation of the Treatment Action Campaign (TAC).

1999 **Jun:** Second democratic election; Mbeki succeeds Mandela as president of South Africa.

2003 **Apr:** final Report of the TRC.

KEY QUESTIONS

- What factors influenced the development of democracy?
- How did the government respond to domestic crises?
- What were the challenges relating to equality, equity and civil protests?

Overview

- The government implemented steps to promote nation-building and adopted new national symbols to encourage a common national identity.
- It also established a Truth and Reconciliation Commission (TRC) to investigate the atrocities of the apartheid era. The TRC found that the apartheid government had been guilty of gross violations of human rights, but it also criticised some actions of the liberation groups and Inkatha.
- Despite the successful political transition, regional diversity created economic problems and ethnic diversity resulted in lingering racism.
- Thabo Mbeki succeeded Mandela as president in 1999, and the focus shifted from reconciliation to transformation. However, Mbeki did not enjoy the same popularity as his predecessor, and there were many critics of his policies and style of leadership.
- Although South Africa was no longer diplomatically isolated, there were some tensions with the US over South Africa's relations with Cuba, Libya and the Palestinians.
- After 1994, incidents of political extremism decreased, except for bombings and attacks by small radical groups, such as the right-wing Afrikaner *Boeremag* and the predominantly Muslim group, People against Gangsterism and Drugs (PAGAD).
- Despite the successful political transition to democracy, xenophobic attacks on refugees from other African countries created problems.
- The high levels of poverty and inequality, characteristic of South Africa before 1994, continued despite the new government's efforts. Although the inequality was no longer strictly defined along racial lines, the overwhelming majority of the desperately poor were black.

- Land reform was a critical issue, but the redistribution and restitution of land was slow, and targets to increase black ownership of arable land were not met.
- The influence of civil society organisations (CSOs), which had played a critical role in the 1980s, declined after the 1994 election, as their leaders moved into government. However, some organisations continued to play important roles in defending civil rights.
- There were tensions between the African National Congress (ANC) and its partners in the Tripartite Alliance, the South African Communist Party (SACP) and Congress of South African Trade Unions (COSATU) especially over the direction of economic policies.

Figure 5.9 In a famous gesture to promote nation-building, Nelson Mandela appeared in a Springbok jersey to support the national rugby team in a game predominantly supported by whites; here he congratulates the Springbok captain Francois Pienaar after South Africa won the 1995 Rugby World Cup

5.5 What factors influenced the development of democracy?

Under the system of apartheid, South Africa had been the most divided society in the world, where every aspect of life was defined by race and ethnicity. Between 1990 and 1994, the laws that had enforced this system were repealed and when the white minority handed over power to the black majority in 1994, institutionalised racism was a thing of the past. Archbishop Tutu called the new society 'the rainbow nation', but it was not easy for South Africans to overcome centuries of division and see themselves as a united nation with a common national identity. In **Source A**, Kenneth Christie explains some of the problems that the government faced.

SOURCE A

Nation building often seems a romantic task, more suited to starry-eyed idealists and visionaries than policy-makers seeking to grapple with the everyday pragmatics of running a large economic infrastructure. Some have argued that there has never been a South African nation, either before or after the colonization of southern Africa by imperial powers. In effect, the South African nation never existed and the present South Africa in itself is a product of colonialism, an invention of the colonial powers.

K. Christie (2000), The South African Truth Commission, *Basingstoke: Palgrave Macmillan, p. 105.*

Fact: New public holidays included:

Human Rights Day (21 March) – the day of the 1960 Sharpeville Massacre.

Freedom Day (27 April) – the date of the first democratic election in 1994.

Youth Day (16 June) – the start of the 1976 Soweto Uprising.

National Women's Day (9 August) – the date of the 1956 march by 26,000 women protesting against the pass laws.

Policies to promote nation-building

Despite the complexities involved, the government tackled the issue by adopting new national symbols in an attempt to promote a common national identity among South Africans for the first time, using elements of different cultural traditions. The new national anthem combined the music and words of the old anthem with the African liberation hymn 'Nkosi Sikelel' iAfrica' ('God Save Africa'). The words of the new anthem combined Xhosa, Zulu, Sesotho, Afrikaans and English. The new national flag included the colours of the old flag, as well as the black, green and yellow of the African nationalist tradition. The intention was that all South Africans could identify with these new symbols, but in a different and unified way.

KEY CONCEPTS QUESTION

Change and Continuity: In what ways did the government's attempts at nation-building reflect both change and continuity?

New public holidays were created to commemorate significant events in the liberation struggle. These replaced public holidays rooted in events in South Africa's colonial and white-dominated history. Some name changes were made, such as the towns, airports and dams named after apartheid-era leaders, but there was no immediate rush to shed all names associated with the past, as had happened in other former colonies.

Monuments to figures and events from the past were not destroyed, as they had been in Russia after the fall of the Soviet Union, but some were removed from public view. Many statues to colonial leaders and monuments such as the Voortrekker Monument (built by Afrikaner nationalists to commemorate the Boer victory over the Zulu) remained. This was part of an attempt to promote diversity and to reconcile different sections of the population. But to provide a balance, new monuments built after 1994 commemorated the struggle against apartheid, such as a monument in Cape Town with statues of South Africa's four Nobel Peace Prize winners – Albert Luthuli, Desmond Tutu, F.W. de Klerk and Nelson Mandela.

Desmond Tutu (b. 1931)

He was the Anglican Archbishop of Cape Town and leader of the South African Council of Churches from 1978. In 1984 he was awarded the Nobel Peace Prize. After the ANC came to power in 1994, Tutu continued to speak out on policies and actions that he believed were morally wrong. He chaired the Truth and Reconciliation Commission, which was set up in 1996 to investigate apartheid-era crimes.

The TRC as an instrument of nation-building

A notable achievement of the new government was the establishment of a mechanism to deal with one of the most problematic legacies of the past: the abuse of human rights under apartheid. In the negotiations leading to the 1994 elections, the African National Congress (ANC) and the National Party had agreed on the establishment of a commission to investigate apartheid-era crimes. In 1995, the Government of National Unity established the Truth and Reconciliation Commission (TRC), under the chairmanship of Archbishop **Desmond Tutu**. Unlike the Nuremberg Trials of Nazi war criminals after the Second World War, the TRC was based on the principle of 'restorative justice', rather than 'retributive justice'.

SOURCE B

The decision to opt for a Truth and Reconciliation Commission was an important compromise. If the ANC had insisted on Nuremberg-style trials for the leaders of the former apartheid government, there would have been no peaceful transition to democracy, and if the former government had insisted on a blanket amnesty then, similarly, the negotiations would have broken down. A bloody revolution sooner rather than later would have been inevitable. The Truth and Reconciliation Commission is a bridge from the old to the new.

Justice ***Richard Goldstone****, quoted in Y. Seleti (ed.) (2004),* Africa Since 1990*, Cape Town: New Africa Education, p. 212.*

Theory of Knowledge

History and ethics:
Restoration implies healing, whereas retribution implies revenge. What are the advantages and disadvantages of each of these forms of justice? Why do you think the negotiators decided that the TRC should apply 'restorative' rather than 'retributive' justice?

The aim of the TRC was to investigate politically motivated violations of human rights during the apartheid era. Its underlying purpose was to uncover the truth about what had happened and, in this way, bring about national reconciliation. Between 1996 and 1998 the TRC held hearings around the country, which were broadcast live on radio and television. At these hearings, more than 22,000 victims told their stories. Some of them were hoping that justice would be done and that the **perpetrators** would be put on trial for their actions. However, the TRC was not a court of law: it could not prosecute people or make judgements. Others who came to the TRC simply wanted to find out what had happened to family members who had disappeared.

The TRC did not only investigate the actions of those who had worked for the apartheid government. The actions of the liberation movement, as well as those of

Richard Goldstone (b. 1938)

He was a prominent South African legal expert who chaired the commission investigating the activities of a 'Third Force', was a judge on the Constitutional Court, and served as chief prosecutor in the UN International Criminal Tribunal investigating war crimes in the former Yugoslavia and Rwanda. His 2009 report on war crimes in Gaza was accepted by the UN but rejected by Israel.

Perpetrator: someone who has committed a crime.

Fact: As part of their transition to democracy, several other countries have also established truth commissions to determine what happened during difficult periods in their history. These include Argentina, Chile, Uganda, Ethiopia and Rwanda. A truth commission was established after the reunification of Germany in 1990, to investigate violations of human rights under communist rule in East Germany between 1949 and 1989.

Figure 5.10 Members of the Truth and Reconciliation Commission at its first hearing in East London, Eastern Cape, in April 1996. In the front row are Dr Alex Boraine, the deputy chair (second from the left), Archbishop Desmond Tutu and Rev Bongani Finca, one of the commissioners

Amnesty: an official pardon granted by the state.

'Necklace' executions: a gruesome form of execution in which a car tyre filled with petrol was placed around the victim's neck and set alight.

Inkatha politicians and supporters in the pre-election violence, also came under scrutiny. The TRC had the power to grant **amnesty** from prosecution to perpetrators whose actions had been politically motivated and who made a full disclosure. However, amnesty was by no means automatic: 1,167 were granted out of 7,116 applications.

The TRC encountered several problems. Some people refused to appear before it, like P.W. Botha, the former president, whose government had allowed the use of death squads to kill its opponents. F.W. de Klerk appeared before the TRC and made a formal apology for apartheid, but insisted that he had never authorised or been aware of the brutal actions of the security forces. He later took legal action to prevent the publication of a paragraph in the final report that held him responsible for the activities of a 'Third Force'.

The ANC was angered by the fact that the TRC made no distinction between the crimes committed by agents of the apartheid state and those committed by the liberation movements. Thabo Mbeki, who represented the ANC at the hearings, felt very strongly about this. It was only when Tutu threatened to resign that members of the ANC agreed to apply for amnesty for deeds committed. The ANC later tried unsuccessfully to block the publication of the whole report.

In its final report the TRC concluded that the National Party government under P.W. Botha was responsible for torture, arson, abduction and sabotage. The report also criticised De Klerk for the activities of the 'Third Force', which had tried to disrupt negotiations. The TRC was critical too of some actions of those fighting apartheid. These included the torture and executions that had taken place in ANC training camps in exile, the attacks by Azanian People's Liberation Army (APLA, the armed wing of the Pan Africanist Congress) guerrillas that had resulted in civilian casualties and the **'necklace' executions** carried out by supporters of the United Democratic Front (UDF) in the 1980s. Buthelezi was held responsible for violations of human rights by members of Inkatha.

Some people believed that there was a strong link between the TRC and nation-building, but others questioned whether it was possible to build a single South African nation in this way. They questioned whether the TRC had in reality brought about reconciliation or whether it had created further divisions.

Opinions about the TRC differed sharply. Some whites tried to ignore the proceedings and thought that the past should be left alone; others denounced it as a witch-hunt. Many blacks believed that justice had not been done and that too many murderers were able to walk free. Many victims received little compensation, partly because the government could not afford it. Some families of victims were critical of the whole process, notably the families of the murdered Black Consciousness leader, Steve Biko, and others who applied unsuccessfully to the Constitutional Court for the whole TRC process to be stopped.

KEY CONCEPTS ACTIVITY

Significance: Explain the significance of the establishment and findings of the TRC as a symbol of democratic process.

Problems of regional and ethnic diversity

Another factor that influenced the development of democracy in South Africa was the great range of differences between the underdeveloped rural provinces and the cities, especially Johannesburg, South Africa's most populous and cosmopolitan city. There was

Figure 5.11 A cartoon about the TRC by **Jonathan Shapiro (Zapiro)**, published in the *Mail and Guardian* in 1998. It suggests that the TRC reached truth but not reconciliation. The figure on the right, Archbishop Tutu, urgently points the way towards reconciliation

ACTIVITY

How does the body language of the central figures in Figure 5.11 reflect different attitudes towards the TRC? How does the cartoonist use visual imagery to reinforce his message?

Jonathan Shapiro (Zapiro) (b. 1958)

He is regarded as South Africa's most talented political cartoonist. During the 1980s, he was an active member of the United Democratic Front and the End Conscription Campaign and was detained by the police for his criticism of the government. He has worked as the editorial cartoonist for the *Sowetan*, the *Mail and Guardian* and the *Sunday Times*.

also great regional diversity among the nine new provinces. Some, such as Gauteng and the Western Cape, offered better job prospects and opportunities for economic growth. Other provinces, however, such as the Eastern Cape and Limpopo, which were made up mainly of former homelands, had high levels of poverty and unemployment, resulting in a significant migration of people from them to the cities in search of work and better services. This population movement gave rise to the spread of informal settlements on the outskirts of towns and cities as well as other social and economic problems associated with rapid urbanisation.

There was also linguistic diversity between the provinces – with, for example, most Zulu-speakers in Kwazulu-Natal, and Xhosa-speakers in the Eastern and Western Cape. There was also ethnic diversity, with most people of Indian descent living in Kwazulu-Natal and most coloured people living in the Western Cape.

Ethnic diversity was one of the biggest challenges facing the new nation. When the white minority handed over power to the black majority in 1994, institutionalised racism was a thing of the past, but the need to change existing attitudes and prejudices based on race remained a huge challenge facing the whole country.

Figure 5.12 Map of post-1994 South Africa, showing the new provinces

During his term of office as president, Nelson Mandela focused on reconciliation between the races, going to extraordinary lengths to allay white fears. He went out of his way to meet and forgive former adversaries, such as the public prosecutor who had demanded the death penalty for him and the other MK leaders when they were sentenced to life imprisonment in 1964. Some critics felt that Mandela devoted more effort to calming white fears than to addressing black grievances.

SOURCE C

In his first months as president, he [Mandela] enjoyed a brilliant honeymoon, particularly with white South Africans, to whom this tolerant old man came as a wondrous relief ... It was a normality which carried its own dangers, as black militants saw the revolution betrayed, and younger ANC leaders including Thabo Mbeki knew they must make reforms which would offend the whites.

A. Sampson (1999), Mandela: The Authorised Biography, *Johannesburg, SA: Jonathan Ball Publishers, p. 504.*

ACTIVITY

Why would some activists believe that Mandela had betrayed the revolution? How does **Source C** suggest that black and white South Africans had different expectations about the future?

However, there was a feeling in black political circles that whites did not reciprocate the gestures of goodwill extended to them by Mandela, according to Xolela Mangcu, a political analyst and director of the Steve Biko Foundation. Mandela himself became more critical of white attitudes and in a speech in 1997 he highlighted their lack of cooperation and their unwillingness to change. When **Thabo Mbeki** succeeded Mandela as president, he publicly criticised the reluctance of whites to give up their privileges and accept transformation. As evidence of white opposition to transformation, black critics cited many examples, such as the composition of the national cricket and rugby teams (which remained predominantly white). They also resented the reluctance of many whites to accept that they had benefitted from apartheid, even if they had not been supporters of the National Party.

Thabo Mbeki (b. 1942)

He joined the ANC Youth League in his teens and left South Africa in 1962 to go into exile, after the banning of the ANC. After studying in Britain and doing military training in the Soviet Union, he played a prominent role in the ANC leadership in exile before returning to South Africa in 1990. He served as deputy president under Mandela and as president from 1999 to 2008, when he was forced to resign by the ANC's National Executive Committee.

A different concern, according to Mangcu, was that the issue of race was used by some ANC leaders as a shield against criticism. Thus, white critics of the government could be accused of being racist and opposed to transformation, and their criticisms ignored.

As South Africans of all races mixed with each other in schools, universities, the army and police force, the civil service and in business, as they had never done before, many people hoped that racial divisions would become a thing of the past, in reality as well as in law. Some analysts pointed out that new divisions, based on class rather than race, were beginning to emerge: integration was happening far more successfully in more affluent areas, as a growing black middle class moved into managerial positions or into suburbs and schools that had formerly been reserved for whites. However, many historians and sociologists believed that racism was an unresolved challenge facing the country (see **Sources D** and **E**).

SOURCE D

South Africa is yet to triumph over lingering and subtle racism. This manifests itself in large sectors of South African society continuing to live in almost complete isolation, experiencing South African multicultural society from the vantage point of their homogeneous **squatter camps**, exclusive suburbs, rural villages, gated security complexes and commercial farms. While the poverty and crime of the townships more often than not enforce racial isolation on poorer black urbanites, the majority of South Africans appear to isolate themselves voluntarily. A SA Reconciliation Barometer national survey revealed that 26% of South Africans claim that they never have contact with members of other races on an average day of the week, while 24% claim that they do so only rarely.

E. *Maloka (2004), 'The Fruits of Freedom', in* Turning Points in History Book 6: Negotiation, Transition and Freedom, *Cape Town: STE Publishers, for the Institute for Justice and Reconciliation and the South African History Project, p. 61.*

Squatter camps: informal settlements on the outskirts of towns and cities, which are a feature of developing countries going through a rapid process of urbanisation.

SOURCE E

South Africa is still one of the most race-conscious societies in the world, so deep are the divides of the past. The legacy of apartheid and institutionalised racism will take decades to rectify. So will the racial attitudes and practices that formed the bedrock of white support for the apartheid system. No longer sanctioned or promoted by the state, racism continues below the surface as disaffected and alienated whites contemplate the implications of the loss of historical privilege.

J. *Crush (2001),* Immigration, Xenophobia and Human Rights in South Africa*, Cape Town: Southern African Migration Project, p. 7.*

ACTIVITY

Compare and contrast the views of the writers in **Sources D** and **E** about the causes and effects of continuing racism in South Africa.

What comment is the cartoonist in **Source F** making about the effectiveness of nation-building strategies in post-1994 South Africa?

QUESTION

What steps did the government take to promote a unified democratic identity? How successful were these efforts?

SOURCE F

Figure 5.13 In 1994, Archbishop Desmond Tutu referred to South Africa as the 'rainbow nation' – a reflection of the optimism that many people felt about the emergence of a new non-racial identity. This Zapiro cartoon, published in *The Sowetan* on 25 August 2000, questions this view of race relations in post-apartheid South Africa

Secular: not connected to any religion; secularism is the view that religion should be separated from government or public education.

Calvinist: puritanical, or strict in religious and moral outlook; following the teachings of the Dutch Reformed Church.

Religious diversity did not play a significant role in South African politics. Although the vast majority of the population were Christian, the new government promoted a **secular** approach, compared to the narrow **Calvinist** outlook of the National Party government. For example, the previous school curriculum had been based on the ideology of 'Christian nationalism', but now a broader and more tolerant outlook was encouraged in the new curriculum. The Bill of Rights in the constitution guaranteed freedom of conscience, religion, thought, belief and opinion.

Foreign affairs

Under the National Party government, South Africa had become increasingly isolated internationally, excluded from many international organisations and the target of economic, cultural, sporting and diplomatic sanctions. Furthermore, it had a hostile relationship with many 'frontline' African states, which had become targets of armed intervention and military reprisals on account of their support for MK.

After 1994, after decades of isolation and sanctions, South Africa rejoined the world community. It became the 53rd member of the Organisation of African Unity (later renamed the African Union), joined the Southern African Development Community (SADC) and, after an absence of thirty-three years, rejoined the Commonwealth. The United Nations (UN) formally lifted the remaining economic sanctions (the arms embargo), and South Africa resumed its full membership of the UN.

The new democratic government did not face any foreign policy crises, but there were some tensions with other governments. For example, although there was initially a close relationship between Mandela and the US president, Bill Clinton, South Africa's open support for Cuba, Libya and the Palestinians angered the US government and led to a cooling of relations. In addition, South Africa's attempt to maintain good relations with both China and Taiwan failed and, in order to satisfy the Chinese government, it severed full diplomatic relations with Taiwan, a country with which South Africa had longstanding and significant trade and investment links.

Fact: According to the 1996 census, more than 75 per cent of South Africans were Christian. The mainstream Christian churches included Anglican, Methodist, Roman Catholic, Reformed, Orthodox, Lutheran and Presbyterian. The largest church was the Zionist Church, an African independent church, with more than ten million members. Minority religions were Hinduism (1.4 per cent), Islam (1.4 per cent) and Judaism (0.2 per cent). In the census, about 21 per cent of people did not specify their religious affiliation or described themselves as having no religion.

5.6 How did the government respond to domestic crises?

At the same time that it was trying to establish a firm foundation for democracy, the government faced opposition from political extremists and had to deal with crises resulting from the arrival of large numbers of migrants from other parts of Africa.

Political extremism and violence

Before 1994, political extremism had been a regular feature of South African politics, and acts of politically motivated violence had reached alarming levels. After the election in 1994, acts of political extremism diminished. The inclusion of Inkatha in the government led to a decrease in levels of violence between supporters of the ANC and Inkatha in Kwazulu-Natal.

Former guerrilla fighters became members of a new national defence force (the SANDF), which integrated the former apartheid-era army with an estimated 27,000 MK operatives and 6,000 members of APLA. Understandably there were some tensions with the amalgamation of these former enemies, as the historian Nigel Worden has pointed out, but these did not include political extremism. However, according to Anthony Butler in *Contemporary South Africa* (2009, p. 203), the merger was done at 'great human cost to many of the younger generation of MK volunteers' who consequently presented a 'potential source of political difficulty for the government in the future'.

A few isolated but violent incidents after 1994 showed that members of the Afrikaner right-wing were not prepared to accept the changes that had happened. The AWB itself appeared to be demoralised after its ill-advised invasion of Bophuthatswana. It was also leaderless, after its leader, Eugène Terre'Blanche, was given a six-year prison sentence in 1997 for assaulting a black petrol attendant and for the attempted murder of a security guard. However, another group calling itself *Die Boeremag* (Boer Force/Power) emerged. Its political aim was the creation of an independent Afrikaner state, or *volkstaat,* and its members were prepared to use terror to achieve it. They were responsible for a number of bombing incidents that targeted places used by black civilians, as well as thefts from army bases of ammunition and weapons, including rocket launchers, machine guns and bombs. The perpetrators of these crimes were convicted and given long prison sentences. After further plans were discovered by police, more Boeremag members were charged with treason, sabotage and terrorism-related charges.

Vigilante: a group that organises itself, without any legal authority, to fight crime.

AK-47s: assault rifles that were exported in vast quantities by the Soviet Union during the Cold War and were used in many civil wars in Africa. Large numbers were smuggled into South Africa during the liberation struggle.

Another form of extremism emerged in 1995, with the formation of People against Gangsterism and Drugs (PAGAD). Originally formed as a **vigilante** group in the poor townships around Cape Town, where gang-related crimes were common, PAGAD was a predominantly Muslim organisation that became increasingly political and anti-Western. It was believed to be responsible for an urban terror campaign in Cape Town between 1998 and 2002 that targeted gang leaders, police stations, synagogues, gay nightclubs, tourist attractions and Western-associated restaurants.

A disturbing feature of post-apartheid South Africa was the high level of violent crime. Although not politically motivated, there were links to the violence and extremism of the apartheid years because of the easy availability of weapons, especially **AK-47s**, and the low level of respect for the police force, which, in the apartheid years, had focused on political opponents rather than criminal activities. The growth of criminal gangs was a significant factor, too. The historian Nigel Worden explains that many township males who had been heroes in the township resistance of the 1980s, and who lacked the education or skills to get jobs, turned to gangsterism to 'maintain their gendered prestige as men of action'. Added to this was a breakdown of family structures, with many youths being socialised in violent street gangs. Historians Giliomee and Mbenga believe that another reason for the high crime rate was the loss of expertise from the criminal justice system, after one-third of public prosecutors resigned between 1994 and 1996, partly due to the government's transformation policies. As a result, South Africa came to have one of the highest rates of murder, armed robbery, rape, assault and car hijackings in the world, with Johannesburg gaining the reputation of being a particularly crime-ridden city.

The steps taken by the government to reduce politically motivated violence – such as the inclusion of Inkatha in the Government of National Unity, the creation of an integrated defence force and the long prison sentences for acts of terrorism – were successful overall. However, many people were highly critical of the government's inability to solve the problem of violent crime, which has remained a seemingly insurmountable challenge in subsequent years.

Issues of xenophobia

Xenophobia: a strong resentment or dislike of foreigners.

From the mid-1990s, a crisis situation concerning migrants and refugees from other African countries developed, and the government seemed unable or unwilling to tackle it effectively. There were disturbing instances of **xenophobia** towards them.

These refugees and migrant workers had been coming to South Africa for several years, but after 1994 the numbers increased substantially. The new South Africa seemed to offer peace and democracy to millions of people displaced by civil wars in Rwanda, the Democratic Republic of the Congo and Somalia, and relative prosperity to millions more escaping economic hardship in countries such as Mozambique, Zimbabwe and Malawi. There were no accurate statistics about how many refugees arrived. Historians put estimates at between three and eight million, although the 2001 official census gave a figure of only one million foreign-born people in South Africa, the majority of them male. Many of them brought valuable skills and a determination to work hard to improve their lives. Most went to live in the black townships and informal settlements of cities and towns around the country, where unemployment levels were high, and there were severe shortages of housing and services.

In many places the refugees were treated with resentment and hostility, with South Africans claiming that they put a strain on the economy and that they contributed to rising crime levels. They were seen as a threat to jobs, houses and livelihoods. As Butler notes in *Contemporary South Africa* (2009, p. 204) they were 'popularly viewed as competitors for work as well as scapegoated for disease and crime'. People called on the government to strengthen border controls and to return refugees to their countries of origin. Some even believed that refugees should be denied basic rights, such as freedom of speech and movement, police protection and access to services. This hostility sometimes turned into acts of violent brutality. Shops and houses belonging to refugees were looted and burnt, and people were attacked and killed, sometimes in the most gruesome manner.

Jonathan Crush, the director of the Southern African Migration Project, noted that 'apartheid-era solidarities between black people of whatever national origin

Figure 5.14 Although government efforts to curb xenophobia were largely ineffective, civil society organisations coordinated protests and campaigns to raise awareness of the issue. However, ongoing violence towards migrants and refugees continued, disturbing signs of intolerance in the new democracy

Fact: The 2001 census showed that the one million foreign-born residents officially counted had a higher level of education than the average South African (more than 20 per cent had post-school qualifications, compared to only 8 per cent of South Africans) and a higher level of employment (61 per cent compared to 33 per cent).

QUESTION

Explain how political extremism and xenophobia threatened the evolution of a working democracy in South Africa.

were crumbling' in the post-apartheid era. In 1997 the South African Human Rights Commission identified xenophobia as a major source of concern to human rights and democracy, and launched a public and media education programme called the 'Roll Back Xenophobia Campaign' to tackle the problem. This created greater awareness of the issue, but did not stop the continuing xenophobic attacks. Government attempts to limit the number of refugees, or to offer them security and protection were largely ineffective. Instead, the new government, which had maintained much of the policing infrastructure of the apartheid government, now used it 'aggressively to curtail the opportunities of migrants to South Africa or to expel them', according to Anthony Butler (2009, *Contemporary South Africa*, p. 204).

5.7 What were the challenges relating to equality, equity and civil protests?

Equality: when everyone is equal and has the same rights and opportunities.

Equity: when everyone is treated fairly and equally; fairness; impartiality.

In addition to political extremism and xenophobia, the government faced other challenges. The most difficult to resolve were the struggle for **equality** and **equity** and land reform. Dissatisfaction with the government's handling of these issues led to the formation of civil society organisations (CSOs) to address them and to tensions within the ruling tripartite alliance.

Issues relating to equality and equity

Colonialism and apartheid had created one of the most unequal societies in the world in South Africa, and the differences were clearly marked along racial lines. In **Source G**, historian Leonard Thompson describes the situation in 1994.

SOURCE G

The country had one of the greatest gaps in the world between rich and poor, and although new multiracial classes were forming, the gap marked primarily a division between races ... Most white South Africans were well-to-do, well educated and well housed. Most Africans, like most people of tropical Africa, were poor, badly educated and ill housed. The conditions of the coloured and Indian members of the population were in between those of whites and Africans.

L. *Thompson (2006),* A History of South Africa, *Cape Town: Jonathan Ball Publishers, p. 258.*

This situation had not changed significantly by 1998 when, in a speech to parliament on the theme of reconciliation and nation-building, Thabo Mbeki referred to South Africa as a land of two nations (see **Source H**).

SOURCE H

South Africa is a country of two nations. One of these nations is white, relatively prosperous, regardless of gender or geographic dispersal. It has ready access to a developed economic, physical, educational, communication and other infrastructure ...

The second and larger nation of South Africa is black and poor, with the worst affected being women in the rural areas, the black rural population in general and the disabled. This nation lives under conditions of a grossly underdeveloped economic, physical, educational, communication and other infrastructure ...

This reality of two nations, underwritten by the perpetuation of the racial, gender and spatial disparities born of a very long period of colonial and apartheid white minority domination, constitutes the material base which reinforces the notion that, indeed, we are not one nation, but two nations. And neither are we becoming one nation. Consequently, also, the objective of national reconciliation is not being realised.

Speech by deputy president Thabo Mbeki to the National Assembly at the opening of a debate on 'Reconciliation and Nation Building', Cape Town, 29 May 1998.

ACTIVITY

Compare and contrast the views expressed in **Sources G** and **H** about the links between poverty, affluence and race in post-apartheid South Africa. What, according to Mbeki, were the causes and effects of this situation? Read **Source I**. Explain whether it confirms or contradicts the views expressed in **Sources G** and **H**.

By the year 2001, the poverty and inequality that were marked features of South Africa were still evident. A study by the Human Sciences Research Council, comparing the results of the 1996 and 2001 census figures, showed that about 57 per cent of the population were still living below the poverty income line, unchanged from 1996, and that the degree of poverty had become worse. It also showed that the gap between rich and poor had widened, and that the **Gini index**, used to measure inequality in societies, had increased from 0.69 in 1996 to 0.77 in 2001, making South Africa one of the most unequal societies in the world.

Table 5.3 The inequality between rich and poor in South Africa in 1998

% of households	% of income	% of population
Richest 10% of households	40	7
Poorest 40% of households	11	50

By 2000, however, this inequality was no longer so clearly defined along racial lines. The highest levels of inequality were among the African population.

Gini index (or Gini coefficient) – used by economists to measure inequality of income or wealth. It can vary between 0 (complete equality) and 1 (high inequality). In 2009, South Africa overtook Brazil as the country with the highest levels of inequality

Theory of Knowledge

History and statistics:
How do statistics, such as those in Table 5.3 or referred to in other parts of this chapter, help historians to reach conclusions about the state of transformation in South Africa? What are the dangers of using statistics as historical sources?

SOURCE I

During the 1990s the black elite – politicians, bureaucrats, entrepreneurs, managers, businessmen – prospered as never before, many acquiring the lifestyle and status symbols so prized in South Africa – executive cars, swimming pools, domestic staff, private-school education, golf handicaps and foreign holidays. Perhaps 5 per cent of the black community reached middle-class status. But for the majority, the same struggle against poverty continued.

M. Meredith (2005), The State of Africa: A History of Fifty Years of Independence, *Cape Town: Jonathan Ball Publishers, p. 662.*

The issue of land reform

One of the key factors responsible for the high levels of inequality was land ownership. Land reform was an issue that people expected the government to address urgently after 1994. Most of the arable land was owned by white commercial farmers, which was a legacy going back to the days of colonialism. The problem had been aggravated by apartheid legislation, under which nearly four million people had been forcibly removed from their houses or land. According to a report compiled by the Democracy and Governance Research Programme of the Human Sciences Research Council in 2003, black farmers controlled only about 16 per cent of arable land in 1994, most of it in the former homelands. An added complication was that ownership of much of the land in these former homelands was held by traditional rulers on behalf of their people.

Redistribution: making grants available for the purchase of land for farming or settlement.

Restitution: the restoration of land lost through racially discriminatory laws or cash compensation for victims of forced removals.

The new government planned to bring about a more just and equitable share of land through **redistribution** and **restitution**. It hoped that, within five years, 30 per cent of all farmland would be owned by black farmers. Parliament established a Land Claims Commission to investigate land claims, and a Land Claims Court to settle disputes. A large number of urban land claims were settled, but the more complicated rural ones, sometimes involving whole communities, were more difficult to resolve. As property rights had been recognised in the constitution, the present owners could not be forced to hand over the land, so the success of the process partly depended on the willingness of white landowners to sell their land to the government, and also on the amount of money the government allocated to land reform. The target of 30 per cent was not achieved, and in five years less than 2 per cent of the land was re-allocated to black owners through redistribution or restitution. In 2000, the distribution of land remained very inequitable.

Many historians and political analysts expressed surprise about the seeming lack of urgency on the part of the government to address land reform issues. They pointed to

KEY CONCEPTS QUESTION

Cause and Consequence: What were the causes and consequences of continuing inequality in South African society after 1994?

Figure 5.15 The slow pace of land reform triggered protests and increasing dissatisfaction with government policies the slow pace of land reform under Robert Mugabe's government in neighbouring Zimbabwe which led to land invasions, the collapse of the agricultural economy and other severe political and economic crises. Many of them predicted that the unresolved issue of land reform would pose critical problems in the future, and create political and ethnic tensions.

Civil society protests

South Africa had a rich history of civil society activism, notably during the 1950s, a decade of non-violent protest and civil disobedience, and more especially during the 1980s when community organisations played a critical role in the mass protests against apartheid.

An important civil society organisation, the Institute for Democracy in South Africa (IDASA), was established in the mid-1980s to explore democratic alternatives to the politics of repression. Between 1990 and 1994, it ran programmes to enable members of the old and new orders to work together to build democratic structures, and after 1994 it focused on promoting a culture of democracy. In a 2003 report, it noted that CSOs were weakened after 1994, when many former civil society leaders moved into positions in government. With the liberation movement in power, they believed that there was less need for them to act as watchdogs. This view is backed up by political analyst Xolela Mangcu (see **Source J**).

SOURCE J

One of the unfortunate consequences of the transition to democracy was the decline in the quantity and quality of civic leadership as former civic leaders took up new roles in government and others pursued opportunities in business and elsewhere. An oft-asked question by those in power was 'what do we need civil society for now that we have a government of the people?' Civil society began to lose its special place in the language of development. Civil society organisations were seen as at best a nuisance and at worst a threat to the democratic government.

X. Mangcu (2008), To the Brink: The State of Democracy in South Africa, *Scottsville: University of Kwazulu-Natal Press, pp. 123–4.*

Some CSOs continued to play an important watchdog role in defending civil rights. One example of this was the Treatment Action Campaign, which appealed successfully to the Constitutional Court to force the government to supply **antiretroviral** medication to HIV-infected people (you will read more about this issue in Unit 5.3). This ruling was also evidence of the importance of the Constitutional Court, as well as other statutory bodies such as the Human Rights Commission, in upholding civil rights.

Other civil society organisations that played important roles included the Freedom of Expression Institute and the Institute for Reconciliation and Justice. Other CSOs focused on land issues: the National Land Committee criticised the slow pace of land reform, while the Landless People's Project focused on the rights of farm workers and the need for more ambitious land reform policies.

Fact: One measure of the strength of a democracy is the participation of civil society organisations as pressure groups. Civil society includes churches, trade unions, human rights and environmental groups as well as a wider variety of organisations often loosely referred to as CSOs (civil society organisations) or NGOs (non-governmental organisations).

Historical debate: According to historian Tom Lodge, another reason for the declining influence of CSOs was that many of them had depended on foreign funding, which dried up when the anti-apartheid struggle came to an end in 1994 and funders redirected their money to government programmes. Nevertheless, Richard Calland, an independent political analyst, believed that CSOs continued to represent a powerful counterbalance to state and corporate power. Giliomee and Mbenga suggest that after 1999 there was a reawakening of civil society, because the government under Mbeki had lost the 'moral authority' it previously had under Mandela.

Antiretrovirals: drugs that have proved effective in slowing down the development of AIDS in HIV-infected patients; they halt the progress of the infection but do not cure it. They were initially very expensive, but cheaper generic drugs are now being produced for use in developing countries.

Figure 5.16 Supporters of the Treatment Action Campaign (TAC) at a rally in Cape Town prior to a protest march on the South African parliament in February 2002; the TAC was demanding that the government announce its intentions about the provision of antiretrovirals for HIV-positive people

Tensions within the Tripartite Alliance

Before the 1994 election, the ANC had formed the Tripartite Alliance with the SACP and COSATU. Some leaders of the alliance partners played crucial roles in the pre-election negotiations. They included Joe Slovo and Chris Hani of the SACP and Cyril Ramaphosa of COSATU. Some important features of the constitution, such as proportional representation and a presidency limited to two terms, were suggested by COSATU. The cooperation between the alliance partners continued after the election, with SACP members holding key positions in government and parliament. In this way the alliance partners formed an important pressure group. This was demonstrated in a series of strikes in the mid-1990s by COSATU-affiliated unions to put pressure on government and business when new labour legislation was being negotiated.

However, there were deep divisions within the alliance over the direction of government policies, especially economic policy and issues relating to the transformation of society. The initial focus of government policy had been on redistribution and transformation in the Reconstruction and Development Programme (RDP) but in 1996 the focus shifted to economic growth, and the Growth, Employment and Reconstruction Programme

(GEAR), which was based on the principles of free market capitalism, replaced the RDP (see Unit 5.3). Many members of the SACP and COSATU believed that the ANC had betrayed the liberation movement and departed from the principles of the Freedom Charter, on which ANC policies had been based since 1955. Relations within the Tripartite Alliance became increasingly strained, and in 1998 both Mandela and Mbeki publicly censured the SACP and COSATU for their criticism of the government's economic policies.

Many political observers predicted that the alliance would disintegrate and that COSATU and the SACP would re-group as a left-wing opposition to the ANC. This did not happen, however, and historian Tom Lodge attributes this to the fact that COSATU leaders preferred to have access to and influence on government, rather than opposition to and exclusion from it.

End of unit activities

1. Design a table to summarise the work of the Truth and Reconciliation Commission (TRC). Include information on each of these aspects: aims; workings; debates; findings; successes; failures.
2. Write a report to summarise the threats posed by political extremism and violence before and after the 1994 election.
3. Design a spider diagram to illustrate the issue of land reform. Include information on the historic causes of the problems, obstacles in the way of their successful resolution, and the results (successes and failures) of government attempts to solve them. Use the information you have read in this unit, and any other information you can find. You may start off by looking at www.overcomingapartheid.msu.edu/unit.php?id=65-24E-4&page=2.
4. Find out about the role played by a civil society organisation, such as the Institute for Democracy in South Africa (IDASA), the Treatment Action Campaign (TAC), the Institute for Justice and Reconciliation (IJR) or the Landless People's Project in promoting human rights.
5. Divide into two groups. One group should work out an argument to support, and the other group an argument to oppose, the following statement: 'In spite of the formidable challenges facing South Africa in 2000, the achievements of the previous decade in establishing a democratic state were truly remarkable.'

3 Unit The impact of democracy on South African society

TIMELINE

1994 **Sept:** Launch of Reconstruction and Development Programme (RDP).

1995 **Feb:** National Economic Development and Labour Council (NEDLAC) established.

Dec: Labour Relations Act.

1996 **Mar:** Trevor Manuel becomes minister of finance; RDP office closes.

Jun: Manuel announces Growth, Employment and Redistribution (GEAR).

1997 **Oct:** Basic Conditions of Employment Act.

Dec: The African National Congress (ANC) adopts policy of Black Economic Empowerment (BEE); Mbeki becomes president of the ANC.

1998 **Dec:** Recognition of Customary Marriages Act; formation of the Treatment Action Campaign (TAC); Employment Equity Act.

1999 **Jun:** Second democratic election; Mbeki succeeds Mandela as president of South Africa.

2000 **Feb:** Promotion of Access to Information Act.

KEY QUESTIONS

- What economic and social policies did the government implement?
- To what extent did people benefit from these policies?
- What was the cultural impact of the establishment of democracy?

Overview

- The government introduced an ambitious Reconstruction and Development Programme (RDP) in 1994 to restructure society and redistribute wealth. But the focus changed from redistribution to economic growth with the introduction of Growth, Employment and Redistribution (GEAR) to replace the RDP.
- Neither economic policy succeeded in reducing unemployment, which reached more than 40 per cent by 2001. However, the informal sector provided a source of income for millions.
- New labour legislation gave greater power to trade unions, provided mechanisms for solving industrial disputes, improved working conditions, and gave preference for employment to those disadvantaged by previous labour practices.
- The government extended the provision of social welfare grants, and the number of families dependent on them grew as the unemployment figures rose.
- Efforts to rectify the inequality and dysfunctions in the education system were unsuccessful, despite a great deal of attention and funding being directed at education reform.
- The focus of government health care moved to primary health care, but progress was overshadowed by the rapid spread of HIV and AIDS. The health policies of the Mbeki government aggravated the AIDS crisis.
- The government used affirmative action to transform the civil service, and introduced Black Economic Empowerment (BEE) to end white domination and control of the economy.
- The position of women improved with the passing of laws to promote equality, and the establishment of a commission to promote and monitor gender equality. The number of women representatives in parliament and government increased substantially.

- The ambitious economic and social policies introduced by the government improved the daily lives of millions of people, but fundamental economic and social transformation was more difficult to achieve; two of the biggest challenges still facing South Africa in 2000 were poverty and inequality.
- Significant challenges affecting the position of women remained, such as the impact of AIDS, high levels of violence against women, the effects of poverty, and inequalities resulting from customary law.
- Before 1994, European notions of art and culture had predominated, but in the new South Africa there was a wider interpretation of what constituted the cultural heritage of the country and a greater emphasis on African cultural traditions.
- The apartheid government had used censorship and restrictions to limit freedom of expression, but democracy brought greater freedom of expression in the arts and media.

5.8 What economic and social policies did the government implement?

Although fundamental political change had taken place in 1994, it was harder to bring about meaningful economic and social transformation. Another legacy of the past was a huge imbalance in the standard of living and the quality of services that had been provided by the apartheid government.

Policies to address the distribution of wealth

Many people, especially those in poor rural communities, had high expectations that the new democratically elected government would provide land, running water, electricity, houses, clinics, schools and jobs. But the challenges facing the new government were considerable, and the economy was not sound. It had been weakened by years of economic sanctions, isolationist economic policies and the high cost of implementing and defending apartheid. The apartheid government had also run up substantial debts.

Before the election, the African National Congress (ANC) had drafted a Reconstruction and Development Programme (RDP), and soon after coming to power in 1994 the Government of National Unity implemented it. It was an ambitious socio-economic plan to restructure society and redistribute wealth. These aims were in line with the traditional policies of the ANC, outlined in the Freedom Charter in 1955, which had called for state ownership of key sectors of the economy. However, by the time it came to power, the ANC had abandoned its support for nationalisation, despite continuing calls for it from the South African Communist Party (SACP) and Congress of South African Trade Unions (COSATU), its partners in the Tripartite Alliance.

The RDP included plans to build 300,000 new houses a year, provide the whole population with access to clean water, sanitation and electricity, and improve health,

Figure 5.17 Under the Reconstruction and Development Programme, thousands of rural communities were supplied with piped water for the first time. This ensured a clean water supply and meant that women no longer had to spend hours each day carrying water from distant well points

Trevor Manuel (b. 1956)

He was a founder member of the United Democratic Front, who was imprisoned several times by the apartheid government. In 1994, he became minister of trade, industries and tourism, and from 1996 served as finance minister. He was highly rated by business leaders and opposition parties, and his policies were credited with creating the longest period of economic growth in decades. COSATU was critical of his support for GEAR.

Privatisation: the transfer of ownership of state enterprises to private companies. Privatisation is a key feature of global capitalist economic policies favoured by the World Bank and the International Monetary Fund.

education and welfare services. The money allocated to welfare services was increased, and free health care was announced for young children.

However, it was soon clear that the goals of the RDP were unrealistic, as there was simply not enough funding to make up the shortfall. In 1996, the economic policy emphasis shifted from redistribution to economic growth when the RDP office was closed and the new minister of finance, **Trevor Manuel**, announced a new Growth, Employment and Reconstruction Programme (GEAR), which included features such as the **privatisation** of state-owned enterprises. This was based on the principles of free market capitalism, which the government hoped would encourage overseas investment, increase exports and make South Africa more competitive in the global economy. It was hoped that these developments would create jobs and economic growth, which would in turn raise revenue to improve living standards and provide services. In spite of the change of focus, however, the government spent nearly 48 per cent of its 1998/9 budget on social services, including education, health, welfare and housing.

The SACP and COSATU were angered by the change of policy and by the fact that they had not been consulted. They believed that GEAR would do little to redress the imbalances of the past and would create even greater inequality. Some of their leaders accused the ANC of betraying the revolution.

SOURCE A

Figure 5.18 A cartoon by Zapiro about the tensions in the Tripartite Alliance caused by a change in economic policy. It was published in the *Mail* and *Guardian* on 25 July 1996. The figure on the left is the finance minister Trevor Manuel, a prominent member of the ANC. With him in the boat are Mbhazima Shilowa and Jeremy Cronin, leading members of COSATU and the SACP respectively

ACTIVITY

What is the message of the cartoon in **Source A**? How does it illustrate the tensions in the Tripartite Alliance? Who do the figures in the background represent? Explain their differing reactions.

GEAR had mixed results. Although foreign investment increased, it was not at the levels that the government had hoped. The legacies of past policies, such as a poorly skilled workforce and low productivity, hampered economic growth and deterred foreign investors. Many South African companies were not sufficiently competitive globally. Despite all this, business leaders credited Trevor Manuel and Tito Mboweni, who became governor of the Reserve Bank in 1999, with creating a stable economy and a sound framework for future economic growth. In 1994, the government had inherited a bankrupt economy, in which people were getting poorer and economic growth was negative, and managed to turn this around. From 1995, South Africa experienced good economic growth at an average of 3.2 per cent per year (until the world economic crisis in 2008), and the rate of inflation dropped to around 6 per cent (from about 15 per cent in 1990).

Policies to reduce unemployment

When the new government came to power in 1994, there were high levels of unemployment. As with so many features of South African society, there was an uneven pattern along racial lines.

Table 5.4 Percentage of the population aged 15 and above who were unemployed in 1995

African	37%
Coloured	22%
Indian	15%
White	6%

Both the RDP and GEAR aimed to increase levels of employment, but neither succeeded in achieving this. COSATU blamed GEAR for the job losses caused by privatisation, claiming in 2000 that half a million jobs had been lost since the ANC came into power. The 2001 census put the overall unemployment rate at 41.6 per cent. However, as in other developing countries, many people were employed in the informal sector, selling simple goods or providing basic services. It was estimated that the informal sector made up more than 20 per cent of the labour market.

Policies to regulate labour relations

Historical debate:
Historians point out that there were negative aspects to the progressive new labour laws. Nigel Worden notes that they ensured that wage levels were well above those in countries in Asia and Latin America, making South Africa less competitive in the global economy. There were also concerns about the continuing lack of skills and low productivity. Leonard Thompson observes that the new labour legislation gave more power to trade unions than was usual in industrialised countries.

Labour relations in the apartheid era were characterised by discrimination, the repression of unions, conflict and authoritarian styles of management. The new government, prompted by the ANC's alliance partner COSATU, set about amending the country's labour legislation by establishing the National Economic Development and Labour Council (NEDLAC), on which the government, organised labour and organised business were represented equally. The basic functions of NEDLAC were to coordinate and integrate economic, labour and social policy.

In 1995, the Labour Relations Act was passed, to resolve the problems created by previous labour legislation, which had resulted in a large number of strikes over workers' rights and working conditions. The new law established a Council for Conciliation, Mediation and Arbitration (CCMA) to resolve industrial disputes, and a Labour Court to interpret the application of the act. In 1998, more than 81,000 cases were referred to the CCMA, most of them involving disputes about the unfair dismissal of workers.

The Labour Relations Act encouraged the growth of trade unions, and by 1998 more than 75 per cent of workers in registered employment belonged to a union. However, as registered employment did not include farm workers, domestic workers or those employed in the informal sector, this represented only about 30 per cent of the economically active population. As a result of the new measures, the number of strikes declined significantly in comparison with the period before the 1994 election.

The Basic Conditions of Employment Act of 1997 outlined detailed regulations regarding hours of work, wages and a range of issues relating to working conditions. The Employment Equity Act of 1998 aimed to reverse previous discriminatory practices by nominating blacks, women and the disabled as workers who had been historically disadvantaged, and who therefore deserved preference in employment. Pressure was put on private companies that employed fifty people or more, to ensure that their workforce was broadly representative of the population.

Policies to extend social welfare

Against the background of changing economic policies, the government was addressing the issue of social welfare. Before the new government took office in 1994, 2.6 million people were receiving some form of social security grant. The system inherited from the apartheid government had favoured the white minority by providing racially differentiated benefits. The challenge facing the new government was to implement the undertaking in the constitution that everybody had the right to social security. However, it would not be financially possible to provide the level of benefits previously available to the white minority. The challenge was therefore to equalise and extend the system of social grants to all those who could not support themselves, by providing state old age pensions, child support, foster care, disability grants and care dependency grants.

There was a significant improvement in social security benefits. Pensions were increased and a child support grant was introduced. These grants, initially provided for children up to the age of seven, were later extended to the age of fourteen, with calls from COSATU to extend this provision even further. With growing levels of unemployment, this was a formidable challenge to government resources, as the proportion of people contributing to government revenues by paying income tax declined.

Reforms in education

One of the worst legacies of the apartheid era was the education system. There were fifteen separate education departments – one for each race, province and homeland. There was a huge disparity in the quality of schools: those for white students generally offered a good standard of education, but those in the townships and rural areas did not. As a result of apartheid policies, black schools were overcrowded and under-resourced, many teachers were underqualified and buildings were run-down. Not surprisingly, drop-out and failure rates were high in these schools.

Table 5.5 Pass rates in 1993, according to population group. The pass rates shown illustrate the disparity in the quality of education provided under the system of apartheid education

Population group (as classified under apartheid)	Percentage of students passing the school leaving examinations, 1993
African	39%
Coloured	86%
Indian	93%
White	95%

Although the legal segregation of schools had ended by 1994, in reality only a relatively small number of black students attended schools formerly reserved for whites. One problem facing many black schools was that a culture of learning and teaching had never recovered from the schools boycotts of the 1980s, when students had demanded 'liberation before education'. Schools were often lawless places, where teachers had little authority and not much learning took place.

The government unified the many departments into one national department of education, and revised the curriculum. Thousands of new schools were built. Student-teacher ratios were improved to reduce class sizes, and primary schooling was made compulsory for all children. Special attention was paid to the more disadvantaged provinces, most of which comprised former homeland areas. The education budget was increased substantially from 1994 onwards, exceeding the proportion of the **gross domestic product (GDP)** spent on education in many other countries.

Gross domestic product (GDP): the total value of goods produced and services provided in a country during a year.

However, despite the reforms, restructuring and increased funding, little progress was made. Conditions in many schools remained chaotic and teacher morale was low. Fewer and fewer people were choosing teaching as a profession, and there was a serious shortage of teachers, especially in mathematics and science, where pass rates were shockingly low. The situation was further aggravated in 1996 when a large number of teachers accepted retrenchment packages offered by the government, resulting in a further drain of skills. There was a decline in the number of students passing the school-leaving examination, from 58 per cent in 1994 to 49 per cent in 1998.

Some education experts believed that a root cause of the problem was a language issue. African students, whose home language was not English, made up 80 per cent of the school-going population. Up until 1993, their mother tongue was used as the language of instruction up until Grade 5 (age ten and eleven), after which lessons were taught in English. After 1994, parents were given the choice of deciding which of the eleven official languages should be used as the medium of instruction, and from which grade. Historians Hermann Giliomee and Bernard Mbenga describe the effects of this new ruling in **Source B**.

SOURCE B

The parents, transfixed by the image of English as the language of economic progress, international achievement and perhaps even of liberation, eschewed [rejected] the proven benefits of home language learning during the early years of schooling, and the use of English has well-nigh exploded. The number of primary schools using English as a medium of instruction increased from 33% in 1991 to 55% in 1998 and then expanded even further.

H. Giliomee and B. Mbenga (2007), New History of South Africa*, Cape Town: Tafelberg, p. 431.*

An additional problem was that not all children attended school because the government could not fulfil its commitment to provide free education for all. Improvements in school infrastructure were slow, and by 2002, 28 per cent of schools still had no running water, 43 per cent no electricity and 78 per cent no libraries.

Health reforms

Another legacy of the apartheid government was a disparity in the provision and quality of health services. Leading city hospitals were well-resourced and offered standards of surgery and health care that were among the best in the world, while the provision of health care in rural areas was extremely poor. Under the new government, the focus shifted from the provision of curative medicines and costly technology to the provision of preventive medicines and primary health care. As part of the RDP, the government reduced funding to city hospitals and focused instead on building clinics in deprived areas.

While all this was happening, South Africa was in the early stages of what later became a national crisis. This was the rapid spread of AIDS and the HIV virus that caused it. The first cases of AIDS in Africa had been confirmed in the early 1980s. Before long, an area of southern Uganda and northern Tanzania became the centre of the first AIDS epidemic anywhere in the world to affect the general population. By 1989, an official survey showed that 800,000 Ugandans were HIV positive. From there the disease spread, mainly along trucking routes and helped by the movement of migrant workers, refugees and soldiers. However, a survey carried out by the World Health Organization in 1990 showed that central Africa was still the region most severely affected by AIDS.

At that stage Southern Africa did not seem to be at risk, although some far-sighted people saw the dangers. One of them was Chris Hani, the SACP and MK leader who was assassinated in 1993. He spoke frankly about the threat of HIV/AIDS in 1990, the year in which the ANC, SACP and PAC were unbanned, and members of the liberation movement started to return to South Africa from exile (see **Source C**).

SOURCE C

Those of us in exile are especially in the unfortunate situation of being in the areas where the incidence of the disease is high. We cannot afford to allow the AIDS epidemic to ruin the realisation of our dreams. Existing statistics indicate that we are still at the beginning of the AIDS epidemic in our country. Unattended, however, this will result in untold damage and suffering by the end of the century.

Chris Hani, quoted in N. Nattrass (2007), Mortal Combat: AIDS Denialism and the Struggle for Antiretrovirals in South Africa, *Scottsville: University of Kwazulu-Natal Press, p. 75.*

QUESTION

Explain how the AIDS epidemic could 'ruin the realisation of our dreams', as Chris Hani believed.

In 1990, the prevalence of the HIV virus was already being detected in regular blood tests of pregnant women attending clinics in rural Kwazulu-Natal. However, neither the apartheid government, nor the Government of National Unity after 1994, took appropriate steps to control the spread of the virus.

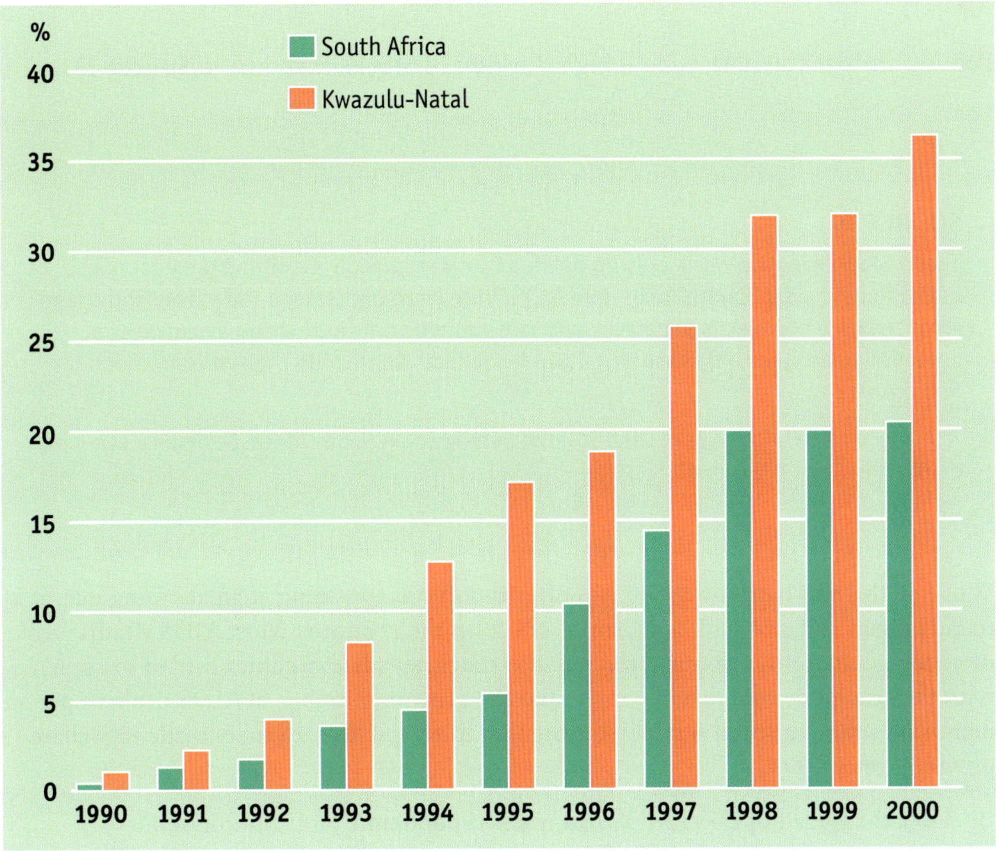

Figure 5.19 This graph from the Department of Community Health at the University of Kwazulu-Natal shows the dramatic growth of HIV infections in South Africa between 1990 and 2000, especially in the province of Kwazulu-Natal. The figures show the percentage of women attending antenatal clinics who were infected with HIV

QUESTION

How did the health policies of the government have both positive and negative effects?

Dissident: someone who opposes the authorities or mainstream views.

Theory of Knowledge

History and language:
The writer of **Source D** is obviously highly critical of Mbeki and uses emotive language to describe the impact of his policies. How could Mbeki's legacy be explained in more neutral language? How is language linked to bias in history?

Pandemic: an infectious disease that spreads on a global scale; the large number of infections makes a pandemic more serious than an epidemic.

Theory of Knowledge

Science versus tradition:
The rapid spread of AIDS in South Africa has sometimes been linked to a conflict between science and tradition in attitudes towards the treatment of AIDS. Some people have rejected modern drugs in favour of traditional 'cures' and beliefs and harmful superstitions. How can health departments in developing countries deal with such issues when combating fatal epidemics?

Although Mandela later became an outspoken supporter of AIDS awareness campaigns, during his term as president he did not focus much attention on it, and it was his deputy president, Thabo Mbeki, who became involved in controversial debates about the causes and treatment of AIDS. Mbeki argued that AIDS was a Western disease and that there was a racist agenda behind reports of the prevalence and spread of the disease in Africa. He questioned the effectiveness of antiretroviral drugs, claiming that they were toxic and suggesting that the pharmaceutical companies had ulterior motives in promoting them.

In a study on the history of AIDS in Africa, historian John Iliffe suggests that the Mandela government could never have prevented the rise in HIV prevalence because of the high levels of migration from other parts of the African continent to South Africa at the time and the different strains of the virus that came with this migration. But medical experts and historians agree that the impact of the disease was aggravated by Mbeki's stance on AIDS. When Mbeki succeeded Mandela as president in 1999, he appointed a controversial minister of health who refused to allow government hospitals and clinics to supply the antiretroviral drugs that had proved to be effective in countries such as Uganda. Mbeki also appointed an AIDS advisory panel that included several international **dissident** scientists who held the minority view that HIV did not cause AIDS.

Political analyst Xolela Mangcu is highly critical of Mbeki, as shown in **Source D**.

SOURCE D

Thabo Mbeki's legacy will largely be defined by his intransigence on the greatest public health threat facing South Africa – HIV/AIDS. In order to understand the gravity and sheer irresponsibility of Mbeki's apparent denialism we need only look at the evolution of a potentially manageable disease into a pandemic that has claimed the lives of millions of South Africans.

X. Mangcu (2008), To the Brink: The State of Democracy in South Africa, *Scottsville: University of Kwazulu-Natal Press, p. 49.*

While all this was happening, the rate of infection was spreading at an alarming rate, at a tragic human cost and with a disastrous effect on the economy. Most AIDS deaths were of young adults, so the labour force was affected; hospitals and clinics battled to cope with the rising tide of infected people; and the growing number of AIDS orphans put an increasing strain on social services, threatening to reverse the advances made in welfare provision since 1994.

By 2000, the spread of HIV/AIDS had reached **pandemic** proportions. About 4.2 million people in South Africa were infected with HIV, more than any other country in the world. Mbeki's denial of the link between HIV and AIDS was taking a devastating human and economic toll.

Policies affecting minorities

Until 1994, South Africa had had a white minority government that discriminated against the indigenous majority of the population. Many whites had feared that a change to majority rule would mean that they in turn would become victims of discrimination.

But ANC policy was based on a long tradition of non-racialism going back to the Freedom Charter in 1955, which had stated that 'South Africa belongs to all who live in it, black and white', so the ANC firmly believed that this concept should become the basis for the new democracy. The new constitution and its Bill of Rights quite clearly upheld the concept of equality for all, regardless of 'race, gender, sex, pregnancy, marital status, ethnic or social origin, colour, sexual orientation, age, disability, religion, conscience, belief, culture, language and birth' – an extensive list that went further than most bills of rights. In addition, the constitution established a Human Rights Commission and a Commission for the Promotion and Protection of the Rights of Cultural, Religious and Linguistic Communities to ensure that minority rights were upheld.

Despite this commitment to non-racialism and equality for all, the transformation of South Africa into a working democracy required a major restructuring of the civil service. A vast bureaucracy of two million civil servants, dominated by male Afrikaners, had administered the country under the apartheid system. Many of them did not share the new government's vision of transformation, but their employment was protected by the sunset clauses. Determined to make the civil service broadly representative of the population, the government advertised 11,000 **affirmative action** positions. Race and gender, rather than individual merit, were to be the key criteria for appointment and promotion. At the same time, attractive early retirement packages were offered to existing civil servants, and by the end of 1998 nearly 57,000 had been granted, and a further 60,000 over the next four years, at a high cost to the government. The process had a dramatic effect on the composition of the civil service: between 1994 and 1999, the percentage of posts held by whites dropped from 44 per cent to 18 per cent.

The government also adopted a policy of Black Economic Empowerment (BEE), to increase black ownership and control of companies, and to create a new class of black small businessmen. It hoped to achieve this by making access to capital more readily available, and by promoting and upgrading skills and management training.

Policies to improve the position of women

South Africa's new constitution enshrined the principle of gender equality, recognising men and women as equal citizens with equal rights, including the right to freedom from unfair discrimination. In addition to race and gender, the Bill of Rights listed other grounds for unfair discrimination that had previously affected the rights of women, such as pregnancy, marital status, sexual orientation, age and disability. As a result, the government assumed a responsibility to transform the lives of women. Furthermore, black women in particular benefitted from the state's commitment to affirmative action policies.

KEY CONCEPTS QUESTION

Cause and Consequence: What were the causes and consequences of the AIDS epidemic in South Africa?

Affirmative action: measures taken to favour people who have been treated unfairly in the past, especially on the grounds of race or gender.

QUESTION

What are the similarities and differences between affirmative action and BEE?

Historical debate: Historians Hermann Giliomee and Bernard Mbenga suggest that the principle of equality enshrined in the constitution was compromised by affirmative action. However, another historian, Christopher Saunders, notes that provision had been made in the constitution to permit race-based legislation to remedy the inequalities of the past.

QUESTION

What evidence is there that the government was committed to improving the position of women?

A Commission on Gender Equality was set up to promote equality in all spheres of society, paying special attention to the most disadvantaged women – those living in rural areas, and those in agricultural or domestic work. It also made recommendations on legislation affecting the status of women. Parliament enacted several new laws aimed at furthering gender equality, covering issues such as domestic violence, the right to terminate pregnancies, employment equity and the abolition of the minority status of women in customary marriages.

Parliament also established a special committee to monitor the government's implementation of United Nations (UN) resolutions adopted at the UN World Conference on Women in 1995. This committee recommended strategies to improve the lives of women most affected by poverty, violence and HIV/AIDS. This had practical results when government departments implemented them in their programmes. For example, the Working for Water Programme of the Department of Water Affairs, set up to clear alien vegetation to improve water catchment areas, stipulated that more than 50 per cent of the jobs created had to go to women, and that more than 60 per cent of them had to be in rural areas.

Within its own ranks, the ANC, as the ruling party, applied a quota for women representatives, and this ensured that a significant number of women became public representatives in parliament and in government.

Figure 5.20 The Working for Water Project was an extended Public Works Programme which aimed to alleviate poverty through job creation and skills development for rural communities, especially women. One of their key activities was to clear alien vegetation from water catchment areas

5.9 To what extent did people benefit from these policies?

The ambitious economic and social policies introduced by the government after 1994 improved the daily lives of millions of people. However, fundamental economic and social transformation was more difficult to achieve. Two of the biggest challenges which still faced South Africa in 2000 were poverty and inequality. Hopes of combating these would largely depend on factors such as good economic growth to reduce unemployment, and improved access to good-quality education to raise skills levels. At the same time, the rapid spread of HIV and AIDS was putting an increasing strain on government resources and productivity levels, and threatening to reverse some of the advances that had been made.

The effects of economic policies

Under the RDP, living conditions for millions of people improved. Hundreds of thousands of state-subsidised houses were built, and progress was made in supplying piped water to remote areas and electricity to townships. A 2001 government report summarised some of the progress that had been made: 1.2 million houses built, more than 7 million people supplied with access to free basic water and 3.5 million electricity grid connections made. However, millions of people still lacked running water or electricity, and many continued to build their own houses in sprawling informal settlements.

Although both the RDP and GEAR put measures in place to create jobs, unemployment remained a serious problem, and contributed to continuing poverty and rising crime levels.

For those in formal employment, however, conditions of work improved. Legislation such as the Basic Conditions of Employment Act regulated hours, wages and working conditions, while the Employment Equity Act gave new opportunities to people historically disadvantaged by previous labour laws.

The effects of social welfare, education and health reforms

There was a significant increase in the number of people receiving social welfare benefits. For some families, this was their sole means of support. By 2002, seven million people, out of a population of forty-five million, were dependent on social grants from the state. By 2014, this number had risen to nearly sixteen million (about 30 per cent of the population), which was more than six times the number receiving welfare benefits before 1994. But although social welfare had improved, millions of people still lacked basic services, and serious inequality remained a striking feature of society.

Figure 5.21 Government policies were unsuccessful in solving the problem of unemployment. In 2014, these unemployed men hold placards at the side of the road about the skills they have and the type of jobs they hope to get. Official figures put the percentage of unemployed at 25 per cent but many economists believed that the real figure was significantly higher than this

The number of children attending school increased substantially after 1994, but the quality of education in many schools remained poor. Huge discrepancies remained between rural and urban schools, as well as between suburban and township schools in the latter. A UNESCO study in 2000 found that Grade 4 South African children (aged eight and nine) had among the worst literacy, numeracy and life skills in Africa. Historian Leonard Thompson described this as a serious omen for the future of a country where a shortage of skills was already one of its greatest weaknesses. Political economist Francis Wilson, in *Dinosaurs, Diamonds and Democracy* (2009, p. 116) goes even further and suggests that the 'failure of the educational system to prepare the next generation for jobs in the 21st century economy contains the seeds of a major social and political catastrophe'.

With the switch in focus of state-funded medical care, the government succeeded in providing access to primary health care for thousands of people who had never had it before. But at the same time the quality of services in public hospitals deteriorated, and those who could afford it, namely most whites and the growing black middle class, switched to private health care, where standards remained high but so did the cost. At the same time the spread of AIDS continued to create social and economic problems for society and for the economy, as well as personal tragedies for the families of those affected.

The position of minorities and women

Although affirmative action policies opened up opportunities for many people who had been disadvantaged under apartheid, there were debates about the fairness and effectiveness of the system. Critics of the system maintained that merit rather than race or gender should be the sole criterion for appointments for jobs or for acceptance for university places. There were also debates about the effectiveness of Black Economic Empowerment (BEE). Supporters claimed that progress was made in increasing black ownership and control of companies, but critics believed that BEE enriched only a small percentage of politically well-connected individuals, while the vast majority of people remained desperately poor.

Fact: The World Economic Forum's Global Gender Gap Index for 2009 ranked South Africa in sixth place in the world, after Iceland, Finland, Norway, Sweden and New Zealand in terms of the representation of women in government. This rating reflected the progress made to empower women politically since 1994.

The legal status of women improved substantially during the first decade of democracy, and by 2000 30 per cent of the seats in the national parliament were held by women. Although they held only 13 per cent of the top management positions in companies, affirmative action policies were ensuring that increasing numbers of women moved into senior management positions. A UN Development Programme report on the position of women in South Africa noted that, compared with the pre-1994 era, South Africa had made progress in terms of gender equality.

However, many serious problems affecting the lives of women remained. These included the effects of poverty, the impact of HIV and AIDS, high levels of violence against women, and inequalities resulting from customary law.

Women, especially those living in rural areas, were the people most affected by adverse social and economic conditions. They formed the majority of the unemployed, landless, illiterate, unskilled and homeless. Although policies were put in place to address these problems, solutions were obviously linked to broader issues of economic development, transformation and the creation of a more equitable society. As Figure 5.22 shows, women in all population groups had higher rates of unemployment than men. African women were the worst affected, and many rural and working-class black women remained trapped by poverty. Pregs Govender, who chaired the parliamentary committee

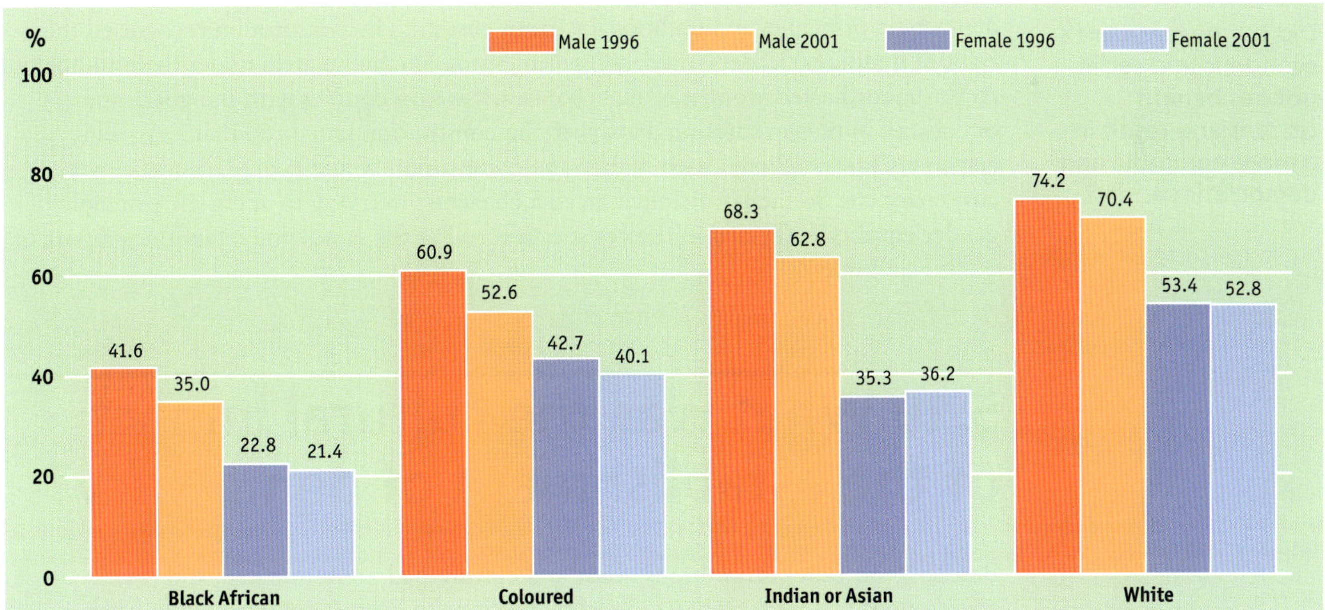

Figure 5.22 This graph, comparing the results of the 1996 and the 2001 census, shows the proportion of the working age population that was employed. It shows that unemployment levels among women were higher than those for men. Source: Statistics South Africa, 2004

on the Quality of Life and the Status of Women between 1994 and 2002, believed that such women could only achieve meaningful equality if there was a genuine commitment by politicians to ensure that the progressive laws and policies they introduced were properly implemented.

Another challenge facing women was the impact of HIV and AIDS. Women and girls were more vulnerable to infection than men and boys: in 2002, the female prevalence rate was 12.8 per cent, compared to 9.5 per cent for males. Young women in their twenties were at a particularly high risk of dying from AIDS-related illnesses. With high levels of teenage pregnancy and single motherhood, many young women, often HIV infected, had to bear the burden of supporting young families.

Other serious problems affecting women were the disturbingly high levels of domestic violence and the fact that South Africa had the highest incidence of rape in the world. The UN Development Programme reported that on average one rape occurred every eighty-three minutes in South Africa. The historian Leonard Thompson attributes this statistic to the 'male chauvinist element in South African culture'. Despite government awareness programmes, the efforts of political and church leaders and projects run by civil society organisations, violence against women and children remained a serious problem.

An important issue for many rural African women was their inequality under **customary law**. They were regarded as legal minors subject to the guardianship of their husbands or male family members, and they did not have the same rights of inheritance and succession as men did. This situation was partially solved in 1998 with a new law that recognised customary marriages. It abolished the minority status of women and gave them equal legal status to their husbands.

Customary law: this is administered by traditional leaders in African societies; marriages formalised in this way are referred to as customary marriages.

However, this law did nothing about women's right to inherit property, or their right to own land under systems of communal landownership (where they were treated as 'subjects' of traditional leaders). Gender activists saw this as a contradiction between democratic principles and traditional African custom. The constitution recognised the right of traditional leaders to apply African customary law in areas under their authority. As this subordinated women to male control, it was in conflict with the guarantee of equality in the constitution. However, the constitution stated too that if African customary law conflicted with it, then the constitution would take precedence over customary law. So the government faced a challenge in trying to apply the principle of gender equality enshrined in the constitution and at the same time retain the support of traditional leaders.

QUESTION

Did the government's economic and social policies benefit citizens and result in a more equitable and democratic society?

5.10 What was the cultural impact of the establishment of democracy?

Before 1994, European notions of art and culture had predominated, and the government had used censorship and restrictions to limit freedom of expression. But in the new South Africa there was a wider interpretation of what constituted the cultural heritage of the country, and greater freedom of expression in the arts and media.

Language, arts and culture

Until 1994, South Africa had only two official languages: English and Afrikaans. The indigenous African languages spoken by more than 75 per cent of the population had no official recognition. The new constitution added nine African languages to the list of official languages. However, although all eleven languages had equal legal status, English was the language used for most purposes, even though it was the home language of only 9 per cent of the population. In fact, English increasingly became the dominant language of government, business, the media and higher education.

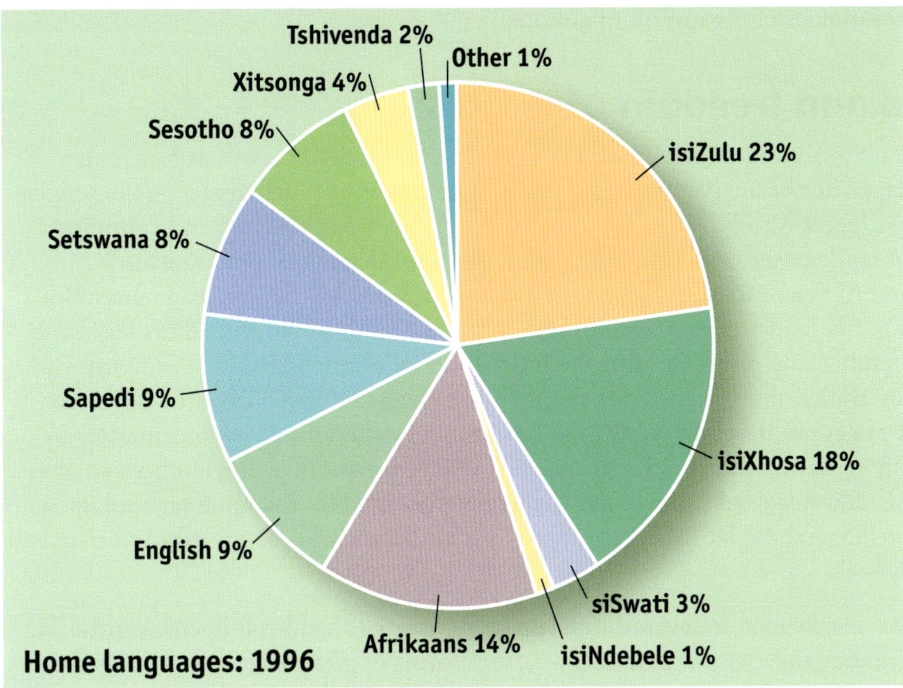

Figure 5.23 The constitution added nine African languages to the only two officially recognised by previous governments, English and Afrikaans

Before 1994, whites had used their economic and political power to enforce their own ideas about what constituted 'culture'. Thus European forms of culture (classical music, fine art, ballet and opera) were seen as 'superior', and government funding had supported them for the sole benefit of white viewers. African or indigenous culture was seen as traditional, tribal or primitive and definitely 'inferior' or quaint.

After 1994, government funding for the arts was directed at previously neglected art forms, and some of the more traditionally Western art forms suffered as a result. One exception to this was opera, in which classically trained black singers excelled both nationally and internationally.

In the new South Africa, many public works of art displayed the vibrant colours and themes of African cultural traditions. These can be seen for example in four large paintings depicting scenes from South African history from 1800 to the present by artist Sipho Ndlovu, commissioned to hang in the newly opened Constitutional Court in Johannesburg.

During the apartheid years, and especially during the 1980s, theatre and music had served as vehicles of protest. But both suffered as foreign funding for these forms of protest came to an end. In addition, after the advent of democracy, the themes that had sustained struggle theatre and protest music had largely disappeared, and so they no longer had the same sense of purpose. A form of uniquely South African popular music – *kwaito* – developed in Johannesburg townships in the 1990s, but it was essentially apolitical.

Although new perceptions of what constituted art and culture were developing, Anthony Butler in *Contemporary South Africa* (2009, p. 172) suggests that the development of a common culture across racial barriers was difficult to achieve: 'The "intercultural dialogue" that a post-apartheid nation so requires is inhibited by historical experiences and understandings of the notion of culture.'

Media and freedom of expression

After 1994, the South African Broadcasting Corporation (SABC), which had been a staunch supporter of the National Party government, was relaunched as a public service broadcaster that was to be independent from government interference and committed to promoting diversity. One new measure was the replacement of predominantly English and Afrikaans television channels with indigenous African-language ones. But the SABC came under pressure from the ANC over news and current affairs reporting and, as a result, many critics felt that the independence of the SABC was compromised, as Anthony Butler observes in *Contemporary South Africa* (2009, p. 179): 'In a return to apartheid-era convention, the SABC has been unwilling to affront senior ministers by aggressively reporting high level corruption, maladministration, or foreign policy failure.' The SABC also struggled to meet the challenges presented by changing technologies such as satellite and digital TV, and so those South Africans who could afford to switched to pay channels.

During the apartheid years, even though some newspapers had been openly critical of the government, they were restricted by various forms of government censorship and harassment, and freedom of expression was not protected. When South Africa adopted a new constitution in 1996, freedom of expression was one of the key principles in the Bill of Rights in this constitution, although some limitations were placed on it:

SOURCE E

Article 16 of the Bill of Rights in the South African constitution (1996):

Everyone has the right to freedom of expression, which includes freedom of the press and other media; freedom to receive or impart information or ideas; freedom of artistic creativity; and academic freedom and freedom of scientific research.

This freedom does not include propaganda for war; incitement of violence; promotion of hatred that is based on race, ethnicity, gender or religion, and that constitutes incitement to cause harm.

KEY CONCEPTS ACTIVITY

Change and Continuity: Explain why the cultural impact of democracy represented change rather than continuity for people in South Africa.

In 2000, the Promotion of Access to Information Act gave all people the right to information held by the government, or by another person, if they needed this information to exercise their rights. This law was regarded as an important step for democracy. However, the government later proposed a new law to limit access to certain information held by the state if this was deemed to be in the interests of state security. Despite vigorous public protests, a modified version of this bill was passed.

However, the press in South Africa was considered to be relatively free and in 2011–12 was ranked 42nd out of 179 countries in the worldwide Press Freedom Index compiled by Reporters Without Borders (or Reporters Sans Frontières), an international organisation that monitors freedom of information and freedom of the press.

End of unit activities

1 Draw up a table to summarise the challenges facing the new government, the policies it implemented to address them, and an evaluation of these policies. Use the example below as a model.

	Challenges facing the government in 1994	**Policies implemented**	**Successes, failures and challenges remaining**
Distribution of wealth			
Unemployment and labour relations			
Social welfare			
Education and health			
Position of women			

2 Design a spider diagram to illustrate the differences between the two different economic policies: the Reconstruction and Development Programme (RDP) and the Growth, Employment and Reconstruction Programme (GEAR).

3 Find out about another African country that handled the AIDS pandemic more effectively than South Africa did, and how it managed to do this.

4 Divide into two groups: one group should work out an argument to support and the other group an argument to oppose the following statement: 'Political transformation in South Africa was a far easier goal to attain than economic and social transformation.'

5 Imagine that you were a journalist working in South Africa in the 1990s. Prepare a list of questions that you would have liked to ask Nelson Mandela about successes and failures during his term of office as president (1994–9), and draft the answers that you think he may have given.

5

End of chapter activities

Paper 1 exam practice

Question

With reference to its origin, purpose and content, analyse the value and limitations of **Source A** for historians investigating the role of F.W. de Klerk in the move towards democracy in South Africa. [4 marks]

Trojan horse: something destructive that appears to be harmless. The term dates from the Trojan War, when the Greeks used a wooden horse to defeat the city of Troy. The Trojans wheeled the horse into their city, unaware that it concealed hidden soldiers, who subsequently opened the city gates to let in the rest of the Greek army, which destroyed the city.

SOURCE A

An extract from a biography of F.W. de Klerk written by his brother, Willem de Klerk, a journalist and political commentator. He explains the impact of the collapse of communism in 1989 on events in South Africa.

The decline and collapse of communism in Eastern Europe and Russia made things look different. The ANC was previously an instrument of Russian expansion in Southern Africa. When that threat fell away, the carpet was pulled from under the ANC. Its base of financing, counselling and moral support had crumbled.

We knew that the ANC enjoyed wide support and that they had to be included in negotiations. The risk that the ANC was being used as a **Trojan horse** by a superpower had drastically diminished.

De Klerk, W. (1991), F.W. de Klerk – the Man in his Time, *Cape Town: Jonathan Ball Publishers, p. 27.*

Skill

Utility/reliability of sources.

Examiner's tips

The main areas you need to consider in relation to the source and the information/view it provides are:

- origin, purpose and content;
- value and limitations.

These areas need to be linked in your answer, showing how the value and limitations of the source to historians relates to the source's origin and purpose. You need to comment specifically on its value to historians studying a particular event or period of history.

Common mistakes

Don't just comment on content and ignore the nature, origin and purpose of the source. Don't say 'a source is/isn't useful because it's primary/secondary'.

Simplified mark scheme

Band		Marks
1	Explicit/developed consideration of **both** origin, purpose and content **and** value and limitations.	3–4
2	Limited consideration/comments on origin, purpose and content **and** value and limitations. **Or** more developed comments on **either** origin, purpose and content **or** value and limitations.	0–2

Student answer

Source A is valuable because it gives an inside view about how F.W. de Klerk saw the state of affairs at the time. It is presumably based on interviews and discussions which the writer had with him (he says 'We knew …'), and it was published soon after the events discussed had taken place. However, the source has limitations as the writer would probably want to portray his brother in a positive light and not admit that he was motivated by the self-interest of his party.

Examiner comments

There is good assessment of the value and limitations of the source. However, there is no explicit comment about its origin, purpose and content and so the answer fails to get into Band 1, and would probably score two marks.

Student task/activity

Look again at the source, the simplified mark scheme and the student answer above. Now try to write a paragraph or two to push the answer up into Band 1, and so obtain the full four marks. Remember to comment about the origin, purpose and content of the source.

Summary activity

Copy these three diagrams and, using the information in this chapter, make point form notes under each heading.

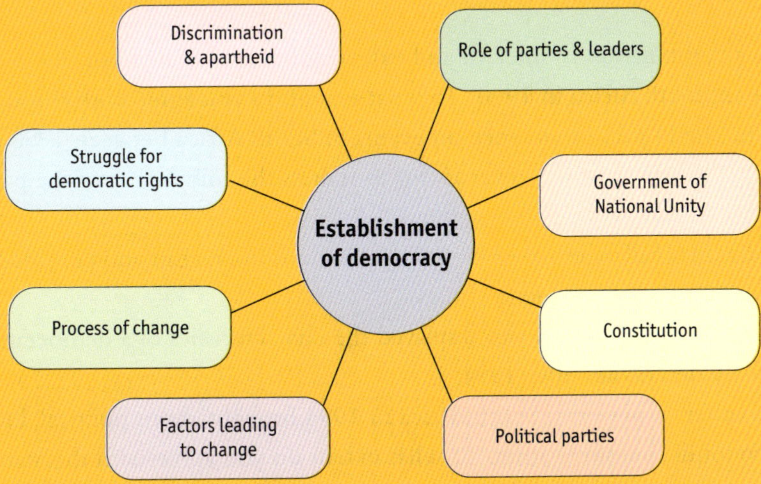

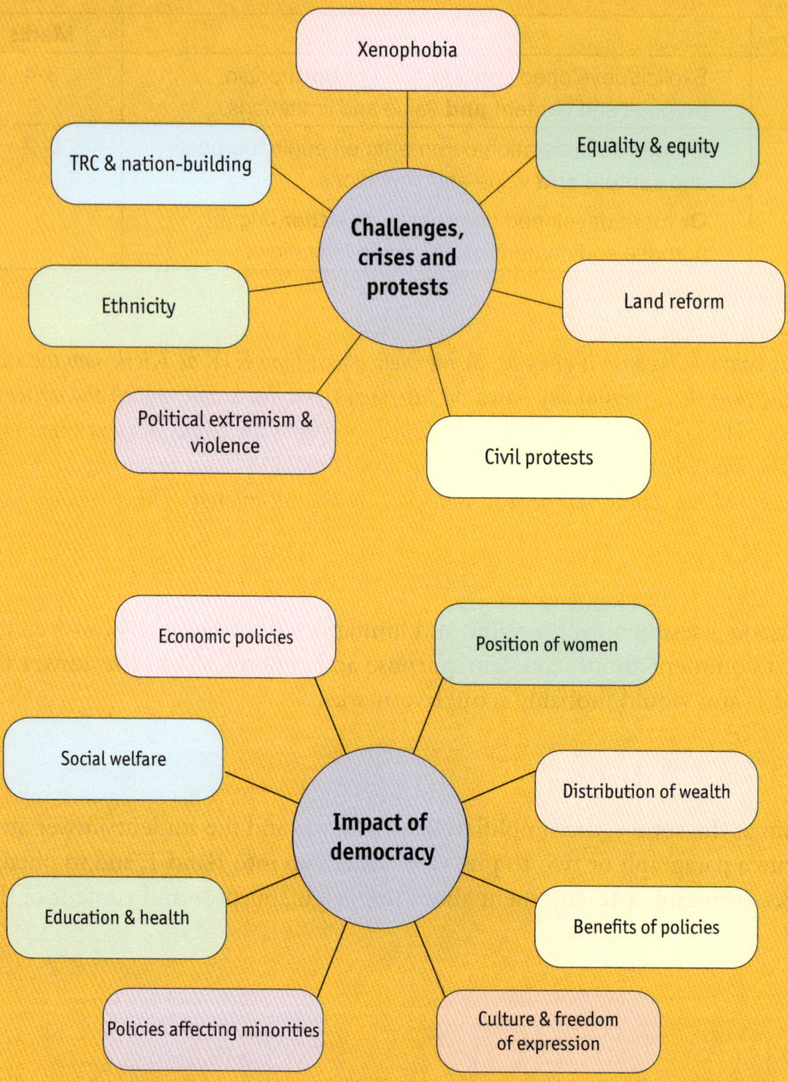

Paper 2 practice questions

1 'It was a combination of internal and external pressures that led to the beginning of change in South Africa in 1990'. To what extent do you agree with this statement?

2 Examine the impact of violence on events in South Africa between 1990 and 1994.

3 Evaluate the efforts of the government to redress the imbalances of the past through its economic and social policies after 1994.

4 Examine the challenges posed by political extremism, racism and continuing inequality to the government.

5 Evaluate whether South Africa displayed the characteristics of a democratic, multiparty democracy after 1994.

6 'The transfer of power in South Africa in 1994 brought about political, but not social and economic, transformation.' To what extent do you agree with this statement?

Further reading

Butler, A. (2009), *Contemporary South Africa*, Basingstoke: Palgrave Macmillan.

Gilomee, H. and Mbenga, B. (2007), *New History of South Africa*, Cape Town: Tafelberg Publishers.

Mandela, N. (2003), *The Illustrated Long Walk to Freedom*, London: Little Brown/ Abacus.

Nasson, B. (ed.) (2004), *Turning Points in History: Negotiation, Transition and Freedom*, Cape Town: STE Publishers for the Institute of Justice and Reconciliation and the South African History Project.

Oates, D. (ed.) (1992), *Illustrated History of South Africa*, Cape Town: Readers' Digest.

Pampallis, J. (1997), *Foundations of the New South Africa*, Cape Town: Maskew Miller Longman.

Seleti, Y. (ed.) (2004), *Africa Since 1990*, Cape Town: New Africa Education.

Sheehan, S. (2002), *South Africa Since Apartheid*, London: Hodder Wayland.

Sparks, A. (2003), *Beyond the Miracle: Inside the New South Africa*, Johannesburg: Jonathan Ball Publishers.

Thompson, L. (2006), *A History of South Africa*, Johannesburg: Jonathan Ball Publishers.

Welsh, D. (2010), *The Rise and Fall of Apartheid: From Racial Domination to Majority Rule*, Johannesburg: Jonathan Ball Publishers.

Wilson, F. (2009), *Dinosaurs, Diamonds and Democracy: A Short, Short History of South Africa*, Cape Town: UMUZI.

Worden, N. (2007), *The Making of Modern South Africa: Conquest, Apartheid, Democracy*, 4th edn, Oxford: Blackwell Publishing.

6 Exam practice

Introduction

You have now completed your study of the evolution and development of democracy in Germany, India, the United States and South Africa. In the previous chapters, you have had practice at answering some of the types of source-based questions you will have to deal with in Paper 1. In this chapter, you will gain experience of dealing with:

- the longer Paper 1 question, which requires you to use both sources and your own knowledge to write a mini-essay
- the essay questions you will meet in Paper 2.

Exam skills needed for IB History

This book is designed primarily to prepare both Standard and Higher Level students for the Paper 2 Evolution and development of democratic states (World History Topic 9). However, by providing the necessary historical knowledge and understanding, as well as an awareness of the key historical debates and perspectives, it will also help you prepare for Paper 1. The skills you need for answering both Paper 1 and Paper 2 exam questions are explained in the following pages.

Paper 1 exam practice

Paper 1 skills

This section of the book is designed to give you the skills and understanding to tackle Paper 1 questions. These are based on the comprehension, critical analysis and evaluation of different types of historical sources as evidence, along with the use of appropriate historical contextual knowledge. For example, you will need to test sources for value and limitations (i.e., their reliability and utility, especially in view of their origin, purpose and content) – a skill essential for historians. A range of sources has been provided, including extracts from official documents, tables of statistics, memoirs and speeches, as well as visual sources such as photographs and cartoons.

In order to analyse and evaluate sources as historical evidence, you will need to ask the following 'W' questions of historical sources:

- **Who** produced it? Were they in a position to know?
- **What** type of source is it? **What** is its nature – is it a primary or secondary source?
- **Where** and **when** was it produced? **What** was happening at the time?
- **Why** was it produced? Was its purpose to inform or to persuade? Is it an accurate attempt to record facts, or is it an example of propaganda?
- **Who** was the intended audience – decision-makers or the general public?

You should then consider how the answers to these questions affect a source's value.

The example below shows you how to find the information related to the 'W' questions. You will need this information in order to evaluate sources for their value and limitations.

SOURCE A

Long years ago we made a tryst with destiny, and now the time comes when we shall redeem our pledge, not wholly or in full measure, but very substantially. At the stroke of the midnight hour, when the world sleeps, India will awake to life and freedom. A moment comes, which comes but rarely in history, when we step out from the old to the new, when an age ends, and when the soul of a nation, long suppressed, finds utterance. It is fitting that at this solemn moment we take the pledge of dedication to the service of India and her people and to the still larger cause of humanity.

Extract from a **radio broadcast** **to the nation** by the Indian prime minister **Jawaharlal Nehru**, **14 August 1947**, formally **announcing India's independence** from Britain.

radio broadcast WHAT? (type of source)

Jawaharlal Nehru WHO? (produced it)

14 August 1947 WHEN? (date/time of production)

announcing India's independence WHY? (possible purpose)

to the nation WHO? (intended audience)

This approach will help you become familiar with interpreting, understanding, analysing and evaluating different types of historical sources. It will also aid you in synthesising critical analysis of sources with historical knowledge when constructing an explanation or analysis of some aspect or development of the past. Remember, for Paper 1, as for Paper 2, you need to acquire, select and deploy relevant historical knowledge to explain causes and consequences, continuity and change. You also need to develop and show (where relevant) an awareness of historical debates, and different perspectives and interpretations.

Paper 1 questions will thus involve examining sources in the light of:

- their origins, purpose and content
- their value and limitations.

The value and limitations of sources to historians will be based on the **origins, purpose** and **content** aspects. For example, a source might be useful because it is primary – the event depicted was witnessed by the person producing it. But was the person in a position to know? Is the view an untypical view of the event? What is its nature? Is it a private diary entry (therefore possibly more likely to be true), or is it a speech or piece of propaganda intended to persuade? The value of a source may be limited by some

origin: the 'who, what, when and where' questions.

purpose: this means 'reasons, what the writer/creator was trying to achieve, who the intended audience was'.

content: this is the information or explanation(s) provided by the source.

Remember: a source doesn't have to be primary to be useful. Remember, too, that content isn't the only aspect to have possible value. The context, the person who produced it, and so on, can also be important in offering an insight.

aspects, but that doesn't mean it has no value at all. For example, it may be valuable as evidence of the types of propaganda put out at the time. Similarly, a secondary – or even a tertiary – source can have more value than some primary sources, for instance, because the author might be writing at a time when new evidence has become available.

Finally, when in the exam room, use the information provided by the Chief Examiner about the four sources, as it can give some useful information and clues to help you construct a good answer.

Paper 1 contains four types of question. The first three of these are:

1 Comprehension/understanding of a source – some will have two marks, others three marks. For such questions, write only a short answer; save your longer answers for the questions carrying the higher marks.
2 Assessing the value and limitations of a source. Remember to deal with all the aspects required: origins, purpose, content, value and limitations (four marks).
3 Cross-referencing/comparing or contrasting two sources – try to write an integrated comparison; for example, comment on how the two sources deal with one aspect, then compare/contrast the sources on another aspect. This will usually score more highly than answers that deal with the sources separately. Try to avoid simply describing each source in turn – there needs to be explicit comparison/contrast (six marks).

These three types of questions are covered in the chapters above. The other, longer, type of Paper 1 question will be dealt with in this section.

Paper 1 – judgement questions

The fourth type of Paper 1 is a judgement question. Judgement questions are a synthesis of source evaluation and own knowledge.

Examiner's tips

- This fourth type of Paper 1 question requires you to produce a mini-essay – with a clear/relevant argument – to address the question/statement given in the question. You should try to develop and present an argument and/or come to a balanced judgement by analysing and using these four sources and your own knowledge.
- Before you write your answer to this kind of question, you may find it useful to draw a rough chart to note what the sources show in relation to the question. This will also make sure you refer to all or at least most of the sources. Note, however, that some sources may hint at more than one factor/result. When using your own knowledge, make sure it is relevant to the question.
- Look carefully at the simplified mark scheme – this will help you focus on what you need to do to reach the top bands and so score the higher marks.

Common mistake

- Don't just deal with sources or your own knowledge! Every year, some candidates (even good ones) do this, and so limit themselves to – at best – only five out of the nine marks available.

Simplified mark scheme

Band		Marks
1	Consistently focused on the question. Developed and balanced analysis, with precise use of **both** sources **and** relevant/accurate own knowledge. Sources and own knowledge are used consistently and effectively together, to support argument/judgement.	8–9
2	Mostly focused on the question. Developed analysis, with relevant use of **both** sources **and** some detailed own knowledge. But sources and own knowledge not always combined to support analysis/judgement.	6–7
3	Some focus on the question. Some analysis, using some of the sources **or** some relevant/accurate own knowledge.	4–5
4	No/limited focus on the question. Limited/ generalised comments on sources **and/or** some limited/ inaccurate/ irrelevant own knowledge.	0–3

Student answers

The student answers below have brief examiner's comments in the margins, as well as a longer overall comment at the end. Those parts of the answers that make use of the sources are highlighted in purple. Those parts that deploy relevant own knowledge are highlighted in red. In this way, you should find it easier to follow why particular bands and marks were – or were not – awarded.

Question 1

Using Sources A, B, C and D and your own knowledge, explain why the US government faced major political and social challenges in the period 1963–73. [9 marks]

SOURCE A

When Betty Friedan interviewed her 1942 Smith college classmates 15 years later, many were bitter about their new loneliness and feelings of social uselessness. Six years later in The Feminine Mystique, Friedan explored the roots of this bitterness. She argued that 'the core of the problem for women today is not sexual, but a problem of identity.' ... [This] became a dominant theme in the new women's writing in the 1970s ... the protest movements of the 1960s provided the training for the women's movement ... in the civil rights and anti-war movements where they were asked to play subordinate roles.

P. Levine and H. Papasotiriou (2005), America Since 1945, *New York: Palgrave Macmillan, p. 167.*

SOURCE B

Children, teenagers and college students were now a major consuming group and called a new world into being by their expenditure. Original popular music became the exclusive property of the young ... a youth market was discovered for clothes, cars, books, pictures, records and drugs, and the suppliers catered for it assiduously. The result was a sub-culture which efficiently insulated its exponents from outsiders. Particularly it insulated them from the men who ran the universities. It is not surprising that in the mid-sixties a widespread challenge was mounted beginning at Berkeley near San Francisco ... rebellion against the men in grey suits spread from one campus to another ... then Lyndon Johnson began to send members of this generation, in large numbers, as conscripts to war.

H. Brogan (2001), The Penguin History of the USA, *London: Penguin Books, p. 658.*

SOURCE C

President Johnson speaking to an adviser in 1968:

I tried to make it possible for every child of every color to grow up in a nice house, eat a solid breakfast, attend a decent school, and get to a good and lasting job. I asked so little in return, just a little thanks. Just a little appreciation. That's all. But look at what I got instead! Riots in 175 cities. Looting. Burning, shooting ... Young people by the thousand leaving the university, marching in the streets, chanting that horrible song about how many kids I had killed that day ... it ruined everything.

W. Chafe (1999), The Unfinished Journey, *New York: Oxford University Press, pp. 338–9.*

SOURCE D

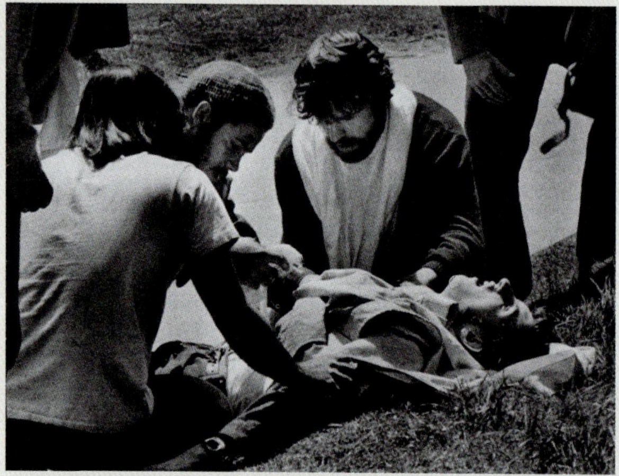

Students mourn a fellow student killed by Ohio National Guards during an anti-war demonstration at Kent State University in May 1970. Four students were killed in total.

Student answer

There are several reasons why America faced political and social challenges during this period, and the four sources given account for some of this, which I will expand upon further with my own knowledge.

First, Source A comments about the development of women's rights in the mid 1960s following the 1963 publication of Betty Friedan's The Feminine Mystique *– this sparked off not only a huge debate, but also made many women aware of an alternative life and career, addressing 'the problem of identity'. The Equal Pay Act of 1963 and other legislation aimed to prohibit bias against women in employment, but many felt they didn't have the same civil rights as African Americans. LBJ's Great Society programme – as referred to in Source C – hadn't protected them enough. By 1967 thousands had joined NOW – National Organization for Women – to protest and campaign for a full Amendment for Equal Rights as well as an end to sex discrimination, the legalisation of abortion, national funding for childcare and housing opportunities for women. Despite disagreements over issues such as the level of radical action to be taken, membership had reached 40,000 by 1974. Many of its members had been vocal in civil rights movements and anti-Vietnam war protests. The women's rights movement was a real challenge to the US government and so much so that Nixon* had *to address these challenges during his presidency and he signed the Equal Rights Amendment and acts ending sex discrimination in schools and athletics and for women obtaining credit.*

Source B also relates to discontent and connects to Source A speaking of another 'widespread challenge' to government, this time emerging at universities. It speaks about 'men in grey suits' being out of touch with increasingly radical popular culture and refers to Johnson's draft for Vietnam, again linking to the anti-war movement referred to in C.

After 1968, the American public increasingly wanted an end to the Vietnam War and to growing casualties: students, feminists and the political left mounted this challenge. Johnson stood down in 1968 over Vietnam and the wider protests incorporating black rights, which Source C shows he took personally. He didn't understand why he should be attacked, with 'riots in 175 cities' as he'd launched so many reforms in his Great Society programme, including the Civil Rights Act and Voting Act.

The Vietnam draft hit blacks and white working-class men worst, with 80% of enlisted men coming from such backgrounds. Many challenged why they should fight in Vietnam when they faced racial discrimination and poverty at home. In 1968 the developing Black Power movement went global when two US black athletes Tommy Smith and John Carlos used one of the Mexico Olympic medal ceremonies to give a black power salute. They instantly had a worldwide audience, although the athletes themselves were suspended by the management of the US Olympic team.

Finally, Source D refers to the killing of four students by the National Guard at Kent State University Ohio, in May 1970. It happened at an anti-war protest following Nixon's bombing of Cambodia in order to destroy Communist supply routes to Vietnam. Nixon's action was viewed as an escalation of the war and led to major protests on US campuses – the one at Kent ending tragically.

In conclusion, these four sources highlight all the main reasons why the US government faced considerable political and social challenges during the period 1963–73. It was a turbulent time, with the radicalisation of issues concerning the role of women in US society (Source A), growing student disenchantment with society in general and Vietnam in particular (Sources A, B and C),

EXAMINER'S COMMENT

This is a good, well-focused, start. **Source A** is referred to and used, along with some excellent own knowledge, and a cross-reference to **Source C**, although the candidate could have dealt with the question of 'why' they challenged the government more explicitly.

EXAMINER'S COMMENT

The **Sources B** and **C** are again clearly referred to and used, showing good understanding, with some good own knowledge. There are also comments linking the challenges not only to cultural change and Vietnam but also to the growing anger about the lack of opportunity for African Americans.

EXAMINER'S COMMENT

Source D is clearly used but in this case not linked. There is some relevant own knowledge. But this section of the answer needs an explicit comment on why the event was a challenge to the US government.

a liberal president struggling to juggle reform with war and racial discontent (C) and continued backlash against government policy, with anxieties over Vietnam even under a new president (D). These merged between the murder of Kennedy (1963) and the end of America's involvement in the Vietnam in 1973.

It was all boosted by a massive artistic change and the growth of a counterculture as musical artists such as Bob Dylan, Jim Morrison and Joan Baez attracted a huge following with their songs of protest. It caused much of America to rethink its attitude to women, students, popular culture, African Americans and to its involvement in foreign wars. There could not be a Great Society with such troubled undercurrents. It was inevitable that it erupted.

Overall examiner's comments

There is good use of the sources, with clear references to them and some very good own knowledge, both integrated with comments on the sources, and developed in addition. Own knowledge might have been used to give other factors not mentioned by the sources; for example, more about some of the women's liberation protests, the death of Martin Luther King, more reference to Black Power and inner-city riots, more on the clash between US culture and counterculture and maybe even mentioning the 1968 Tet Offensive in Vietnam.

The candidate must be careful not to list reasons or tell stories, but always focus on explanation of 'why' there were these political and social challenges. Also a little more balance is needed; for example, an argument as to whether or not the challenges were actually 'major', since America remained one of the richest, most successful and stable countries, putting a man on the moon in 1969 and not facing a civil war or revolution. Hence this answer fails to get into Band 1 – but is a sound top Band 2 answer and so probably scores seven marks out of the nine available.

Activity

Look again at all the sources, the simplified mark scheme, and the student answer above. Then try to write a few more sentences to push the answer up into Band 1, and so obtain the full nine marks. Continue to use all/most of the sources, and some precise own knowledge, but also try to integrate the sources with your own knowledge to a greater degree, rather than dealing with sources and own knowledge separately, or going through the sources in order (Source A says, Source B says, etc., which doesn't sound good). Also, don't lose sight of the need to use the sources and your own knowledge to explain why the US government faced these major challenges.

Question 2

Using the sources and your own knowledge, evaluate the success of the South African government in addressing the challenges that it faced between 1994 and 2000. [9 marks]

SOURCE A

In the few years since the promulgation of the Constitution, a large number of important challenges have been brought before the Constitutional Court. While it is still early to pass judgement on the vibrancy of the Constitution, there is little doubt that it has become part of our daily diet of public debate and discussion. Perhaps more exciting is the fact that despite these vigorous debates, there has been little argument – if any – related to the legitimacy of the Constitution itself.

H. Ebrahim (2004), 'The South African Constitution: Birth Certificate of a Nation', in B. Nasson (ed.), Turning Points in History: Negotiation, Transition and Freedom, *Cape Town: STE Publishers for the Institute of Justice and Reconciliation and the South African History Project, p. 51.*

SOURCE B

Though in some respects post-apartheid South Africa did successfully integrate itself into the world economy, and economic growth increased after 1994, such growth was not nearly sufficient to mop up unemployment and provide the means for social development on the vast scale needed. Over half a million jobs in the formal economy were lost as a result of restructuring, and poverty did not decline but increased. What did 'freedom' mean, asked the critics, to those without food or the ability to pay for the new services now available?

C. Saunders (2004), 'The Making of a Democratic South Africa', in Y. Seleti (ed.), Africa Since 1990, *Cape Town: New Africa Education, p. 201.*

SOURCE C

Despite the emergence of a black middle class, levels of poverty and income inequality actually rose in the late 1990s. Two issues which dominated debates in South Africa in the early 2000s reflect this dilemma. One was the high incidence of HIV/AIDS infection ... A second issue which concerned all South Africans, and a factor which at least partially inhibited external investment, was the high level of violent crime. This was not surprising in a society with such economic inequalities amongst its population. It was particularly evident in the cities, where migration from impoverished rural areas continued unabated and adult unemployment levels reached well over 40%.

N. Worden (2007), The Making of Modern South Africa: Conquest, Apartheid, Democracy, *Oxford: Blackwell Publishing, p. 162.*

SOURCE D

In 1994, Archbishop Desmond Tutu referred to South Africa as the 'rainbow nation' – a reflection of the optimism that many people felt about the emergence of a new non-racial identity. This Zapiro cartoon, published in *The Sowetan* on 25 August 2000, questions this view of race relations in post-apartheid South Africa

Student answer

The Government of National Unity, which took office after South Africa's first democratic election in 1994, faced many challenges. These four sources give information about some of them and show that, although a few were tackled successfully, many challenges remained unresolved.

A fundamental challenge was to draw up a constitution to transform South Africa into a democracy. Source A suggests that this was achieved successfully and that the 'legitimacy' of the constitution was generally accepted. One of the safeguards put in place to protect and uphold the constitution was a Constitutional Court, which had to rule on many important issues, such as the death penalty, in its first few years. Source A implies that the constitution was successful in generating awareness of and debate about issues fundamental to the workings of a democratic state.

Sources B and C deal with the social and economic challenges facing the government. Source B acknowledges the achievements of the government in becoming part of the world economy once again and in promoting economic growth. This was partly as a result of South Africa's re-acceptance into the world community after the isolation of the apartheid years. But the source points out that this economic growth was insufficient to provide enough employment or to provide

EXAMINER'S COMMENT

This is a good, well-focused start. It shows how the student intends to answer the question, and supplies a little own knowledge to explain the historical context. Source A is referred to and the information from it is used effectively.

the revenue for the government to fund social transformation. The source explains that the 'restructuring' of the economy, which was part of the economic policy known as GEAR, caused further job losses, and that poverty increased, making it impossible for people to realise the benefits of the new freedom they had achieved. There had been political transformation without economic and social transformation.

Source C refers to the emergence of a black middle class as a positive change, but mentions increasing poverty and inequality. The source also refers to two further social challenges – the HIV/AIDS pandemic, which was made worse by the policies of Thabo Mbeki, and the high levels of violent crime, especially in the cities. The move to the cities was caused by rural poverty, especially in the former homeland areas. The source links the crime levels to the high levels of inequality in South Africa.

Another challenge facing the government was the lack of unity among the population. Although people had been optimistic after the success of the negotiations between the ANC and the National Party, underlying divisions along racial lines remained. The cartoonist in Source D suggests that the concept of a multi-racial 'rainbow nation' was an illusion and that the nation was still divided into black and white. Although there was an emerging black middle class (referred to in Source C), inequality of income was still largely defined along racial lines.

Another enormous challenge that the government faced was to upgrade the education system. Under the policy of apartheid, black children had received inferior schooling to prepare them for work as manual labourers, under the system of Bantu Education. Although the governments spent vast sums of money on education, the quality of education in most rural and township schools remained poor. This had negative implications for the government's plans to increase employment as many children lacked the necessary skills. It also affected plans to promote economic growth, on which many plans for social and economic transformation depended.

The four sources and the additional information suggest that the government was not very successful in addressing the challenges it faced between 1994 and 2000. Although it had overseen the introduction of a democratic constitution, it had not managed to solve the many social and economic challenges it faced.

Overall examiner's comments

There is good use of the sources, with clear references to them. There is also some good own knowledge, some of which is integrated with information from the sources. The inclusion of a paragraph about the problems in education is good selection of own knowledge. However, there are some omissions – own knowledge could also have included other challenges not mentioned in the sources, such as the position of rural African women. A more critical answer might also point out that three of the sources focus on failures of the government to *meet* the challenges. The answer does not mention the policies adopted to *address* some of them (which is what the question refers to); nor does it mention the achievements of the government in overcoming political extremism or laying the foundations for democracy. Not all the links between the sources are fully explored (for example, the candidate does not point out that Source C's suggestion that the high levels of crime which 'inhibited external investment' might be a reason for the fact that economic growth did not meet expectations, as stated in Source B). Hence this answer fails to get into Band 1 – but this is a sound Band 2 answer and so probably scores 7 marks out of the 9 available.

EXAMINER'S COMMENT

Sources B and **C** are clearly referred to and used, showing good understanding, and there is some helpful own knowledge to clarify some of the issues raised. But the student needs to refer to the overlap between the sources, by pointing out that both refer to poverty and unemployment, and comparing the information about each of these in the two sources.

EXAMINER'S COMMENT

There is a good observation showing a not very obvious link between **Sources C** and **D**. Perhaps the student could have made some comment about the visual imagery in the cartoon – the disillusion in the rather dejected-looking figures, and the rainbow normally being a symbol of hope.

EXAMINER'S COMMENT

The student provides useful own knowledge in the second last paragraph about a key challenge that is not mentioned in any of the sources.

Activity

Look again at all the sources, the simplified mark scheme, and the student answer above. Then try to write a few paragraphs to push the answer up into Band 1, and so obtain the full nine marks.

Paper 2 exam practice

Paper 2 skills and questions

For Paper 2, you have to answer **two** essay questions – chosen from two **different** topics from the twelve options offered. Very often, you will be asked to comment on two states from two different IB regions of the world. Although each question has a specific mark scheme, you can get a good general idea of what examiners are looking for in order to be able to put answers into the higher bands from the general 'generic' mark scheme. In particular, you will need to acquire reasonably precise historical knowledge in order to address issues such as cause and effect, or change and continuity, and to learn how to explain historical developments in a clear, coherent, well-supported and relevant way. You will also need to understand and be able to refer to aspects relating to historical debates, perspectives and interpretations.

Make sure you read the questions carefully and select your questions wisely. It is important to produce a rough essay plan for each of your essays before you start to write an answer, and you may find it helpful to plan both your essays before you begin to write. That way, you will soon know whether you have enough own knowledge to answer them adequately.

Remember, too, to keep your answers relevant and focused on the question. For example, don't go outside the dates mentioned in the question, or answer on individuals/states different from the ones identified in the question. Don't just describe the events or developments – sometimes, students just focus on one key word or individual, and then write down all they know about it. Instead, select your own knowledge carefully, and pin the relevant information to the key features raised by the question. Also, if the question asks for 'causes/reasons' and 'consequences/results', or two different countries/leaders, make sure you deal with all the parts of the question. Otherwise, you will limit yourself to half marks at best.

Examiner's tips

For Paper 2 answers, examiners are looking for clear/precise analysis, and a balanced argument, linked to the question, with the use of good, precise and relevant own knowledge. In order to obtain the highest marks, you should be able to refer, where appropriate, to historical debate and/or different historical perspectives and interpretations, or historians' knowledge, making sure it is both relevant to the question **and** integrated into your answer.

Common mistakes

- When answering Paper 2 questions, try to avoid simply describing what happened. A detailed narrative, with no explicit attempts to link the knowledge to the question, will only get you half marks at most.

- If the question asks you to select examples from two different regions, make sure you don't chose two states from the same region. Every year, some candidates do this, and so limit themselves to – at best – only eight out of the fifteen marks available for each question.

Simplified mark scheme

Band		Marks
1	Consistently **clear focus** on the question, with **all main aspects addressed**. Answer is **fully analytical** and **well-structured/organised**. There is **sound understanding** of historical concepts. The answer also integrates **evaluation** of different historical debates/perspectives, and reaches a **clear/consistent judgement/conclusion**.	13–15
2	**Clear understanding** of the question, and most of its **main aspects** are addressed. Answer is **mostly well-structured and developed**, with supporting own knowledge **mostly relevant/accurate**. Answer is **mainly analytical**, with **attempts at a consistent conclusion**; and shows **some understanding** of historical concepts and debates/perspectives.	10–12
3	Demands of the question are understood – but **some aspects not fully developed/addressed**. Relevant/accurate supporting own knowledge, but **attempts at analysis are limited/inconsistent**.	7–9
4	**Some understanding** of the question. **Some relevant own knowledge**, with **some factors identified** – but with **limited explanation. Some attempts at analysis,** but answer is **mainly description/narrative**.	4-6
5	**Limited understanding** of the question. **Short/general answer**, with **very little accurate/relevant own knowledge**. Some **unsupported assertions**, with **no real analysis**.	0–3

Student answers

Those parts of the student answer which follow will have brief examiner's comments in the margins, as well as a longer overall comment at the end. Those parts that are particularly strong and well-focused will be highlighted in red. Errors/confusions/loss of focus will be highlighted in blue. In this way, you should find it easier to follow why marks were – or were not – awarded.

Question 1

In what ways, and for what reasons, were social issues such as health care and education important for the Weimar government (1919–33)? [15 marks]

Skills

Analysis/argument/evaluation.

Examiner's tip

Look carefully at the wording of this question, which asks for the ways in which social issues such as health care and education were important in Germany during the Weimar Republic, and the reasons for this. **Both** aspects of the question will need addressing if high marks are to be achieved. Don't just describe what happened; give explicit analysis and explanation, with precise/accurate supporting knowledge.

Student answer

Social policies were a key component of Weimar's Social Democrat dominated government, and positive attempts were made to improve health care and education the reason being that success here would not only improve the well-being and contentment of a demoralised country, but lay the foundations for a more stable, democratic society, with a better educated future generation. It would also swing people behind supporting Weimar, itself handicapped by unpopular association with Versailles.

> **EXAMINER'S COMMENT**
>
> This is a crisp and well-focused introduction, showing a grasp of one of the key requirements of the question – explaining reasons behind certain social issues.

Weimar inherited a basic insurance and health care scheme from the 1880s. This was set up under the Chancellorship of Bismarck in the days of the Empire and was one of the first of its kind in Europe. Ebert knew the medical profession had worked with government so he pushed for further co-operation. It was needed after 1919, with malnutrition, a flu pandemic and the care of many war wounded and crippled all presenting problems. Weimar wanted health care for all citizens.

Existing health insurance was extended to cover wives and daughters without income, which was crucial given the level of injured soldiers and the number of orphans and widows after the war; as well as the number of people incapable of finding employment.

Gradually, physicians, nurses, midwives and apothecaries all became part of Weimar's expanding health and welfare network. Sympathetic physicians called for a single state agency to oversee this, with the focus shifting from private practice to public health, from treating disease to preventable health care. Many doctors envisaged a bigger state role – responsibility for national health and not just the individual patient. Weimar passed laws to assist in disease prevention, especially the fight against tuberculosis and established alcohol treatment centres. Other centres opened to advise people with social, financial and legal problems.

Good health care is vital for social, moral and, psychological improvement, and for maintaining a healthy industrial workforce. Politicians knew this was crucial for Germany's success. So there had to be improved public health with laws to help fight tuberculosis, venereal disease and alcoholism; new centres for chemical dependency, as well as counselling bureaux; and compulsory unemployment insurance was introduced in 1927. But these reforms were short-lived.

> **EXAMINER'S COMMENT**
>
> This focuses on health care, digressing unnecessarily about Bismarck and the Empire, but the candidate addresses the question, showing how or in what way health care policies were introduced, the reasons for them, and the consequences. The requirements of the question are met, and the answer does have some good specific own knowledge about policy.

After the 1929 crash, state expenditure on health and welfare was reduced. Rehabilitation clinics and maternal and paediatric health suffered. Economic efficiency became the mantra and health care a question of cost and benefit. But in the time available they did have some success.

Reforming education was necessary as Weimar tried to develop a new generation of supportive citizens in peacetime. Before 1914 poor children had no access to secondary schooling and undergraduate study. Weimar established free, universal four-year elementary schooling with a minimum of eight years' primary school attendance, continuing education to eighteen and free education and teaching materials. Upon passing a rigorous entrance exam, pupils could also enter one of four types of secondary school. They aimed to standardise teacher training and improve quality, stating that women must be educated on the same basis as men – a key ruling.

The Youth Welfare Act of 1922 then obliged all municipalities and states to set up youth offices in charge of child protection, and also codified further the fundamental right to education for all children, with the teaching of religion and morality being made more flexible, thus suggesting the beginnings of a move towards a more secular state. This was important since religion was linked closely to education and it influenced it with many church leaders being opposed to the egalitarian and democratic institutions of Weimar.

They feared what form of education the government planned for the adults of the future, noting that Germany was losing traditional values by adopting popular styles from abroad, particularly America, and were shocked by jazz, general decadence and open sexuality – seen especially in places like Berlin in the mid-1920s. But the constitution of 1919 declared that 'there is no state church' and everybody had freedom to worship or not to worship. Weimar sought to take greater control of education and sought to separate church and state, as well as to give a new generation of German children a better start.

It all seemed to offer the chance to maximise the talents of a post-war generation, leading to equality of opportunity – something necessary to shake off the past. But much never came to fruition, due to the government instability, financial cutbacks and the need for political compromise in order to survive in office. Also critics queried the wisdom of greater state control over education, when there weren't jobs available at the end, due to the unemployment and financial situation.

In conclusion, Weimar was handicapped and eventually doomed by economic problems and the rise of political extremes. Dozens of political parties were represented in the federal parliament. This prevented stable government, or carrying social policies to their fullest potential. Hyperinflation, world depression and social unrest stemming from resentment toward the conditions of the Versailles Treaty all worked to destroy the government. Weimar had limited success in the areas of health care and education. These areas were important to overall well-being and giving a depressed nation a new start – crucial to bringing about the ultimate success/failure of a liberal, democratic republic and safeguarding the future. It was less sure how to 'secularise' or modernise the church and arguably drove many to look for the hierarchy and salvation offered by Nazism.

EXAMINER'S COMMENT

There is supporting evidence linked to the question and coherent analysis and argument of the problems present in education. Explicit comments and good own knowledge about attitudes to morality, decadence, tradition and the role of religion, linked to the Weimar Constitution and its provisions for education

Overall examiner's comments

This is a good, focused, analytical answer with a minimum of digression, and some precise and accurate own knowledge to support the points made. The answer is good enough to be awarded a mark at the very top of Band 2 – twelve marks. However more comment on the importance of these social policies is required, or some judgement as to whether some policies were more important than others, in order to push the answer into Band 1. This would give a more balanced answer. Some reference to historiography and the mention of a historian would also definitely cement it into Band 1.

Activity

Look again at the simplified mark scheme and the student answer. Then try to write a few extra paragraphs to push the answer up firmly into Band 1, and so obtain the full fifteen marks. As well as making sure you address all aspects of the question, try to integrate some more specific own knowledge examples and maybe extend references to relevant historians/historical interpretations.

Question 2

Compare and contrast the policies of **two** of the following: Stresemann; Kennedy; Nehru. [15 marks]

Skills

Analysis/argument/evaluation.

Examiner's tip

Look at the question's wording, which requires assessment of the policies of the two leaders chosen. You will need to compare and contrast their policies and time in office, with analysis and precise supporting own knowledge, in order to achieve high marks.

Student answer

This essay will compare and contrast Gustav Stresemann, chancellor and foreign minister of Germany 1924–9, and John F. Kennedy, US president 1961–3. Both men were talented, committed, hard-working politicians who served for short periods of time and who both died in office prematurely with much more to offer their countries, yet each with a legacy of success and failure. They both had the respect of international leaders and both assumed office during economic recessions. They followed progressive policies designed to advance their countries domestically and internationally and both were mourned upon their untimely deaths. Apart from being separated by a time difference of forty years when in office, their arenas were different, as they operated in different circumstances and within different environments. What happened in each country after their deaths also differed.

EXAMINER'S COMMENT

This is a good introduction, showing appreciation of the demands of the question – the need to compare and contrast. The candidate must avoid drifting into narrative or unnecessary detail.

Stresemann and Kennedy were both accomplished academically, although Stresemann was originally pro-monarchist and anti-Weimar, while Kennedy was always firmly associated with liberal democrat politics. Coming from a Boston Irish background, he was no lover of imperialism or monarchy.

Stresemann originally approved of actions taken against Spartacists, fearing that Liebknecht, Luxemburg and their followers might trigger a chain of events that would lead Germany into Soviet-style communism. However, he was uncomfortable with the Kapp Putsch and knew Germany's future survival depended on Weimar's success. He became chancellor in 1923, leading a moderate all-party coalition, including socialists and Centrists.

Conversely, Kennedy's pathway to the presidency occurred in a successful, powerful, economically self-sufficient superpower. Elected Democrat president in 1960, he succeeded the Second World War hero, General Dwight Eisenhower who had helped to bring prosperity to 1950s post-war America, although by 1961, the USA was in recession. Kennedy therefore headed a reforming liberal administration against a background of relative economic stability, but was aware of growing unemployment and business failures.

Stresemann, however, inherited no such relative stability and assumed office during the deep recession and hyperinflation that followed the French occupation of the Ruhr. It was a desperate time with much unemployment, but he led a government that established a new currency, the Rentenmark. This succeeded, along with other measures, in cutting inflation and balancing the budget. Unfortunately this meant sacking many civil servants and public employees, so adding to unemployment. But the new currency succeeded and Germany came back from the brink. He further ensured stability by negotiating the Dawes and Young plans. These arrangements limited the reparations that were payable, and used loans to stabilise the new currency. Without these plans negotiated by Stresemann, Weimar might have come to an end there and then. They gave the republic a much-needed chance to take stock and plot the way forward carefully.

Although Stresemann was only chancellor for a few months, he continued as an influential foreign minister for five years. Sensible and progressive foreign policies enabled Germany to come out of imposed isolation and join the League of Nations in 1926, following the Locarno treaties.

This improved German national self-esteem. Cashing in on apparent improvement, large firms borrowed money, depending heavily on American loans. German banks sought loans to invest in businesses, and many woes of the early 1920s were forgotten as life improved. This appeared to be the start of a recovery, leading to a greater share of 'the good times' for people.

But it was based on shaky foundations – US loans – and by October 1929 the economy was declining with little or no growth in production and unemployment at 2.5 million. Stresemann died just before the Wall Street Crash, leaving a country without a dynamic political figure – apart from Hitler! – and a nation sinking into economic depression. He might have achieved more if Germany hadn't been politically unstable, which meant that decision-making was difficult and plans might overturn at the whim of a minority of parliamentarians seeking compromise.

Kennedy assumed office in 1961 also during a recession, when bankruptcies had reached the highest level since 1932, with six million unemployed. Many had overstretched themselves with debt through easy hire purchase and credit. Unlike Stresemann, Kennedy did not face an unstable currency; by contrast, the dollar was a powerful world currency. But Kennedy had to tackle a stagnant situation. He tried to lower taxes, protect the unemployed, increase the minimum wage, and pumped money into the US economy to stimulate it; creating jobs and reducing unemployment. As a result of pumping money into domestic and military spending, the recession had eased by late 1961, and unemployment began to fall.

Kennedy called his domestic programme, the 'New Frontier', promising funding for education and medical care for the elderly, with help for the poor and the marginalised: but Kennedy's narrow election victory meant that he had a weak mandate. He was frequently obstructed in Congress by hostile committees and a conservative coalition of both Republicans and Democrats from the south. Like Stresemann, much of what he proposed was hampered by compromise, although unlike Stresemann, Kennedy did not face political instability, nor were his policies bankrolled by foreign loans.

Unlike Stresemann, Kennedy faced an unanticipated issue: the growing Civil Rights Movement led by Martin Luther King. Kennedy had his eye on the 1964 election and was treading warily with Southern Democrats, many of whom opposed civil rights legislation. But he felt racism could no longer be ignored. His Civil Rights Bill planned to give African Americans federal enforcement of equality; but no legislation was passed until after his death, due to obstruction in Congress. Likewise, other items of legislation that Kennedy would have liked, such as Medicare and Medicaid, passed under Johnson.

Unlike Stresemann, Kennedy's legacy was the unfulfilled social policies developed under Johnson. In Germany the Grand Coalition collapsed, little or no legislation was passed, and Weimar drifted into Nazism – although the USA drifted into conflict in Vietnam and social upheaval within another two to three years. But overall, there were two different legacies for two leaders who perhaps had more in common than first imagined.

EXAMINER'S COMMENT

There is clearly excellent depth of knowledge shown here and significant points are made. However, the student must beware of drifting off into narrative or including superfluous material about Eisenhower or Weimar in general, especially in an exam when writing against the clock.

EXAMINER'S COMMENT

There is some accurate supporting own knowledge, explicitly linked to Stresemann's background and the financial problems and foreign policy successes. Some good analysis, but some aspects are vague or a bit clichéd (e.g., a greater share of the good times, etc.) or not sufficiently developed (e.g., Stresemann and Kennedy were both accomplished academically). Also, references to Kennedy look slotted in and this section should have just discussed Stresemann.

EXAMINER'S COMMENT

There is some accurate supporting own knowledge, and a comparison/contrast between the two men is attempted. But again it seems pushed together.

EXAMINER'S COMMENT

The student makes a good point about the impact of civil rights and this highlights a contrasting situation to that faced by Stresemann. The references to Medicare need expanding.

EXAMINER'S COMMENT

The conclusion is brief and while it continues the pattern of comparing and contrasting, it is rather vague. Yet it tries to keep the question in focus.

Overall examiner's comments

Comparison questions like this are quite difficult to attempt and are often better tackled either thematically, by writing about each relevant policy and analysing/comparing/contrasting it according to each leader, or by dealing individually with each person and their policies in their entirety and then coming to a synoptic conclusion.

This is a brave attempt, which falls somewhere between the two methods described above. It is occasionally muddled, with some vagueness, omissions and passages that need sharper explanation of policies. Yet there are very relevant pieces of own knowledge and definite attempts to focus on the question and to analyse. The approach is slightly narrative, though the conclusion attempts to bring it together analytically, albeit briefly. The answer is in Band 3, at about nine marks. To reach Band 2, better comparison and contrast of policies is needed. Further factors need identifying and explaining, plus more precise examples, more analysis and a crisper conclusion.

Question 3

In 1994, Nelson Mandela wrote in his autobiography, *Long Walk to Freedom*: 'I have walked that long road to freedom. But I have discovered that after climbing a great hill, one only finds that there are many more hills to climb.' To what extent is this assessment of South Africa's emergence as a democracy between 1990 and 1994 accurate? [15 marks]

Skills

Analysis/argument/evaluation.

Examiner's tip

Look carefully at the wording of this question, which asks for an assessment of the events between 1990 and 1994, when negotiations took place to transform South Africa into a democracy. You need to be sure that you analyse these events in relation to Mandela's statement, and decide whether it is an accurate assessment or not. Above all, you must avoid simply giving a narrative account of the negotiation process.

EXAMINER'S COMMENT

This is a clear and well-focused introduction, which shows a good appreciation of the demands of the question. This is a good start.

EXAMINER'S COMMENT

There is good focus on the essay topic, but try to avoid giving unnecessary details outside the time period stipulated in the essay question.

Student answer

When Nelson Mandela was released from prison in 1990, it seemed as though a 'great hill' or obstacle to a peaceful settlement in South Africa had been overcome. However, during the next four years, many more obstacles had to be faced before negotiations succeeded in transforming South Africa politically. So Mandela's assessment that there were still many 'hills to climb' is an accurate assessment of South Africa's emergence as a democracy.

Although Mandela was free and the ANC had been unbanned, the struggle for democracy was not over. First of all, the ANC had to transform itself from a liberation movement to a political party. It had been banned for more than thirty years and needed to form organisational structures. Many ANC supporters, especially thousands of township residents who had been involved in the sustained resistance of the 1980s, had unrealistic expectations that the ANC would bring freedom and transformation immediately. Extremists within the ANC opposed the idea of negotiating with the government and wanted instead to continue the armed struggle. The National Party also faced opposition to change from within its own ranks, and supporters were leaving to join the right-wing Conservative Party or AWB. So making preparations to start the negotiations was the first obstacle that had to be overcome.

Once the negotiations began, it became clear that there were fundamental differences between the two parties. The ANC wanted majority rule and a new constitution to be drawn up by a democratically elected assembly. The NP called for protection for 'minority rights' and wanted to play a leading role in any decisions about a new constitution. In other words, it wanted to retain some control over the negotiations, and ensure a future both for the NP and for whites in South Africa. Before talks began in earnest, both sides agreed to make concessions – the government lifted the state of emergency and the ANC suspended the armed struggle. When the talks finally got underway at CODESA in December 1991, it seemed that another small hill had been climbed.

However, negotiations made slow progress against a background of violence and political extremism. Massacres at Sebokeng, Boipatong and Bisho led to the collapse of the talks. There were also acts of extremism by right-wing Afrikaners in the AWB who were opposed to any form of negotiation with the ANC. They crashed an armoured car into the building where the CODESA talks were taking place, and they invaded the homeland of Bophuthatswana. The assassination of Chris Hani, the SACP and MK leader, posed a serious threat, and only appeals for calm by Mandela and other leaders prevented a civil war. Attacks on civilians by extremists in APLA, the armed wing of the Pan Africanist Congress, and by right-wing Afrikaners, intensified the tensions. The death of thousands of people in politically related violence made a peaceful transition to democracy seem unlikely and this was possibly the greatest obstacle facing South Africa.

Tensions between the ANC and Inkatha also impeded negotiations. There was on-going violence between supporters of the two parties, especially in Kwazulu-Natal, and in the townships east of Johannesburg, where Inkatha hostel dwellers fought the 'comrades'. The violence was fuelled by a 'Third Force' of units in the police and army secretly supporting Inkatha. Inkatha's refusal to take part was a serious threat to a peaceful settlement until its agreement one week before the election.

Nelson Mandela's famous words in his autobiography are therefore a true assessment of South Africa's emergence as a democracy. There had been 'many more hills to climb' between 1990, when Mandela was released and the ANC unbanned, and 1994, when South Africa finally became a democracy. The new government now faced new challenges, such as national reconciliation and the legacy of inequality.

EXAMINER'S COMMENT

Again there is good focus on the essay topic, and a good attempt at analysis.

EXAMINER'S COMMENT

Many important issues are mentioned in this paragraph without proper explanation, and the answer is a bit vague about the incidents of violence mentioned. Remember to **analyse**, and not simply **relate**. As the paragraph acknowledges, acts of violence were a key obstacle, so more explanation is needed here.

EXAMINER'S COMMENT

The student has missed an opportunity to say something here on different historians' views on the role of the 'Third Force'.

EXAMINER'S COMMENT

This is a well-focused concluding paragraph, which makes a comment on the quotation as required.

Overall examiner's comments

This is a good answer, with some precise knowledge to support the points made, although there is no real analysis of the violence that threatened the process. The answer is thus good enough to be awarded a mark towards the top of Band 2 – probably about 11 or 12 marks. However, a topic like this also calls for some mention of relevant specific historians/historical interpretations.

Activity

Look again at the simplified mark scheme, and the student answer above. Then try to write a few extra paragraphs to push the answer up into Band 1, and so obtain the full fifteen marks. Try to integrate some references to relevant historians/historical interpretations.

Index

Acknowledgements

The author and publishers acknowledge the following sources of copyright material and are grateful for the permissions granted. While every effort has been made, it has not always been possible to identify the sources of all the material used, or to trace all copyright holders. If any omissions are brought to our notice, we will be happy to include the appropriate acknowledgements on reprinting.

Text

Extract on page 189 Source E P. Levine and H. Papasotiriou, America Since 1945, 2005), New York: Palgrave Macmillan, reproduced with permission of Palgrave Macmillan.

Extracts on pages 25, 57, 82, 338 G. Layton (2009), Democracy and Dictatorship in Germany 1919–63, London: Hodder. Reproduced by permission of Hodder Education.

Images

Cover © Louise Gubb/CORBIS SABA; 1.1 © Peter Turnley/CORBIS; 2.3 Bain News Service/Buyenlarge/Getty Images; 2.4 © World History Archive/Alamy Stock Photo; 2.5 akg-images; 2.6 © Rohwedder/dpa/Corbis; 2.7 © dpa/dpa/Corbis; 2.8 Hulton Archive/Getty Images; 2.1 Keystone-France/Gamma-Keystone via Getty Images; 2.11 Three Lions/Getty Images; 2.12 bpk/Kunstbibliothek, Staatliche Museen zu Berlin; 2.13 © dpa/dpa/Corbis; 2.14 Albert Harlingue/Roger Viollet/Getty Images; 2.15 © DACS 2015; 2.16 akg-images/ullstein bild; 2.17 AFP/Getty Images; 2.18 © Berliner Verlag/Archiv/dpa/Corbis; 2.19 Popperfoto/Getty Images; 2.20 EUROVISION/EBU; 3.3 Dungan/Pix Inc./The LIFE Images Collection/Getty Images; 3.6 © TopFoto; 3.8 AFP/Getty Images; 3.1 Arif Ali/AFP/Getty Images; 3.11 New York Times Co./Getty Images; 3.12 Frank Bienewald/LightRocket via Getty Images; 3.13 Popperfoto/Getty Images; 3.14 James Burke/The LIFE Picture Collection/Getty Images; 3.15 Keystone-France/Gamma-Rapho via Getty Images; 3.16 Margaret Bourke-White/The LIFE Picture Collection/Getty Images; 3.17 © Steve Speller/Alamy Stock Photo; 3.18 PRAKASH SINGH/AFP/Getty Images; 4.2 Library of Congress; 4.4 © CORBIS; 4.5 © Bettmann/CORBIS; 4.6 Cecil Stoughton, White House, in the John F. Kennedy Presidential Library and Museum; 4.7 © Wally McNamee/Corbis; 4.8 Michael Rougier/The LIFE Picture Collection/Getty Images; 4.9 FPG/Getty Images; 4.12 Margaret Bourke-White/Time & Life Pictures/Getty Images; 4.13 Library of Congress; 4.16 AP/Press Association Images; 4.17 © World History Archive/Alamy Stock Photo; 4.19 Francis Miller/The LIFE Picture Collection/Getty Images; 4.20 NY Daily News Archive via Getty Images; 4.21 © Camerique/ClassicStock/Corbis; 5.1 WALTER DHLADHLA/AFP/Getty Images; 5.3 © Gideon Mendel/Corbis; 5.4 © Rafs Mayet/Africa Media Online; 5.5 WALTER DHLADHLA/AFP/Getty Images;

5.8 KEITH SCHAMOTTA/AFP/Getty Images; 5.9 JEAN-PIERRE MULLER/AFP/Getty Images; 5.1 Oryx Media Archive/Gallo Images/Getty Images; 5.11 © 1995-2015 Zapiro; 5.13 © 1995-2015 Zapiro; 5.14 Ashraf Hendricks/Anadolu Agency/Getty Images; 5.15 Africa Media Online TBC; 5.16 © Gideon Mendel/Corbis; 5.17 Universal Images Group via Getty Images; 5.18 © 1995-2015 Zapiro; 5.20 Scott Ramsey; 5.21 © Gallo Images/Alamy Stock Photo; 6.1 Howard Ruffner/The LIFE Images Collection/Getty Images; Source D © 1995-2015 Zapiro